Watching Cambodia

Watching Cambodia

Ten Paths to
Enter the Cambodian Tangle

Serge Thion

White Lotus
Bangkok   Cheney

White Lotus Co., Ltd
G.P.O. Box 1141
Bangkok 10501

Published 1993. First Edition

Printed in Thailand

Typeset by COMSET Limited, Partnership

ISBN 974-8495-91-4   White Lotus Co., Ltd.; Bangkok
ISBN 974-8495-91-6   pbk. White Lotus Co., Ltd.; Bangkok
ISBN 1-879155-20-6   White Lotus Co., Ltd.; Cheney
ISBN 1-879155-19-2   pbk. White Lotus Co., Ltd.; Cheney

Contents

Contents

Contents

Acknowledgements

A very large number of people have helped me over the years to slowly build up my own understanding of things Cambodian. It would make a book in itself to list all these people, the circumstances of our meetings and the food for thought they, consciously or not, brought with them. Among my Khmer acquaintances, many suffered a tragic fate but I wish to mention at least two of them because we had intense exchanges from which I learned a great deal, Nourn Khoeun and Ros Chet Thor. To my many Khmer friends who fortunately are alive, I apologize for not naming them. The hazards of political life in Cambodia are such that I do not want anyone to be associated with judgements which are my own only, and may be seen as obnoxious by present or future rulers. I fear this trend of Cambodian politics which conceives of people as "linked" into "networks", and the need to eliminate these networks. I have no such network and my friends belong to a large array of political persuasions.

Among foreigners, many people helped me in one way or another. And again, because I write about politics, I am not sure it would be wise to name all of them. I wish to thank those who helped with translations or revisions, Laura Summers, William Mahder, Donald Nicholson Smith, Ian Noble, David Chandler and most of all Helen Jarvis, who did a tremendous job. Susan Faircloth, for White Lotus, to my shame but to the serious improvement of the book, identified a myriad of small errors and inconsistencies. I learned much from her. I received Chandler's *Tragedy of Cambodian History* too late to use it but this book will remain a classic for a long time to come. Because we have worked in the same field, I wish to mention the long friendly discussions I had over the years with my friends and colleagues, exchanging ideas, including many heated debates, documents, books and all sorts of tips, Ben Kiernan, Steve Heder, Michael Vickery, David Chandler and May Ebihara whom I met in that order. From the Border emerged two long-lasting friendships with François Grünewald and Christophe Peschoux. Among the press corps, I would like to name Jean-Claude Pomonti, Tiziano Terzani "the

Magnificent", Nayan Chanda and Nate Thayer with whom, over the years, talking was always exciting and thought provoking. We had our agreements and disagreements which, in my view, were all very useful. This book owes them a lot but, of course, I stand alone for its content.

December 1992

Introduction

These articles have been written over a span of twenty years. They describe several facets of a rather small group of our brother humans, living, and sometimes suffering, in a place which is, at the same time, notorious and generally unknown: Cambodia.

Notorious for the ruins of Angkor, an amazing place indeed, an art marvel of all time, the so-called "smile" of the Khmers being carved on the huge stones of the towers of the Bayon, near the middle of the former Angkorian capital city, now populated by none apart from the *bandar logs*, the monkeys roaming in the ruins of a lost city, carved too in our young minds by Kipling's *Jungle Books*. Equally notorious for its endless war and one of the worst political catastrophes of our time, which the media industry labelled the "killing fields" of Pol Pot. The population was small, indeed, but the scale of the murder was huge, even compared to the grim record of our time.

Generally unknown because Khmer reality lies shrouded by many veils. Khmers usually are retiring, in a peasant way, and believe that only fools expose themselves and speak their minds. They have a long experience: as far back as memory can go, they have lived under authoritarian rulers. During the colonial period, French rule was quite heavy handed. Law and order was rigidly maintained but the burden of taxes was not negotiable. The colonial system crumbled after World War II but soon guerrillas and bandits of every description started to swarm around. For several years, insecurity was widespread. Armed bands roamed the countryside and, if you were a Khmer, you had to accommodate them. Then, in the mid-1950s, the French left and Sihanouk took over. You had to show enthusiasm and refrain from criticism, which the prince did not like. Usurers and corrupt police pocketed a sizeable amount of your income. Outspoken people disappeared or landed in jail.

Then, in 1970, the prince was overthrown and war broke out. At the beginning, Americans and Vietnamese were locked in furious battles. But then, you were either in the countryside under the Khmer Rouge and the giant American bombs, or in town under Lon Nol and his cronies, violent, corrupt and greedy. An extreme moralism on the one hand, a total absence of morality on the other. In either case, you had better keep your thoughts to yourself. But the worst was still to come, after the war ended in April 1975. The "Organization" (*Angkar*) of the Khmer Rouge took complete control. You had to do what you were told immediately. These youngsters with guns had no patience or humanity. Walk, work or die. You were not supposed to utter a single word of comment. People could disappear because of a single frown. You even had to pretend to be happy. You were frightened all the time. And hungry. You had to hide everything, your past, your knowledge, your feelings, your tastes.

And then, by 1979, that system crumbled too. It meant freedom, but you had lost everything. It was difficult to be happy to have survived when so many members of your family had perished. Probably more than one million people were missing.

The struggle for life went on. A new regime for Cambodia was created by the Vietnamese. The war continued but then the Vietnamese did most of the fighting against the Pol Pot forces. Since you had to start everything from scratch, you had the choice: you could stay and face whatever difficulties came up, or leave the country and try to start a new life abroad, if you could avoid being trapped in the camps at the Thai border. Those camps were another hell, with mines, bandits, warriors, treating the refugees like cattle. Foreign workers brought amenities in some places, but they were in the camps only eight hours a day. This hell has been maintained by the UN until now. Many educated people chose to seek asylum in a third country, leaving the country even more depleted.

If you chose to stay, you had to accommodate to the Vietnamese presence, and the new regime, if somewhat less authoritarian than the previous one had been, was obsessed by security. It was better to keep your mouth shut. Vietnamese troops withdrew in 1989 and the regime slowly started to depart from its communistic origins.

Now, in 1992, things are changing. The prince came back from exile and secluded himself in the royal palace. Good for him. A huge crowd of foreigners have invaded the country. They are constantly to be seen in big white cars with "UN" stamped on them. They have a stupendous amount of dollars in their pockets. They say we shall have to vote, that Cambodians should express themselves. But they know nothing. They will come and go, like the rain clouds. And we are like the frogs. If there is no noise, if everything is quiet, we may dare to raise our heads above the water. But at the first noise, we had better hide. Raised heads are easily cut off. We know that because we have seen it. All these people who have been, or dream of becoming our rulers again are ready to cut each others' throats. There is room for only one water buffalo in the pond. And when big people fight among themselves, small people die. Violence is everywhere, lying in wait. Fear is everywhere too. It is not easy to be Cambodian.

This I had not discovered immediately. I had come for a short visit at the end of 1967. While a massive war had engulfed Vietnam, Cambodia was, supposedly, still an island of peace. I came back a year later to teach, in a Phnom Penh high school. It was the *lycée* Chau Ponhea Yât, taking its name from the king who, according to some chronicles, decided to move the centre of the Khmer kingdom away from Angkor, around 1431. The pupils were not interested in Ponhea Yât, nor in Angkor, nor, in fact, in any historical considerations. But they were interested in contemporary politics. They could not talk openly but I felt that questions were boiling in their heads. And the more people I came to know, the more I felt the regime was gasping for air. Prince Sihanouk was losing his grip. Things were collapsing from the inside, but the process was not visible because people could not talk. The fear itself was hidden. I left in June 1969 with a very pessimistic assessment.

In January 1970, when I came back, the political war-game was in full swing. The end of Sihanouk was written on the wall and people were starting to talk. The bourgeoisie and a large part of the state bureaucracy had become bold enough to claim power for themselves. When the coup occurred in March, I was in Paris and I guessed that Cambodians who had to realign their loyalties quickly would again be prisoners of their new involvements (in favour of Sihanouk or against him). Among rightists, the rage against the former sovereign turned politician was leading to indiscriminate and sometimes slanderous accusations while the leftists, using his name as a shield and a symbol, would never criticize the man who, long before his overthrow, had unleashed a savage repression against them.

I then decided to try to describe what the Sihanouk regime had been and how it had dug its own grave. I joined forces with Jean-Claude Pomonti who had covered the coup and its aftermath for *Le Monde*, and we produced a book, *Des Courtisans aux partisans*, by the end of the year. We were fortunate enough to have Cambodian readers of all political shades, quite happy, most of them, to see in print what they had known in silence for a long time, except for leaders who disliked the exposure. Sihanouk, who had never lost an opportunity to rebut criticism, always avoided mentioning the book and had his wife write us an angry letter. Lon Nol (or someone among his cronies who could read) put us on the black list of people not permitted to enter Cambodia.

This did not make Cambodia watching an easy task. But an opportunity soon arose when word came from the Phnom Penh underground that the Khmer Rouge Special Zone was requesting the visit of a journalist to report about the situation in the guerrilla zone. I made an arrangement with *Le Monde* and flew to Bangkok. I then caught a train to the border, figuring that the blacklisting would be efficient in Paris or Phnom Penh but not in the border village of Poipet. I walked across the bridge that marked the frontier and a sleepy soldier let me in. I then proceeded to Phnom Penh where I could wait in hiding. Several of my friends worked with a kind of underground network which supplied the guerrillas with medicines and other needed commodities. My departure was delayed for several weeks because the former Foreign Minister, Prince Norodom Phurissara, felt threatened and had decided to cross over to the other side; his departure had to be organized first. (He was to become minister in the guerrilla government and chairman of the Phnom Penh NUFK committee.) It gave me an opportunity to see how Phnom Penh had been changed by the war. The irruption of American, Thai and South Vietnamese military influence had quickly reduced the new regime to a powerless clique where the benefits of corruption were unleashing endless quarrels. Since its best troops had already been trounced by seasoned North Vietnamese regulars, the Lon Nol army had obviously lost the war.[1] The political personnel were more or less the same as under Sihanouk and had not improved. With few exceptions, these people seemed without hope. When I returned from the Khmer Rouge zone, I had feverish conversations with some selected Khmer friends who knew where I had gone and wanted to have news from the other side; many of their friends had already "crossed over". I told them that Cambodia's future was there, that the Lon Nol side was condemned, that intellectuals I had met in the forest seemed quite happy, that skills would be needed and that it would be better for them to cross over before it was too late. My former colleague at Ponhea Yât and very good friend, Nourn Khoeun, followed the advice one year later. He was to be killed in the purges in 1977–8.

I do not know if what I told him had any part in his decision but one thing is sure: I shall never forgive myself for having given him such bad advice. The truth is that in 1972 Khmer Rouge rule was still quite lenient. In the villages, people took part spontaneously, mostly because they were bombed and machine-gunned by the Lon Nol air force. And Sihanouk even though in exile in Peking was their leader; this made things easy for them to accept. The cadres were obviously quite rigid but some were quite familiar, merry, open persons. Nothing I saw warned me of an impending catastrophe. The first very harsh measures were taken later, in 1973, under the heavy bombardments of the US Air Force. For an observer like me, everything in the guerrilla zone seemed organized along the same lines as in neighbouring Vietnam. The Vietnamese communists were going a long way to convince their own people, using terror in a rather discriminatory way, although occasional excesses did happen, with no apologies. Historically, this deep influence of the old Vietnamese communist tradition on the Cambodian left wing movement is a fact. Because it had never expressed itself publicly, and because when it did so, this was done under the vague formulas of a frontist policy, we knew nothing of the real political thought of the Pol Pot group and its secret resolve to break away from the Vietnamese, this hidden agenda being the main source of its extremism. The speeches always referred to the "solidarity" between the two movements. And, anyway, they were in the same boat: they were fighting the same American enemy.

We knew of course that Stalinist communism has a strong nationalist component but no observer was ready, at the time, to gauge the amount of irrationality that promptly led the Khmer Rouge regime to orchestrate its own demise. The most common mistake of analysts when they try to evaluate a political situation — and I must confess my share in this sin — is that we tend to believe political actors will behave in a rational way, or at least work to continue or increase their own power. This was not the case of the Pol Pot group: in 1975, they won absolute power but, even before reaching the apex, they had started to destroy its base, destroying the people, the economy, the Party, the army in less than ten years. I did not foresee that outcome, although I had unknowingly met one of the members of the Pol Pot group, Vorn Vet. His importance could be deduced from the fact that he was driven on a motorbike and he had several bodyguards. Some monks passed by during our short conversation. He kneeled in front of them, but while we talked together his words sounded quite Maoist to me. This was not exactly Vietnamese thought, it had overtones of the *Little Red Book*. The veils of secrecy were so numerous around him that it was several years before I knew who he really was: a member of the Political Bureau, who rose to be No. 3 of the regime before his downfall and execution at the end of 1978. At the time we knew almost nothing about the man later called Pol Pot, nothing about the tiny Party apparatus he had built. And nobody else knew either. Only the Vietnamese and

Chinese leaders knew about him and certainly did not, at the time, know exactly what his real inner thoughts were.

The article I wrote when I came back is reproduced here as Chapter 1. It has become a kind of source because, as it turned out later, mine was the only visit into the Khmer Rouge zone by a Western observer. Some Westerners had been prisoners, either of the Viet Cong or of the Khmers and could bring back their observations, like Richard Dudman, Jean-François Bizot, Xavier Baron, Lydie Nicaise and several others. They were soon released. But many other journalists, like Dana Stone, and Sean Flynn were never seen again. These two friends of mine were based in Saigon. The photographer Tim Page followed their tracks twenty years later and found villagers who remembered. They had been handed over by the Viet Cong to the Khmer Rouge and, after several months, a local chief shot them. A young Japanese journalist tried in 1973 to repeat my trip and disappeared. In 1980, commissioned by NHK, the Japanese network, Steve Heder found out that he had been held in a village, near the Phnom Aural, became sick and died from lack of medical attention. My friend Naoki Mabuchi published a book in Japan on this promising young writer who had been his colleague. The single reason why I had been able to travel around and report — as they had not — was that I had been invited. Furthermore, my visit was to the Phnom Penh area. Otherwise, foreigners were not welcomed and more than two dozen members of the press died during or after their capture.

I felt the need to seek the roots of these problems. The rejection of colonialism was an obvious factor. But others were embedded in the social fabric. As Vietnam and Cambodia were two peasant societies, I thought it would be useful to do research into the agrarian problem. I combed the literature and came up with contrasting pictures of social history of the peasantry in these two countries. These are given here in Chapter 2.

In early 1975, I was once again in Saigon. Soon after my arrival the South Vietnamese regime started to collapse, bit by bit, like a cardboard castle. I had an eye on Cambodia, of course. Several flights a day were carrying food to an embattled Phnom Penh. I considered going back. I had to wait until the Pochentong airport was sufficiently disorganized by rocket attacks to sneak in, since I was still quite high on the black list. By then landing had become extremely hazardous and watching the coming fall of Saigon was very interesting too. I still remember the shock of learning from the radio of the evacuation of Phnom Penh after it had fallen to the Khmer Rouge. I knew this town, I knew the common folk would accept the new masters because they were bringing a long-awaited peace. I of course expected

Vietnam and Cambodia to throw the foreigners out, at least for a while, because they had been in a way recolonized during the war. But emptying all of Cambodia's cities struck me as monstrous, maniacal and self-defeating. I could not find any rationality in such a decision. I could not accept such an inhuman move. Abolishing money was another stupid and crazy act. Both showed a complete perversion of what the idea of revolution stood for. From that point onwards, I felt totally estranged from those people.

Watching Cambodia directly at this point was out of the question. When the first alarming missionary reports were published, three months later, I paid them little attention. Missionaries in Indochina had been a particular brand of ultra-conservative, rabid anti-communists anyway. Propaganda, as a concept and a word, had been invented by the Church. The ones I had met in the field had given me no reason to trust them. But in the following year refugee reports started to filter from the Thai border. Their veracity was of course open to question but two facts gave them weight: the mad decision to evacuate the cities and the total absence of foreign observers. Even "friendlies" were not allowed in. Suspicion was then legitimate. It took some time to find out who at the border could be trusted to report the refugee accounts accurately. I must say that, as in other instances where I knew certain situations at first hand, I have rated the accuracy of the press as quite poor. Distortions, mistranslations, selective reporting were quite common. Noam Chomsky has discussed all this in a large study that remains perfectly valid.[2] The fact that real horrors had taken place in Cambodia (or is taking place in other countries, for instance Yugoslavia) does not excuse falsifications or selective and biased reporting. Reality is never black and white as the press, or the moral need of the readers, would have it. And to add some more confusion, Chomsky or people like myself criticizing the press, have been accused of supporting Pol Pot and applauding the bloodbath. The only reply to this ridiculous accusation is one simple question: are the facts important to us or not?

Anyway, I took the opportunity presented by the publication of a book by a missionary, F. Ponchaud, to say what I thought about the "new" Cambodia (reproduced here in Appendix 1) and I maintained a tenuous contact with the very unofficial small group of Cambodians in Paris who still had a link with Phnom Penh. In fact, their link was the reception from the Democratic Kampuchea embassy in Peking of transcripts of Radio Phnom Penh and of some pamphlets. By 1978, after the public declaration by the DK officials in Peking on 1 January that there was a state of war between them and Vietnam, more foreign delegations were invited to Cambodia. Most of them were representatives of tiny Maoist groups but some more credible guests, like a Yugoslav television team, were invited. Obviously, the Pol Pot regime was trying, in its heavy manner, to open up a little because it needed support to face the Vietnamese reaction to their own aggressions. By the end of the year, I was told that I would go sometime in 1979. Some non-Maoist foreigners were already going, like Malcolm Caldwell whom I saw in London some weeks before his departure for Phnom Penh. We discussed what he should ask but he knew what he wanted to say. He was to be shot there in December 1978, a victim of the internal struggle for power, of which we knew nothing. The Khmer Rouge had just published a long and garbled justification of their position and I started to scrutinize this document in order to figure out exactly what their political concepts might be. My analysis is reprinted here as Chapter 3.

The fall of Phnom Penh to the invading Vietnamese army, on 7 January 1979, was, I felt, a blessing for the Khmer population. Most people in Cambodia also felt that way. Soon after, stories started to flow from inside the country. The DK sent its former ambassador in Laos to Geneva for a UN meeting. He was the first official to come to Europe. I spent an evening with him and Chan Youran trying to test the hypothesis of a Vietnamese infiltration, given by the Pol Potists as the cause of their demise. I could not find anything convincing to support the idea. Both at the border and inside the country there were now people with enough basic knowledge of the country to pick up pieces which could be used to reconstruct the course of events. There again, however, propaganda was still mixed with facts. A hotel room with a blood-stained floor, presented as the one where Malcolm Caldwell had been shot, was shown to visitors, but it turned out later the murder had occurred at a different place. The most outlandish rumours, spread by CIA-sponsored journalists at the border, were now echoed in Hanoi and Moscow. Again, we had to disentangle fact from fiction.

The discovery of the Tuol Sleng interrogation centre was to provide not only facts but documents. The Khmer Rouge leadership had been so confident that they had had to flee at the last minute from the advancing Vietnamese troops. They had left behind piles of documents. Another set of documents, the Central Committee papers, was captured in April by the Vietnamese. These they kept for themselves. They were Party business. But in Phnom Penh the first period was rather chaotic. The Vietnamese decided to turn Tuol Sleng into a museum for propaganda purposes. From far away, I realized Tuol Sleng was my old *lycée*, Chau Ponhea Yât. The thought that this place where I had shared so many good moments with nice pupils had been turned into a torture centre, where false confessions were extracted from so many honest and dedicated militants, several of whom were my friends, was unbearable. Several thousand deaths were thus explained, rationalized in the paranoid suggestions included in the handwritten and typed confessions, and even shown in an atrocious collection of photographs, many of them taken "before" and "after". In early 1980, Anthony Barnett brought back a copy of Hu Nim's confession, which was later presented by him, Ben Kiernan and Chanthou Boua in *The New Statesman* (2 May 1980). Hu Nim was the Information Minister in Pol Pot's government. His "confession", clearly signed by himself, is representative of all the others: an incredible mixture of truths, half-truths and suggested inventions which makes the question of sincerity meaningless. At one point, he wrote: "I am not a human being, I am an animal." A cold note in the margin indicates that after this absurd exercise, he has been "crushed to pieces" on 6 July 1977.[3]

In 1981, I visited Tuol Sleng. I recognized the place, even with the transformations of the Khmer Rouge period and the "adaptation" by the Polish-trained Vietnamese experts. It is impossible to describe my emotion. I understand the idea of a "museum" dedicated to mass killing but I am not convinced that such places should exist. I do not believe reality can be shown in this way. A historical event can be reconstructed only by people who already know a great deal about the time and the circumstances. Otherwise, it belongs to the realm of fantasy. Moreover, the place is not what it was when the torturers fled. The need to rearrange the stage is in itself proof that it does not "speak" enough, that some transformation will help the onlooker, provide him with pictures he could not formulate by himself. A conscious attempt was made to introduce images drawn from the German concentration camps, like the mountain of clothing seen in so many 1945 pictures. Later, some of this reconstructed evidence, like the one just mentioned, was removed. Tuol Sleng was slightly different when I visited it again in 1991. The clothing and the busts of Pol Pot had disappeared. Traces of disorder left by the flight of the tormentors had been cleaned up. The interrogators' office, the former teachers' room, has been turned into a salon for VIPs, and so on. I disapprove of making use of death, even for the best motives, because death has no meaning in itself; it is always useless and should not be used. The dead belong to themselves, not to us. Nobody has to tell survivors to remember: they do. As for the others, to whom this kind of memorial is offered as an incentive to resist the return of such atrocities, they, instead of concentrating on a vanished past, should rather worry about other atrocities committed now, here or there, sometimes with their implicit approval. More thoughts on this problem will be found in Chapter 9.

I finally returned to Cambodia in 1981, having recently shared my findings with some colleagues in an attempt to understand what had happened.[4] On this return visit we interviewed many people and travelled around, sometimes alone, sometimes together. As for the people we had known before, we met very few. Material and psychological destruction was widespread. The towns had been spared and only ordinary decay was visible there. But the population had changed. The old urban classes were very much depleted and peasants had taken over. Village life was the way to save the country. The formidable resilience of the Cambodians had its source in rural poverty. Poor people know better how to survive. Food was still scarce but babies were to be seen everywhere. There was an unwilling and probably unconscious wish to re-establish the old society. Michael Vickery and I worried about this (see Chapter 5). I was convinced the Vietnamese could not stay very long in Cambodia. Everything they might do to re-establish a state and the normal functioning of a society would become less and less bearable for the Khmers with the passage of time.

I expressed this view in Hanoi which I visited soon after my trip to Cambodia and I met many who were willing to listen. I attempted to demonstrate to some of the Vietnamese leaders in charge of the Cambodian question that they would never succeed in convincing Cambodians, and that willingly or not they would have to adapt to the Khmer way of thinking and doing. At the same time, I argued, they would be wise to prepare an orderly withdrawal rather than face a crisis like the one faced by Vietnamese Emperor Minh Mang in the 1841.[5] I think Western observers, including myself, always underestimated the degree of confusion and puzzlement the Cambodian question sparked in the minds of the Vietnamese leaders. Much of what they did and said was improvised and beneath a thin layer of dogmatic speech lay many unanswered questions. The overall assessment should be done now, but the fact that mistakes were made is privately accepted in Hanoi. If the Vietnamese leaders never fully grasped all the complexities of the Cambodian problem, one of the main reasons is that their first priority has been all along the security of their own country.

Watching Cambodia, in the 1980s, was not easy. What was permitted to foreigners was very superficial. Cambodian citizens could not speak freely. Travelling was complicated. Everything required permission. Under these conditions, nothing very useful could be done in the country by people like me. Over the next few years, I visited all the main camps along the Thai–Cambodian border. I avoided the camp authorities and spoke mostly with ordinary people. In my view, those places were a shame on the West which had established them, ran them and paid for them. The underdogs, that is to say most people, lived there in terror, most of the time. Thefts, rapes, pressures to recruit and enforced idleness were some of the most negative aspects. For many years, the Thais prevented schooling for the young people, so that boys had no alternative to joining the guerrillas. The Thai military controlled absolutely everything and can thus be held responsible for the inhuman side of camp life. But the United Nations system has been a willing accomplice in maintaining the whole network and paying for it. The food emergency in Cambodia lasted until 1981–2 and the camps should have been closed after it was over. Then people could have gone home. The existence of the camps was purely artificial and was the consequence of a political calculation. The Non-Governmental Organizations active in the camps were accomplices too. They provided the manpower, paid by the UN, to maintain attractive facilities, such as the medical ones, in an attempt to hide the political motivations. They themselves were politically motivated but never recognized the fact in front of their donors at home. They drew prestige, growth and money out of their presence on the border. This is a scandalous misuse of human misery. I was depressed and frustrated each time I visited the camps and heard so many stories of fear, despair and hopelessness. Of course, many individuals in the camp population, the camp administration or the NGO volunteers were excellent, dedicated and caring. Many, after some months, could not stomach what they saw and what they were supposed to do. But it remained a private concern. They left out of disgust and never fought the system. These drops of humanity were falling in an ocean of bitterness, injustice and cruelty. Nothing was ever stabilized and insecurity was the rule for 12 years. The history of the border, with it deceptions, its cynical use of the refugees' misery, the corruption of the Thai military, the brutality of the Khmer warlords, has yet to be written. As for me, I did what I could, inquiring into the conditions of the refugees after they had settled in France. The picture was far from rosy and is given here as Chapter 8.

The clouds started to dissipate slowly. By 1987, returning once more from the border, I was convinced the negotiations would sooner or later succeed. The basic reason for my cautious optimism was the new course adopted in the Soviet Union. Although a host of political analysts warned against trusting Gorbachev's resolve to reform, I thought it was clear the man was not another Khrushchev and the new leadership was jumping into the unknown. They clearly wanted to reverse the expansionist policy and withdraw from costly and politically useless involvements. For Indochina, it meant the Vietnamese would have to adapt and follow.

The withdrawal of the Vietnamese army would open up the possibility of a return of the Khmers Rouges but at the same time would provide a golden opportunity to reorganize a healthy Khmer state system. I then wrote a piece, not to suggest any particular idea but to urge the various Khmer factions to start a discussion on this topic (see Chapter 7). I argued that if the Khmers did not reach an agreement on the political future of their country, foreigners would take decisions instead. I guessed these decisions would fit foreign interests but would not be workable.

Of course, I entertained no illusions. The institutional problem in Cambodia is generated precisely by the inability of the political actors to agree on rules to set up compromises. They were in a vicious circle and the probability they would escape from it was limited. But watching Cambodia is not always a passive activity. It sometimes implies taking a stand and telling what needs to be told in the circumstances. Political leaders live surrounded by flattery and truth may be a bitter beverage. But they deserve it.

December 2nd is celebrated in France as the anniversary of the most famous of all Napoleonic victories, the battle of Austerlitz. That day, the sun goes down exactly in the middle of the Arc de Triomphe. Symbolic language in war and politics is nobody's privilege. In 1987, this very day saw the first meeting between Prince Sihanouk and M. Hun Sen, the Prime Minister of Phnom Penh. There had been attempts to meet before. In 1985, the prince had requested the French Government to facilitate such a meeting and had later balked at it, lamely complaining about the Chinese rebuttal of his intention. But finally, with Gorbachev helping, the meeting was made possible.

It took place at Fère en Tardenois, in a sixteenth–century castle, 110 kilometres from Paris, at the heart of the old royal domain. The castle had been transformed into a luxury hotel. The restaurant, with one star in the *Guide Michelin*, had a speciality ranking high in the prince's tastes, a famous *étuvée de foie gras au jus de racines* and a cellar of good wines from nearby Champagne. In these royal surroundings, Sihanouk felt at home. Arriving in the mist of a cold morning from a third rate motel in Soissons, Hun Sen looked like a happy young man. With some advisers he secluded himself with Sihanouk, his wife Monique and his son Ranariddh. While the small press crowd was milling around trying to guess the mood of the meeting, I sneaked into the kitchen. Knowing my man, I thought his ordering of the lunch would reflect his inner disposition. The menu was sumptuous, with all sorts of *foie gras* and wild game. The list of wines provided the final clue.

I came back and informed a startled press that everything was going smoothly and there were reasons to be optimistic. Later we learned that Sihanouk had been charming. Sihanouk had performed the role of the father welcoming home a long lost son, and Hun Sen had nicely played his part as a respectful loving son. This was explicated by Ranariddh when he talked to the press, saying that the prince had "many sons" around the table. At the end of the three-day discussion, Hun Sen went so far as to say he had told the prince that he had joined the guerrilla following the call of the prince against Lon Nol, after the coup. And he had lost an eye fighting for the prince. It was a well intended lie because he had in fact joined the Khmer Rouge as a young courier long before the coup, probably in March 1967.

But beneath the warm atmosphere, the repetition that "we are among fellow Khmers", the struggle was intense between the old man who thought of himself as an embodiment of the country, but who had nothing, no power, not even reliable advisers, a lone figure representing the vanished glories of the past, and this young man, a commoner, as Monique who hated him said dryly, a usurper in the former king's view, who had everything in his hand, the power, the trappings, the influence over men, a soft-spoken word with real weight, a sharp intelligence which alone explained his position. He found out on the spot how to behave with the prince. It was clear he would pay any price in non-essential political commodities to bring back to Phnom Penh the old symbol, embodied in the person of the former king. Sihanouk was dying to go back because real power was in Phnom Penh and nowhere else. He trusted his own ability to outmanoeuvre anyone, including this young farmer who had the crown in his luggage. But he was not free. Every word he said he would have to repeat to his Chinese mentors and plead for their acceptance of his views. He did not lack courage or tenacity. But time was running out. How long could he dance on the tightrope?

A long string of negotiations followed, in France, in Pyong Yang and Jakarta leading to the conclusion in October 1991 of the Paris Agreements. Four years of ups and downs, during which I sometimes, with some other people, tried to facilitate communication between parties who did not use the same language. At the beginning, the French authorities were extremely unfair to Hun Sen while giving Sihanouk the red carpet treatment. This was not conducive to a balanced situation. But the Quai d'Orsay (the Foreign Ministry) was under a kind of Chinese spell. Opposing this irrational and useless submission to the masters of Peking was not always an easy task. The two main bones of contention had been, for Phnom Penh, to include a condemnation of the "genocidal practice" in the agreements, so that the Pol Potists would be excluded from power but reintro-duced at a low level into the political game, and for the so-called Coalition (the Khmer Rouge plus the two other factions) to obtain a dismantling of the Phnom Penh administration. Finally, there was a kind of trade-off, and both requests were dropped. In this formal exchange lies the root cause of the failure of the Agree-ments, as we shall see in Chapter 10.

What I had feared in 1987 was happening. The Americans, together with the French and the Chinese, were writing down their own solution to the Cambodian question. I thought it was a very bad solution. It gave to the four political-military factions a key role in the UN-controlled transitory period and provided for the continuation of this role into the future. The freedom of choice was thus very limited. Moreover, the record of these factions did not justify this protection. The major consequence was to reintroduce the Khmer Rouge into the political system. Because they had enjoyed asylum on Thai territory, the Khmers Rouges could not be destroyed. But giving them a stake in the peace process was a continuation of the cynical support they were given by China and the West. Although I thought peace was the most desirable achievement, I believed that peace was not possible with the Khmer Rouge unless they were obliged by force to lay down their arms. This was not a moral reaction but a cold assessment of the aims of the Khmer Rouge. They are a centralized military organization, a kind of Teutonic Order, and only naive minds believe they can accept some form of demilitarization. The Paris Agreements offered them enough opportunities to combine a political and a military struggle, of which they had a long experience in the years 1963–70, with a phoney demobilization of their army.

But the Agreements are ambiguous enough to be read as a process by which a new legitimate government will possibly be promoted in 1993 with the means to deal with the Khmer Rouge threat. The outcome of the game is not fixed in advance. I thought it would be interesting to watch on the spot and in November 1991, I went to Cambodia, in time for the return of Prince Sihanouk, obviously one of the key players. This is the subject of Chapter 10. I entertained no great illusions about the United Nations system but I did not anticipate such a lack of effectiveness. This is why I choose to give as the title of this chapter my own translation of UNTAC — the name of the UN body in Cambodia — "United Nations Traditional Apathy in Cambodia".

Someone once said of the bourgeoisie that it would choose a frightful end rather than an endless fright. The Khmers had both, a frightful end under Pol Pot, and an endless fright, for 13 years, that he would return. But at one point the threat will have to be removed. The Khmers and nobody else will have to do it. Those well wishers, who are now ready to lavish on the Khmers all the benefits of democratic happiness-cum-consumerism, would be well inspired to provide them with the political and material means to do it.

1

Cambodia 1972: Within the Khmer Rouge

*To the memory of Ros Chet Thor who was my guide in this
venture and then my friend. He perished at the hands of those
he had faithfully served.*

On the Footpaths of the War

Three women are cooking in the shade of a tree, where criss-crossing rice-field dams meet. One by one, peasants arrive; they were probably fishing because they now wring out their clothes. I am still quite close to the big road. I see the traffic of military trucks and Chinese buses. From the bushes, the farmers retrieve grenade belts and US carbines. They don their military attire and start moving. I am in the liberated zone, escorted by the guerrillas. I glance at my watch. I left the centre of Phnom Penh, in a car, one hour ago.

I had thought we would drive a long way and we would need to travel far from the road to reach our rendezvous with the Front. In fact the control post at the exit from the capital was only one to two kilometres behind me when I descended into the rice fields. The zone in which armed guerrillas circulate in daylight, and openly, commences on the outskirts of the city. In Phnom Penh this fact is ignored or denied.

A long walk starts. The first day, to get me far from the area of confrontation, I was conveyed by bullock cart, then by motorbike along the wide sandy paths that cut through the dry rice fields. But now I am invited to follow the trails of the war on foot. I am going to see the country on the level of peasant life.

My first impression is surprise at having crossed this invisible border line. We are still within binocular sight and already the spirit of the villagers and fighters is visible. Farmers in their fields as well as busy villagers whom we meet while walking treat us as usual passers-by. They quip with my guides and do not show any concern at this small troop escorting a bizarre foreigner. In about two weeks of walking in this wet rice field region, rather more populated than the average, I went through about fifty villages. Almost always, we stopped for some minutes or some hours, to talk with the villagers, look at the destruction caused by the bombings, and accept, when time permitted, invitations offered with a dignified sense of hospitality.

The cadres' and soldiers' austerity has often been put under pressure in this way. To the two regular quick meals, at seven in the morning and five in the afternoon, is often added an improvised banquet by which peasants show their solidarity and appreciation for those who fight.

My first impression has remained unchanged. There was never any need to hide my presence. Inside the zone held by the Khmer National United Front (NUFK), political and physical security is total. The cadres walk around, often alone, and unarmed. Troop movements are seen and known by all who live there. Spies who might infiltrate are feared but the relationship between the partisans and the villagers is obviously based on trust.

Air Attacks

Danger comes principally from the air, not from the ground. Seen from the countryside, war is not permanent. Since the summer of 1970, the territory controlled by the Lon Nol regime has been gradually cut back. The battles which liven up the front, more or less, occur close to the towns and the big arterial roads and, consequently, far away from the villages in the interior. Regions in which there was still fighting in 1971 have become quiet following the withdrawal of Phnom Penh's troops to positions further back. The weakness of these troops and of their offensive capability gives to this conflict an appearance quite different from that taking place in neighbouring Vietnam. In Cambodia, the *maquis* is much more protected against incursions of the enemy foot soldiers. Only the air force may bring its daily share of destruction.

It is easy to establish a balance sheet. All the villages through which I travelled had been attacked by aircraft, with bombs and napalm, at least once, and often many times. From what one can see on the ground, these attacks were frequently carried out at random. Here a corpse burned, there a field is cratered in the middle with a deep gulley six yards deep and twenty-five yards wide, elsewhere a group of houses blown apart. Observation planes, L-19s or OV-lOs, mark the target with a cloud of smoke. "Then", they warned me, "you must run straight away, very fast. You have two minutes. Generally that is enough." Two or three minutes later, T-28 propeller fighter-bombers or Phantom jets start their thunderous ballet. At some other times, and particularly when there is some fighting, come the old and slow DC3s. They remain airborne for hours, blasting their guns or their electronic machine-guns. The six-thousand shots per minute roar like big organs you can hear miles away.

But on the ground there is no terror. People hear the planes coming. They always have several minutes to disappear in the vegetation or to reach a shelter. These are to be found in every village, in the pagodas, often in the fields and sometimes beside the paths. They are simple trenches (the French word *tranchée* is used by the Khmers) covered with logs of wood and earth. In case of direct hit, this offers no protection. The victims are usually old people, the deaf and the sick, or babies, killed by surprise.

These shelters very much reduce the loss of human life, but they don't protect houses or cattle. In many cases, villages are partly evacuated. The peasants build temporary refuges in the surrounding woods or in the rice fields, in the shelter of a clump of trees. The villagers disperse; they merge into the surrounding landscape. This complicates everyday life. Their huts are less comfortable than their houses. Many huts have to be abandoned or moved during the rainy season. But physical security is increased.

Peasants know and passionately comment on every bombhole, every burned palm tree and the circumstances of the attack. Obviously these holes mean something: beyond the physical reality, they puncture the rural fabric where time, as it is perceived by the villagers, is woven into the space of their territory. This you can see in the rings of earth surrounding the bombholes, making them look like ugly scars.

Our ancestors looked for signs of the future in the flight of birds. Here one studies the flight of planes. One recognizes their typical noise, implies their function from their way of moving, and one makes some kind of psychological guess about their behaviour. One can predict if the incoming bird of ill omen is a threat or is just passing through. But in all cases, the reflex is to hide. That is what I did when, on my way back to Phnom Penh, I was overflown by the regular Air France plane, coming in to land…

A Rustic Economy

Contrary to my fears, the war has not upset the material life of the peasants. The former economy — with its statistics, international trade, state resources, money, and so on — has dropped into the abyss. The rustic economy, with its village production and exchanges, was not very much involved in the modern sector before the war. As a consequence, the rupture was not dramatic. "We have not yet met to put the results together", says a farmer, "but I believe the rice crop will be a bit smaller than last year. Of course, the planes are a nuisance for our work in the fields but the main reason is the poor rains."

Soon the peasants will be holding meetings in the villages to decide how to apportion the harvest: one share for families' food, another for seeds and reserves, another to be given to the Front, another share to be sold either to the Front or to other villages. Prices are somewhat higher since 1970, but, under the control of the Front, they remain much lower than those in the city. The Front's cadres vehemently insist that sales must not be made to the enemy zone. As a monk said at a meeting: "The cadres are right. If you strengthen the enemy, they will kill you more easily. And if they kill you, they kill me too. That is why I tell you they are right."

Blockade the enemy zone, suffocate the cities, develop regional autonomy — these are the aims of the Front in this sphere. The large Chenla 2 operation by the Lon Nol troops in the autumn of 1971, which ended up in disaster, had one objective: to reopen the "rice road" to Kompong Thom in time for the harvest. The Front seems to have important reserves, since the countryside's stocks from 1970–1 are not yet used up. And, in any case, the pillaging and violence which accompany the passing of Lon Nol's troops scarcely encourage the peasants to trade with them. "Yesterday," someone told me, "they captured two peasants who were driving carts loaded with rice and decapitated the two drivers. Their heads were hung up on the gates of the barracks."

But some peasants would like to sell because the difference in prices is very attractive. "Those are the most wealthy," explains the president of a village committee, "and they want to get richer. We explain to them that we don't agree and that our common interest must prevail completely." But very rare are the peasants in the Cambodian countryside who produce enough to save. Most are barely able to eke out a living. Nothing demonstrates this fact better than the absence of manufactured objects in the countryside before the war. The situation has hardly changed and local craftsmen satisfy, through a system of barter, all material needs. The only innovation is the presence of arms. The weapons are very varied. There are old French rifles, Chinese rifles and even American M-16s which have been taken from the enemy. Only the regular troops have the best weapon in this war, the Chinese AK-47 assault rifle. There is plenty of ammunition, and the peasants are proud to show their boxes of bullets freshly arrived from the United States.

Every village has a militia. Its function is to check unknown people's identity, observe enemy moves and take part in ambushes. Young and old men take part in turns, depending on the day's tasks. They take very seriously activities which seem to be more symbolic and educative than military. But they are sometimes thrown into the battle. Both by their many auxiliary functions in support of the fighting and their role as a reservoir for soldiers in training, the village militias are the basic element of the whole political military structure of the resistance.

The Story of a Battle

"We are at Bat Doeung, twenty-five kilometres by train from Phnom Penh and only sixteen kilometres as the crow flies. This was one of the key posts in the defence circle around the capital and the deepest inside the liberated zone." The man who was speaking in a strong voice was seated on the trunk of a felled palm tree in the middle of an indescribable field of ruins as he unfolded an American military map. Small, with greying hair, he was the head of Battalion 113 which had assaulted and taken the post at Bat Doeung in the month of December 1971.

The closer we came to this little trading town on the railway, the more militiamen left their villages to come with us. We were in zone No. 1, where the line of contact with the enemy is. Surprise attacks cannot be ruled out.

Just outside the town, we passed a monastery, Wat Sokkharam. All the monks' houses had been burned. Some debris of burned vessels, cinders and broken tiles were evidence of this. The Superior of the pagoda greeted us warmly. He wanted people to know about the attack. His monastery had been attacked by planes, a young monk had been killed, others were wounded. The outer walls of the sanctuary were marked with stains of napalm. This normally jovial man was in despair. Twenty-one years of his life he had spent in building that pagoda, in teaching and social work in that region. And not only do Lon Nol's men destroy religious buildings, they even accuse the "North Vietnamese" of the crimes they perpetrate.

He is indignant about this but he hopes that when peace comes back, Prince Sihanouk, who had consecrated the pagoda in 1969, will come back to bless the rebuilt sanctuary. As a farewell present, the monk extracts from his cabinet the most delicious palm sugar and his best *prahok* (fishpaste). Equipped with his food and blessings, we walk into the town.

The fighting must have been violent. Houses are riddled with bullet holes. The tin roof of the market looks torn by suffering. The large streets are empty: the whole population is gone; most of them, including many Chinese traders, went into the liberated zone where I met several of them, as refugees. They all complain of having been mistreated and looted by the government soldiers before the fall of the garrison.

The barracks and the command post are desolate; they have been shelled and stormed and then everything useful has been methodically ripped out, weapons, ammunition, radios, exercise books, pens, and even cartridges, smelted by the peasants into kitchen utensils. Earthen fortifications have been flattened. A half skeleton lies amidst shell cases. "In spite of our insistence, the peasants did not put much energy into digging to bury those people", says a cadre. "Must be some dogs…"

The Assault

Van Rit, leader of the battalion, told the story:

These installations housed the 396th Infantry Battalion of the special military region of Phnom Penh, under the command of Captain Theim Siem. Its actual strength was more than 250 men, without counting the 25 provincial guards in the administrative post. This garrison was mostly made up of former Khmer Serei [commandos organized by the CIA in the border regions before the *coup d'état* of 18 March 1970] and it was notorious for its extortions of the people, forced labour, assassinations, and blind machine-gunnings. We responded to the wishes of the people, shocked by these crimes. We struck first between Bat Doeung and Phnom Penh, taking the post at Tuol Leap on 18 November and capturing that at Trapeang Thnot five kilometres from here on the 29th. We cut the bridges and told the garrison, with leaflets, that we controlled the neighbouring posts. At night, we pounded them with mortars and dug approach trenches. In the daytime, we repeated through loudspeakers appeals for surrender. They called in air support, but our dugouts were solidly built.

Every night, we moved closer. We began to fire with individual arms. We cleared the mines and traps and cut the barbed wire. On the night of the 6th we were so close that air support had to stop. The soldiers began to flee and we entered the post. The staff captain was captured and the soldiers who fled were picked up by the peasants. We took 130 prisoners. The rest were dead or seriously wounded.

I had just seen the trenches and the individual dugouts showing the progress of the siege. The rest of the story I got from peasants who continued to recount episodes in which they had taken part, with great animation. It was a hot battle and they will talk of it for a long time.

Only the regular battalion of the People's Liberation Army took part in the assault. The provincial troops supplemented the encirclement at a distance. As for the village militia, recruited for the occasion, their job was to intercept possible reinforcements and to collect abandoned supplies. Just after the capture, a crowd of farmers swooped down on the place. Waiting oxcarts were loaded with weapons and ammunition and immediately sped away. "Women were fantastic", says a witness. "They picked up the scattered bullets and put them in big sacks, not caring about the airplanes. We got the radios. At the beginning, the peasants did not know what it was and broke them down. We had to explain a lot", he adds with a laugh.

They love to tell each other funny stories about the runaways. "And the one who hid naked in the river… And this other one who had only a loincloth. I got near to him and said: 'Hey boy, I don't feel you belong to here…'" Everyone burst into laughter. "We had brought nylon strings but there was not enough to tie down all the prisoners. We had to cut lianas." Kids still find guns the runaways discarded in the bush. Villagers in the area feel more secure now. They are very proud of having taken part in the assault and in this way they identify with the Liberation Army.

It is not only at a political level that this battle serves as an example. Its military significance is clear. Certainly, the press in Phnom Penh ignored it, simply reporting that the army had had to evacuate Bat Doeung. But Phnom Penh is surrounded by dozens of Bat Doeungs. If a post held by a well-armed and well-trained battalion can fall in three days without artillery, aviation or infantry being able to save it, it is because the army that is defending it has no more reserves.

Of course, since its lines are only five kilometres away, the army could retake Bat Doeung. But it would have to wage a battle and bring reinforcements from other positions.

On February 5th, a column led by two APCs, with two infantry groups and several trucks, started moving from Oudong [says a soldier in the provincial troops].

We ambushed them two kilometres from Damnak Smak, before the station. There were only about ten of us. We first shot at the guys on foot to stop them and then one of us fired a B-40 rocket. The leading APC burst into flames, just like a match, with around twenty people inside. Then they fired at us with the six 12.7 machine-guns and we ran for cover. They gathered the bodies and turned back. Driving on the dirt track makes them afraid, so, you see, going down in the rice fields…

The "Soft" Fronts

So, because this is a guerrilla war, an observer on the spot, like myself, comes to the odd conclusion that it would be better to describe it as a sort of war of "soft" fronts without any rigidity. It winds around the villages and stretches out along certain arterial roads. The regular troops are distributed on either side of this front line. The capture of Bat Doeung was a classical defeat of a "bulge" in the line. The defence position often call in the artillery, particularly at night, to clear their own surroundings and forbid concentration.

For all that, the situation is not stabilized. At some points, Phnom Penh's troops, benefiting from American, South Vietnamese and even Thai air support, can make a breakthrough and recapture some ground, but only for a limited time. For when they advance, the guerrillas press on other points of the front and open up new operations to re-establish the initial equilibrium. For the guerrillas, progress can only be slow. It is not that they lack men. It is more a question of seasoned fighters.

Commenting on the Cambodian situation, a Viet Cong cadre told me in 1970: "As for us, we need two years training to create a battalion and its field commanding staff." Now I was attending a popular meeting where elements of the provincial forces who had participated in several operations around Phnom Penh, like the battle of Bat Doeung and the attack on oil storage facilities, were "promoted" into a battalion of the regular forces. Heavy weapons (Chinese and US mortars, one recoilless gun, about 15 machine-guns) have been taken from the enemy.

It is the third such battalion created by this province. Starting from this, it will take at least one or two years to merge these units into operational regiments. If they want to smash the 120,000-man army (the real figure, not the inflated one currently on paper) which faces them, the guerrillas will have to go a step further and combine regiments into full-blown divisions. This has not yet happened. The guerrillas' equipment is still light, they have scarcely any artillery and very few anti-aircraft guns. As for armoured cars, they have only little B-40s which, it is true, achieve miracles, but only at a very short range.

For, at least in the provinces I visited to the west of Phnom Penh, there was no trace of foreign aid. The Chinese arms came from the Khmer Army's old stocks and the supply of munitions could, one day, pose problems. Certainly, communications are very slow and logistical services are poorly equipped. Radios are rare. Above all, it seems that the modern arms which are transported through Laos are not destined for the Khmer guerrillas. "The Vietnamese keep the supplies they transport for themselves", a cadre told me without allowing me to distinguish between his regret or his satisfaction at not depending on anyone.

The idea is hammered in every occasion: "Depend only on our own forces." At the meeting centred on the new battalion, its future commander expressed it in this way: "Our armed forces do not put their hope in the numbers or in the equipment, but in courage, sacrifice, solidarity, morality and also in the discipline you have freely accepted in order to be able to serve the people."

Political choice and material necessity therefore meet in the building of an entirely autonomous force. As long as the US finances the war by giving money and military hardware to their cronies, as long as the survival of Phnom Penh is ensured by the threat of rapid intervention of one or two South Vietnamese divisions sent by Saigon, the war cannot reach a point of decision.

But the overriding impression is that, today, Phnom Penh is in the same position as Saigon towards the end of 1964. Only a massive intervention of American ground troops was then able to save the capital of South Vietnam from asphyxiation. Now, the Americans seem able to keep their Cambodian ally alive only drop by drop.

The Deepest Forces

The flimsy buildings which serve as dormitory, kitchen and lecture rooms for the cadres' school are so well camouflaged in this little wood that I can scarcely make them out from 15 yards away. I am received by the director of the school who is also chairman of the Front's district (*srok*) committee. They call him, jokingly, Mr One Hundred, because he has so many pseudonyms. Three close rows of benches; 80 listeners from 18 to 20 years old, of whom a good third are women; eight hours of courses daily for two weeks plus two hours every evening to talk over the day's instruction. These are the cadres of the future chosen by the province committee from the most active of the local militants. They have responsibilities in the villages (*phum*) and in the communes (*khum*).

They are nearly all farmers except for a few who have fled from Phnom Penh. Most of them have only briefly attended primary school. So the classes are given in simple, repetitive language and the answers to the students' questions are aimed more at ensuring that they have assimilated the doctrine than at developing their intellectual curiosity.

The purpose is to teach them the political line of the Front, as defined in the programme adopted on 3 May 1970. Each part is repeated and commented on at length. One aspect or another is given particular attention according to the cadres whom they are teaching, their political level and the nature of their work. For peasants at the first stage, for example, they pass over international affairs very quickly but give great emphasis to relations with the people, respect for religious beliefs and land problems.

I believe the aim is to find a way to implement the political line by teaching the principles at all levels of the hierarchy. The idea is to create in the bosom of Khmer society channels through which to infiltrate analyses and decisions coming from the top in order effectively to reach large masses. The training of the cadres is precisely designed to help them to thoroughly understand and interpret the directives of the Front. The language of the peasants does not offer a direct route for this because their vision of the world and of politics is scarcely adequate for the particular rationality of a modern liberation struggle.

Consequently the function of the schools for cadres is to give the rural people who attend them a *language* to use, new but comprehensible. It is simple, constructed of certain basic ideas acquired through repetition. The values it establishes are not, in themselves, new to the peasants; they even have a reassuring conformity. But this new language allows them to rethink the conditions of their lives and to apply this to the vaster panorama of national politics. It is basically effective. In the past, they have thought as a village with everyday words. With these new ideas, they will now think as a nation.

This is the essential factor in unifying their struggle. Regional autonomy is a necessity because there is a real absence of communication between one region and another. That is not a new phenomenon here, but the war has helped to amplify it. Thus, the radio has a unifying role. In all the villages they listen to Radio NUFK, broadcast from Khmer territory, and to Radio Peking which sends out several programmes a day in Khmer. But it is still necessary that they understand what is said.

So, in this way informed of significant events and of the priorities of the moment, the cadres carry the directives for action and propaganda from the top to the bottom of the organization and from there to the villagers. At the time of my visit, on the eve of President Nixon's visit to Peking, when the Phnom Penh politicians were attacking their rivals in expectation of contacts with the other side, a vast campaign was about to be launched against "Nixon's false peace" and the "traitors' manoeuvre" with which "no compromise" could be envisaged.

"Do you think that these big diplomatic moves can have any immediate effect here in the field?" I asked a journalist from the Front's press, who was accompanying me [Ros Chet Thor]. "Probably not," he replied, "but we cannot take too many precautions. We must continue to increase the level of mobilization of the masses." The best way to do this seems to be through holding meetings of the people. I attended three of these, in different areas.

A Meeting at Night

The first meeting was held after sunset. It was a strange sight to see these silent nocturnal columns coming together from far away along the paths. The platform is already in place, with two neon tubes powered by a small generator, with red cloth banners on which are slogans like "Enlarge the Liberated Zone"; "Invite the People from the Enemy Zone To Join Us"; "Down with the False Republic"; "Long Live the Heroic People's Armed Forces for National Liberation". The crowd grows. The monks are already there when the top leaders of the province arrive. They are dressed like everyone else in black pyjamas but we recognize them because they arrive by motorbike with their "chauffeur".

Greeted with the same humility by all taking part, the monks recite the litanies for the occasion, then the cadres take over the microphone — the chairmen of the district committees, the chairman of the province committee, military chiefs, delegates from local organizations of the Front, from the Union of Patriotic Women, and so on. In the second half, the audience will be entertained with songs and dances, traditional in form and very patriotic.

Three to four thousand people are assembled together. A good number of them come from the zone held by Phnom Penh's troops and they will return there the next day.

The military campaign around Phnom Penh has been a strategic success [says a cadre]. We have captured bastions supposed to be impregnable in Phnom Penh's security belt.

We have struck even inside the capital. The enemy is on the defensive and cannot fill the gaps. Our people accept every sacrifice. They prefer to abandon their land for the time being rather than remain under the control of the enemy. Our people have withstood all temptation for personal advantages by refusing to supply the enemy.

Sometimes, during speeches such as this, guns thunder in the distance.."Lon Nol is shaking out his carpet", they say. All the speeches end with chants which the crowd is invited to repeat in chorus — "Long live the National Front of Kampuchea, presided over by Samdech Norodom Sihanouk", "Long live the National United Government of Kampuchea, with Samdech Penn Nouth as President and Khieu Samphân as Vice-President", "Long live the Buddhist religion", "Down with American imperialism and its valets, Lon Nol, Sirik Matak, Son Ngoc Thanh".

The message hardly changes from one speech to another. The military cadres stress the good relations between the army and the people. "The People's Liberation armed forces are your sons, dear compatriots, and your pupils, venerable monks. You have given your hearts to create them, to form them, to educate them. Their first duty to you, in return, is to show themselves ever more resolute in serving the people and the nation." "The armed forces", says another, "must be educated by you in order to acquire the character of a true people's army, modest and courageous." That is the main role of the family heads, and even more of the monks: to educate.

The Commitment of the Clergy

The reactions of the Buddhist clergy are perhaps the sharpest and most astonishing feature for a foreign observer. Accustomed to the majestic unction with which ordinary monks receive the homage of the faithful, aware of the enormous influence possessed by the clergy, all of rural extraction, such an observer would presume this spiritual power to be wholly conservative.

The new authorities in Phnom Penh, after 18 March 1970, staked everything on this card. Since then, they have never ceased to speak of a "holy war" (*chambaing sasna*) against the *Thmil*, the atheists. Marshal Lon Nol, now Head of State, is an expert in appealing to religious fanaticism. "For a year", he said on the Khmer New Year's Day in 1971, "we have fought the expansionist Thmil with their lacquered teeth, the Viet Cong, and the Pathet Lao. The whole world admires us. Our Buddhist religion will survive for five thousand years as preordained".[1]

Not only has this operation been a complete failure, it has rebounded on its authors. In spite of the difficulty of obtaining precise information on this subject, it seems that a large part of the clergy was overtaken by anxiety and indecision after the ousting of Prince Sihanouk. Many monks waited to see how events would turn out and how their flock would respond. Gradually, they have taken sides. In the course of the year 1971, the Front organized a Congress for pagoda leaders.

We sent out many invitations and we expected about two hundred Superiors [said a cadre who worked on this]. Three hundred and fifty came and with those accompanying them there were fifteen hundred people who had to be worthily fed, decently lodged with respect for the hierarchy and, above all, protected and camouflaged for many days. An exhausting task, and I don't know how we managed it. But in the end the Congress was an enormous political success. That is to be expected. They wanted to know what we were worth. Now they know.

Even more than the cadres, the monks themselves confirmed this.

It has become impossible to fulfil all our prescribed religious duties [declared the Superior (*chau athicar*) of the pagoda of Ang-Pralung]. We can no longer carry out some of the rites, because of Lon Nol's planes. His propaganda is a tissue of lies. His actions show no respect for religion. He says the Viet Cong have burned pagodas when it was his planes which were responsible. Here, our immediate surroundings have been bombed more than 15 times. We no longer go out in the daytime and we are obliged to practise passive defence. A look-out watches the sky and gives the alert several times a day.

He added:

Lon Nol's soldiers hold religion in contempt. They install themselves in monasteries. They turn them into barracks. They steal the animals which they kill even in the inner sanctuary of the monastery. They profane the sanctuaries and mistreat the novices. The Front's soldiers do not behave like that. They only pass by and they show respect. Our monks are not political propagandists. They don't concern themselves with that. When we take part in a public meeting, it is in order to bear witness, to show that religion also suffers in this war.

A few days later, I heard a monk speaking at a people's meeting.

> Formerly, the nation, religion and the throne were a trinity. The nation– that is you and me. Attacks on the nation are also attacks on religion and on the throne. The nation is the base of everything. Without it, neither religion nor the throne could survive. The enemy pretends that this is a communist war. They try to frighten those who practise religion and if there are any among you who have fallen into that trap [laughter from the audience] I say to you that religion cannot disappear because it is education. Who does not get education? It shows us the difference between good and evil, between the good and the false. And even communism, I believe, distinguishes between good and evil, in its own way. Our religion is tolerant. Everyone has the right to seek and find the truth, according to one's conscience. If the Front's cadres do good, they will reap a good harvest. As for the American imperialists, they are strong and rich but, I tell you, they are insatiable. They are our mortal enemies.

And he ended his speech with a ringing *cheio pracheachon* (long live the people).

At a third meeting, it was a member of the aristocratic order Thammayut who spoke, the *chau athicar* of the pagoda of Ang Talek in the district of Samrong Tong.

> Emotion troubles me this evening. It is already three months since I was forced to leave my pagoda. I could no longer suffer the yoke of the demon Lon Nol. I say to the monks and to the people: Unite in your hearts with the Front and throw away any idea of compromise with imperialism and its valet Lon Nol. Come, all of you, and live in the liberated zone. If you wait for the can of milk, the fragment of cloth or the blanket which occasionally the enemy offers you, the war won't end for a long time. I have been to the liberated zone. I have seen with my own eyes that there is plenty of land available. I can assure you that there will be no lack of rice nor of land to cultivate. I guarantee this. If, on going back to the Lon Nol zone, you fear you will not be believed or will suffer reprisals, give my name, say that you only echo my words.

One could easily see from the reactions of the crowd that this speech, so concrete and vital, went down very well. The support of the monks, the gift of their authority to the resistance forces, is a trump card. Truly, no one expresses the deep feelings of the rural masses with greater weight than these peasant-monks.

Mustering the People

Province of Kompong Chhnang. In speeches as in discussion, the term *kamaphibal* (cadre) often comes up. The cadres as in the Vietnamese NLF and in the Pathet Lao are the mainspring of the machine. Near and far, they are the leaders. From what I could see, there are not many of them, but they move around ceaselessly, equipped with their ubiquitous brief cases, frequently sending and receiving messages written on the leaves of a notebook and sealed with a grain of cooked rice. The messengers, on foot or on bicycle, always seem to know where to find the recipients, an ability which surpasses my comprehension. Obviously, they refuse to talk about themselves and their past life, but it is probable that a large proportion belong to the small Cambodian Left who had to disarm in 1954 and after that to operate clandestinely because of brutal police repression, especially after 1966. Even in the most difficult circumstances they continued to proclaim their support for anti-imperialism, national unity and neutrality. Today, there has been an abrupt change and the Left is now able to use that old policy against those who for a long time forced them to keep it hidden.

The partisans of that political line are generally recruited from intellectuals of modest origins, sons of farmers or of small employees. Many made a career in education at a low level. Others were barred from this by their lack of familiarity with French culture, a privilege reserved for the rich bourgeoisie. So one could take as typical the case of the chairman of the provincial committee. He had been a monk for five years during which time he studied the classics in his native tongue. Then he became a low-level municipal employee and finally a Khmer-language monitor in a pagoda school. He was a gentle, affable man who understood a little French but did not speak it. A peasant intellectual, he was not from the upper crust, but his word counted in the villages. Others have come and will come to join this initial core — bourgeois intellectuals, rich and poor, like two engineers with diplomas from the public works high school in Paris whom I met by chance as I travelled around. We talked about the cost of life in the Quartier Latin. "When all this is over, I'll go back to visit Paris", says one of them. Maybe. Meanwhile it is hard to become a peasant.

Others were peasants who had passed through the cadres' school. The older ones will remain active at the village level, but the younger ones have a very open future. They take their responsibilities very seriously. In principle, the organizational pyramid of these cadres plays the role of an administrative structure but this also seems to be in an embryonic stage. The villages administer themselves. They have their committees, appointed according to proposals from higher up in the Front but reflecting the general wishes of the inhabitants. Above this, there is a group of cadres whose powers are fixed but whose roles are, in reality, many sided. There are practically no medical services, which is nothing new in the Cambodian countryside. So far as education is concerned, literacy is ensured, but the programme has not gone very far beyond that.

This is the provincial apparatus. Now, a regional committee (Cambodia is divided in four regions) seems to have responsibilities little different from those of the national leadership of a dozen ministers and vice-ministers who are inside the country. Among them, Khieu Samphân is notable as Deputy Prime Minister, Minister of Defence and Commander of the armed forces. In the region I visited, Hou Yuon, Minister of the Interior, was as well known. He had just toured the area and held several big meetings close to Phnom Penh. People were impressed by his talent as a speaker. Nonetheless, the key personality in the situation remains Prince Sihanouk.

The Role of the Prince

On 18 March 1970, everything was over in a few hours. The conspirators had not wished, or known how, or been able to rally Prince Sihanouk to their cause. The countryside was, therefore, immediately at boiling point. All the peasants I interviewed confirmed that. "In our village we were very angry." The massacre of the peasants who went in protest to Phnom Penh, instigated by Colonel Les Kacem, roused very great indignation among them. Certainly, in political speeches today, the prince is valued for what he symbolizes: national independence, neutrality, and unity. But the attachment is at the same time personal and emotional, a mixture of political and religious symbolism, more directly understood in the peasants' mentality. He is a royal figure, a worker of miracles, whether one likes it or not, and this is an aspect which the peasants often say has an impact on them.

It is clear that if the prince had not called for an insurrection and had not supported the Front in his messages over the air on Radio Peking, the guerrillas would still be hard put to extend their influence in the heart of the country, in the rice-growing plains. One could call it legitimacy, but that is too legalistic a word, too Western. It would be more accurate to speak of the "mandate of heaven", if one may presume to transplant that Chinese and Confucian idea to this country. Let us say "authority" and add that no one here dreams of contesting it.

Old grudges have been buried. Only the broadest and strongest unity can guarantee success. Division would be the real enemy, for the prime task is to kick out the foreign interventionists. The presence of the prince is at one and the same time the guarantee and the cement of that unity. In that role, not so new as it seems, the prince has not entirely renounced his sometimes undiplomatic style. But that scarcely raises problems for the moment. They don't know, in the *maquis*, about the quarrel between Prince Sihanouk and the Soviet leaders. As it does not touch questions which are explicitly included in the Front's programme, what the prince does or says remains ignored by most of the cadres and the population because the radio does not mention it. But that does not mean that the prince's moves would be disapproved of by the leading cadres.

With skilful equilibrium, very much in the Cambodian manner, the prince and the Front support each other, and if one adds the clergy, this reciprocal and necessary support becomes triangular. These three elements emanate from the aspirations of the Khmer peasantry and although different, they complement each other and can only move in step along the same path. Without this, all would be threatened with chaos. It is the interplay of these component forces which give the Cambodian situation its originality, compared to neighbouring countries.

Indochinese Solidarity

Some sad spirits may regret, perhaps, that one cannot discover the "hordes from Hanoi" to which Phnom Penh's propaganda attributes all its problems.[2] It is a fact that, even according to American intelligence, the North Vietnamese forces and those of the Provisional Revolutionary Government have wholly recaptured their old "sanctuaries" in the border regions. Certain sectors, strategic for the guerrilla communications, are still probably defended by the Vietnamese, who also defend the plantations where, one should remember, the workers were mostly of Vietnamese origin. The local cadres were all the less talkative on this subject because they had never had Vietnamese troops in their sector. But the various indications one can collect, as much in the zone held by the NUFK as in Phnom Penh, show that the presence of troops or of military advisers of the NLF has been greatly reduced since March–April 1970, by the extent to which the NUFK has established its own political-military structure. Its military capacity can only grow over time. Even if one admits that the international situation will determine the moment when the battle will end, it is from now on clear that the Cambodians are carrying on their struggle themselves and that there are in the *maquis* the elements of a government ready to assume its national and international responsibilities, in harmony with its Indochinese allies.

Village Society and People's Unity

"Before, life was quiet here. Now, there's no more pagoda, no more school, that's no life." This grumbling old woman feels the weight of the war at her own level. She does not even mention the fact that bombings chased her away from her home to a temporary hut in middle of the fields. What is important is the breaking of the social order, the injured morality.

The bombs are certainly a decisive factor in the determination to fight to the end which animates the Khmers, young and old. But other factors are at work. One sees them in the contrast between the day to day morality in one zone and another. In Phnom Penh, bars, prostitution, gambling dens and thieves have invaded the streets in a good part of the city. The military police have implanted their gangsterism. Corruption is everywhere and it isn't only military chiefs who demand money before sending reinforcements to a colleague in difficulty.

On the other hand, in the zone held by the NUFK, a few weeks of propaganda was enough to suppress gambling and drunkenness, to the great relief of the wives. Corruption does not exist and the morality of the troops is such that families are easily persuaded to allow their young daughters to join cultural groups or production units which tour the countryside. That morality which has been recaptured in the twinkling of an eye is certainly the sort of security to which the traditional peasantry aspires — fervent, and very different from the caricatured modernism which makes life in so many Asian cities so derisory and painful. It is a conservative reflex. It feeds the energy of a society which knows with confidence it is not condemned.

In moulding itself closely in these ways the Front has captured for its policy of national unity the physical dynamism of the peasantry. Solidly founded on these beliefs and aspirations, the Front, under the princely umbrella, can draw other social groups to it — workers, not very numerous, but politically motivated for a long time; shopkeepers, when desire for profit does not entirely obscure their judgement; officials, whose situation may be profitable today but possibly precarious tomorrow; and young school boys, among whom the Lon Nol army tries to recruit, offering hazardous perspectives. To realize the largest possible unity, merge together all the social strata — this is the obsession of the cadres, the key to final victory.

They hope, in addition, that this unity which they have acquired will survive victory, that it may become the soil in which this new power can spread its roots. When a cadre insisted that this democratic power must know how to respect the interests of the workers and, at the same time, of "patriotic capitalists", I objected that elsewhere their interests have appeared to be contradictory. "In Cambodia", he replied, "we usually resolve our problems through discussion." A beautiful habit, indeed.

These problems of the future don't yet, in any case, seem to be the order of the day. The Cambodian *maquis* is only two years old. The war increases its ravages. American military supplies continue to flood in at night to the airport at Pochentong. The order of the day is total war.

But, in collecting under its banner the greatest possible range of forces, the Front hopes to grow capable of restoring liberty to a people that has lost it — a liberty which is needed to conserve its intimate rustic relationships, on the edges of an all too brutal history.[3]

2

The Agrarian Question in Indochina

For thirty years now, the thunder of guns has almost made us forget the propelling themes of Indochinese history. It is for this reason that we should investigate them, as their significance will no doubt re-emerge.

"Whoever wins the peasantry wins China. Whoever solves the agrarian problem will win over the peasantry", said the Chinese communists in the 1930s.[1] "The agrarian question in Vietnam has always been the key to the peasant question, which is itself the essence of the national question; that's what dominates the internal development of South Vietnamese society", say the North Vietnamese communists, in their turn.[2] And although the Vietnamese formula (a matter of how to resolve the "national question") differs slightly from the Chinese one, the thought is the same. Its application is even more universal: "In non-industrialized Asiatic countries, no class can seize power without first *resolving* the land problem." Or even: "A new political order will be established and consolidated because it is seen as the harbinger of new production relations in the countryside, which conform more to the peasants' aspirations." Various conditions can obscure the significance of this principle. It remains a fact that it lights the way for the political traveller in Asia, for those who aim to achieve power.

Actually this obvious truth is accepted by all parties involved in the conflict. But very little attention has been given to understanding the land problem in Indochina, because of the preoccupation with world power politics. Firstly, then, the agrarian question is spacewise fragmented and timewise evolving. The Cambodian and Vietnamese problems differ greatly from each other. The land laws and the nature of agricultural economic processes have changed dramatically several times over the past hundred years.

Several logical threads are tied into this problem: what is the nature of the movements in which the Indochinese peasants today have risen up in rebellion? What agrarian question do they have to resolve and how are they going about it?

How can one learn from this phenomenon of two peasant masses seemingly involved in identical uprisings, even though one has profound social roots and the causes of the other are obviously institutional? What sort of revolution takes place when these movements come to power, as in Hanoi in 1954? What solution do the revolutionaries impose on the land problem and how closely does it follow Marxist analysis? Can it be considered at any particular moment that the revolutionaries have really been able to "solve" the agrarian problem? We cannot at once find answers to all these questions. The following guidelines are intended to gather together, after dipping into the huge barrel of assorted material available, some themes which throw light on the nature of these problems.[3]

The Traditional Land-Holding Systems

The "populating virtue" of Chinese civilization[4] is not just a cultural phenomenon; it has its economic roots in wet rice agriculture and its high yields. Rice and irrigation are responsible for the great population densities of Asia. Rather than discuss the hypotheses of Karl Wittfogel in his work *Oriental Despotism,* it is enough here to stress the importance of water control and its political ramifications.

Rice has been grown in Indochina since the Bronze Age, and perhaps before. We know little enough about the old land laws, but we do know about the different politics of water control in the Indianized states (Cambodia, Champa) and the Sinicized ones (Vietnam). In the former, a complex system of reservoirs and run-off canals enabled the discharge of water needed for irrigation and had to be completely regulated. But these great water control constructions were even more difficult to maintain than to build, and their decay seems to account satisfactorily for the collapse of Angkorian power in medieval Indochina.[5] Apart from the huge protective river dikes in the northern Delta, the Vietnamese, especially during their southward movement, instead of keeping the tank system of Indian origin, utilized small-scale water control systems of local design, and so maintenance did not depend entirely on the vigour of the central authority.[6] This difference of technique has had its influence on modes of appropriation and occupation of land.

Vietnamese land customs have gone through several fairly distinct periods. But the beginnings of the dominant role of private landed property in agricultural production can be traced back to 1722. In that year, the authorities took action on a developing situation which had for a long time been contained, and drafted a fiscal reform which imposed land taxes, for the first time, not only on communal lands, but also on privately owned land. For several centuries, in fact, the Viet-namese monarchy did its best to restrict the accumulation of large estates. As in China, high officials were assigned lands from which they would receive revenue, but the rights over those lands were tied to the position and were not hereditary. By preventing the development of a landed nobility, the regime assured its control of the administration, which was recruited by competitive examination, and performed what the political ideology of the period necessitated: the provision of a constant means of subsistence to the peasants, who were spread over a difficult and very dispersed area.

> The large estates were condemned because they demanded much less labour per hectare than the peasant's small life tenancy concession. That's why the large landholdings very soon became the target of restrictive, even prohibitive measures. By the end of the fourteenth century, Hô Qùy-Ly, in his struggle against the growth of these *latifundia*, decreed that from then on, no-one, except princes and princesses by blood, could own more than 10 mau of riceland[7] [that is, 3.6 hectares].

But be that as it may, amongst the minor royal aristocracy, or in the mandarin class, the tendency to accumulate land remained strong. In periods of weak central control, the large estates reappeared, by appropriation of communal land, by purchase or by subjection of the small farmers.

The war between the family cliques which dominated the north and the south of the country led, in the north at the end of the eighteenth century, to an important administrative and fiscal reform. Officials, instead of being assigned benefices from the produce of certain lands, were given rights of taxation over a certain number of villages. Taxation demands thus became a powerful tool in the hands of "devious village tyrants".[8] The spread of large estates resulted in the eviction of many peasants, a reduction in the amount of cultivated land and a decline in production. Finally, the great peasant upsurge which led to the Tây Son revolt (1770–1800), swept away the dynasty and the ruling cliques and reunified the country, but it failed to transform the agrarian structure.

The heir of the southern clique, Nguyên Anh, the future Emperor Gia-Long, partly because he was supported by foreign intervention (Siam and France) and no doubt also because of the disillusionment of the rural people with the way the Tây Son chiefs had discarded their revolutionary ideals, managed to recapture the capital and assume power over the whole country. The situation, a turning point in history, demanded social changes that would endure. But, on its revamped political base, the new Nguyên dynasty set about preserving the spirit of the old land regulations.

It was all organized at the communal village level. The lands were entered into the cadastral records, the *dia bô*, detailing their surface area, fertility, usage (rice or otherwise), and owner (peasant, communal ownership, religious land). Periodically, in theory every three years, more often every six, the communal land was redistributed hierarchically: the most powerful notables had the right to the greater part. The purpose of this was to guarantee the survival of the least fortunate and to adapt farming conditions to demographic changes within the village.[9]

Right through the nineteenth century, imperial edicts proclaimed that public lands, *công diên*, were inalienable, thus indicating that they were continually threatened.

> The villages have always had a tendency to ignore this prescription of public policy, by selling the communal rice lands and retaining the right to repurchase them. In an attempt to increase resources in the short term, they get hold of funds by alienating their most productive lands in this way; they intend this to be merely temporary, but, if they lack capital at the date of required payment, it risks becoming permanent.[10]

Apart from a small head tax, the main form of taxation was on land. It was annual and based on the number of *mau* of cultivated land. If a peasant ceased cultivation of a plot for three years, he would no longer own the plot nor would he pay taxes on it. Most of the tax was paid in kind; the amount depended on the quality of the soil or more accurately on the information written down in the *dia bô*. Allowances were made for depressed geographical areas (there were four of them in the country), and for the hand of nature, so that taxes were reduced in times of natural disasters. The aggregate tax level was determined by the numbers of inhabitants officially "registered" and it was up to the commune to collect the tax from amongst all the members. Those "registered" were often the descendants of the founders of the village; the non-registered were of more recent origin. According to the prevailing administrative principles, the number "registered" was never to decrease. This distinction of status, a very important one for the individuals concerned, was embodied in the complex hierarchy which regulated the relationships between villagers. The elders, the landowners, the former officials, former soldiers, and the scholars were at the top of the social ladder. It was from among them that the village council was elected, without outside interference.

By falsifying the real number of local inhabitants, the village council shared out the tax burden as they saw fit, taking into account those exempted by law, and they were allowed to reserve some of the financial resources for local purposes and interests.

All the fiscal institutions created by the sovereign were distorted in practice; the land register was inaccurate, the census incomplete. That higher authorities were powerless to ensure that their intentions were carried out is evidenced by the large number of penal regulations. The reason for this state of affairs can be found in the political constitution of Annamite [Vietnamese] society. All its components crystallize in social communities: only the communes, the religious congregations, and the guilds would stand up to face the central power. The Empire was a government of collectives and not of individuals.[11]

The black-and-white generalizations on which the opinion of this colonial official is based are a good example of the prevailing ideas of the period; colonial administrators loved to draw the distinction between Europe and Asia as one of Western individual values face to face with the collective anonymity of the Asiatic masses. The latter view, they said, was a wrong done to humanity, and they set out to redress it — at their own profit incidentally. But to do this, they had to ignore the considerable freedom that Vietnamese had to play out their own game in a society whose only static quality was the opinion that Europeans had of it.

The colonization of southern Cochinchina, that is to say the Mekong Delta, opened new horizons to the dynamic Vietnamese. Having subdued the power of the Chams and the Khmers, the Vietnamese — landless peasants from the north, adventurers, beggars, soldiers and pioneers — were able to set up their own village structure, their own irrigation system and their own mode of cultivation and production. In the delta of the Red River and in the narrow plains of central Vietnam, the communes were the product of a long evolution directly controlled by the state. But the colonization of the south was the combined effort of state action and private initiative; the latter was actually encouraged by the authorities, who were anxious to consolidate their occupation of vast, recently acquired territories. Freedom to clear and settle on land was very soon guaranteed to new arrivals: "The process of colonisation by individuals can take place, in those conditions, on a large or a small scale, depending on the means of each settler. Because of the vast tracts of land available, the setting up of large estates was not incompatible with the existence of individual plots".[12] So during the initial period of colonization, one could find small cultivators living side by side with large landowners; the latter would often employ serfs,[13] or tenant farmers, sometimes the original Khmer inhabitants. In contrast to custom, this process was not always even, and some settlements only became communes a long time after their establishment. This explains why the communal land area is often very small compared to the average in older agricultural areas. This scantiness of communal land has contributed to the process of proletarianization.

Under these conditions, in southern Cochinchina in the nineteenth century, there developed both large landlordism and a class of farmers producing a marketable surplus. Population pressures remained weak, as tracts of arable land still remained to be cultivated. The socio-economic system which developed had important differences from the prevailing tradition in the rest of the country. It was there that the colonial initiative made its first advances.

In Cambodia, land problems developed under completely different conditions. The decline of the Angkorian Empire, in about the fourteenth century, and the end of an efficient political centralization of water control, as well as wars, the weakness of the monarchy (the king was often forced to hand over provincial power or face a feudal rebellion), all combined to leave the king only a negligible role to play in the agricultural economy. Up until the modern period, population pressure was weak and land remained available for settlement. Competition for land was therefore not very intense. This became obvious in the eighteenth and nineteenth centuries in the Mekong Delta; in the face of the Vietnamese advance, Khmer peasants remained on the land or just dismantled their houses and moved elsewhere.

We know very little about the social and economic history of Cambodia, but we can deduce, from the fact that the king possessed vast estates which were worked for him by servile labourers, that the important nobles who held revenue rights over one or more provinces must also have owned large estates.[14] Although subject to corvée labour requirements, the greater part of the population were free and tilled their own land.

The Cambodian communal institution was far from having the same strong internal cohesion that was so noticeable in neighbouring Vietnam. The real nucleus of the Khmer village is the pagoda. This difference in political organization is obvious at first sight even today. As distinct from the traditional Vietnamese village which is turned in on itself and hidden behind its protective hedge of tropical growth, the Khmer village is spread out, or dispersed along a river bank, open to the world. This arrangement also prevails quite often in the Vietnamese regions of the Mekong Delta where the communal organization is much less rigid. The principal official of the *srok* (the Khmer word for district), who probably was once elected by the notables, is now appointed by the provincial authorities. He acts as an intermediary between them and the villagers.

In Cambodia, then, there is no communal land and no land registry. The different system is clearly evident in the mode of taxation: not the land, but the harvest, is subject to tax.[15] The procedure is revealing: a high official of the house which holds revenue rights over the province (King, Queen Mother, *Obareach* or Crown Prince, Minister, etc.) traverses the province, evaluates the harvest, fixes the total amount of the tithe, and then waits for it be collected.[16] It also seems that over a long period — from the sixteenth century till the end of the eighteenth — client-patron relationships were developed between aristocrats and commoners, and that the produce taxed from the clients went to the patron with whom they aligned.[17]

On the eve of the colonial era, then, the land laws of Vietnam and Cambodia were radically different. The following similarities and differences may be enumerated:

— In both countries, the sovereign possessed a theoretically absolute right over the soil.[18]
— In both countries, cultivation gave ownership. Cessation of cultivation led, after several years, to the disqualification of ownership rights.
— Feudal revenue for religious institutions.
— In both countries, the mandarins were remunerated by the direct allocation of taxes raised in their district.
— There existed in Cambodia revenue rights of a feudal character which had long since disappeared in Vietnam.
— Serfdom was rather widespread in Cambodia and played an important economic role. It was much rarer in Vietnam, where it only played a transitory role in the settlement of the south.
— Tax was on land in Vietnam, on the harvest in Cambodia.
— Land was surveyed and registered by the mandarins in Vietnam. Local acceptance was the proof of possession in Cambodia.
— The Vietnamese commune, run by the notables, owned land collectively and shared out the tax burden. There was no equivalent institution in Cambodia.

It would seem from this summary that the Vietnamese land law in the second half of the nineteenth century was closer than the Cambodian to a modernized system of agriculture and marketing, and that the way appeared clear for the introduction of a capitalist land rent system.

Let us take this opportunity to remark, as others have before us, that very little research has been carried out to analyse the origins of capitalism in Asiatic societies, or, to put it another way, the factors which have combined to prevent its development. However, the question has been posed for a good many years, at least since Max Weber published the first volume of his *Religionssoziologie* (1920). Karl Wittfogel, when he was a Marxist, said of him: "Weber is the only bourgeois historian who has ever seriously posed the question of why China did not of its own accord arrive at industrial capitalism. But his eclectic and non-Marxist method prevented him from finding a convincing answer to the questions which he had correctly recognised as crucial".[19] A former pupil of Wittfogel's at the seminary in Frankfurt, Etienne Balazs, has contributed to the economic history of China and has reformulated the question.[20] But it remains almost completely unanswered as far as the other Asiatic societies are concerned (except for Japan), and particularly in Indochina.

The Colonial Intervention

Whatever their real role, large estates did not seem, to the first administrators sent out to manage colonial affairs, to be the dominant aspect of the Indochinese countryside. Some even went so far as to deny their existence and to find reasons for their absence:

> Private individuals, in spite of their desire to preserve their property, would never try to extend their landed wealth, otherwise they would have to meet the tax requirements of officials. They are content to produce as much as possible on their land, to sell the harvest profitably, and to waste the profits on gambling, most of the time, even though they could turn them to better account. Because of this, *landownership* in Annam is on a very small scale, and *large landholdings* do not exist.[21]

Now, large estates can easily exist side by side with very small plots, that is, where they are not the direct cause of such fragmentation of landholdings.

It is true that to a Frenchman accustomed to land transactions, especially those vast property transfers of nineteenth-century France, the market for land in Vietnam would have appeared to be unusually tight, and there are various reasons for this. As well as noting that (Vietnamese) peasants were unwilling to divest themselves of their land, where their ancestors' tombs are frequently to be found, C. Lejeune points out: "Apart from this moral restriction, the low market value of land and the enormous interest rates preclude land transactions and speculation."[22]

Pierre Gourou, using the Tonkinese example, sums up clearly the different attitudes, psychological as well as economic, that obstruct the development of large landholdings in overpopulated regions:

> Laws and customs were traditionally hostile to large estates. The royal government periodically ordered their redistribution; the peasants on their part united strongly against anyone attempting to establish large estates. It was difficult to buy land outside of one's native village; the buyer could be swindled and, after paying a reasonable price, clash with the true owner. The village authorities could create a thousand problems for a landowner who was not a native of the commune. The buyer would not be able to get his land cultivated; the locals would refuse to lend him aid; as a last resort, the new owner would be reduced to taking on the seller as a tenant, and accept his outrages.... The seller would often retain right of repurchase. These conditions pleased the peasants who hated to be separated from their ancestral lands, without the hope of recovering them.[23]

This situation, on the whole, raised grave problems for the colonists. Their military and technical weaknesses prevented them from massive expropriations of land belonging to local cultivators, for fear of revolt, of which the process of conquest had given them a foretaste. In fact the existing landholding system had to be guaranteed, and any modifications left until such a time as settlers could be introduced. However, the disposal of unoccupied land could be done immediately: "In Cochinchina ... all lands not appropriated or occupied by the natives were, by virtue of the decree of 20th February, 1862, confiscated by the State, and the transfer of this property was regulated by the same decree."[24] But at the stage when the authorities in France decided to sanction a programme to develop these areas, the situation had to be taken as it was:

> The principle always referred to in this matter [explains C. Lejeune,] is that Annamite laws must serve as the basis for our judicial system, and that there is only cause to apply our laws as binding in the absence of native texts. In Annam and Tonkin, by virtue of the Treaty of 6th June, 1884, and of other conventions, the Annamites were promised that their land laws would be preserved.[25]

So it was presumably for this reason that, in good time, translations were made of the *Code Annamite*, by Aubaret (1865), then a better one, by Philastre (1876) and the *Codes cambodgiens*, by Adhémard Leclère (1898).

In Cambodia the situation was even more delicate since property laws seemed more vague; they were not complemented, as in Vietnam, by the existence of the communal institution and the *dia bô*. Article IX of the Convention of 17 June 1884 (imposed on the king under threat of bombardment) stipulates that "the land of the kingdom, up until today the exclusive property of the Crown, will no longer be inalienable. The French and Cambodian authorities will proceed to establish private property in Cambodia." This dream of the colonial Lycurgues was going to be shattered the following year by a widespread peasant revolt.

Still, the settlers demanded guarantees, and, in 1897, the colonial authorities returned to the fray. "The government reserves the right to alienate and to assign all the free lands of the kingdom. The buyers and the grantees will enjoy full property rights over the land sold or assigned to them."[26] The application form stressed the necessity "to increase over and over again the wealth and prosperity of the country, since immense tracts are available and unoccupied."[27]

But that was not enough. The French, still anxious to "establish private property", made Sisowath, the new king they had just put on the throne, deliver the following words as part of his coronation speech: "I am absolutely resolved to give land, which up till now has been the exclusive domain of the Crown, over to individual private property, to the villagers who cultivate it, for the well-being and prosperity of the kingdom."[28] In 1920, the authorities had to try again, and promulgated a new civil code which, as regards landownership, went back to the principles outlined five years before by M. Boudillon, an inspector in the office of registry of lands and public domains, who had come out in favour of a single landholding system. He was under no illusions as to the possibility of applying a body of regulations derived from Roman law to a system founded on possession by common acceptance:

This new organization can still only be considered for the distant future, after a slow transformation of the customs and needs of the natives and the development of means of communication which are crucial to agricultural modernization; only then will land acquire a higher market value, and also new value as collateral for credit.[29]

And that was the point. Beyond the short term interests of the European *colons*, who were frequently given virgin lands on which to establish plantations, the general aim of the colonizers was to increase land values; in other words, according to Marx, capitalized rents. It was also important to raise the level of production, so capital would be created for payment and credit that would become the necessary source of investment for colonial development.

Very early, in fact, the administrators of French Indochina had complained of the lack of capital available to them for the exploitation of the colony. Paul Doumer, the General Governor, went so far as to collect forced taxes for two years to enable him to present Paris with an inflated colonial budget capable of guaranteeing a large loan to finance a trans-Indochinese railway line. But it was impossible to keep pressuring a peasantry that was already very poor. Leaving aside the revolts that this policy provoked,[30] it was counterproductive. The fiscal returns of the following years betrayed a significant decline.

One classical solution was available; to impose, as far as possible, French land laws and tax system. In Cambodia, this was seen as a long process by those who had an interest in it:

> In this era, with no private property, and land registration only embryonic, a land tax suitable for some time yet would have to be of a very special kind, and consequently would necessitate the maintaining of special levying procedures. But it was still necessary to look ahead. So, the Ordinance of 25 April 1902, which prescribed the posting of a notice in each village bearing the name of all landowners and the area of land they occupied, was submitted to the king for his signature. Unfortunately, though, this Ordinance was not followed up.

These words were written in 1925, sixty years after the arrival of French colonialism.[31]

In spite of the slow pace of change and the difficulties of conformity between French and Vietnamese law,[32] colonization assumed an economic importance which modified the basis of the land question. In Cambodia, huge rubber plantations began to encroach upon the jungle. Most of the labour was recruited, often pressganged, from among the landless peasants of Tonkin.

In Vietnam, public projects extended the cultivated areas in the Mekong Delta, and the southward flow of immigrants from the north and centre continued. Large landholdings increased in size and number. Some of these vast estates, made up of hundreds or thousands of small plots rented out to tenant farmers, were owned by Frenchmen, but the greater part were owned by Vietnamese in reward for co-operating with the colonial authorities. By the beginning of this century, a powerful group of big landlords began to emerge as the dominant class in the Mekong Delta and in Saigon.

The process was different in the centre and in the north. Centuries of settlement, and the resultant scarcity of virgin lands, the population density, and the rigidity of the village structure weighed heavily against land transfers and land accumulation. Nevertheless, plantations were established in the upland regions on the fringes of the Red River Delta. The process developed thus:

> Around 1890, there were 116 European-owned estates in Indochina, 100 of them in Cochinchina, and they extended over 11,390 hectares. In 1900, the total area of European concessions reached 322,000 hectares, 70,000 in Cochinchina and 193,000 in Tonkin. And now, there are about a million hectares, 110,000 in Tonkin and 610,000 in Cochinchina; of this million hectares, 400,000 were under cultivation on 1st January 1937.[33]

And of course the amount of land bought annually is important: 133,000 hectares in 1930.[34]

It is useful to compare these figures with those indicating the increase of the cultivated area in the Mekong delta, after the public works programmes (land reclamation, the digging of canals, and so on):

1880	522,000 hectares
1900	1,175,000 hectares
1937	2,200,000 hectares[35]

The greater part of these new lands were carved out of the public estate, marshes and forest. Areas of up to 300 hectares were given away freely. But this was not exactly all "virgin" land, particularly in the highlands where the non-Vietnamese ethnic minorities lived.

> It is absolutely false [writes Robequain] to say that these very vast expanses of the backwoods which are not under permanent cultivation, are unclaimed and unused. In fact, they nearly always belong to agricultural nomads, each year crops are planted in predetermined plots... And the rest of the highlands are not unoccupied either; they are reserves which revert season by season to the disposal of a collective. The territory of each village or tribe is perfectly well defined by tradition.[36]

Most of these European estates were situated on the fringes of the local peasant realm. There were plantations of rubber, tea, coffee, and various industrial crops. More important, from our point of view, is the development of a vast network of large estates (*latifundia*), the emergence of a Vietnamese absentee landlord class and the deterioration of tenancy conditions for the mass of the peasants. The establishment of land titles not only led to the clearing of virgin lands, but also to the enlargement of the big landholdings through usurious practices and the increasing number of mortgages. In town, the landlord-moneylenders received credit from the banks on terms that were much less harsh than they themselves imposed on their tenants: for peasants, 100 per cent interest per year was quite commonplace.

The reform of the land tax and its payment in cash, the transformation of corvée labour requirements into a personal tax, along with the abolition of the *sapèque*, a copper coin used only locally, brought about an important change in rural production relations. The peasants were thenceforth obliged to deal in cash, and therefore were drawn into the local market system, which was itself increasingly dependent on the colonial market and its relationship to the world market. From generation to generation, the impact of these changes became more drastic.

The crisis of 1929 had an immediate impact in the rural areas, when the big landlords found their access to credit severely restricted by the banks. Their economic subjection of the peasants increased proportionately. The unrest this provoked broke out in the form of sporadic uprisings, such as in Nghê An in 1930, where embryonic peasant soviets were set up. But it is worth noting that these economic changes did not usher in any significant technical transformation. Rural social conditions underwent few changes and the old mode of production was preserved. Only the new landed bourgeoisie embraced modernization.[37] In spite of the views of Vietnamese or Russian theoreticians who appeal to Marxism and who see in this period a "feudal" or "semi-feudal" Vietnam, capital was definitely at work in the rice field mud, even if its effect on the peasants' consciousness at the beginning of the twentieth century was not very obvious.

The role of capital is illustrated by a supporter of the colonial system:

The French government and its colonial administration have been criticized for having sheltered an antisocial class of large landowners in Cochinchina, for having depended on this group in the past, and in fact even for using them to establish the autonomous government of Cochinchina in 1946. This is partly true, but the facts must be seen in historical and economic perspective. Besides, this class of large and medium landlords only grew up in the west of Cochinchina. This fertile region was wasteland scarcely 50 years ago, and it was only exploited thanks to the magnificent and formidable technical achievements of the French irrigation projects in Cochinchina. In this uncultivated, abandoned region, the exploitation of the soil could only lead to the dominance of large and medium landowners, given the political atmosphere of the last 50 years. In fact, only with private holdings on that scale could the accumulation of private capital, upon which the private financing of the development of western Cochinchina depended be assured, by the concentration of profit from the export of rice. This avoided the need to establish and levy taxes which would have been necessary for public financing of the development of western Cochinchina. By the same token, the hardships that the public sector avoided imposing in the form of taxes, existed nevertheless in the relationship between the landowners on the one hand, and the tenants and sharecroppers on the other.[38]

The Vietnamese Insurrection: The Soil Below

The history of peasant rebellions in Indochina remains, we believe, to be written. But it is a less ambitious project to outline the approach to the agrarian problem taken by the political movement which established itself at the head of the insurrection, under different names, the ICP, the Viet Minh, the Lao Dong, the NLF. At this stage we will just set out a few guidelines.

Founded in 1930 from several small groups, the Indochinese Communist Party (ICP) viewed itself as a working class movement and adopted a simply conceived and radical programme: the distribution of land to rural workers.[39] During the peasant insurrections in the provinces of Nghê An and Ha Tinh (1930–1), peasant unions, in which the communists played a dominant role, set out to distribute communal land, to confiscate land belonging to "reactionary landlords", to reduce land rents and interest rates, and to organize production. These peasant soviets were soon crushed by the army. The Nghê-Tinh insurrection seems to have had exactly the opposite effect on the leadership of the ICP to that which the destruction of the Canton commune had on the leaders of the Chinese CP; battered in the countryside, and decimated (the Secretary-General, Tran Phu, was killed), the Vietnamese communists were thrown back into agitation among the urban proletariat.

In 1936 the new policy adopted by the 7th Congress of the Comintern served to modify considerably the ICP's peasant programme. The Congress recommended the creation of democratic fronts throughout the world. So in November 1939, the National United Front was created to oppose the French colonialists and imperialist war, and to prepare for insurrection. To attract landowners to the national front, the slogan "confiscate the estates of landlords and divide them up amongst the peasants" was played down.[40] The platform of the ICP during this period was quite moderate: reduction of rents, which were not to exceed one-third of the crop; exemption from rents and taxes in case of a bad harvest; equitable distribution of communal lands; freedom to clear, and settle on, virgin land; prohibition of usury; guarantees of basic democratic rights.[41]

The exigencies of the war meant even further moderation:

In May 1941, the 8th Plenum of the Central Committee was held. The revolution in Vietnam had to be seen, in the short term, as a war of national liberation, and this necessitated the creation of the *League for National Independence* (Viet Minh). The principal slogans were: unite the whole people, resist the Japanese and the French, reassert independence by force, and postpone the agrarian revolution.[42]

The first guerrilla bands had appeared in 1940, in the mountains of the north-east; they became "armed propaganda units" in 1943, but played only a minor role in the seething unrest that inflamed the Tonkinese peasantry, who could no longer tolerate food requisitions and famine. It was only after the take-over of power in August 1945 and the retreat to the *maquis* in December 1946 that the Viet Minh appealed to the toilers in the paddy fields to rise up in rebellion, and it was only then that they trained them and led them.

So in the period 1930–45, two themes were prominent: peasant rebellions, often provoked by miserable conditions, were frequent and violent, and sometimes exploited by particular political movements. At the same time, the communist movement downgraded the land problem for the sake of the national front; when they took it up again it was not at the grass-roots level, but when circumstances briefly gave them control of the machinery of state. Meanwhile social tension mounted, and the war increased the burden on the peasantry. The collapse of the successive dominating powers created a desperate and violent atmosphere. As Paul Mus summed it up: "Once they accepted it all. Now they won't have any of it."[43]

The most celebrated aspect of the Viet Minh's agrarian policy was the confiscation of the estates of absentee landowners, both French and Vietnamese, and their redistribution in small plots to "poor peasants", agricultural workers or tenants. Most often, the tenants were assigned the land that they were already working: and they no longer had to pay rent. But the French-owned rice estates (300,000 hectares throughout Indochina, in the 1940s, of which 80 per cent was in Cochinchina) were far from enough for a distribution which, as it was done locally, varied from region to region.

The Viet Minh founded their policy on a distinction between five "rural classes", following the Russian and Chinese communist models.

    (1) *dia chu,* or big landlord, in possession of more than 50 hectares;

    (2) *phu nong,* or rich peasant, owning from 5 to 50 hectares;

(3) *trung nong*, or middle peasant, owning less than 5 hectares;

(4) *ban nong*, or poor peasant, or even a simple tenant;

(5) *co nong*, or landless peasant.[44]

The estates of large landlords who had fled were divided up amongst families, according to the needs of each family, and, of course, the amount of land available. The average seems to have been less than a hectare. If the landlord did not flee, he was forced to reduce his rent demands, often by three-quarters. Previously rents had been as much as half the annual harvest.

In March 1953, apparently for tactical reasons, the Viet Minh leadership pushed for an acceleration of this programme. The Central Committee approved a report on "the principles of land ownership", which advocated "land to the tiller". Along with this, they published a *List of the social classes determined by the government (temporary list)*.[45] Although we have not located the complete text or a translation of it, the title calls up visions of the ups and downs of Marxist thought. Whatever the case may be, after these texts were approved, the rural people were "reclassified": the members of the landlord class multiplied by five, as numbers of "rich peasants" and even some "middle peasants" joined their ranks. Their lands were then confiscated and redistributed. This programme was interrupted by the Geneva Accords and the cessation of hostilities.

The outcome varied a lot from region to region, according to the local military balance, that is. Lê Chau says that "the urgent task of armed combat relegated the political education of the peasantry to second place". The "associations of peasants for national salvation", inadequately organized and strengthened, were much less favoured than other mass movements. As a result one leader of the Resistance later declared "that the role of the peasantry had been underestimated".[46] This and other evidence combine to indicate rather clearly that the autonomous demands of the peasants, that is the political basis of the land question, were kept in check because it was deemed necessary to "educate" the peasants, that is to say, to get them to expect something other than their low level of political awareness and their own views led them to seek. The statistical results as Lê Chau gives them were the following: the poor peasants possessed 62 per cent of the cultivated land in 1954, as against 40 per cent in 1945. In South Vietnam, 600,000 hectares had been distributed to tenant farmers and to the families of soldiers.

This situation was the result of the very principles which inspired the Viet Minh to action. Here Truong Chinh, Secretary of the Workers Party (the Communist Party of North Vietnam), outlines the necessary conditions for the implementation of a radical agrarian reform:

After the liberation of an extensive and relatively secure region, it is possible to implement the land policy as planned. But it must be done step by step. Agrarian reform can only be undertaken when the conditions are favourable. The conditions that must apply in our free zone while the war is still going on, are:

— political stability;
— a strong demand for reform on the part of the peasant masses;
— sufficient cadres to provide proper leadership.[47]

The central question was a political one. The popularity that the partisans enjoyed was found to be, in practice, inadequate as an instrument for a policy that was designed to break up the rural social structure; to sever, at one brutal stroke the impact of which was cushioned as much as possible, the traditional psychological chains which bind the different actors on the rural stage. The dead weight of the past promoted the feeling, amongst both oppressors and oppressed, that it was necessary to remain in one's place.[48] The Confucian social structure was rigid. Capitalism had not yet weakened the old network of social and economic obligations, the demands of which many considered as designed for eternity.

The intervention of the activists, many of whom were of urban background, took place precisely at the heart of local power: the village administration, curiously christened "local feudalism" by the Vietnamese Marxists. It was run by notables, landlords, former officials, and so on, and in general elderly and influential people who shared power amongst themselves. This power was built on a local consensus and remained dependent on it. To be sure, the French later tried to make them submit to a vote; but real power remained in the shadows and stooges were put up for election; later still, Diêm finished off the system by appointing village chiefs. In the traditional organization, and this did not change under the colonial administration, the village leaders chose among themselves. They rarely stood up to behind-the-scene pressures and they no doubt represented the interests of the powerful. It is probable, or at least very arguable, that the village organizations reflected the relations of production which were prevalent in the region. And the relations of production had long since lost their "feudal" characteristics.

In determining to destroy the village institutions, by force if necessary, the Viet Minh counted on the emergence of a new pressure group inside the village, that of the poor tenant farmers. These peasants could not afford to lose sight of the fact that they owed their new privileges (land and local power) to the continued large-scale military and political dominance of the Viet Minh. From this violent overthrow of the village notables stems a great deal of the violent anti-communism of some Vietnamese.[49]

As early as 1951 the French, under the guise of Bao Dai, had drawn up a project of agrarian reform which they considered capable of taking the ground out from under the feet of the "rebels". But it was too little, too late, and never saw the light of day.

It fell to Ngô Dinh Diêm and his American advisers to take up the idea. The end of the war seemed to provide the chance to put it into practice. The Americans, for their part, conceived of a radical agrarian reform which they felt would eliminate the legacies of colonialism which US domestic public opinion condemned, and which would give rise to a "liberal democracy", which they insisted could alone protect the State against all forms of subversion. They saw land inequality as the root of all political evil in Asia. In Japan, MacArthur's first concern was to implement agrarian reform that would favour the individual small landowner, who could then be mobilized to form a solid base for a conservative regime that would be favourable to American interests. Even today, a liberal-conservative party is in power in Tokyo and it owes its electoral majority to the rural constituencies. American specialists then set off for Korea, Taiwan, and the Philippines to help realize this political strategy. In 1955, the interest that they had long shown in the Vietnamese conflict brought them along to advise Ngô Dinh Diêm as well.

In 1956, Ordinance 57 was promulgated, limiting private landholdings to 100 hectares.[50] Excess land was to be registered, appropriated, and sold, in order of priority, to: (1) current tenants; (2) victims of the war against the Viet Minh; (3) refugees from the north; (4) unemployed persons, etc. The government paid the owner 10 per cent of the value of the land and the rest in twelve-year government bonds. The buyer had to pay the 10 per cent on transfer and the rest in six annual instalments, and he would only receive the title to the land on payment of the full amount.

For many reasons, the reform aborted and brought hardly any change in ownership patterns. Many landowners managed to disguise part of their holdings by registering them in the names of their relatives. Land titles sank into the bureaucratic morass and very few were ever distributed. Corruption and the insecurity in certain areas muzzled legal measures. In the case of a large proportion of the expropriated land (and also in the case of French lands bought back by the Vietnamese government in 1958 with the help of French grants), the farmers could not obtain the necessary credit to make their purchase. In that case they had to keep paying rent, and they had to pay it to the State. In the same spate of reforms, various measures provided for the registration of tenancy contracts and a ceiling level on rents. In practice, though, even if a small number of contracts were duly registered with the correct official rent, tenants continued to pay higher rents.

The results of all this were the following, ascertained by American experts in their preparations for a second attempt at land reform:

> Although land redistribution carried out under ordinance 57 increased the portion of land owned by the smaller owners, it was not substantial. Comparing tax data results, the curves show that 10 per cent of the large owners held 65 per cent of the [rice]land in 1955 and that land reform reduced this ownership to 55 per cent of the riceland.[51]

This ineffectual reform is almost wholly explained by the politically opportunistic aims of the Saigon authorities. On the one hand it was vital for them to alleviate rural tensions to protect themselves from a storm of revolutionary agitation, but on the other they had to create a class of small landowners loyal to the regime. So they had to uphold the validity of private landed property; above all, it was inconceivable that the powerful class of large landlords would go along with a revolutionary redistribution of their own land. Furthermore, the land reform implemented by the Viet Minh had to be rendered null and void. The return of peace, in 1954, soon meant the return of the landlords and their managers, whom the people greatly detested, supported by the police and the army in villages where they had not dared to venture for almost ten years. The villagers had become well accustomed to not paying rent, and they did not take the reimposition of the old laws lying down, especially in those frequent cases where arrears were demanded. Then the peasants saw, looming up, the shadow of an impoverishment that they perhaps thought had disappeared. The Viet Minh had laid down their arms and their political agitation against this step back into the past met with increasingly fierce repression. The White Terror entrenched itself little by little, and seemed as though it was going to last. Under these conditions, the peasants could only regard the Diêmist reform as a direct threat to the rights that their participation in the Resistance had earned them.[52]

There is very little doubt that from 1954 to 1964 the south Vietnamese peasantry demonstrated their scorn and hostility towards the Saigon regime, especially because of its dismantling of the achievements of 1954: the reduction or abolition of land rents in most areas. All the available evidence, although fragmentary, points to this. The sale of communal lands to the highest bidder, the decision to appoint instead of elect village heads (sometimes in spite of their wishes), the refusal to recognize that new social relations had been established in the country-side, the inability of the government to send, instead of its soldiers, funds which would have been more effective if carefully employed, all combined to spark, and add fuel to, the fire of civil war.[53]

Hunted down and massacred, losing the confidence that they once could inspire in the poor peasants whom they had propelled into a position of power in the village, the communist cadres were forced on to the defensive and then, five years after Geneva, into their agony. The reasons of international politics which obliged the communists to cling on desperately to the Geneva Accords, even though Diêm violated them in many ways, and to a policy of peaceful coexistence, were in fact counterproductive. The need for survival finally drove them to make a clear-cut decision. The choice was either to follow the mounting wave of peasant anger, and assume the leadership of it with their already weak organization, or just accept the annihilation of their movement in the south, and the prospect of the outbreak of violent peasant uprisings followed by fierce repression.

It was in these circumstances that the Central Committee, in May 1959, made the decision to recommence armed resistance. From its very beginnings, the National Liberation Front (NLF) paid great attention to agrarian problems. The principles which the Viet Minh had followed during the war against the colonial power were again adopted: elimination of large landlords, reduction of rents, distribution of unoccupied land and redistribution of communal land to poor or landless peasants, the struggle against "feudal" elements in the villages and the agents of the Saigon administration. These measures were implemented with discretion, taking into account the local military strength of the Front, the local political balance, the amount of land at their disposal and the social structure of the area. Thus, in areas where large landlord estates existed, rich peasants who tilled their own land and rented the rest out were hardly disturbed, while in regions where rich peasants predominated (such as some valleys of the Centre), they were forced to renounce their demands for rent and even to give up some of their land for redistribution.

This policy was shown to be much more flexible than that of the Saigon administration, as an American study has attested:

> Higher echelons in the Viet Cong call for the gathering and evaluation of vast amounts of detailed demographic information at the village and hamlet levels. As a result, Viet Cong estimates of the situation are exceedingly thorough and display an insight into the

problems encountered at these levels that can only be attributed to excellent intelligence and extensive experience. Thus, while the lower echelons are given the flexibility they require to adapt their resources to the Viet Cong land reform policy and to the local situation, they are monitored continuously. If a serious problem arises at the local level, there is an immediate response to define its nature and to apply the leadership and resources required to correct the situation.[54]

The flexibility — one may well call it fluidity — of this programme of redistribution is evidently motivated by a political aim, the United Front tactic of the union of all social classes against "imperialism and its lackeys". According to the same American study,

repeated references in captured documents indicate that the Viet Cong need the financial support of the middle and upper segments of the old rural society and are reluctant to alienate them through the direct expropriation of their land. Even when Viet Cong control was complete, the Viet Cong did not confiscate land indiscriminately. Instead, the Viet Cong let the natural processes of the conflict operate to provide land for distribution. As taxation of well-to-do peasants by the Viet Cong became unbearable, these peasants turned land over to the Viet Cong voluntarily. Even the land of those who fled the bombing and shelling for the more protected GVN [Government of Vietnam, Saigon] areas was held "in trust" as an incentive for them to return when conditions allowed. Those who left permanently or had dealings with the GVN did not qualify for this concession, and their land was immediately expropriated and redistributed.[55]

Here again we find the dilemma of 1936: no radical reform; the movement must simultaneously rely on the underprivileged rural groups (hence the suppression of land rents) and ally itself with the landowning class. However, the context has changed. The big landlord class was not the same: evicted from the countryside by the Viet Minh, they never really managed to reinstate themselves. They were already absentee landlords in the 1920s and 1930s; as a result of the modern education they gave to their children and the investments they made in the urban economy (and abroad), they managed to acquire a new economic base. Perhaps not as wealthy as before, they became well entrenched in the State administration. Finally the Diêm regime was not able to guarantee their landed interests and they were obliged, by necessity, to give them up for the most part. The official figures, paradoxically enough, exaggerate the real importance of large estates. There was in 1960 less land in need of redistribution than in 1945. If the peasantry took up the cause of the guerrillas *en masse,* it was because they were the only ones who lightened, indeed disposed of, the burden of land rent.

With the passing of time, the growing influence of US strategy, and the reconversion of the large estates, the Saigon regime tried to break out of the contradiction in which the Diêm regime had been bogged down before its collapse. The principle was to recognize the actual situation and to propose to the tillers free legal titles of ownership, which guaranteed them less precarious possession than they had before, whether they received their land under Ordinance 57 or from the NLF.

Law 003/70, passed in March 1970, prescribed that peasants who rented land from the State would be able to assume immediate ownership of it upon simply lodging their request with the village council. But then again, this measure came too late to seriously change the land situation. The war and the repressive methods of the military administration justify the view that when, forty years too late, the government of the day takes into account the old slogan "land to the tiller".[56] It represents no real change in policy.[57]

The Cambodian Insurrection: The Sky Above

It has been said of Cambodia, and it is true compared to other Asian countries, that there is no "land problem", meaning that land is readily available for the peasants to use to their own account. The population density is not very high: 150 peasants per square kilometre of arable land, whereas in Thailand the figure is 210; 400 in Indonesia; 460 in South Vietnam and 730 in North Vietnam.[58]

Custom has not been completely replaced by Roman law. Even though the heartland of the rice-growing areas is more or less registered as private property, virgin land is regularly being cleared and there, as is the custom, occupation means ownership. The abolition of the feudal regime, the law which the colonial authorities passed early preventing the Chinese (the wealthy class) from acquiring land, the low level of development of local capitalism, which was as much French as it was indigenous, all contributed, as Boudillon had predicted, to the maintenance of very low market values for land and to the prevention of private land accumulation. Although the peasants were exploited in many ways, by administrative corruption, or by commercial fraud, we cannot really talk about land rents which are directly transferred from the toiler to the coffers of a landlord.

While the figures must be treated with care, it is still noticeable that they have changed little over the last half century: according to Yves Henri, in 1930, 93 per cent of the land was divided up into plots of less than five hectares, and 1.2 per cent was over ten hectares.[59] In 1956, according to Jean Delvert, the figures were 92 per cent and 1.2 per cent respectively.[60] In 1962, Hu Nim says 86 per cent and 4 per cent.[61] In spite of a degree of uncertainty, various reports show a noticeable trend since independence in 1953: the beginnings of land accumulation in areas of rich rice land (Battambang, for instance), the buying up of land on the outskirts of towns by wealthy urban dwellers (officials or businessmen). An economist has noted that "in 1962, there were more than 30,000 non-agricultural households who owned land".[62] The census of 1962 showed that out of 800,000 agricultural families, 84 per cent were "owners only", that is, neither tenants nor share croppers.

This freedom, a gift of demography, which allows rural Cambodians to avoid, for the most part, becoming landless labourers or paying rent for their land, does not protect them from usury. Even in an egalitarian society, a little capital is necessary for exploitation to initiate development. Credit is mostly borrowed from a Chinese merchant at an exorbitant rate, from 100 per cent to 200 per cent per annum. As a result the Khmer peasantry finds itself deeply in debt.[63] Elsewhere we have referred to this point made by Khieu Samphân, who is in fact the military leader of the Cambodian resistance:[64]

> The peasants might just as well be working for the moneylender, on their own land. But the mystique of "owning" their own plot makes them stick to it and not give it up if they possibly can, even under the most difficult conditions, while they hope for "better days". It is very much in the interests of the moneylenders, the landowners and the merchants to perpetuate this mystique and they do not consider it wise to go ahead and take over land in the event of peasant involvency.[65]

A sharecropping agreement for half the harvest would provide less profit for the moneylender. It is only true in a local barter economy where money is still scarce.

To remedy this, the authorities organized a system of co-operatives and agricultural credit.[66] However, it proved to be quite ineffective as it was kept out of the hands of the peasants and manipulated by officials and merchants. But another problem was destined to highlight real peasant discontent. In a north-west border region, at Samlaut, a peasant uprising broke out briefly in 1967, sparked off by the arrival of new settlers and especially by the flagrant appropriation of land already in use. Manipulating the legal regulations, officials and army officers assigned themselves titles to lands which had recently been cleared by the local cultivators.

They claimed their titles invalidated the customary possession by occupation, and they put the district to fire and the sword. The outbreak subsided but the regime of Prince Sihanouk had been dealt a severe blow. This peasant revolt provoked widespread repression of those whose loyalty the authorities considered doubtful or suspect; many such people only managed to avoid the crackdown by taking to the forest where some cadres from the small Khmer communist movement, which had been virtually driven underground after the Geneva Accords, gathered together once more.

The most significant aspect of the period 1967–70 is not the existence of these small groups of rebels hiding out in remote areas, but rather their slow progress. The peasants undoubtedly had little cause for satisfaction with their poverty, driven home by the arrogance of the new mandarins. But from all the evidence it seems that they found ways of surviving on the fringes of society, clustered around the village pagoda which administered consolation to their spirits. Moreover, nothing in Khmer social history involved a build-up of power at the local level, and so in Khmer villages there were no notables like the ones whose elimination was precisely the focal point of the class struggle in the heart of the Vietnamese village. The *maquis* therefore remained "dormant" (inactive) at least as much because, lacking a mass base, the revolutionaries' political influence was not extensive, as because that was what was demanded by the communist strategy of coexistence and support for Sihanouk's neutrality.

On the eve of the *coup d'état* of 18 March 1970, the rebels numbered 1,500 to 3,000 men. The overthrow of Prince Sihanouk and his call to arms against the new regime had the immediate effect of throwing several tens of thousands of peasants into the ranks of the armed resistance. In several towns, in particular Kompong Cham, thousands of peasants demonstrated spontaneously to demand the return of the prince. Observers all agreed: in every village, the peasants' bewilderment and anger produced spirited reactions. The cadres of the communist movement were to ride the wave of this powerful rural opposition and, in fact, train, arm and mould the peasantry, and lead them into battle. Since then the Phnom Penh regime's zones of activity have been increasingly eaten away until becoming restricted to the suburbs of the capital itself.

From what I was able to observe on the spot in February 1972, the structure of the revolution is similar to that in operation in Vietnam.[67] The villagers have been encouraged to form committees responsible for communal affairs, to set up militias, to increase production, and so on. On the land question, two problems seemed to predominate; that of the organization of production and that of unoccupied land.

Relying on the traditional custom of mutual aid, the cadres encouraged the peasants to work co-operatively. Land remained in the hands of its owners, but the mutual aid teams worked on every plot, even on those which were bigger than their owners needed. Needy peasants were helped out by being assigned a portion of the surplus, the amount and allocation of which were determined by discussion in the village assembly. The only regulation which hurts, indirectly, the "rich" peasants is the Front's general prohibition against selling agricultural products in the markets in the enemy zone where prices are very much higher. At the village committee level, the peasants who are divested of their surplus are the most vigilant about the strict application of this rule.

Some land is unoccupied, either because its owner, often a moneylender, has fled into town, or because it belongs to an official or a soldier who has gone over to the side of the Phnom Penh authorities. The cadres try to prevent the peasants from taking over this land immediately — and here again we see the principles of the United Front being applied — in order to protect the rights of landowners living in town, so long as they have not chosen to take an active part in the struggle against the resistance. Therefore, in principle, a long investigation must always be carried out before unoccupied land is taken over and redistributed. However, in places, land becomes scarce because of the influx of refugees fleeing the combat zones. Rents and interest payments are no longer met, in the absence of their collectors. This occurs side by side with the process of demonetization of the village economy as it becomes self-sufficient once again.

The policy of the Front is to protect property rights, to "set up an equitable system of land rents and rates of interest on loans, to help the peasants solve the agrarian problem by finding an equitable solution to unjust debts".[68] But the word "equitable" has nowhere been defined. At the moment the war itself acts as a moratorium on the payment of large rural debts.

So it seems that the insurgency of the Khmer peasants can only be attributed to factors that we would call political. Despite the very limited *jacquerie* of 1967, it cannot be said that Cambodia's agrarian problems were responsible for setting in motion a political movement in the rural areas, or for calling into question the relations of production, archaic as they were in an Asia on the road to development. The massive participation of peasants in the insurgency, schooled by their local monks and led by minor officials or intellectuals usually from rural backgrounds, can only be explained in terms of the highly symbolic political and even religious upheaval that was precipitated from outside by the *coup d'état* of March 1970.

The works of Indochinese Marxists provide hardly any definite guidelines for an analysis of land rents, of the organic components of agricultural capital, the value of labour-intensive farming and of surpluses. They usually restrict themselves to defining rural "classes" and to investigating the penetration of the money economy. The strategy of the struggle for power and the priority given to nationalism and its United Front policies have obscured this very important problem.

From the earliest colonial days, the French, like the Americans, have treated the land question as a simple *political* problem to be settled amongst others. But how can we understand, for example, that a province like Nghê An has risen up in rebellion time and time again in 1874, 1883, 1885, 1930, 1941, 1945 and 1956 without seeing its cause in the rigidity of the landholding system and the mode of production? Why did it take a religious historian, concerned with the ways of thinking and the beliefs passed down as the heritage of an ancient civilization, to advise the observer to wade into the mud of the rice fields? "You cannot move a single piece without returning to the chequerboard. And this analogy is a useful one, because the morcellization of plots of rice land takes on the form of a chequerboard".[69]

3

The Ingratitude of the Crocodiles: The 1978 Cambodian *Black Paper*

Our political bestiary is growing. One new entry is "the [Soviet] paper polar bear", whose moustache Deng Xiaoping tickled while "touching the [Vietnamese] tiger's buttocks". In a long document published in September 1978, the Cambodian government denounces the Vietnamese as being "even more ungrateful than crocodiles". Entitled *Black Paper; Facts and Evidences of the Vietnamese Acts of Aggression and Annexation Against Kampuchea,* this text airs the whole range of grievances of the Khmer communists against their former Vietnamese comrades. For this reason, it merits careful examination (since its authors are not usually very talkative) and a critical assessment of its implications.[1] The first chapter exposes "the annexationist nature of Vietnam" by arguing that, historically, the Vietnamese have never stopped trying to "devour" Cambodia. We are first told of the conquest of Champa, the Hinduized state close to Malay culture which ruled over what today is central Vietnam. Then came the conquest of the territories of the great South, the Mekong Delta, which had been under Khmer suzerainty. This is not a difficult thesis to sustain. No one — certainly no Vietnamese — would dispute that the southern territories, what the Europeans later named Cochinchina, were formerly part of the Khmer empire.[2] However this incontestable truth hardly seems to have been recalled out of concern for historical accuracy. To understand this centuries-old feature of Vietnamese history, this *Drang nach Süden,* we must remember that we are dealing with a feature of Chinese civilization which heavily conditioned the Vietnamese one. For a long time this military and administrative expansion was carried out at the expense of the Vietnamese themselves in their Tonkin enclave. Besides wanting to occupy all the countries "between the four seas", the Chinese saw solid profit in maritime commerce and were irresistibly attracted by exotic objects from the South Seas.

46

For evidence of this, one need only refer to the excellent Sinologist, Edward Schafer.[3]

We should also remember that neither the Chams nor the Khmers of antiquity were just innocent victims. The Chams were tough; they carried out a naval expedition against Tonkin and even against Angkor, which they totally sacked. One can still see them waging war on the sculpted frescoes of the Bayon temple. The Khmer empire never missed a chance to expand at the Chams' expense or to impose a vassalage tax on them. The reason why the Angkor empire decayed was a weakness in its political system. Its successors let its immense territory be broken up to the advantage of more enterprising neighbours, and, despite its much greater economic potential, it shrank away. It is rather paradoxical to see the Cambodian communists speaking the same old language as the defunct monarchy, as if to absolve its past incompetence and put the blame on its eternally evil neighbours. The *Black Paper* wishes to convince us that Vietnamese are expansionist because of some mysterious "nature". As if Cambodians were not expansionist when they had the means.

To take just a few details: "The Cham race was totally exterminated by the Vietnamese" (p. 3). The defeat and annexation of Champa in the seventeenth century certainly entailed major massacres. Nonetheless, a population of Chams numbering in the tens of thousands still lives in Vietnam today. Despite undeniable pressure to assimilate, they exist. They existed in even greater numbers in Cambodia, since many Chams sought refuge there after losing their independence. This community, which had converted to Islam, dominated certain areas of the country and totalled roughly 200,000 people. It suffered a great deal from the Indochina War; some of its leaders went along with the shady games of Lon Nol, who dreamed of re-establishing Cambodian influence over the high plateau of Vietnam by using the Chams as intermediaries with their Montagnard cousins. Other Chams took an active part in the resistance. The Pol Pot regime apparently was suspicious of them and forbade them not only to practise their religion (which happened to all Cambodians), but also to dress in their customary way. Above all, the regime's officials assert that their country is 99 per cent Khmer, thus denying the very existence of the Chams, the hundreds of thousands of Chinese and Sino-Khmers, the small groups of Burmese and Laotians, the Montagnards and other Khmer minorities (Kuy, Pear, Samrê, and so on). Here, allegedly, is a happy country without any problem of "national minorities".

Another revealing point: the *Black Paper* says that in 1715 the Vietnamese "through their adventurers practically controlled" the Cochinchina provinces of

Hà Tien and Rach Gia to which it gives their old Khmer names, as it does to the other provinces of what is now South Vietnam (p. 7). Perhaps it was distraction that caused them to neglect one important bit of information: these adventurers were Chinese émigrés fleeing the new Manchu dynasty; and their leaders carved out a personal fiefdom in those underdeveloped regions at the tip of the peninsula. Intriguing with both courts, Cambodian and Vietnamese, they ended up under the banner of Huê.[4] The Chinese, all kinds of Chinese, have always been present, in all sorts of ways, in this area. There has not been a political game played out there within the last 2,000 years that has not had the local Chinese mixed up in it — and with *Zong guo,* the Middle Kingdom, always watchful of what is going on in its periphery.

For the authors of the *Black Paper* to say (*ibid.,* p. 7) that "the whole nation and people of Kampuchea have always fought against Vietnamese invasions and annexations" is to throw a crude veil over all the requests for intervention, addressed to both Bangkok and Huê, by Khmer princes fighting for the throne. When all is said and done, national sentiment is a rather recent thing in Cambodian history, and the little survey of the past presented in the *Black Paper* is a web of anachronisms.

The most surprising thing in this rewriting of history is perhaps the attribution to the Vietnamese of the measures taken by the French colonial authorities to unite (with their colony, Cochinchina) territories or islands which had belonged to Cambodia or had in fact escaped any political suzerainty, like the Highlands of South Vietnam.[5] The French authorities obviously saw an advantage in expanding the colony — a political structure they had well under control — at the expense of the protectorates (Cambodia, Annam, Tonkin), where, especially at the beginning, they had only superimposed themselves on an indigenous authority that was still endowed with its ancient legitimacy. According to the *Black Paper,* "the process used by the Vietnamese consisted of nibbling away at the territories, encroaching upon the borders and purely and simply establishing geographical maps by themselves. In fact all agents of the cadastral department were Vietnamese. The French just signed" (p. 9). It is hard to believe that the same people who had this finicky and strict French colonial government on their backs could imagine it so naive. As in a good many other places in this document, we see here a veritable political paranoia, which attributes to its evil neighbour all the ills of the universe.

A small paragraph entitled "The sordid use of Vietnamese girls" is an example of this. "The French called Kampuchea Krom [or lower, Southern Cambodia]

"Cochinchine". This word is made up of the Vietnamese words Co-Chin-Xin; "Co" means "Miss", "Chin" is the name of a girl, and "Xin" means "ask for". Thus, "Co-Chin-Xin" means "Miss Chin asks for". The *Black Paper* goes on to tell the story of a Khmer king who married a daughter of the sovereign of Annam who is supposed to have requested permission in 1623 for his subjects to settle in the Saigon area to do business. The Annamites soon thereafter colonized the area, according to the *Black Paper* and the Vietnamese army came in to put the finishing touches to the occupation in 1699.[6]

The interesting thing is not that this account is a mixture of historical facts and legends. Rather, it is that this kind of episodic word game is given as irrefutable proof of the "sordid use" of young girls. The translation of the three Vietnamese words is in fact correct (disregarding the tones). The problem is that the word "Cochinchine" is not Vietnamese! It came into French usage from Portuguese, the language of the first European navigators in this area of the world. We know, moreover that it designated different parts of the Indochina coast — Tonkin and Annam — and that the French use of the term in the nineteenth century extended it to central and southern Vietnam, to the point where the delta region was called "*basse* Cochinchine" [lower Cochinchina]. The term *basse* went out of use because Annam (from the old Sino-Vietnamese name that the Empire was given before the nineteenth century), became the customary name of the centre. But the Portuguese must have found this name somewhere. In fact, its origin is given by one of the first Western travellers in the country, the Jesuit Father Christoforo Borri. In 1618 he wrote:

> But having worked their way into Annam with the aid of the Japanese to do business there, the Portuguese, from the same word Coci [Cochi] of the Japanese and from this other word, Cina [China] created a third, word, Cocincina, applying it to that kingdom as if they had said Cochin of China to distinguish it better from Cocin [=Cochin], a city in India also frequented by the Portuguese.[7]

As for the first part of the word, one can recognize the Japanese pronunciation of the two characters that the Chinese pronounced *Kiao Che* and the Vietnamese *Giao Chi*. This was the name of the Viet country, that is, approximately Tonkin, at the time of the Chinese colonization, the first ten centuries of our era. To be more precise, this was the name of the capital of the Chinese protectorate, probably in the Hanoi area. It was customary to call a country by the name of its capital or the dynasty that ruled it. This is how the name "China" came to us.

Let us spend a moment on this problem of appellations. There are some linguistic usages that are particularly revealing. The reader will have noticed that I continue to use the word "Cambodia". In the constitution they gave the country on 5 January 1976, the victors of 1975 baptized their state "Democratic Kampuchea", rejecting the term republic, which was too closely associated with Lon Nol, and at the same time renouncing the principle of a kingdom. They did not spell out their reasons but in the documents translated by them, the word "Cambodia" has not reappeared.

A lot of smart pedants straightaway renounced the dirty colonialist word Cambodia for a rejuvenated Kampuchea, free of the past, for better or worse. Can such a grotesque rush to this cheap symbol be attributed to ignorance? Who can not see that Cambodia and Kampuchea are one and the same word, that they simply come from different phonetic contexts? When what used to be French Sudan rebaptized itself Mali, albeit a historical mistake (the Mali Empire was in another part of West Africa), this was at least a real change, the recovery of a political past which had been abolished by a colonial presence. But the Cambodia case is nothing like this. The term Kambuja is found in Sanskrit writings around the seventh and eighth centuries, when the ruling dynasty settled in Angkor. Previously, the country had been known only by the name given it in Chinese annals, Chen La (probably pronounced *Chinrap*).

The Portuguese navigators again tried to find a written form that corresponded to what they had heard, and came up with Cambogia. The first French missionary in the country tried to do the same thing: in 1783, he wrote *Kamphoxa*.[8] It was the French version of the Portuguese transcription that was adopted by the first travellers and Orientalists. But also, how can one render the true sound of the Khmer word? The transcription "Kampuchea" is just about as far removed from the original. It is an approximation which, moreover, has been in use for a very long time. Prince Sihanouk, who often mixes French and Khmer in his speeches, used it quite a lot. Similarly, he named a monthly magazine that he ran *Kambuja*, which is the Sanskrit transcription later modified to suit Cambodian phonetics. Should we end this squabble over transcriptions by proposing a new one just a bit closer to the original, and henceforth write "Kamppoutchi"?

As to the origins and meaning of the word itself, we are rather in the dark. Khmer myths claim a certain Kambu as an eponymous ancestor who is said to have united with a serpent goddess. There are many reasons to think that this is a case of the Khmers remoulding mythical material which, like much of the local culture, originates in India. Although we do not know anything about the local origins of this name, in the geography of classical India it is quite well known that there was a region of the northwest periphery, perhaps roughly what is now Afghanistan, named Kamboja. It seems highly probable the Indianization, reinforced by the subsequent diffusion of Buddhism, transferred to Southeast Asia a geographic representation based on India and its Gangetic centre. (The name Mekong is probably a doublet of Ganges.) In his remarkable work on Cambodian chronicles, Michael Vickery demonstrates the existence of this transfer by the fact that other regions of Burma and Thailand were called Kamboja during some periods: "What is certain is that in medieval Burmese and Thai traditions "Kamboja" does not refer to Cambodia, and that the confusion is not due to the fact that the Khmers once ruled over central and southern Siam, as Cœdès believed, but rather results from the displacement of classical geography".[9]

One could give a thousand examples of this kind of phenomenon. Greeks and Romans easily transposed their own toponyms to the peoples they subjugated. The Crusades brought us a good number of Biblical place-names which became scattered over the map of Europe. Europe's colonial expansion littered the world map with New Scotlands, Hebrides, Caledonias, York, Amsterdams, and so on, not to mention the bewildering toponymy of the United States. That the northwest part of classical India should thus be transferred at an early time to the northwest of what was undoubtedly the first centre of Hinduization in the Indochina peninsula, in the lower Mekong Delta, seems highly probable. This is how history mocks fledging nationalisms. After all, what does France owe a few handfuls of Germanic warriors who crossed the Rhine in 454 A.D.? Nothing, just its name.

Before finishing with these name traps, I would like to focus for a moment on a statement in the *Black Paper*: "Yuon is the name given by Kampuchea's people to the Vietnamese since the epoch of Angkor and it means 'savage'. The words 'Vietnam' and 'Vietnamese' are very recent and not often used by Kampuchea's people". All press commentators, without exception, have adopted this assertion that the ordinary name used by the Khmers to refer to their neighbours is pejorative. This fits perfectly with the assertion, also repeated a thousand times, of the hereditary antagonism that divides them. Not very convinced, I questioned various Cambodians. Apart from the word "Viet" which is a foreign word (like the French term "les Britiches"), there is no other word besides "yuon" in Khmer to refer to the Vietnamese. Moreover, no one finds the word pejorative in itself; it designates in a neutral way — but the connotation is obviously the reflection of the sentiments of the speakers towards the Vietnamese. And with things as they are…

Though I do not know if it is mentioned in the Angkor inscriptions (Cambodia and Vietnam did not have a common border then since Champa was between them), the antiquity of the term can be accepted. It exists in Thai and Cham. This is where we can find the key to it, thanks again to Edward Schafer: "In a few villages of Binh Thuan in southern Vietnam, no longer in touch with their former Chinese neighbours, are the remnants of the once rich and powerful Chams, now trifling enclaves among the Vietnamese, whom they contemptuously style *yu'o'n* — that is, Yavana (to use the Sanskrit original), or, ultimately, 'Ionians' — a term suggesting subnormal, devilish men".[10] These inhabitants of Iona, or Ionaka (that is, Ionia, the oriental Aegean coast of Greece), cropped up rather abruptly on the borders of the Indus, brought there by Alexander the Great in 326 B.C. The commotion was felt in the rest of the subcontinent. These intruders were not your ordinary barbarians; they came with an organized army, a script and a government, not to mention the arts which produced the magnificent Gandara sculptures. Transplanted on to the Indochina coast, where, in their words, they civilized the naked tattooed savages, the pilgrims and merchants from India quickly realized that to the north lay a threat to their trading posts and settlements, the threat of an organized force equipped with an army, a script, a government, a technology, a body of art, and so on. The term Yavana fitted them like a glove. It designated the Chinese colony of Giao Chi before it freed itself to become Vietnam. We know that the Chinese army made many incursions in response to Cham attacks. In the common cultural flux of Hinduization, the Cambodians just adopted the term which was already detached from the area to which it originally referred. The innocent writer of the *Black Paper,* absorbed in his desire to show that the Cambodians have hated the Vietnamese from time immemorial, could certainly not have known that he was repeating a term historically marked by ambiguity, that is, both admiration and fear, and born out of the clash of two civilizations that are different but equally full of themselves.[11]

According to the *Black Paper* the "manœuvres used by the Vietnamese" to annex Cambodian territory were of several types, including the sordid use of young girls and drawing maps, as we have seen. But there were others as well. In 1966–7, the Hanoi and Viet Cong authorities are said to have been planning to bring hundreds of thousands of Vietnamese nationals into the country and settle them along the rivers and in the border zone. It seems the *Black Paper* is alluding here to the refugees who fled the escalation of the war in South Vietnam that followed the introduction of American combat units. This paragraph, which describes the settling of the Vietnamese, contains a phrase which I find interesting: "If measures had not been taken, they would have totally annexed the districts of Saang and Koh Thom."

Naturally, the *Black Paper* never states what everyone knows, which is that Vietnamese nationals were almost all expelled from Cambodia immediately after the Communist Party took power. They are estimated to have totalled 300,000, of whom some were evacuated by special river convoys that came from Vietnam for this purpose. But the reference to Saang, which is not far from Phnom Penh, recalls another evacuation, the one Lon Nol troops provoked in 1970 when they launched their anti-Vietnamese pogroms. Saang had been taken by the guerrilla forces and, to get it back, General Sosthenes Fernandez' troops advanced behind rows of Vietnamese hostages from the local Catholic community. The others were shoved into camps. Does the *Black Paper,* in recalling "the measures taken" to avoid "the total annexation" of Saang, wish to congratulate the Lon Nol regime for its exactions?

Another practice of the Vietnamese which the *Black Paper* later re-examines at length is "the use of the flag of the revolution". There must be reasons for the relentlessness of their evil neighbours. First of all, of course, there is poverty. These Cambodians — the ultranationalists who wrote the *Black Paper* [12] — whose country is one of the poorest in the area, whose agriculture is distinguished by its archaic techniques and by yields which are among the lowest in the world, believe themselves to be the object of economic desire. Let's wish good luck to the potential investors and return to the political factor:

> As they had made the revolution, the Vietnamese enjoyed some prestige in Southeast Asia. At that time, the international community gave them aid and support. The Vietnamese have taken advantage of this support and used it as a political tool in order to carry out their scheme of expansion and annexation. They wanted to dominate all of "Indochina".... They want to take possession of Kampuchea in order to use her as a springboard for their expansion in Southeast Asia. (pp. 12–13).

The *Black Paper* mentions an anecdote: in 1965, at the time of the first visit by a CPK (Communist Party of Kampuchea) delegation to a foreign country (Vietnam, and then China), the Khmers say they called Hô Chi Minh "Comrade President", which reportedly made him and his entourage livid with anger; the Vietnamese insisted he be called "Uncle Hô".

A strange story. It is hardly possible to reconstruct the real incident which lies behind this delirious account. But we can see that the Khmers thus want to reject any avuncular relationship inherited from the communist "family" past. For *bac,* "uncle", in Vietnamese, is the eldest uncle, the one who is owed the same respect as one's father. In their relations with the Cambodian communists and with the Cambodians in general, have the Vietnamese always managed to avoid a slightly paternalistic attitude to which solidly rooted prejudices might easily have made them prone? I do not think so. In the *Black Paper* as in many other documents, there are traces of hurt feelings. The blame lies with the Vietnamese, who were always stronger.

We all know that relations between communist powers are generally characterized by flippant cynicism. The revelation of Sino-Soviet relations and the Yugoslav stories about the 1948 confrontation taught us a lot. The way the Chinese dumped the Albanians, as if brushing an insect off their sleeve, set off some interesting revelations in Tirana. Around 1965 and later, the Vietnamese would have needed an almost inconceivable supply of urbanity to treat their Khmer comrades without a hint of condescension, given their own prestigious past, long experience of struggle and political-military resources that bear no comparison with the several hundred ragged guerrillas who had experienced more hardship than success. In an April 1970 internal document, an officer from a Viet Cong-North Vietnamese security unit stationed in Cambodia notes that

> forces are available but the ideology and sense of organization of our [Cambodian] friends are poor. Therefore, we must be patient in providing help for their movement. (because their capability of learning is slow we must use explanations that suit their level of understanding when we request their help, they request us to provide them with weapons, medicine, food, provisions, and so on).[13]

Finally, after the economic and political factors, comes the military factor: the Vietnamese would need a powerful base to subjugate Southeast Asia. "One might object that the Vietnamese have no possibility of building up military bases, because they are not as rich as the United States imperialists"[14] (p. 13). But, the *Black Paper* goes on, they created their own armies in the neighbouring countries. "In Kampuchea, for instance, between 1946 and 1954, they had several times created separately an army composed of Khmers in their pay in order to use them as a tool of their policy of annexation" (*ibid.*). This phrase gives a curious feeling of *déjà-vu.* This is not only Sihanouk's thesis, but was also that of the French military command in Indochina which could not swallow the fact that the Viet Minh came to attack them in Cambodia as well as in Vietnam and used to denounce their "work of Annamization".[15]

To avoid a long digression, suffice it to recall here that there was no revolutionary Khmer movement apart from the one involved with the Viet Minh, and which was largely Viet Minh-trained and officered. The communists of the time participated fully in it and the young intellectuals who were studying in Paris during this period, and who had joined the French Communist Party, wanted to send a delegation to the rebels. The delegation went and some of the presumed authors of the *Black Paper* played a role in it. This "army composed of Khmers" was "separate" only for the Cambodian right and its French protectors. This kind of declaration, which borders on the absurd, also represents a rather curious reversal of perspective. After the Khmer guerrilla delegation was denied right of representation at Geneva, with the agreement of the Eastern countries (first given by Chou Enlai), the communists' hope relied entirely on the tenuous thread of proletarian internationalism, that is, that the foreign policy of the countries called socialist might guarantee the Geneva Accords and thus the political representation of the Khmer left. They looked to Hanoi for this safeguard but nothing came. The international context, the difficulties in launching collectivization and, in an inverse and complementary way, the opportunities to construct a bureaucracy, all were such that the Vietnamese Communist Party was in no way inclined to take risks at that time, neither for its Khmer comrades, nor for its brothers in the South, alone under Diêm's repression. The former resistance fighters in the South were hunted down and cornered before they could ignite a movement and thus force the Hanoi leadership to accept its existence. It was then taken over by high-ranking cadres dispatched to the South, five years after Geneva.

In South Vietnam this bitterness and deception which followed Geneva were erased. But this was not the case in Cambodia. The VCP did not commit itself to action until after the *coup d'état* of 18 March 1970. In the meantime, the Khmer communists had lost trust in them. Today we see that they have also lost their memory of those difficult times.

Chapter 11 of the *Black Paper* deals with "Hô Chi Minh's Indochinese Communist Party's" strategy of an Indochina federation. "The choice of the name of a party has its political significance", it says, after stating that "the Vietnamese Party was founded in 1930, under the name of the 'Indochinese Communist Party'".This is false. It is not very difficult to find out that the party founded in February 1930 came from regrouping three communist cells, all Vietnamese, which the Comintern had asked to unite. Nguyên Ai Quôc, the future Hô, did the federating and gave the new party the name "Vietnamese Communist Party". It was later, in November, on Comintern orders and herded along by Tran Phu, a militant fresh from Moscow who was to be elected Secretary General, that the party changed its name and became "Indochinese". The Comintern's directive was clearly aimed at unifying the different groups which were challenging each other for recognition by the "Centre"; this recognition only came in April 1931, after Moscow was satisfied that the programme conformed to Comintern strategy.[16] From Moscow's point of view, it would have seemed absurd to decree the existence of one party or of several different parties for a territory which drew its unity from colonization. There were certainly social, cultural, linguistic and even national differences, but what country is devoid of them? Entities like the Soviet Union, China, India and Indonesia were endowed with a single party, even if, like India or Indonesia, they did not have a tradition of a centralized state. The decision to create a single party for Indochina seems to have been determined by ordinary common sense. And perhaps, moreover, we should not expect a Moscow bureaucrat of the time to distinguish between a Vietnamese and a Cambodian. Even today (under Brezhnhev), any Asian in the streets of Moscow runs a heavy risk of being considered a dangerous "Chink".

Though scornful of these details, the *Black Paper* correctly notes that the Indochinese Communist Party (ICP) statutes called for the creation of a "totally independent Indochina", but it neglects to mention that the phrase is followed, in the 1930 text, by the following formula: "Recognize the peoples' right to self-determination",[17] phrases which certainly lack precision, and which can even be considered standard clauses (we know what happened to Menshevik Georgia, which was self-determined by the Red Army in February 1921); but if one wants to go back to the texts to prove intent, one must recognize that those which date from the foundation of the party prove only one thing: the Indochinese colonial space was the space of the anti-colonial struggle. The future lay in the "institution of the power of worker and peasant soviets", which is still being awaited, in Vietnam as well as in Cambodia.

From the time it was formed, the Communist Party won out over the traditional and bourgeois nationalist movement in Vietnam. This is why in August 1945, when Japan's attempt at hegemony collapsed, it was in an excellent position to present itself and be welcomed as the representative of national legitimacy. The VCP is one of the few communist parties, along with those in Yugoslavia and China, to bring off this feat. Bourgeois nationalism was never again to succeed in challenging the party's plans, and in 1975 was forced to leave the scene, completely discredited. On the other hand, this ability to ride nationalism limits control to the territory of the nation in question. The Indochinese Communist

Party, by the very principle that served as its impetus, had to confine itself to Vietnam. The *Black Paper* notes that it was totally absent from Cambodia from 1930 to 1945, but is indifferent to the fact that after 1951, when the ICP split up into three national parties (of which two, the Lao and the Khmer were rather embryonic), the Vietnamese never again spoke of an "Indochina Federation".

Coming from bureaucrats known for their obsession with compiling report after report, the fact seems significant to me. The war against the French made the whole of Indochina a theatre of operations. The *Black Paper* is entirely correct in reminding us that, in Cambodia, operations on the Viet Minh side were directed by a Vietnamese committee presided over by Nguyên Thanh Son. The country was divided into several operational zones and an intense effort at political organization was carried out among the Khmer population.[18] It had some success, which contradicts those who believe in the supposed hereditary hatred between Khmers and Vietnamese. It needs to be said again that whether in 1885, 1950, 1970, or, it seems to me (at least in certain areas), in 1980, Khmers and Vietnamese have fought side by side against their enemies, the French, then the Americans, and now Pol Pot. This is why, when the *Black Paper* states that the Viet Minh, with a support base among some of the Khmers Krom in Cochinchina, "kidnapped several[19] Khmers in order to train and supervise them, with a view to furthering their strategy of an "Indochinese Federation" in Kampuchea" (p. 18), we can not believe a word of it. This is just a logical trick to be able to say that, at the time of the Geneva Agreements, all the Khmer cadres in the resistance were Vietnamese puppets, trained in their school.

Curiously enough, the *Black Paper* does not mention one of the arrangements set out in the Accords: the regrouping of the guerrilla forces and the departure for North Vietnam of some two to three thousand fighters. The main leader of the Khmer resistance at the time, the former monk Mean, alias Son Ngoc Minh, also went to Hanoi. All those men who came back to Cambodia from 1970 onwards and took up important positions in the war against the Lon Nol regime and the US intervention are ignored here. Further on, they are called "agents" of the Vietnamese, as if it were impossible for a Khmer militant to be persuaded that the general line of the Vietnamese revolution is correct, and even that it is the best in contemporary Indochina. The policy of denying cadres the right to make a free assessment of the situation, eliminating and "unmasking" these militants and in a good number of cases killing them has undoubtedly led to serious convulsions within the CPK, of which we find only a muffled echo in the *Black Paper.* In any case it is people who followed this trajectory who are now trying to run the government in Phnom Penh. Admittedly they arrived in Vietnamese army trucks, but this is because they had to flee their country and leave their organization in order to survive. If you want to drown your dog you say it has rabies, but then you should not be surprised if it bites.

The end of this chapter surveys in broad outline the period 1954–70. From the beginning of the 1960s on, this period was marked by the installation of Viet Cong elements on the Cambodian side of the border. This fact is universally known, although the Vietnamese, to my knowledge, have never explicitly acknowledged it.[20] "We have not respected the territorial integrity of Cambodia", says one of the internal documents cited above. All the Western intelligence agencies agreed that this "occupation" did not go deeper than a few kilometres, mostly in lightly populated areas. This is why the astronomical figures given by the *Black Paper* are so astounding: 150,000 Viet Cong in 1965 (undoubtedly the equivalent of the whole liberation army), 200,000 in 1966, "between 1.5 and 2 million" in 1970. This is totally absurd.

It is explained by an ingenious theory: the Viet Cong had a mistaken political-military line.

> It consisted of waging the struggle on the spot, of controlling the population, and keeping them on the spot. In the Southern part of Vietnam, the members of the Vietnamese party who lived in the strategic hamlets were all enlisted in the army of the Thieu clique. Seventy to eighty per cent of the youth, members of the Vietnamese party's organizations, were enlisted in the enemy's army. The remaining 20 to 30 per cent complied with the enemy and gave up the struggle. There was nobody to lead the struggle of the population who, as a whole, were under the control of the US imperialists and the Thieu clique" (p. 20).

The Pentagon brass would surely have been delighted to learn this bit of news. Without going on about such blatant falsehoods, we can try to find out what they mean. To say that all the Vietnamese were stationed in Cambodia both prepares the way for the statement that they were only able to win the war *thanks to the assistance of the Khmer communists,* who can thus denounce the ungrateful crocodiles, and explains it by their mistaken line. The Khmer communist military officers did not try to keep the population on the spot; they evacuated them. In a war which, more than in Vietnam, had front lines, evacuation of the population from areas recently conquered or threatened amounted to political control. We know that this measure, applied to the entire urban population, served as an instrument of the specifically political victory. It is also the tactic used by the CPK resistance against the invasion of the Vietnamese army. It was also the tactic used by Kutuzof against Napoleon, but now it is the paddy-fields and bamboo, and without the Russian winter.

The *Black Paper* then lists the advantages the Vietnamese resistance fighters derived from being in Cambodia: sanctuaries, particularly for various leadership bodies; supplies bought on the spot or through the local government; communications; and especially supplies through the port of Kompong Som (Sihanoukville), which greatly lightened the perilous Hô Chi Minh Trail traffic. These benefits were considerable, but they were due to a tacit agreement with the Sihanouk regime which could not help but reinforce the latter in its policy of repression of the left.

The chapter ends on an enigmatic point: "In 1966 the Communist Party of Kampuchea consolidated and strengthened its position of independence, sovereignty and self-reliance, and clearly discerned the true nature of the Vietnamese" (p. 22). To start with the chronological point, nothing of note happened in 1966. The CPK, which consisted of only a few hundred stalwarts, had bases in a few rural and peripheral mountainous areas, but was not conducting armed struggle. Its leadership was in the northeast — that is, judging by the balance of power, under the protection of Viet Cong troops.[21]

So why 1966 in particular? The previous year, a CPK delegation headed by Saloth Sar, alias Pol Pot, went to Hanoi for the first time. This was the beginning of massive US troop intervention in the south. One can assume that, despite their confidence, the Vietnamese leaders were a bit worried by this. They must have emphasized to their Khmer comrades the absolute necessity of having elbow room in Cambodia, whose strategic importance had become crucial. According to the CPK, the Vietnamese at the time recommended patience, saying that after victory in the south, which was certain, they would come to their aid. In short, still the same post-Geneva line: stay calm, we need the Sihanouk regime and when our national interests — which are those of the revolution — are satisfied, we'll look out for yours. But the perspective, disheartening as it must have been to people hiding out in the underground to survive, became even more and more remote. It is tempting to date the real rupture from this period — by which I mean the Khmer communists' decision for a political line deliberately contrary to what Hanoi wished. We have a CPK document which dates the Central Committee's decision to adopt the name "Communist Party of Kampuchea" from September 1966.[22] If this analysis is correct, CPK history as written today by Pol Pot must be considered a "revision". The date 1960 that he gives as the origin of the CPK's independent line, but which has not been visible in actual facts, must be the date when a new generation of communists moved into leadership positions, a generation which came out of the experience with the French CP and only distinguished itself slowly from the "Indochinese" past of the party set up in 1951. The turning point of 1965 made them realize that they were running a major risk of being sacrificed again, that continuing to support Sihanouk's policy of neutrality while being hunted down by his henchmen was not a position that could be sustained for ever. Between the egotism of the Vietnamese and the nationalism that was Sihanouk's forte, only some sort of ultranationalist leftism could provide a way out of the impasse into which Indochinese solidarity led. The whole ambiguity of the situation is summed up nicely in this sentence from the *Black Paper*: "From 1967 on, the people and cadres vigorously opposed all these activities of the Vietnamese, but the leaders of the Kampuchean revolution always recommended to them that they develop solidarity and mutual aid with the Vietnamese" (p. 21).

Chapter III in fact deals with "the struggle between Kampuchea and Vietnam over the question of the political line from 1954 to 1970". The reasoning goes like this. There were the bad guys; the people installed by the Vietnamese were "the old cadres they had trained before the 1954 Geneva Agreements and that afterwards belonged to the Pracheachon group", the legal party of the former resistance movement (p. 25). "Once the 1955 elections were over, the enemy started their repression. The people trained by the Vietnamese were scattered. Some of them abandoned the struggle and some others turned traitor and went over to the enemy" (p. 30). This is undeniable: the Party's general secretary, Sieu Heng, went over to the Sihanouk regime in 1959.

On the other side, there were the good guys.

> But there were some real Kampuchean revolutionaries who faced up to the situation. They continued to carry out their revolutionary tasks. Some of them took responsibility for activities in the capital and prepared for the 1955 elections. In order to carry out these preparations successfully, some revolutionaries came from the countryside to make contact with those in the capital, which allowed the Phnom Penh leaders to get to know cadres from all over the country. Through these contacts and acquaintances, the Phnom Penh revolutionary leaders ipso facto played the role of liaison committee for the whole country (p. 30).

Here we have an outline history of the formation of the Pol Pot group and of the origins of the experiences that shocked the whole world (and made Cambodia a famous myth: if anyone is massacred somewhere, it is a new Cambodia). The hard reality is the intellectual and political confusion that reigned in Phnom Penh after 1954. The small Khmer left was still inexperienced. After being formed hurriedly in a situation of guerrilla war, it had to jump into an election campaign with its advisors away in Hanoi. The *Black Paper* is essentially the Pol Pot group's version of history, the version of the men who came to control the leadership of the CPK during the 1960s and controlled the military apparatus during the 1970–75 war, ran the country from 1975 to 1978 and have been since waging guerrilla warfare against the Vietnamese forces. The best known are Pol Pot, Ieng Sary, who is in charge of foreign relations, Son Sen, head of the military apparatus, and others like Nuon Chea, the party's deputy secretary general. There are also other important figures whose pre-1975 political careers are not well known.

Apart from throwing discredit on the Pracheachon, the text shows that the Pol Pot group was part of it at that time, which is confirmed by other sources, and that they therefore were a long way away from their later positions, which did not separate and crystallize until around 1965–6. In my opinion, the determining influence on this change was the version of Maoism which was vulgarized and "Linbiaoized" by the Cultural Revolution in a late paroxysm of the Stalinist vulgate.

The Pol Pot group dates its own emergence to 1960, the moment of the formation of the Communist Party, or, more precisely, of the change in name of the former People's Revolutionary Party. I have stated my doubts about the date of this change. It was hardly to be expected that the confusion would be cleared up since the party secretary general at the time was Tou Samouth, a former bonze recruited by the Viet Minh in Cochinchina in 1946, the president of the United National Front in 1950 and thus a typical product of the policy of the Indochinese Communist Party so fiercely criticized in the *Black Paper*. Saloth Sar, the future Pol Pot, who was without a doubt a key person in the Phnom Penh organization, was named deputy secretary general. He owed his later promotion to party secretary general Tou Samouth's disappearance in murky circumstances.[23] The communists' legal arm, the Pracheachon, dissolved in 1962. It was at this very moment that the Pol Pot group went to the forest, to the zone where the Hô Chi Minh Trail came out into Cambodia.

According to the *Black Paper*, it seems the Vietnamese communists did not approve of what was happening.

In 1961 … they worked out a political line for the Communist Party of Kampuchea and handed over this document in Vietnamese to the leaders of the Communist Party of

Kampuchea. This document mentioned neither the struggle against US imperialism nor class struggle.... They were against the analysis of the Communist Party of Kampuchea concerning the division of Kampuchean society into classes. They claimed that Kampuchea had not yet reached the stage of a society divided into classes. They asserted that Kampuchean society had the same characteristics as that of Laos.... They also opposed the line of waging armed struggle and political struggle in combination. (p. 30)

It would obviously be of the greatest interest if the authorities in Hanoi would publish this document and several others of the same ilk mentioned in the *Black Paper*. The lack of eagerness, not to say complete inertia, of the VCP leaders about making public the basic documents of their relations with the Khmers is regrettable. All there is in the *Kampuchea Dossiers* I and II published in Hanoi in 1978 is emotional reportage, virtuous editorials and diplomatic notes. The heart of the problem is systematically side-stepped. The *Black Paper* has innumerable defects, but at least it has the merit of trying to recount the history of relations between the two communist parties, in abundant detail. It is a partial, biased history which nonetheless carries weight because of its ounce of truth compared with the awkward silence from Hanoi. To those who ask for more detail, the Vietnamese respond with nothing, or at least nothing serious. Nor is repeating the Western press' worst output, like the *Reader's Digest* book on the atrocities in Cambodia, in a radio series and in *Nhan Dan,* the party daily, the way to convince people you are serious.[24]

For, basically, the discussion is not without interest. How should we understand Cambodian society? Is it composed of classes? Which ones? This is a vast subject on which to reflect. What we know of the Cambodian communists' class analysis, most of which comes from Pol Pot's major speech of 30 September 1977, which made public the existence of the CPK, is appallingly weak. It uses the Soviet schema of the 1930s, which was mechanically adopted by the other Asian communists before and after World War II,[25] but which is even more simplified and rigidified in its Cambodian version. Eighty-five per cent of the country is made up of poor and medium-poor peasants. The exploiting classes constitute the rest, but they include a lot of patriots who joined the revolution. This is the 1975–8 version; we do not know what the 1960 version was like. But, when one knows how this kind of sociological analysis can be used to justify the party line, especially when it is in power, one can imagine that the discussion must have been highly theoretical — and a long way from Marx.

In 1965, a delegation led by Pol Pot went to Hanoi — as mentioned — and to Peking, but the *Black Paper* passes over this latter interesting detail in silence. The CPK line "worried the Vietnamese because, if the Kampuchean revolution went on, this would affect their collaboration with the ruling classes in Phnom Penh" (p. 27). This is more than likely. The discussion seems to have been bitter, and without appreciable results for the moment.

> They then intensified their activities against the Communist Party of Kampuchea. In the East and Southwest revolutionary bases, the Vietnamese carried out activities aimed at creating confusion and division in the ranks of the Kampuchean revolution. They both acted themselves and also manipulated Khmer elements whom they had been organizing for a long time and had infiltrated into the ranks of the Communist Party of Kampuchea. They also conducted many divisive activities abroad. They distributed Lenin's *"Left Wing" Communism, an Infantile Disorder* so that the Hanoi Khmers [evacuated in 1954] would intensify their attacks against the CPK (pp. 27–28).

The *Black Paper* here raises a poisonous question which it is undoubtedly impossible to resolve. The Vietnamese communists had allies in the ranks of the CPK. Many of them were former members of the ICP, whose political motives were without any doubt honourable. In a tiny, scattered party without a press, threatened by repression and with precarious communications, homogeneity was an inaccessible goal. The small group that ran the party certainly did not have the means to get its own way completely. The same situation continued to prevail after 1975 and this explains how directives from above, from the *Angkar loeu* (top-level organization), were so diversely applied, even according to refugees. For a long time, therefore, there have been — have always been, it seems — serious clashes within the party. The *Black Paper* unwittingly confirms this with its long list of conspiracies and plots which are now invariably attributed to the wickedness of the Vietnamese. But, leaving aside the actions of real opponents, can we dismiss the accusations of Vietnam-inspired manipulation and interference which Pol Pot complains about now? The Cambodians' version is more likely, but they do not offer a shadow of proof. And when they state that certain "agents" of the Vietnamese were simultaneously in the pay of the CIA (which is something they had not previously made public), and they claim to have found this out only from confessions by these "agents", we have a right to find all this fairly suspect. It would be better to wait until we know more. Perhaps some day we will find out what is in the archives of Pol Pot's political police which fell into the hands of the Vietnamese in January 1979.[26]

Chapter IV brings us close to events fresher in our memories: "Vietnamese attempts at smashing the independent political line of the Communist Party of Kampuchea from 1970 to 1975". What emerges first is that around the summer of 1969, undoubtedly just as Sihanouk was setting up a very rightist Lon Nol-Sirik Matak government, the CPK leadership had foreseen that a *coup d'état* was going to take place to the advantage of the Americans. They had therefore "elaborated a document fixing the Party's line of the National United Front" (p. 33). In this document the leadership criticizes "the statements of the intellectuals who have joined the *maquis* and attacked Samdech Norodom Sihanouk" (*ibid.*). It seems that this is an allusion to the three members of the National Assembly who went underground in 1967, Hou Yuon, Khieu Samphân and Hu Nim. According to Sihanouk, in villages in areas where they had some influence, their supporters passed round tracts, little ditties and even playlets castigating Sihanouk's corrupt regime and Sihanouk himself. These three intellectuals (in Cambodia, this is almost a political label, enough to qualify for politics) and the others in their sphere of influence had a political trajectory quite different from that of the Pol Pot group, even though they had the same origin: student life in France and 1950s PCF influence (the good old days) They are the only ones who attempted to carry out a Marxist style analysis of Khmer society and make it more widely known. The Pol Pot group produced no analysis or text before the major 1976–8 triumphal speeches in stilted, stereotyped language.

While the Pol Pot group worked in Pracheachon (and more discreetly, in the Democrat Party) and little by little lost their illusions about the impact of this kind of work, the group of Marxist intellectuals joined the Sangkum, the party organized by Sihanouk, and ended up becoming ministers (with limited power). I find it hard to believe that such an operation was concerted, that one group fled to the forest while the other had its eye on ministerial portfolios within a coordinated general strategy. The divergence was real. One need only read the newspaper published in 1959–60 by Khieu Samphân, *L'Observateur*: the tone could be called reminiscent of Khrushchev, with homilies on peace, peaceful coexistence, the beauties of the construction of socialism, and so on — nuanced, of course, because of the censor, but with an influence of the PCF that is still quite marked.

Then came the Cultural Revolution in China. The Phnom Penh milieu, which was heavily Chinese, was receptive to it. Several of these intellectuals were militants in the Khmer-Chinese Friendship Association, which circulated propaganda put out by the embassy on Mao Tsetung Boulevard. The upsurge in youth protests, the Samlaut peasant revolt and the closing of the KCF Association by Sihanouk drove these intellectuals underground in 1967, where they found the tiny CPK apparatus in the hands of Pol Pot supporters. There followed a "rectification of errors" (p. 33). But I tend to believe that at least some of them held ultra-Maoist positions and that they kept a certain autonomy, indicated by a congress in the *maquis* in May 1970 of a so-called "Union of People's Struggle Movement", which was curiously short-lived since it was never mentioned again. In my opinion, what happened was that a third tendency within the CPK, the ultra-Maoist faction, was then formed, which coalesced for a long time with the moderately Maoist faction of Pol Pot, and which seems to have lost its influence only around 1977, after the fall of the Gang of Four in Peking. As for those who, like Khieu Samphân, survived all these crises physically and politically, they must have been able to bend with the wind and yet be tough enough when needed.

The elaboration of this policy of a United National Front would soon prove to be of crucial value. Were the Vietnamese against it? The *Black Paper* does not blame them. It would have been surprising if the Vietnamese had been against it, coming from a party that had its greatest successes by practising a frontist policy (Viet Minh, NLF). Near the end of 1969, when another delegation from the CPK travelled up the Hô Chi Minh Trail for a new journey abroad, the main Vietnamese criticism was over the launching of armed struggle, on a reduced scale, which the CPK had decided on at the beginning of 1968. In Cambodia, things had started to heat up and the emerging government of Lon Nol and Sirik Matak closed the port of Sihanoukville to profitable trade which supplied the Viet Cong on the borders. The *Black Paper* indicates that in the discussion between the two parties, the Vietnamese tried to "get the CPK to give up the armed struggle" (p. 34). This is exactly what Sihanouk was publicly requesting from the Vietnamese and which was the aim of his trip to Moscow and Peking during which he was overthrown. He wanted the allies of Hanoi to pressure the Vietnamese into withdrawing their troops from the border zones and stop deploying the "Khmer Viet Minh". Neither he nor anyone outside the Indochinese communist movement could imagine the gulf that already separated them.

We have a good example of the dialogue of the deaf that went on in Hanoi that winter. The Vietnamese asked the CPK delegation:

Where and how will the CPK procure arms, ammunitions and other materials? How will it get doctors and medicine? Where and how will it find the necessary finances? The CPK delegation did not take account of the objections raised by the Vietnamese because the CPK had the situation well in hand before the decision to start armed struggle. If the CPK carried on armed struggle, it was because the concrete situation did not allow it to do otherwise. If it did not, it would be condemned to disappear. But if it persisted in this struggle, its continued existence would be assured (p. 34).[27]

Perhaps this modest attitude towards its objectives indicates that, basically, the two parties were not discussing the same thing. The Vietnamese were faced with problems of fighting to seize power; presumably they thought the means to take over political power in Cambodia were very slim and they considered Khmer strategy adventurist. As for the Khmers, after a few initial successes in 1968, they were hunted down hard in 1969 and were fighting to stay alive. The presence of the Vietnamese at the border, even if the aid which went with it was very small or even non-existent, nonetheless was a guarantee of safe refuge. Since 1963, moreover, the ruling organs of the CPK were based where the Hô Chi Minh Trail hits Cambodia. It should be noted too, that at the time, the CPK never called for the departure of the Viet Cong.

In any case, the relations among the leaders of the two parties seem to have been very strained: "The Vietnamese used open threats against the Communist Party of Kampuchea and all the members of the CPK delegation were unanimous in saying that the Vietnamese were furious and were capable of doing away with them" (p. 35).

The *Black Paper* then tells us that, at the time of the *coup d'état* and Sihanouk's arrival in Peking, the CPK delegation was also there *en route* from Hanoi. The prince seems to have ignored the CPK delegation, and negotiations were carried out through the Chinese. We learn also that the "CPK delegation examined and modified the political programme of the National United Front drawn up by Prince Sihanouk", adding that in the prince's appeal of March 23 to overthrow the traitorous regime and form the FUNK "there was no question of socialism or communism in this document". This must be considered a sure sign of success of the united front policy, since elements as far removed from socialism and communism as the prince could be integrated into it. But foreign observers, and a good number of Cambodians, too, considered there was an enormous element of deception in this policy's success. Again in February 1975, at the time when the decision seems to have been made to evacuate the cities immediately after the forthcoming military victory, a FUNK congress reaffirmed its intention to establish a regime with a democratic, liberal, rather social-democratic appearance.

Nothing in the public declarations indicated the kind of pressure that was to be applied to make Cambodia give birth to the new communist society desired by the Pol Pot group and the ultra-Maoists (although it is impossible to separate their roles in the decisions of this period). Some will point out that the Vietnamese did the same by not giving any substantial power to any members of the "third force" recognized by the 1973 Paris Agreements, the neutralist patriots, victims of Thieu and the Americans. Although representative of a large part of South Vietnamese public opinion, they were entirely forgotten in 1975, when not thrown in jail.

The question raised here is not of historical interest only. We have the same situation again today. On 5 January 1979, immediately after a party congress, and before leaving Phnom Penh, Pol Pot launched an appeal to resist the invaders. He returned to a theme which had been abandoned for several years: a united front, a union between the "democratic" (that is, controlled by the CP) and "patriotic" forces (the others, especially those in Sihanouk's sphere of influence). This proposal attracted little support among Cambodian *émigrés*. The non-communists had already paid dearly to learn how limited their place was to be under Cambodian communism. Those who considered this turnaround by Pol Pot to be the result of Chinese influence rather than a sound evaluation of the balance of power were confronted by the staggering news coming from Prince Sihanouk in Peking. He said that, according to Han Nianlong, Chinese vice-minister of foreign affairs, Peking was recruiting troops to be armed, equipped and transported in Cambodia by the Chinese from among former Khmer Serei, old Son Ngoc Thanh heavies in the pay of the CIA and the Thai and Saigon intelligence services.[28] This Holy Alliance of a new sort promised some pretty good bloodletting.

When does Chinese interference in this aspect of Cambodian communist affairs date from? The *Black Paper* says March–April 1970.

When the CPK delegation was in Peking, the Chinese comrades told it that Pham Van Dông [who was also there] had informed them of the serious difficulties encountered by the Vietnamese and that he had asked them to intercede with the CPK so that the latter would agree to help them. The Chinese comrades themselves were perplexed. They had always heard that the Vietnamese had helped Kampuchea. The CPK delegation told them about the real situation: the Vietnamese had no territory at home [in Vietnam] and were taking refuge in Kampuchea. They had set up there their organs of leadership and command, quarters for their troops, hospitals, and so on.... The Chinese comrades discovered the truth for the first time, because the Vietnamese had carefully hidden it from them until then (p. 48).

How much credit can we give to this statement? Is it possible that the Chinese were never kept informed about what was going on in the sporadic guerrilla war in the forests of Cambodia? They were playing the Sihanouk card, too, like everyone else, but could there have been no contact with the fraternal party? This is hard to believe. But we can also accept the *Black Paper*'s statement if we see this as the beginning of a real *rapprochement*, an active commitment on the part of the Chinese. With the CPK in the stronger position in the underground organization, the Chinese could see a new card being added to what was already a very good hand containing: Sihanouk, the master trump; the Viet Cong, a major trump, being resupplied through Chinese merchants in Phnom Penh via deals financed by the Chinese embassy; and down to the Lon Nol card, which they played as long as possible. The Chinese involvement in the affairs of Indochinese communism was to have heavy consequences since it is the direct origin of the military flare-up in the peninsula in 1978–9. This is a subject on which the CPK has been totally silent. It does not fit very well with the doctrine of "sovereignty — independence — relying only on one's own forces".

On the way back, when they stopped off in Hanoi after the 18 March *coup d'état,* the Khmer delegation found a completely changed atmosphere. Hugs and kisses instead of grimaces, "but in the middle of the embraces, Vô Nguyên Giap, ever boorish and undiplomatic, let this remark escape: 'This is a historic occasion that allows our three parties to unite once again'" (pp. 48–9). The proud Cambodians did shudder. They saw right away that even though the Vietnamese were grappling with serious difficulties, they "did not for a moment give up their ambition to annex and devour Kampuchea" (p. 49). Try negotiating with such sensitive people…

However, there were urgent affairs to discuss. The Vietnamese made a number of proposals, the most important of which was the establishment of joint military commands — "which would be joint in name only", adds the ever perfidious *Black Paper*. The Khmers obviously refused. There then follows a murky story of a telegram from the guerrilla zone which was given to Pol Pot in truncated form, which it is hard to know quite how to assess. Further negotiations took place in Cambodia upon the return of the leaders. We learn incidentally that the Vietnamese offered a hospital with 200 beds and a full staff, including cooks. "The Vietnamese even wanted to teach Kampuchea how to cook rice" adds the *Black Paper* hysterically (p. 52). In the same delirious tone, among the types of co-operation proposed by the Vietnamese the text mentions aid in organizing women, which elicits this vengeful barb:

Even with regard to work among women, the Vietnamese Nguyên Thi Dinh [the name indicates a woman] offered to come and educate the women of Kampuchea, to teach them how to work. In fact, this Nguyên Thi Dinh did not know how to do anything, either housework or mass political work, nor military work. What the Vietnamese really wanted was to control the people of Kampuchea like they did at the time of the fight against the French colonialists (p. 55).

I will not pass judgement on Nguyen Thi Dinh's competence at housework, but I recall that she was Deputy Chief of Staff of the Liberation Armed Forces in the South and that she was anything but ignorant of "military work".[29]

The *Black Paper* is very discreet about the positive results which must have emerged from the many negotiations. From the evidence of what happened on the ground in 1970, there was very considerable political, administrative and military collaboration. Here it is passed over in complete silence. It is also true that it extended to large areas where the CPK's hold was minimal and where the Viet Cong's partners were more likely to be Sihanoukists of diverse allegiance who in Cambodia were called "Khmers Rumdoh" (liberation) to distinguish them from the Rouges, the "Khmers Krahom". The existence of this wing of the resistance, which was gradually eliminated, is never mentioned in CPK literature, unless this is what the *Black Paper* is referring to when it speaks of a "parallel army" organized "in secret" in the east and southwest, which the CPK demanded should be handed over to them. It apparently amounted to only four battalions. Some of these troops were perhaps auxiliary forces of the sort that the Vietnamese maintained along their communication lines for various protection and supply duties. For the same purpose, the Vietnamese had organized a certain number of their nationals residing in Cambodia. According to the *Black Paper,* they were more "cruel in their repression than their compatriots from North Vietnam because they knew the Khmer language and the inhabitants.… The CPK launched a struggle against them both in an official way and by mobilizing the popular masses to organize large demonstrations against them" (p. 56). It is not very clear what the text is referring to here.

Collaboration must have been thorny. Military and medical training schools set up by the Vietnamese were closed on the orders of the Khmer party. "In fact, the party had already opened military and medical training schools for the whole country. These schools devoted more time to political education than to technical training" (p. 55). Note that at the time, the CPK had had only a very brief military experience. As for medicine, the less said the better. The health situation was catastrophic in 1975–6 and producing simple traditional medicines did not relieve the situation much. Malaria in particular wrought serious havoc. But it was undoubtedly better to die at the hands of a quack if at least he had a good political education...

The following episode, which is meant to show once again the malice of the Vietnamese, seems to be taken from a second-rate thriller. In November 1970, a meeting took place between Pol Pot and his associate Nuon Chea, and two high Vietnamese officials to discuss problems "of development of solidarity and co-operation". The negotiations were held in the northern zone and were organized by the CPK secretary of that region, Koy Thuon, a member of the central committee, vice-minister of the economy and finances of the royal national union government. We do not know much about the content of these discussions, which lasted eight days. The *Black Paper* states: "As to their offers of aid to Kampuchea,[30] the Kampuchean side politely told them that it was completely self-sufficient, both in state power and in the army. At the same time, the CPK already had a fairly large quantity of weapons and in each zone there were already numerous battalions" (p. 56). This is without a doubt the biggest and most blatant lie in the whole text. Everyone, from Sihanouk to Lon Nol, the Americans and the Khmer Rouge whom I interviewed on the spot in 1972, all said that a major part of the weapons came down the Hô Chi Minh Trail. But this is not the really interesting part about the story.

Koy Thuon was arrested in April 1976. He confessed, reportedly in written form. These confessions conform perfectly to the classic pattern of Stalinist psychopathology. Koy Thuon was born in 1928 in the province of Kompong Cham and was a former pupil of Son Sen at the Pedagogic Institute and apparently followed him underground in 1963 or 1964. There is no trace of him again until 1970, when he surfaced as a member of the central committee of the clandestine CPK, and was also a member of the FUNK central committee, a deputy minister and secretary of the northern zone. In 1973 he welcomed Sihanouk to Angkor as secretary of the area but he was not part of the Democratic Kampuchea government set up on 14 April 1976. There are rumours that he tried to stage a pro-Vietnamese coup.

His "confessions" have not, of course, been made public; but the *Black Paper* tells us that he had been an agent of the CIA since 1958, that he joined the party in 1960 and that, on the orders of a double agent in the service of the CIA and the Vietnamese communists, he wanted to poison Pol Pot during the November 1970 meeting, through his wife "who was doing the cooking on that occasion" (p. 59). However, it does not appear that he actually tried because this story only surfaced in 1976.[31] Other facts thus become "clear": the reason the revolutionary forces did not succeed in taking Kompong Cham during their vigorous 1974 offensive was because the operation was led by Koy Thuon, who was a CIA agent. Will we be disingenuous enough to lend credence to this murky story? The CIA undoubtedly had its informers; but we old sceptics were immunized a long time ago by Victor Serge and others. Who will tell us the real story of Koy Thuon? He well personifies what is tragic in the history of Khmer communism, the last born of the communist parties which have gained power.

For good measure, the *Black Paper* criticizes the behaviour of Vietnamese soldiers stationed in Cambodia. Passing over a grotesque story of discontented soldiers overturning the chicken soup offered them by some nice village people, there is not much under this heading except for an incident that occurred in July 1973 in the southwest, not far from Kampot, in which six village people are said to have perished, burned alive in a house. This quickly degenerated into a military confrontation and the Viet Cong withdrew toward the Vietnamese border after senior political officials intervened. Perhaps what is most interesting is what the *Black Paper* does not say. In this same sector, serious incidents between Khmer Rouge and Khmer Rumdoh occurred in November and December 1973 which also degenerated into military confrontations. At the bottom of it all lay a campaign by the communists against Sihanouk and their desire to control the paddy crop. The villagers chased out the communists, who were only able to have their way the following year.[32] One cannot help but think that there is a connection between these two series of incidents and that they form the framework of the slow and sometimes difficult takeover of the guerrilla apparatus by the communists, and especially by the Pol Pot group. In this game the Viet Cong were trouble-makers since they also gave their support to the Sihanoukists, whom they considered an essential component of any political settlement in Cambodia. The Chinese, then as now, thought the same. In its own way, the small group of CPK hard-liners also recognized this, which is why they tried to eliminate the Sihanoukists during the war (the reverse was undoubtedly true locally) and the Lon Nol supporters after the war, since, ultimately, they were the same political class. Apart from the fervent supporters of Son Ngoc Thanh and some of the communists, who in Cambodia was not a Sihanoukist at one time or another, to a greater or lesser extent? In 1959 Khieu Samphân respectfully dedicated his thesis to Monseigneur Sihanouk. Hou Yuon did not do this.

We shall stop here on this brilliant sophism: "The CPK representative told the Chinese comrades that the Kampuchean revolution is independent and sovereign but that if the Kampuchean revolution had bound itself to Vietnam, it would not have been able to carry on the fight because there would not have been unanimity within the party" (p. 59). This chapter ends with the year 1975 showing that without the victory of the Khmer communists, the poor Vietnamese would have had trouble taking Saigon. Suddenly, "their plan to seize Kampuchea automatically collapsed" (p. 62).

The next brief chapter deals with the Paris negotiations. Without getting into the inventive explanations the *Black Paper* gives on the profound reasons of the Vietnamese for negotiating, one can accept the assertion that they exerted considerable pressure on the Khmers to get them, too, to negotiate with the Americans and Lon Nol. It had been known for a long time, and the Khmer Rouge had let it be known more than once, that they did not want another Geneva. They thought, not without reason, that the Lon Nol regime was collapsing from within and did not have long to go. Why give up on a sure thing? One thing which can never be repeated too often is the appalling price the country paid for what was, basically, a refusal to allow a political solution to be dictated from outside, which was modelled on the American-Vietnamese compromise, and which was a short-lived mutant anyway. Besides, the Americans did not want a real compromise. In order to try to enforce their solution, between 27 January and 15 August 1973, Kissinger and Nixon concentrated all the air strike power at their disposal in Southeast Asia. The British journalist William Shawcross, who obtained them through the Freedom of Information Act, published American maps showing, month by month, the places that were subjected to massive B-52 bombings. One might have expected the bombings to have had strictly military targets and to be concentrated on the sanctuaries, communication lines and rear areas where fighters were likely to be regrouping and gathering their forces to attack Phnom Penh. But the bombing pattern is hallucinating: it is concentrated on the most densely populated areas, on the paddies of the central plain.[33] The action of devastating the fields and villages with giant bombs ensured that the economy was certain to be severely hit. Phnom Penh, surrounded by a devastated void, was condemned to live solely on the river and air supplies decided upon annually by the Americans, depending on the good will of Congress.

I am not one of those who think that the reasons for the 1975 evacuation of the cities were primarily economic or humanitarian. I think that political considerations were predominant. But who can be surprised that these bombings, straight out of the tradition of Tokyo, Dresden and Hiroshima, had some consequences, economic and political and psychological? The last chapter deals with the period following 1975. Curiously, it is the least informative. It begins thus: after April 1975 "the Vietnamese had to leave Kampuchea and return to their own country. The CPK told the Vietnamese to withdraw before the end of May 1975 and at the latest the end of June 1975. But in fact they withdrew partially" (p. 71). As in the previous chapter, the *Black Paper* neglects to say here that, with the exception of the border zones that they traditionally used as sanctuary, the Vietnamese troops withdrew from Cambodia around the end of 1972 and the beginning of 1973. This was one of the clauses in the Paris Agreements and the reports of the American intelligence agencies confirmed this withdrawal. The 1975 withdrawal, therefore, concerns only a very small portion of Cambodian territory. On the subject of omissions, I would add Sihanouk's trip to the liberated zones in February and March 1973. I have much trouble imagining that such a trip, for which Sihanouk had pressed over such a long time, could really have been to the liking of communist officials who had embarked on a full-scale campaign to eliminate Sihanouk's followers from all positions of responsibility, and before they launched the agrarian reform movement which was radically to change the face of the Cambodian countryside. Only the prince could make political mileage out of this, and only the Vietnamese could give him the means to do so, by letting him go down the Hô Chi Minh Trail in an automobile convoy. Here they used a lever they had on their Khmer comrades. Rumour had it later that the Khmers confined the prince and made it impossible for him to have direct contact with the peasant masses.

The *Black Paper* thus acknowledges that in 1975 the majority of Vietnamese had left. Besides, the text does not distinguish between Viet Cong and North Vietnamese soldiers on the one hand, and civilians on the other — the latter often being long-time residents in some places: "Their forces numbered more than a thousand men, scattered here and there in groups varying from 10 to 100" (p. 71). There were a few incidents and the Vietnamese withdrew. Probably these were in places where the boundary is not perfectly demarcated. The question of Cambodia's borders is a nightmare which would fill several volumes.[34] The French colonial authorities had marked out administrative boundaries, which most often were favourable to the colony of Cochinchina and to the detriment of the protectorate kingdom of Cambodia. The numerous protests from the Cambodian throne were never taken into consideration. After independence the French boundaries had to be accepted, with some imperfections. When Saigon and then Bangkok put forward territorial claims, the Cambodian authorities became alarmed; they reiterated that they were ready to give up all their rights to the lost provinces and asked the international community to recognize the "current borders" and declare them inviolable. For a while, Sihanouk even made this the precondition for diplomatic relations with any country. Saigon, Bangkok and (for a long time) Washington refused to go along. Negotiations with the NLF failed in 1964 and 1966 because of claims which the Vietnamese termed "unreasonable",[35] improbable though this may seem. Finally, in May–June 1967, the NLF and Hanoi responded to Sihanouk's demands and recognized the "current borders".[36] It seems that, as the Khmers saw it, this meant there were no grounds for negotiating further about the borders and that for special cases where the demarcation was imprecise (because of discrepancies between maps, absence of physical evidence on the ground, or imprecise colonial directives, and so on), the Khmers were given latitude to define the border precisely, according to the principle that villages composed of Khmers and formerly administered by mandarins answerable to Phnom Penh should be on the Cambodian side. Judging from their number, geographical distribution and total surface area (roughly 100 square kilometres), these are the cases that came up again in 1975. The Cambodians did not want to get into discussions and evacuated them under duress. Furthermore, it is interesting to note that the *Black Paper* mentions the border problem only in relation to the CPK–VCP encounter in June 1975 and is completely silent about the negotiations in April–May 1976, when a Vietnamese delegation went to Phnom Penh to prepare a summit meeting on this question planned for June. Without explanation, the Khmers abandoned the discussion.

It seems certain that the maritime border question was the cause. It is even more complicated than the land border by the fact that the notions basic to its existence have evolved considerably since the colonial period. The problem has taken on considerable significance with the onset of oil prospecting in 1972–3. Judging from what the Vietnamese themselves say, it is clear that they have not accepted the Brévié line which was used as the administrative demarcation line during the colonial period; the pretext being that it had not been recognized as such in practice under the Thieu and Lon Nol govemments. The Cambodians were certainly justified in considering their interlocutors to be in bad faith and in viewing this as a manœuvre aimed at renegotiating the border — in this case the border between the maritime zones which are dotted with islets, most of which are uninhabited. Renegotiation contradicted the solemn declarations of 1967.

The reason the *Black Paper* is silent about this episode, although it would provide material for criticizing the Vietnamese for their obvious bad faith, is undoubtedly because the border problem has largely been overtaken by events; for Phnom Penh the intention is to establish an indictment designed to go beyond any possible negotiations. Another, more understandable omission, concerns the attacks by Cambodian commandos on Vietnamese border settlements from January 1977 on. This raises the question of who attacked first. Here we must pause for a moment and ask how such things are known. I propose adopting a simple method: record the complaints of whoever claims to be attacked. Sometimes there is a third party confirmation, in this case the American agencies and their observation satellites. Usually one side will say: the other side struck me, on such and such a day, at such and such a place. The striker says nothing. The Manichaeans will choose their side. It seems preferable to me to choose them both at the same time. I find thus that after the 1975 incidents which involved both sides but which seemed to be resolved amicably in 1976 — a year of relatively good relations between the two countries — the year 1977 marks the beginning of what became a real war. The Vietnamese report Cambodian attacks in January, March, April, May and all the following months of the year. The *Black Paper* tells us: "In December 1977, the Vietnamese launched large-scale attacks of invasion and aggression against Democratic Kampuchea" (p. 74), a fact confirmed by Western sources. It seems equally unquestionable that, as the document says, the Cambodian army cut the attackers to pieces. One can imagine the shock in Hanoi. The December 1978 offensive and the January 1979 occupation clearly originate in the lessons the Vietnamese generals learned from this failure.

It may be noted incidentally that this Vietnamese invasion, which stirred up profound emotions in international public opinion, had not always been set in the context of the true war which had been going on in the area for two years, and that it is not too rare, even if it is highly regrettable, that wars end or are pursued by military means. In my humble opinion, it would be proper to critique this kind of undertaking not according to nationalist principles (all the more so since we are dealing with the nationalism of others), but according to the degree of political liberty this kind of action brings to or takes away from a given situation. We recognize it implicitly in not criticizing Nyerere for invading Uganda (in order to topple Idi Amin Dada), because obviously the Ugandans are the gainers. As for the Cambodians, how are we to know?

The *Black Paper*, written in September 1978, asserts that the Vietnamese "blitzkrieg" strategy is and will be undone by long-term war, people's war and its classical doctrine. At the same time, Pol Pot was telling foreign visitors that, if his regime was as unpopular as the Western press said it was, it would not last a second against the Vietnamese. The test of truth was going to come and we would see.

We have not stopped seeing. The Vietnamese maintain a stubborn silence about their occupation while their supporters rewrite history. The serenity displayed by the Khmer communists does not reflect the real setbacks they have suffered. If one listens to some of the more informed observers with experience in Cambodia, who speak Khmer and who talked recently with refugees on the borders, their impressions are conflicting. The Vietnamese were welcomed as liberators in certain places and violently opposed in others. All is shifting, nothing is decided. Everything that has been said and written about Cambodia for almost four years now is an inextricable mixture of truth and lies. The press as a whole played its usual role, that of a huge ideological machine. This is clear from the very small amount of space it gave to accounts by those who had actually been there, which were less rare than one might think. A political assessment of this period should be re-undertaken by first of all trying to establish the facts. A document like the *Black Paper,* with all its excesses, its racism and its omissions, is nonetheless rich in facts which call for further explanation. Neither the Chinese, nor the Vietnamese, nor even Western officials who are better informed than one would think, have said anything very useful. Nor have the sensationalist journalists, the churches or the ideology shops. For them, inevitably, truth is always simple, and simply always on their side.

4

The Cambodian Idea of Revolution

In pre-colonial Cambodia, as in most traditional polities, the concept of revolution as the replacement of one ruling social stratum by another, was nonexistent. But if we take the word in its old European usage, that is the violent replacement of a ruler, or a dynasty, by another one, then revolutions did occur. Slight or slow social changes may have followed them, but the distribution of social power remained basically unaltered.

> The people had no idea of any kind of political system other than that under which they lived, and there was no cleavage of class interests to produce revolutions, aiming at a different kind of social order: The conflicts that arose in the nation over the king's actions and his trespasses on the right of his subjects, were thus directed by their institutionalized loyalties and allegiances within the political system to support kingship and royal family. Over a period of time the cohesion of the system absorbed the conflicts which the system itself set up.

Any student of traditional Cambodia would easily recognize in this passage the local form of rebellion in the nineteenth century, but this was written by an observer of Southern and Central African traditional states — the sadly missed Max Gluckman.[1] For him, this was an explicitly comparative view. Discussing the Wars of the Roses, he wrote that "when I go to a Shakespearian historical play I feel that I am back in Africa, sitting at my campfire, discussing the politics of rebellion with Zulu or Barotse".[2] It has been my own privilege also, to discuss the politics of revolution at their campfires, with Zulu, Arab, Khmer and other guerrillas and I feel certain a comparative approach is not only in order, but an absolute necessity. Gluckman went on to suggest that:

until a State has an integrated economic system, rebellion against the king, and struggle for the kingship, inhibit the achievement of independence. All sections struggle for the kingship, and this unifies them. They work to place their own prince on the throne; they do not try to become independent from the kingship. A whole series of customs — the ritual of kingship, the distribution of the royal family, and so forth — produces social order out of the conflicts set up by the same customs.... The ritual sacredness of kingship prevents anyone but another prince taking the throne.[3]

This also applies to nineteenth-century Cambodia, with rebellions breaking out even when colonial rule maintained kingship under strong pressure without destroying its ritual value. Most, if not all rebellious leaders claimed royal descent, genuine or not: Leai Tai, the Phnom Srok rebel in 1889, said he was the king's fourth brother; Achar Soa pretended to be Ang Chan's nephew; Pou Kombo claimed he was Ang Chan's grandson; Si Votha was a full brother of king Norodom, and so on. As Maurice Comte aptly remarks: "Thus we see important rebellions ending with general amnesties, with only a few 'leaders' being executed. The most serious crime, it seems, was not to have killed, fought, and ravaged the countryside, but to have openly opposed the king."[4]

The backbone of the traditional political structure was the patron-client system of dyadic relationships. It has been noted that this system, both through the effects of its functioning and the psychological categories it implies, prevents the rise of a global political consciousness. Only factional groups may emerge from personal linear loyalties. On the cultural constraints produced by the system, David Chandler's comment on the subject at least avoids the old anthem of Buddhist resignation: "The rectitude of these intransitive, graded relationships has been drummed into everyone from birth. Cambodian proverbs and didactic literature are filled with references to the helplessness of the individual and to the importance of accepting power relationships as they are".[5]

It seems then that the political system and the basic culture made the concept of revolution wholly unthinkable in traditional terms. Instead the rebellion model might be labelled "millenarian": promises of riches, a golden age, invulnerability, a just ruler, heralded as a saint, a messiah, a *nak mien bon*, an archetype which has haunted Khmer lore since time immemorial. A journalist reported recently that people in the Siem Reap area speculated about the coming of a blond messiah from the West. The greatest regional actualization of this model was the Tai Ping rebellion and it might be valuable, in another context, to draw some comparisons between the Tai Ping and the Khmer Rouge.[6]

The gradual loss of substance suffered by Khmer kingship under French rule is the obvious reason for the waning of cultural constraints which impeded the growth of a new concept of political change. Although it would be interesting to assess some recent French studies of colonial Cambodia,[7] I shall not discuss here to what extent the patron client system and the related concept of *komlang* ("force", or a hierarchical network of clients) have survived and permeated post-independence politics. I assume that they did, and in a significant way; I shall return to this point later.

The Cambodian economy underwent significant changes after the beginning of colonization. Although they were rather slow and not spectacular, fundamental changes in the economic sphere did prompt reactions of hostility among the rural Khmers. Collard is being a better Marxist than most when he remarks that one of the origins of the 1885 insurrection was the abolition of slavery: "But slavery was just what one called upon in difficult times! With slavery abolished, how could anyone pay fines? How could anyone pay legal judgments? How could a bar of silver be obtained, without performing some labour? The people, so little disposed to making an effort, felt the necessity of work and the risks of independence germinating in article VII of the 1884 convention."[8]

Here the meaning of independence is the economic independence of the individual. The introduction of capitalist production and the related economic reorganization during this century was slow, superficial and incomplete. It put growing pressure on the old agrarian system but failed to destroy it and to extract from it the resources and manpower that could have been diverted towards more profitable activities. Martel's description of a village in 1961–2 shows that the traditional features of a pre-capitalist economy, with its limited trade, high rate of auto-consumption, dire poverty and great indebtedness, were still dominant, even in a supposedly rather rich area of the country.[9]

In the late 1960s, Cambodia was probably reaching a point where the pressures of the world market would have severely disrupted the old agrarian pattern, forcing it to raise productivity and eliminate a growing number of redundant peasants. As an FAO expert pointed out in the conclusion of his thorough analysis, in 1968:

> The country has reached the point where it must choose between an agriculture whose traditional sector has reached the limit of its possibilities and whose production the law of diminishing returns will ineluctably reduce, and changing over to an agriculture of growing productivity, based on the step-by-step imposition of procedures capable of arriving at it.[10]

The means are, of course, investment of capital and modern technology, with the correlative social effects.

The taking over of political power by the right in 1969 could have been the opportunity for a kind of bourgeois revolution, removing obstacles and paving the way for a capitalist modernization of the countryside. The war of 1970–5 destroyed this possibility, which has yet to re-emerge. When it started, the process of class formation was still in its infancy. The old system of status hierarchy was still dominant, as there was no objective basis in peasant experience to relate their very real poverty to the consciousness of an exploitation that had not yet reached them and stripped them of their former normal lives. Under these circumstances, their reaction was massively conservative.

In Cambodia, there are two sources for the idea of revolution, namely the French school syllabus and the international communist movement. The two are not unrelated.

The French were very slow in establishing a modern type of educational system in Cambodia. The first French school, in the 1880s, "catered chiefly for Chinese and Vietnamese children".[11] In 1905, probably no more than 500 Khmer children were attending Protectorate schools. A *lycée* was not established in Phnom Penh until the 1930s, but a tiny number of young aristocrats, like Sihanouk, generally were sent to Saigon or Hanoi to attend a *lycée*. Under the centralized French educational system, all pupils, whether in Phnom Penh or any French town, were expected to master the same knowledge. History was taught with no adaptation to local conditions, so that future citizens and colonial subjects alike would identify with French history and with French political values. Since 1870, in the republican education system, the 1789 revolution has appeared as a central event, not only in French, but in world history. It is hailed as the destruction of an arch-evil *ancien régime* and the first victory of a universal bourgeoisie, representative of the whole population. Every nation is supposed to go through such a redeeming experience. The most subversive ideas, figures and groups are carefully erased from the official picture, so as to make this troubled period more an object of reverence than a source of inspiration.

However, for young pupils in the colonies, metropolitan history was difficult to master, especially since their own past was almost totally ignored. While teaching history in a Khmer *lycée* in 1969, I soon discovered the bewilderment which was produced by the history courses among these youngsters. With few exceptions, they could not grasp what a chronology was about, nor conceive that another country could differ from the Cambodian landscape. World history for them was an obscure struggle, with all great historical contenders, from Caesar to Napoleon and Bismarck, fighting one another, probably in a vast rice field dotted with *thnot* (sugar palm trees).

Even before World War II, the very word "revolution" existed in political language, although I am not able to say when it first crept into Cambodian usage. The Khmer word *padiwat* is derived, as is its Thai equivalent, from Pali *pattivattam*. The *Dictionary of the Pali Language,* by R.C. Childers (London, 1909) shows that *pati* means "towards, back in return, against" and *vattam* means "going on, continuance, succession", also "a circle, region, realm", as in *samsaravattam*, "revolution or realm of transmigrations". The general meaning of "moving against", implying also a circular motion, was then an apt translation, in several Southeast Asian languages, of the Latin "revolution". It can safely be assumed that this Pali word was first introduced into modern political speech in countries other than Cambodia. Thailand, with the birth of an indigenous CP in the thirties, is a most likely place. The 1932 coup which established both military power and constitutional monarchy was also a *padiwat*, and many military coups since then have been named *padiwat*.

Although a nationalist consciousness developed in Cambodia in the late 1930s among the small cultured élite, mainly around Son Ngoc Thanh's paper *Nagaravatta*, it was the events of World War II which led to a real broadening of political consciousness in the country. The French colonial administration was first shattered and then overturned by the Japanese military occupation. With the handing out of bogus independence to Cambodia, as to many other Asian nations, the Japanese triggered, in the local élite, an impulse toward power. The way the French protectorate was reinstated after Japan's fall was conducive to a broader contest for the political system. It was all too obvious that Cambodian kings had been used as protective screens by French rulers. In 1945–6, for the first time, the king's legitimacy was open to question. The idea of dispensing altogether with monarchy and replacing it with another system became conceivable for a handful of young, educated, would-be leaders, who started to spread this thought among their colleagues. Thus the idea of a revolution akin to the one in 1789, against a corrupt and sold-out monarchy, gained ground for the first time in Cambodia. The events in neighbouring Vietnam, with the deposition of Emperor Bao Dai, could only be seen as moving in the same direction.

We have an interesting testimony from a student in that period, Saloth Sar, who later achieved fame under the alias "Pol Pot". His little-known article, "Monarchy or Democracy?" has recently been reprinted. In it, Saloth Sar says: "The king is absolute. He seeks to destroy the interests of the people when the people are in a position of weakness and he is disturbed to see that the more people are educated, the more clearly they can see the faults of kings. The absolute king uses nice words, but his heart remains wicked."[12] This sounds like a typical 1789 speech. He contrasts the corrupt *ancien régime* with the revolution — France 1789, Russia 1917, China 1924, meaning the overthrow of the monarchy and the establishment of democracy: "Democracy is the government which all people everywhere adopt nowadays; it is as precious as a diamond, and cannot be compared with any other kind of government." Hence, perhaps, the paradoxical name of "Democratic Kampuchea".

The 1917 model is superimposed on to the 1789 one. The left-wing critique which described the early Soviet regime either as non-revolutionary or counterrevolutionary, and which originated in Rosa Luxemburg's writings (later expanded in the German ultra-left and other European leftist groups), was never understood by people outside the workers' movement revolutionary tradition, such as bourgeois politicians and colonial emancipation leaders. With many others in the European working classes, these people often identified revolution with the Soviet regime in the 1920s and 1930s and reacted accordingly. The failure of Bolshevik-type revolution in Central and Western Europe in the aftermath of World War I, and its spread to the underdeveloped parts of the Tsarist Empire, suggested to them that it could be used as a model for colonial emancipation, provided that verbal concern for such things as capital accumulation processes and class struggle were reduced to insignificance. Gaining political power became the object of revolutionary struggle. Another was to weaken the enemies of the Soviet regime in their rear bases. Special schools were established in the USSR to train cadres from colonial areas. Slowly, and with the active contribution of the Russian leaders of the Comintern, the concept of revolution as a seizure of power by a communist party in a colonial situation emerged as an acceptable theoretical view, whereas Marx's analyses of revolution as an end-product of capitalist evolution were altered or even dropped.

The stumbling block, of course, was nationalism, induced by colonial pressure and the related deprivation of political autonomy. Early attempts to weld nationalism to Communism were repressed in the Soviet Union because nationalism transcended class boundaries.[13] China provided the ground for painfully elaborating tactics of class compromise as a recipe to promote working class (that is, Communist Party) control over the otherwise bourgeois and peasant nationalism.[14] With its doctrinal variations and successive labels, this nationalist communist policy did not achieve real success before the 1940s, because bourgeois nationalism was also vigorously expanding. The war provided nationalism with a clearcut enemy. By freezing the special claims of each particular class and providing a unified and dedicated military framework for resistance, communists in many places were able to win over large parts of the population and identify with national legitimacy — events in China, Yugoslavia, Albania and Vietnam testify to this.[15] But where nationalism was weak or divided, and could not therefore provide the impetus, communist tactics failed to achieve power (Malaya, the Philippines, Korea and, with qualifications, most of Europe).

The preceding remarks are irrelevant if we try to apply them to Cambodia before and during World War II. Political nationalism did not surface there publicly before the 1930s, and was limited mainly to intellectuals, secular and religious. For a long period, in most of the nationalist movement, the idea of revolution, inherited from the French schools, was hardly present, breaking through only after the 1970 coup against Sihanouk. Even then, in spite of republican rhetoric, the political élite remained deeply imbued with the values of the *ancien régime*. Disaffected Lon Nol supporters, for example, often regretted that a new king had not been put on the throne in the wake of their coup.

Two sets of people, in search of a way to achieve revolutionary nationalism, to dispense with kingship and to reach national independence, were exposed to the Russian model: those who joined the Viet Minh guerrilla struggle, and those who went to France as students.

As far as Cambodia was concerned, the social content of the revolution promoted by the Viet Minh and its Khmer allies was unimpressive: first, the country was not plagued by a potential agrarian crisis as were the big Vietnamese deltas, where vast numbers of tillers had been evicted from their land by landlordism and consequences of the 1929 crisis. But whatever social differentiation existed in the Cambodian society — and inequality was great — was to be played down by the communist leadership, which had embarked, since the late thirties, on "frontist" policies.

In the Comintern view, defence of the Soviet Union was the foremost aim, and it was considered most urgent to regroup all political forces in "front" organizations, striving for independence, to deny bases for colonial and imperialist anti-Soviet powers. Social conflicts, which had been seen by the Comintern as the main asset of the growing revolutionary movement, were now considered as disruptive of the union of social classes. Demands by the most alienated classes should be met only with the utmost care in order not to jeopardize the rallying of the ruling classes. The Soviets had direct experience with their advisers working in China to build up a front that included Chiang Kai-shek and other warlords. In the Cambodian countryside, although the economic situation was far from generally good, there was not much demand for social change. This frontist policy had some adverse consequences in Vietnam, where a long frustrated landless peasantry voiced its discontent about the mildness of measures taken by the Viet Minh leadership to put a limit to landlords' exploitation. The pressure reached a point where the Viet Minh leaders felt the need to give way to these demands, if they were to be able to enlarge and speed up peasant support in the last phase of the war. They launched an agrarian reform in 1953, which was to take its full course mainly after Geneva, and to lead to some "excesses", as was officially recognized in 1956. All that was very much shaped on the Chinese model. But in Cambodia nothing of the sort was even proposed. Still the front policy of organizing all the Issarak (anti-French freedom fighters) groups in close co-ordination with the Viet Minh was largely a failure, since many Issarak groups had either joined the king or gone out of action, for there was no other alternative. National union, or its pretence, was the best cover for alien intervention against a foreign overlord, and revolutionary activities without deep-rooted cause.

So small was the concern for social justice that no theoretical device, such as a class analysis, is known to have been produced at the time. When, in 1951, the Khmer communist movement was officially separated from its Indochinese source, it was meant by the Vietnamese leadership as a gesture toward a more closely knit Khmer united front. It was not considered to be a full-grown CP in its own right, but more like a proto-CP (hence its name of People's Revolutionary Party) because its class basis and its programme were still so vague. In this context, "revolution" was thought of mainly as the slow building of the Party, emerging from the (phantom) working class and preparing to lead all the dominated classes in the struggle for power.

In France, young Khmer nationalists were exposed to a more diverse political experience. They had to probe by themselves, urged on by their solid defiance of the throne. They soon had a Marxist discussion group; several of them belonged to a marginal cell of the CPF; but that did not deter some of them, like Saloth Sar (the future Pol Pot), from having long formative talks with other radical nationalists, like Ea Sichau, or those far removed from any Marxist attachments, like Son Ngoc Thanh, then (1947–51) under forced residence in Poitiers. It was only after the schism between Tito and Stalin that Pol Pot says that he visited Yugoslavia, made attractive to him, perhaps, by its newly won independence from "Big Brother".

The Khmers in France were constantly thinking of another "big brother" — Vietnam — and they resented the prominence given the Viet Minh representatives and their Khmer allies, like Keo Meas, on the Parisian scene and in the international conferences which they attended. Upon his return to Cambodia in 1953, Pol Pot soon landed in the *maquis;* it was the end of the war and he does not seem to have played a very significant role. I think we might fairly assume that this group of young nationalists was, for a long time, not entirely clear about what methods would be the most efficient for carrying out a true 1789 type of revolution. Communism certainly appeared to be the most sophisticated tool, but objective conditions were not favourable to it. They were probably fully committed to the building of a communist party only when all other avenues appeared blocked, and the 1960 Party Congress may be seen as much as a start of a new era, as the dead end of an unsuccessful search for a bourgeois revolution which never materialized. In the meantime, Sihanouk had gained hegemony by combining traditional charisma, political acuity, and foreign support. He outmanœuvred the opposition by appearing to be the most outspoken leading nationalist.

Sihanouk's victory was made easier because Khmer nationalism has always been fundamentally conservative. By regional standards, the demand for social change had been very low. Although there were large pockets of rural poverty and increasing exploitation of resources and manpower, capital was lacking and thus had been unable to transform the old economic pattern. Conditions were not ripe for revolution. Only a totally different *political* set-up, such as a foreign invasion, could transform the odds.

In the race for nationalist achievement before 1970, the revolutionaries were on the losing side, whatever they did. In the meantime they had turned to a more sophisticated revolutionary model than that of 1789; they had opted for a Chinese way. In their Paris period, they had already felt an attraction for the new China. China's experience was more akin to theirs, socially and culturally, and also more contemporary than Russia's in 1917.

Imitation of Vietnam was out of the question for purely nationalistic reasons. The reality was, of course, that Vietnamese methods were practically the only ones which those with guerrilla experience knew. In that respect, the difference between the Chinese and the Vietnamese ways did not look very great. The Chinese influence on the Vietnamese Party had been very deep. Local guerrillas and those exiled in Vietnam could well have followed a Vietnamese line, if the former Paris students, strong in the urban Party Centre, had not pretended they knew better. The adoption of a Khmerized version of Maoism was a gradual and almost clandestine process, starting with the leadership and transmitted downwards, along with rigid disciplinarian rule.

The Japanese occupation had been a blessing in disguise for the Chinese Communist Party, and many lessons could be drawn from that period for other communist parties struggling for national liberation. Most of Mao Tsetung's writings were of pre-victory vintage. For most CPK members and Phnom Penh leftists, China was seen as a general abstract pattern of socialist revolution, with a complete package of ways and means to realize national union against foreign intervention, control over the peasant masses, strict methods to organize the Party and the army, and so on. All this was rather abstract. Chinese propaganda, particularly after the start of the so-called Cultural Revolution, was aiming at the most simplistic views: the sheer strength of will, whatever the sacrifices, was to overcome all material difficulties. Such a simple moral solution had a quasi-religious appeal to the Cambodian Party's rank-and-file. This was probably not the case for a small group of Party leaders, in particular Pol Pot, who made a secret visit to North Vietnam and China in 1965.

The group apparently was converted to the peculiar set of ideas now known as Maoism. It might seem easy nowadays to reject Maoism as a doctrinal fantasy, when the Chinese leaders themselves are in the process of throwing it into the "dustbin of history". But it should be remembered that it infected a host of dedicated activists and groups everywhere, who never found much attraction for Soviet policies. For anyone with a slight acquaintance with Marx's thought it was, from the start, manifest that the political groups embracing this backward pseudo-theory would unavoidably end in dismal failure, out of a complete disregard for social and economic realities, as they eventually did in India, Bengal, France, Italy, Turkey, Japan, and even China, not to speak of Cambodia.[16]

The strong moral overtones of Maoism and its disregard for material trivialities ("I don't understand much about economics", Mao said to a group of startled Red Guards) fit comfortably with the Confucian mixture of morality, righteousness and intellectualism, linked together in a cosmic and mundane order. This peculiarly Chinese background is generally lacking overseas, of course, and this means that Maoism has to impose its political values with a set of ethics which may prove less palatable to foreign national communities. The rigid, some say fanatical, style of the Khmer Rouge derives in large part from this effort to comply with impractical ethical demands, for although Chinese and Cambodian culture have much in common, there are nevertheless many differences between them, in terms of individual and collective behaviour.

The Maoist framework of thought was further strained by the factional struggling which erupted in 1966, known as the Cultural Revolution. The basic issues were related to the scramble for power in China, but its ideological fall-out was disastrous for Cambodia, where many angry young men were comforted by the idea that revolution was at hand, and that social reality was nothing to worry about. The movement propelled many young urban radicals into the guerrilla movement, particularly in the northeast, where they learned to cater for a somewhat mythical "people". They met some seasoned partisans who probably had a more realistic approach. Feelings of defiance between the two generations later became mortal distrust.

The launching of armed struggle in early 1968, and its stagnation under Lon Nol's subsequent repression, could only reinforce the idea that revolution was a military struggle, and that violence, if applied with a just spirit, provided the best way to achieve it. A rudimentary class analysis was in use, borrowed from Stalinist Russia of the late 1920s and handed down by the Chinese and the Vietnamese, which, far from reflecting real economic relations, was a mere catalogue of peasant ownership status and non-peasant professional categories. Later refinements included political attitudes; this analysis proved to be a useless sociological tool since there was never any serious attempt to manipulate socio-economic factors.[17] Old structures were just erased and replaced by artificial militarized organizations. This led, among other things, to complete mismanagement of the economy.

After all, the most striking feature of the idea of revolution entertained by the Khmer communists was that it was **unexpressed**. In the 1960s, opposition to government policies and calls for an anti-imperialist stand made up the platform of the left wing. In January 1968 the setting up of a secret and embryonic "Revolutionary Army" signalled the official beginning of armed struggle. But there is no evidence that the qualifications of this army were elaborated in propaganda at the time, and it made no breakthroughs under that little-known name.

Revolution was never a major propaganda theme because peasants could not be convinced by, and would have shied away from, any involvement in a complete overturning of their world (and cosmic) order. In fact, revolution and the existence of a revolutionary party were not only played down in propaganda, they were completely hidden truths, revealed only to the enlightened few who could achieve senior positions in the apparatus. Revolution was not an asset but an ultimate goal, which had to be achieved by devious and clandestine means, since even the beneficiaries could not be led towards paradise.

It is clear that under these circumstances, the CPK leadership was not in a position to experiment with revolutionary formulas or draw lessons from the social responses which they evoked. In China and Vietnam, communist parties have had a long involvement in actual struggles taking place in large industrial concentrations. They have had to organize trade unions and striking workers, and their rather bourgeois leadership has learned immensely from this involvement. "Proletariat" was a harsh reality for those who had to organize political rallies in the 1920s and 1930s. Although the proletarian nature of the CPs remained a matter of rhetoric, this original experience was never forgotten, even in subsequent rural and militaristic developments.[18]

The Khmer leadership, as we have seen, had a wholly different starting point. The most "advanced" concentration of workers, on the rubber plantations, was largely Vietnamese, and for a long time a Viet Minh/Viet Cong constituency, therefore rejected by Pol Pot and his colleagues. Endowed for the most part with bourgeois backgrounds, communist leaders made their headquarters in the tribal areas of the northeast. There, local people had the most slender relationship, if any, with the general economy of the country. Although this could be a matter for discussion among anthropologists, these remote tribal populations (mixed with various types of outlaws) could be seen, in a simplistic Marxist view, as embodying primitive communism. This social experience was unique, if we ignore the Lolo episode of the Long March, and it certainly had an impact on Cambodia's revolutionary leaders.[19]

In that light, it is very striking that when the real war started in 1970, there was a strong insistence on a generalized local economic autarky. Every region, every district, if not every village, had to be self-sufficient, not only in food, but in other commodities, such as cotton, handicrafts, and so on. Of course, transportation was an acute problem. But it might seem strange that self-sufficiency had become such a paradigmatic solution to a war-torn economy that it was also to be applied to the co-operatives after the war. Trade was practically banned, as it was believed to harbour the seeds of capitalism and to carry an evil moral value, not an economic one.

By 1978, and possibly earlier, the co-operative system appeared to be a failure. The lack of an efficient local and central bureaucracy made any control over the co-operatives purely formal. It has been said by members of the 1980 Democratic Kampuchea government, that by 1978 the central authorities had only vague ideas about what was happening in more than half of the country's co-operatives. The reason is clear: central authorities determined the quotas of rice and other foodstuffs to be delivered by each co-operative, each region and each zone. Cadres had to find a way to fulfil these quotas, or they might have been suspected of treason or sabotage. So their reports to the Centre were very often designed to cover up the real situation, and the havoc created by the often absurd demands sent by the Centre.

This has to be related to the most original assertion coming from the CPK: that the Cambodians did not need *transition phases*. This term belongs to a strictly internal discussion which takes place periodically among post-Leninist economists. They have to face the fact that revolutions, where they have occurred, did not take place *after* the final phase of capitalist evolution and that, therefore, the concentration of productive forces has to be achieved under revolutionary control. That is the meaning of "building socialism." And in order to achieve socialism and proceed towards communism, transition phases must be carefully understood and put into practice. This strangely uncanonical view had been widely accepted and refined by Western Marxist economists and Eastern bloc governments, as a matter of necessity. But the Khmers misunderstood it as a "reformist" or "revisionist" scheme that they had better avoid. Spokesmen occasionally boasted that the regime had jumped over the transitions and achieved instant socialism. As for the land reform initiated in 1973, they even said that in some areas peasants did not notice the reform was taking place, suggesting that they already lived under some kind of primitive communism and there was nothing to reform.

In 1978, when the failure of the system became blatant, a more cautious approach was fashioned. A Central Committee resolution, dated 10 October, introduced a timid version of the transition phases and called for the creation of "advanced co-operatives".[20] "Each advanced co-operative", said Phnom Penh Radio, "must have more than economic or rice-production characteristics. It must have all kinds of characteristics, particularly political ones. This is a complete change in Kampuchean society". This "complete change" was just the opening of a well-known road, leading towards *kolkhozian* and *sovkhozian* economic miracles. Were the Khmer communists the last people on earth to ignore the fact that in all socialist countries, private plot production is an absolute necessity, without which starvation lingers? They were probably told as much by powerful friends, but they were never prepared to learn from foreign experiences. Certainly the Khmer communists entertained the illusion they were not "Maoist" and that they were devising some sort of original version of the old dogma, even though Pol Pot paid tribute, when Mao died, to the power of his "Thought". But the true originality of the Kampuchean experiment is more on the side of oversimplification and emphasis on the authoritarian aspects of ruling methods in the "Chinese way".

Similar results stem from similar causes. As a brief and penetrating analysis of China in 1949 points out: "The truth of the Chinese communist revolution is the encounter between the smallest of the social groups, the thin layer of the modern intellectuals, and the largest social force, the peasantry."[21] As a group standing outside the power structure, but nurturing the idea of modernization as a reaction to Western domination, the radical intelligentsia in China suffered from the failure of the Republic in the 1920s, and, after 1927, adhered to the motto of one of its most admired thinkers, Li Tachao, who said, long after the Russian *narodniki*: "Go to the village." One aspect of Maoism is the rationalization of this breakaway from the ruling class, and the subsequent reorientation of political activities towards the countryside. "Rectification campaigns" are the way for the Party to adapt to, and adopt the new social environment. This broad outline of events applies perfectly to Cambodia. The leadership of the CPK is made up of "outcast" intellectuals who could never gain control inside the power system (although some Khmer Marxists, later purged by Pol Pot, tried hard to do so) and who were rejected by the traditional body politic. They then "went to the village" (1963–8) and had to place themselves under extreme pressure in order to become professional peasant leaders. The theorization of their evolution was then, quite normally, very close to Maoism, that is, an ideology which rationalizes the substitution of the radical intelligentsia for a powerless, and occasionally privileged, working class. To maintain its grip, this small élite had to look like a peasant class, and had to destroy, within its ranks, all those who were thought to retain anything of their former class background. Class background, after all, was considered the bridge by which the former ruling classes could infiltrate the Party and re-establish their power. Hence the need to promote uneducated peasants, and to "purify" the Party and the population with purges which became more and more frantic.

What was the most remarkable feat of Asian communists? A very great ability to manipulate the peasantry, to infiltrate closed villages, observe inner conflicts, develop them and use them as levers to change the local political balance and orient peasant motivations toward collective goals, which had not been those most cherished by the peasants themselves. I use the term manipulation with no moral judgement attached. Social engineering might be a more apt description. Mao's first recognition abroad came in the 1920s, with his description of village conditions in Hunan, which was approved by Trotsky, then still in Moscow. I remember long conversations with low-ranking Vietnamese cadres, in the 1960s and 1970s, as they explained to me how they had had to settle down in a village, alone, with no protection, to study it in depth, work out its internal "contradictions" in order to destabilize it from inside, using its own social dynamics, much as judo uses the adversary's strength. It made them remarkable practical sociologists, much to the shame of Westerners of more established scholarly reputations.

If there was ever any attempt to carry out that painful and dangerous work in Cambodia, it was short-lived and its results are not on record. Instead, in the aftermath of the 1970 coup, an authoritarian machine was imposed from above on the peasantry, and social manipulation was minimal.[22]

This, and other reasons derived from the general pattern of communist operations, led to the total absence of democratic processes, and the corresponding political weakness of any organization based more on imposed subservience than on voluntary participation. War conditions and militarism usually set back democratic processes, but here the end of the war meant an increase in militarization and a gradual disappearance of what was left of voluntary adhesion to the new system.

This complete inability in the field of social engineering was best illustrated with the sacrosanct question of the working class. Though tiny, it existed, scattered in the towns. But instead of cultivating it, the Khmer communists proceeded to liquidate it as if it were a decadent legacy of the past, and undertook to replace it with young uneducated peasant soldiers. As is shown in Chinese and Yugoslav films, the plants and workshops were designed primarily to produce not goods, but "new" workers.

Another striking feature of the Khmer revolution is the deep contradiction between its ultranationalist claim, bordering on racism, and its radical incapability to have a *national* policy that could effectively be carried out. It is safe to say, I think, that at no time between 1975 and the end of 1978 were the central authorities close to having complete control over the national economy, the state power system, the army, the Party, and possibly even the State security office, S-21. All of these were riddled with political factions, military brotherhoods, regional powers, personal networks, all contending for influence and the purging of rival forces. The State never stood on its feet (and this had nothing to do with the predicted degeneration of the State). Continual purges and the indiscriminate use of terror created a semblance of political unity, but the damage was so great that the shell was empty when the Vietnamese set out to crack it.

We find here again that kind of clan structure of political divisions, already noted in Cambodian history. It is true that clandestine politics often produces this kind of side-effect. But the multiplication of subgroups, regional or subregional, inside the Party and the "State power" attained unusual dimensions. It looks very much like a re-enactment of the old *komlang* concept of linear loyalties linking people upward to a leader.

As a hypothesis, I would suggest that Cambodian systemic hierarchy, noticeable in political behaviour and linguistic usage, has been much less operative than is usually believed. Since a rather large number of people thought themselves fit for a leader's role, fierce competition arose from sheer numbers. Of course, the collapse of the old society in 1975 could have favoured the appearance of a wide range of new leaders emerging from the lowest strata of the peasantry. The Party was unable to provide a framework to channel this emergence, which soon erupted in a murderous competition between locally based "organizations" — even more acute when they all had to retreat under Vietnamese pressure, and to fight with each other for food. Many of them merely disintegrated.

This lack of efficiency of a hierarchical system, in traditional politics as well as in the communist rule, may be ascribed — and this is a further hypothesis — to a lack of intermediary social groups which could relate the nuclear family to the national community as a whole. A loosely structured village community, drawn together by the *wat*, was not a strongly binding tie among the villagers. It could well be that the French colonial authorities, by introducing paid officials into the villages, contributed to dissolving elders' councils which possibly played a role in ancient times, and were, until recently, more prominent in marginal areas.[23]

The real power of the CPK, I think, did not lie in any particular type of social (re)organization, but rather in two factors — the psychological manipulation of individuals, and the monopolization and the distribution of food. Because class consciousness could not be considered to be the main source of revolutionary dynamics, the need to create such consciousness was soon embodied in a set of ethical rules, which were based on two main principles: the rectification of the self and the integration and subordination of the individual into a collective unit. The implementation resulted in a system of intense psychological pressures on collective meetings, where individuals had to tell their life stories again and again in order to criticize their own bad "trends" and to relinquish any control over their own behaviour. Drawing on the Buddhist traditional exercise of self-examination and the Stalinist concept of the "New Man", these pressures were effective in reducing individuals to servility. The fear of hard labour or execution was well founded, and led to the complete psychological isolation of the individual, making him suspicious of everybody, totally identified with, and dependent upon his group and its leaders. Suspicions were aired, as rumours, "targets" were defined before they were actually struck, in order for everyone to feel that he himself might be the target of the next purification move.

Towards the end of 1978, it was said that the purges were to be decreased as the Organization was considered to be 50–70 per cent pure, with some regional variations. Purges were considered "battles", involving "victories", which could conveniently explain current difficulties. Thus, the Minister of Defence, Son Sen, was denounced as a traitor in high administrative circles for at least a month before the Vietnamese intervention saved him from being purged. He hid himself in the forest for eighteen months, with a handful of bodyguards, before resurfacing in the DK apparatus, apparently with strong Chinese and Thai support.[24]

The monopolization of food strongly complemented psychological pressures and could be used on a wider scale on non-Party people who could not be put under so much scrutiny. Such a perverse situation was previously achieved only in the vast concentration camp complexes known in Nazi Germany, the Soviet Union, communist China and lesser imitators. It had never before been extended to a whole nation. The idea of revolution, as benefiting at least some classes or sections of the population, vanished in the process, while the threat and the use of starvation and death were the only means to gradually expand domination by the CPK (or a diminishing fraction thereof) over a largely demoralized and frightened populace.

The most recent avatar is the abandonment of all pretence of a revolutionary meaning to this tragedy. The Pol Pot communists now explain to visitors that all they really want is free elections, with no more reference to socialism and revolution. But the very same people are using the very same authoritarian methods as before, and cannot be taken at their word, since they have proven all along to almost everybody in the country, that their promises have been grossly deceptive. The extent of this deception will also affect the new Vietnamese-dominated regime with its bureaucratic conception of socialism, since there is now a wide consensus in Cambodia which holds that revolution is the worst thing that can happen. The self-proclaimed dissolution of the CPK (December 1981) is the latest deception since the Party remains the only structure that can keep the DK guerrillas alive. It is painting a red banner white, but the banner is still there.

The social revolution — "*la sociale*" as the French workers used to say with fervent hope at the turn of the century — is not far advanced anywhere, to be sure. But what happened in Cambodia cannot be described as a "perverted" or "traitorous" interpretation of the term; it is just a total misunderstanding of what it represents. Blood was all that the Democratic Kampuchea songs were calling for. Blood was all the nefarious State Security was after. To "save the Kampuchean blood", they had to spill it all over, and turn this ancient land into a bloody mess.

5

Cambodia 1981:
Background and Issues[*]

The Geopolitical Situation of Cambodia

Cambodia is basically divided into two ecological zones: the smaller one is the central and southern flat plain which allows wet rice cultivation. Up to perhaps nine-tenths of the population is concentrated in this zone. The river banks have the greatest agricultural potential and the most valuable non-rice cash-crops are cultivated there. The central lake with the riverine system is the key to the Cambodian economy, as the annual flood brings water and silt to relatively poor soils. The conditions are ideal for an enormous fish population and produce a decisive amount of animal protein. Except for some periods of particularly adverse weather in the 1920s, Cambodia never experienced mass starvation, although individual cases of malnutrition could be observed, mainly in remote areas. In most years of this century, before 1970, Cambodia exported food, rice, fish and cattle. For the country to have to import food at all is a very abnormal situation. But this should not be understood as meaning that the country is rich. Most of the cultivated soils rank between average and very poor. The only very rich soils, those on the river banks, called *chamkar*, are of limited extent. In the past decades, they were intensively cultivated (tobacco, vegetables) mainly by Chinese, Vietnamese and Cham market gardeners. Other very good volcanic soils in the forested areas have been earmarked for rubber tree cultivation. The Cambodian rubber plantations ranked among the best in Southeast Asia. The Chup modern processing plant was destroyed by the South Vietnamese Air Force in 1970, without military justification.

The second and larger part of Cambodia is composed of mountains and plateaus, either densely forested or covered with savannah-type overgrowth. Lack

---

[*]   Written with Michael Vickery.

of water prevents wet-rice cultivation, but dry-rice cultivation is fairly common. The population is extremely scattered, sometimes only half-Khmerized.[1] The forest does not provide much food and then only to those who master the traditional knowledge of wild plants and animals. Khmers usually consider the forest a dreadful and dangerous place and would not choose, except under duress as under Pol Pot, to settle in forest areas.

It is fair to say that they never had to live in the forest, other than when taking temporary refuge in time of war, because flat land has always been available. The potential area where normal cultivation could be undertaken is probably slightly larger than the area cultivated before the war. This explains why there was never in Cambodia a high pressure on land, or on productivity. This pressure began to be felt in the 1960s around the urban centres but was nothing to compare with that in other large Asian rice plains.

The average yield, one ton per hectare or less, is about the lowest in the world, and matches that of Laos. The basic technology does not seem to have changed much since the Angkorian period and might be much more ancient than Angkor itself. Programmes for agricultural development and modernization, including irrigation works, seed-selection, experimental State farms, have been quite consistent and were applied during the Sihanouk period. Their relative lack of efficiency in raising the level of productivity is to be found in the reluctance of a large part of the peasantry to produce a surplus which might well be taken by moneylenders, tax-gouging petty officials or through corrupt administrative practices, like the royal co-operatives, or the military collection of paddy. For other more entrepreneurial farmers, the lack of capital and the cost of credit also deterred efforts to increase production. Peasants were thus mostly doomed to remain poor. They were above starvation but access to consumption goods was practically out of the question, unless someone in the family went to work in the towns. Its long-time landlocked position (Kompong Som harbour was not opened until the 1960s), the small size of its population, its lack of any significant industry and its cultural isolation made Cambodia a small and weak nation compared with most other Asian countries.

Cambodian Society: A Selective Historical Survey

Traditional Cambodian society was formed essentially of three classes — peasants, officials, and royalty. Very few Khmers became merchants, and to the extent an urban population apart from the court and officials existed, it was composed mainly of non-Khmers, generally Chinese. This division of society probably goes back to the Angkor period when national wealth was produced from the land and collected by the officials who channelled it to the court and religious apparatus, where it was used largely for building the temples and supporting the specialized population attached to them. A part of the wealth collected by officials remained in their hands for their support in lieu of salary, but this was accepted as the way in which the system naturally functioned. Each of the classes had a function believed essential for the welfare of the society, and in which the king's role was quasi-religious and ritual.

Although the Angkorian State declined and disappeared, the old divisions of society persisted. For the mass of the population, social position was fixed, and it would have been almost unthinkable to imagine rising above the class into which one was born. Occasionally, perhaps in time of war, or for exceptional services to a powerful patron, someone from a peasant background might rise into the official class and thereby change the status of his immediate family; and clever children might be educated in an official family or at court to become officials; but such occurrences were too rare for any expectation of social mobility to be part of public consciousness.

The possibilities of wealth accumulation were also limited. Land was not personal property, but in theory belonged to the king. An energetic peasant could thus not accumulate land and wealth through hard work and abstemiousness and move up the scale to rich farmer, entrepreneur, or whatever. The only possibility for wealth accumulation lay in an official career. Even there life was hazardous. Officials were of course more or less wealthy, and the official status of a family might continue for generations; but their status was not assured by any formal legality, and could be ended precipitously at royal displeasure — for instance, if an official showed signs of accumulating too much wealth or power. Even if a career did not end in disgrace, wealth accumulated in the form of gold, jewels, other precious goods, or dependents (slaves), might revert to the State at an official's death rather than passing in inheritance to his family. There was thus no incentive, or possibility, to use wealth for long-term constructive purposes or entrepreneurial investment.

Nevertheless, in pre-modern times the wealth squeezed out of the peasantry by the officials and the court — the State apparatus — did not in general represent a loss to the national economy, for little of it was spent abroad. It was used for conspicuous consumption within the country in the construction of dwellings and temples, the support of large service retinues, and the patronage of local artisans. Much of it was returned whence it came, and the propensity to accumulate wealth by the élites must have been restricted to some extent by the limits of consumption, or use, within the country.

Village and family organization, especially if compared to that of China, Vietnam or India, was extremely weak. Khmer villages were not cohesive units, as in Vietnam, dealing collectively with officials; and beyond the nuclear household, families easily disintegrated. Extended family did not exist, records of previous generations were not kept, ancestors were not the object of a religious cult. Corporate discipline over the individual by extended families or by village organizations was weak, and once a person had fulfilled his obligations to the State — through tax or corvée — there was little constraint on his activities. It is thus likely that a paradoxical situation of great anarchic individual freedom prevailed in a society in which there was no formal freedom at all.

Compensating for the absence of any possibility of secure accumulation of wealth or amelioration of status in the present life, Buddhism offered the possibility of both in the future. The performance of meritorious work in this life in theory opened the way to rebirth at higher status: thus the vast amount of wealth and voluntary co-operative work which went into construction and maintenance of temples. For the Cambodian who believed in rebirth, this was a practical investment. This aspect of Buddhism also served to justify social inequality and injustice. The wealthy and powerful were such because of meritorious past lives; and if they were abusive in the present their position would decline in their next existence. Fate would punish them, and it was not for the common man to criticize or resist them in the present. Except for the construction of religious edifices, there was little or no voluntary investment for a long-term purpose; and the purpose of individual wealth was immediate consumption.

In such a society in which the present was fixed and development or mobility reserved for future existences, all education and knowledge was of an immediate practical nature. Literacy and literature were mainly religious, and even in that field had the practical purpose of preparing for the cosmic future. Theoretical or speculative intellectuality, which presupposes a possibility of change in the present human condition through deeper understanding of the immediate world, found no ground in which to grow.

Since the fifteenth century at least, and particularly during the eighteenth and nineteenth centuries, Cambodian society was subject to nearly continuous disruption and instability. Frequent warfare meant displacement of large segments of the population, movement of the capital, disappearance of villages, and thus continued weakening of all organization beyond the immediate family. One of the important causes of the eighteenth and nineteenth century warfare was rivalry between expanding new regimes in Siam and Vietnam, both of which sought to incorporate all or parts of Cambodia.

The colonial period, beginning for Cambodia in 1863, ended the instability caused by foreign invasions, and in a way stabilized the traditional society in that the French tried to rule indirectly, through the old Cambodian administration. Taxation, however, increased, forcing peasants to seek more cash income than before, and the colonial authorities attempted repeatedly to establish legal private property of the land to transform it into a commodity and to provide an inducement to higher productivity. But these measures were opposed by peasant inertia and it is only in the latest period that land accumulation could possibly become a form of wealth. As commerce and foreign trade developed, towns grew, but the urban commercial groups remained non-Khmer; and even after World War II, Phnom Penh was mainly a Chinese and Vietnamese city with a small élite Cambodian royal and official class and a French administration at the top.

Of particular interest is the development of modern education, begun by the French. Although the colonial powers in Asia were ultimately found guilty of neglecting education, it must be remembered that at the very beginning of European rule in Burma, Cambodia, and Vietnam, more education was offered than the local population was willing to accept.

The subjects offered by the new schools were strange, traditional knowledge was neglected, and the utility of modern education was not recognized until it was seen that careers in the growing administration — the only traditional non-peasant education for a Cambodian — could be opened up by a knowledge of French and certain other European subjects. This traditional channel of upward mobility was widened by the French administration; and the first people to take advantage of it were often not of the traditional élite. The rapid rise of the new civil servants in French service sometimes provoked hostility from their erstwhile social superiors, as in the famous Prince Yukanthor affair in 1901, when the French were blamed for allowing upstarts to subvert the position of the traditional élite.[2]

Of course, modern education established by the French was limited to what they felt was required for their administration, but similar limitations were imposed by the contemporary, and independent, Siamese government, and for the same reason — recognition that a large body of educated, but unemployable, youth would be socially and politically disturbing.

In spite of the restructuring of the top levels of the Cambodian government according to European forms, and recognition of the utility of European education, there was little change in attitudes and values. Officials continued to see their positions as ends in themselves, as situations in which to accumulate, for consumption, part of the wealth extracted from the peasantry and passed upwards to the rulers. After they were put on salary by the French, such additional accumulation was illegal, but as a traditional practice was not felt to be immoral, and the corruption which later became such a serious problem began thus as a continuation of an accepted traditional practice. The exploitative character of colonialism thus merged easily with the exploitative character of traditional society, and intensified it; and for many members of the Cambodian élite the evil of colonialism probably resided less in its exploitation than in the fact that they were not in ultimate control.

Between 1945 and 1954, the Cambodians gradually took over the administration of the country from the French and the process was completed by the granting of independence in 1953 and the arrangements of the Geneva Conference of 1954. Cambodian officials thus succeeded to all the offices and privileges once held by the French. Along with official prerogatives went a desire for the life-style of the French élite; and soon upper-class Cambodians came to believe they should possess the same luxuries and material conveniences as their counterparts in Paris or New York. In contrast to the pre-1940 period, when the top level of administration was foreign, the demonstration effect of new luxuries in the hands of Cambodian officials influenced ever wider circles who sought to acquire consumer goods which neither they as individuals, nor the country as a whole, could afford.

Thus in the new independent Cambodia, in contrast to the old, pre-French society, wealth squeezed from the peasantry did not go into patronage of local arts or maintenance of local retinues, but was exchanged abroad for Western luxuries, invested in Paris real estate, or deposited in foreign banks. Development for such a consumption-oriented élite meant luxury housing, Western-style restaurants and bars, importation of automobiles. The type of growth experience of Saigon and Bangkok in the 1960s and 1970s, ending for the former in 1975, and which most Westerners would consider a tragedy, was regarded by Cambodians with envy; and those who opposed Sihanouk's rejection of American aid in 1963–4 argued that such growth would thereby be impeded in Phnom Penh. Even when whole industries were set up as foreign aid projects, as was done by China in the 1960s, such industries were valued mainly for the possibilities of personal enrichment inherent in them; and one observed the interesting circumstance that an industry might show deficits while its management personnel accumulated great wealth. It was still the traditional practice of officials to extract a percentage of what they collected for the State; and no member of the élite was ever severely called to account or forced to repay what he had collected from the public till.

After World War II, and particularly after independence (1953–4), education underwent very rapid growth, but the results were not always as positive as might have been assumed. Whatever indifference to the *forms* of Western education remained soon disappeared once it was realized that the new Cambodian administration required more employees and that the key to State employment was some kind of diploma from modern schools. The only traditional way out of peasant status, entrance into the official class, was maintained and reinforced; and not only did those who went to school hope for State employment, but if more than basic primary education had been obtained, return to peasant status was seen as intolerable. Any kind of petty service occupation in Phnom Penh, however precarious, was preferable to life in the old home village.

Both because of the employment function of education and because its development made Cambodia appear modern and progressive, the construction of schools was a popular State activity and great attention was given to it; and much propaganda value was derived both for domestic and foreign consumption. Much less attention was given to the ultimate goals of education and its effects on the rapidly expanding student population. The school syllabus was copied from the French, and was thus designed for a quite different type of society and, with the exception of those few who went on to tertiary education, it produced a class of semi-intellectuals too conscious of their new status and unwilling to try any occupation but office work. School subjects were learned by rote in order to pass exams, often with little appreciation of the content, perhaps even with some disbelief in its veracity or utility.

Already by 1961 the problem was acute. The bureaucracy was over-filled and Sihanouk announced that the 600,000 or so students still in school could not possibly be absorbed. It was in fact an insoluble problem. Cambodia on its own is inevitably a peasant country, with only small possibilities for local industrial development; and a literary education of the mass of the people can only be disruptive, not progressive. The type of education appropriate for turning peasants into more productive farmers would be quite different, and it is probably not to any developed country that one should look for a model.

In Cambodia of the 1960s, there were no new developing sectors to absorb the new schools' graduates, such youth refused to placidly return to the villages, and it was politically impossible to limit schooling. One palliative was the creation, beginning in 1965, of dozens of new "university faculties", which would permit thousands of the educated youth to continue their education for a few more years. But this only delayed the day of reckoning since the problem of their ultimate absorption, quite apart from the question of the quality of these "universities" still remained. The educated youth, who by the end of the 1960s numbered in the hundreds of thousands, were an economic problem as an expensive but unemployable resource, and a political problem in that they became increasingly critical of the regime, partly no doubt just because they could find no place in it.

The educated youth also joined the ranks of those clamouring for more and more of the luxuries of the West, and the obsession with such goods from the top to the bottom of Cambodian society, led to increasing corruption at all levels. To satisfy the demands of the élites, the peasantry had to be squeezed ever harder, and that led to increasing disaffection in the countryside, and ultimately to peasant revolts.

Some of the traditional features of Cambodian society — inability to impose organizational discipline, accumulation of wealth mainly for immediate consumption, and persistence of the peasant-official-State social pattern — were reinforced and exacerbated between 1945 and 1970, and are important in explaining why war and revolution came to Cambodia and affected the country as they did.

By 1970 the State apparatus, the official class, was discredited both in the eyes of the peasantry and of the educated youth. The former, however, generally saw Sihanouk as above, and not responsible for, the evils of the administration, while the latter realized that he was an integral part of the system. The coup of 1970 represented a conflict between two factions of the State apparatus for control of its wealth-generating potential, and the war which ensued was also viewed by the élite as a source of personal enrichment. At a time when strict rationing, for example, should have been rigidly enforced, market forces were freed as never before, luxuries continued to be imported, corruption increased with army officers inventing phantom battalions whose salaries they pocketed. By 1975, demoralization was total, and most people probably at first welcomed the Communist victory.

The War and its Effects on Cambodian Society

The coup of 18 March 1970 against Sihanouk triggered two main political responses. First, in the towns, the bureaucratic élite, the merchant class and the educated youth hailed the downfall of a tyrant and the new opportunities promised by the country going over to the American side. On the other hand, the rural response was massively hostile. More than the passionate calls to rebel, launched by Sihanouk in Peking, more than the sweeping military moves of the VC/NVA, more than the thinly spread influence of the local communists, it was the distrust and rejection by the peasantry of the new totally urban-centred regime which widened the rift between town and countryside to such an extent that it would never be bridged. The Lon Nol regime and its sponsors were responsible for the most savage onslaught ever launched against a peasantry. By late 1971, almost all Cambodian villages had been visited by the Air Force. Between January and August 1973, following the Paris Agreements and the cessation of the bombings of North Vietnam, the total firepower of all the strategic US bombers operating in Asia was concentrated on the densely populated central rice plain. There had never been such an intensive bombing of populated areas in any war before. Terror from the sky was total and indiscriminate and, not surprisingly, this was the time when the Cambodian communist guerrillas set a new course of action, dropping all pretence of compromise, and established new authoritarian methods, including terror, to maintain themselves and the local population in a ravaged landscape. Unlike the ordinary tactical bombings, B52s cannot be seen or heard before their larger bombs explode, and it is quite likely that this saturation bombing campaign produced a half of the 600,000 deaths which are usually considered by both sides as having been produced by that five-year war. The massive bombing also destroyed a large proportion of the draught animals on which Cambodians rely in preparing for the slow return to self-sufficiency in rice production even today.

In the towns, the rising expectations of April 1970 were soon doomed as the old élite refused to loosen its grip on power and to share its substantial benefits. American gold never materialized and instead general impoverishment, along with an ever-growing swell of refugees from the countryside to the city, produced a gradual deterioration of urban life. By the end of the war, perhaps half of the rural population had been driven into refugee status in the cities and starvation had already begun. The population of the city of Phnom Penh increased during this period from *about 600,000 to over two million.* Cambodian social life was disrupted in a way it had never been before.

At the beginning of the war, the already active Communist guerrillas numbered less than 4,000, a quarter of them with weapons, scattered mostly in remote areas. They had some influence in several rural areas but were quite unable to maintain any control, except near the Vietnamese sanctuaries. The Party itself had no more than a few hundred members, a number of them having been involved in the anti-

French guerrilla war, some others having had education abroad. Since 1965–6, they had secretly chosen a Maoist strategy which was not much to the taste of their Vietnamese communist counterparts, and which stressed independence from the latter.

In spite of these weaknesses, the military aid provided by the Vietnamese communist troops pushed the Lon Nol government army into the towns and permitted the Khmer guerrillas to gain control of the countryside.

As most of the country fell easily into guerrilla hands, Khmer communist control expanded rapidly, first at provincial levels and then downward. Very large areas set up a revolutionary administration staffed with Sihanoukist civil servants or military who had gone over to the guerrillas, under Vietnamese military protection. But after early 1973 and the Paris Agreements, Vietnamese troops pulled out and control was taken over by Cambodian communists. Purges of non-communist cadres started. The Party recruited members from its élite military outfits, themselves selected from local militias, mainly drawn from the poorest sections of the village population. These elements, whose loyalty had already been tested in very difficult battle conditions, were to fill local and district level administrative and military positions. By the end of the war, the Party had several thousands of these young, tough, uneducated and disciplined cadres. Their performances were to be extremely unequal, to say the least.

Post-War Development, 1975

The so-called Pol Pot period was a negation, and reversal, of all that had gone before. No longer could Cambodia be dependent on others. It would live by and within its own means, using human labour in place of unavailable machines; and the formerly parasitic classes would either have to adapt or be destroyed.

That experiment proved a failure, its excesses beyond excuse, and it deserves no defence; but some of its features deserve more careful attention.

In the world as it is today, countries like Cambodia must learn to live increasingly by their own means. Large quantities of international aid which can be diverted to luxury consumption will not be forthcoming; and such countries must learn to organize their populations efficiently and productively. In certain respects, the Pol Pot experience should have left Cambodia in a favourable position for such reorganization — the parasitic groups were severely weakened if not completely destroyed, excessive urban growth was reversed, and the entire population was inured to hard work. If redevelopment of the urban sector had been more carefully controlled and a more strict organization of the population carried on, without Pol Pot excesses, some of the problems of the past two years, still visible today, might have been less serious.

Instead Phnom Penh has rapidly inflated to nearly its pre-war size without the services necessary for healthy city; and much of the population seems to live on mutual petty trading while labour is unavailable to clean the city, repair its buildings or water supply or drainage system, or to repair the roads over which essential aid has to be carried to the countryside. Some Westerners have apparently seen the rapid growth of a "free" market as a sign of healthy development, but that view may take insufficient account of local conditions and traditions. Much of the market trading involves goods which are non-essential, perhaps even noxious (such as uncontrolled, or even fake, medicine from Thailand), and the historical record shows that the market in Cambodia will not be a channel for accumulating capital to invest in productive activities. Instead, it will channel Cambodian wealth abroad or into domestic hoards of gold or items of conspicuous consumption. In the conditions of the past two years, the market may have been the most efficient way to acquire and distribute certain needed consumer goods, but its continued free development is not necessarily healthy, and it could certainly bear more control and *taxation* for the benefit of the State budget.

In this connection, however, we must note another side of the Pol Pot legacy. Because of the oppressive character of that regime, the imposition of even minimal discipline and organization is more difficult than before. Any kind of regulations may be interpreted as a return to Pol Potism; and a reaction to the penury of 1975–9 may be a consumption-leisure psychology even stronger than before. Because of the destruction of the administrative and intellectual groups, the present administration below the very top level of old revolutionaries is staffed by people who are generally at a much higher rank now than they could ever have hoped for in the past; and it would not be surprising if the first desire of many of them were to acquire the bourgeois trappings of the pre-1975 élite.

There are two major external constraints which make any imposition of discipline and efficiency even more than usually difficult: (1) the nature of the Cambodian-Vietnamese alliance and (2) the international situation on the Thai-Cambodian border.

Since the present government has been installed and maintained with Vietnamese support, any unpopular measure it takes may be interpreted as Vietnamese domination; and it is likely that the extreme freedom which has been allowed people in their choice of work (or non-work) and place of residence has been to gain popular support and avoid any hint of Vietnamese interference in everyday life.

On the Thai border the refugee operations mounted since 1979 were only in part for humanitarian reasons. They were also in part to put pressure on, and to destabilize Phnom Penh and Vietnam; and they have served to draw off many surviving professionals and intellectuals who are badly needed in Cambodia. Unpopular measures taken here could send still more people across the border; and their movement would be interpreted abroad as "voting with the feet" against an oppressive "socialist" regime. Until the border operations are closed it will be extremely difficult for Phnom Penh to take some of the organizational measures which are necessary.

Foreign Relief Agencies

Since the largest component of the Vietnamese presence, the army, is here to protect the country from the Pol Pot guerrillas, and since those guerrillas are largely supported from across the Thai border, the two constraints on development organization mentioned above are closely related to the actions of unfriendly foreign countries, first of all China, the United States and Thailand. One of the greatest services which agencies interested in helping Cambodia could perform would be the energetic dissemination of propaganda against the nefarious effects of the refugee camp system and the land bridge, neither of which is any longer needed for the humanitarian purposes alleged at its inception.

The cause of Cambodian recovery would best be served by an end to all support for the Pol Pot or Khmer Serei remnants, the closure of border relief activities, the recognition of the present Phnom Penh government, and the direct supply of all necessary aid directly to Phnom Penh.

Of course, the cause of Cambodian recovery is not first among the interests of some of the governments and agencies involved; and if considerations of international power politics continue to be given precedence, Cambodian recovery may be delayed indefinitely. Voluntary agencies with humanitarian goals, however, should not feel bound by the political interests and prejudices of their governments, and might often perform their tasks better in opposition.

With respect to aid programmes within the country, emergency conditions seem to have ended, and aid inputs should be studied much more carefully. Of course, the Cambodian government is entitled to its own policies and preferences, and must develop as it wishes, even if certain policies seem wasteful or unproductive. But there is no need for foreign agencies to co-operate in or support ventures of which they do not approve. An agency, such as CWS, should adopt as its first principle that it will only support strictly humanitarian projects or economic projects which have a reasonable chance of being cost effective.

The Cambodian government and its organizations should be asked to formulate careful plans for what they need; and the foreign agencies should then decide whether they wish to participate in any particular project. Hardware should be limited to what is absolutely essential and for which maintenance service is available. The maximum use of human labour rather than overly sophisticated machinery should be required, for example, in road repair and reconstruction of the city. Here foreign agencies might encourage the Cambodian government to bid successfully for the surplus food now traded in the market and use it as payment for work projects to mobilize the population by carrot rather than stick measures.

In the end, however, exclusively carrot measures might be prohibitively expensive. All Cambodian "infrastructural" works, beginning with the Angkor temples, through the French roads and Pol Pot's dams were built with forced labour of one sort or another, and the mass of the population probably saw very little utility in any of them. Necessary large scale construction in the future will probably require some kind of "stick" in the form of labour tax, or *krom samakki* labour groups from the urban areas.

International Aid and the Concept of Emergency

When, in September 1979, tens of thousands of exhausted and dying Cambodians flocked across the Thai border, world opinion was shocked and a vast movement of aid was prompted and channelled through various relief agencies. Only those who took care to analyse facts first could realize that this ghastly picture, true as it was, did not represent the general situation inside the whole country, and was even a grossly distorted view of it. These parched and starved crowds were the remnants of the 800,000 or so people who, willing or not, had followed the retreat of Pol Pot's troops into the forested areas. Routed from one place to another by successive Vietnamese thrusts, they had lost or consumed any food they could have taken with them, or found at prepared storage points. Whatever food was left was going to the military and for a long time civilians were forcibly prevented from crossing over to Thailand although starvation was already taking a heavy toll. They had reached the ultimate level of misery before the Khmer Rouge high command allowed them to cross over the border. It was a time of total disruption for the Pol Pot politico-military structure. Morale, discipline, organization — all had been dissipated in this long agony. At that point, the Khmer Rouge had ceased to exist, except as a collective traumatic memory.

Thus an emergency was created, because of Pol Pot's own political miscalculations. It is quite clear that whatever ulterior political goals might also be served, the duty of the international community was to rush aid to the people and save them from imminent death.

At that time, the food situation in the country as a whole was rather bad but still a far cry from disaster. Most of the 1978–9 crop had been consumed. Some food had already been given by the Soviet Union. Storage facilities and transport were very difficult problems. Only in a few places, mainly around the towns, where food resources fell far below the needs of the number of people who tried to make their way back, were there pockets of severe malnutrition. However, if this situation as a whole was not too bad at the time, the prospects for the future were very grim. Due to the war and the sudden breakdown of the Draconian co-operative system only 20–25 per cent of the fields had been planted in time. The crop to be harvested by December 1979 to January 1980 would last for only about three months. Starvation, comparable to the scenes on the border in September, could begin to occur inside the country by April or May 1980. In anticipation, and since the emergency had triggered food donation on the border, a vast number of people started to trek towards the Thai border in order to receive, or barter, or buy food and bring it back into the country.

The fortunate consequence of the misunderstood emergency of September 1979 is that it contributed decisively to averting months ahead a more serious and widespread one. All this was very good. The detailed story is of course much more complicated, as the motivations of the international agencies were not always clear, and diverging political interests could hardly be patched up. The new Phnom Penh government was, for instance, accused of favouring starvation by holding back international aid at a time when there was as yet no starvation and the main crop was just being harvested and stored.

In retrospect it is apparent that the timing and even-handed delivery of international aid resulted in the restoration of the Pol Pot military apparatus. For almost two years now, Pol Pot's army and its reduced civilian base (around 100,000 persons in all), including its worst killers and those who ordered those lethal policies, have been fed — to the extent of around two-thirds of their food requirement — out of international humanitarian help. For those nations intent on preventing the consolidation of the Vietnam backed Heng Samrin regime in Phnom Penh, this might have been good politics. It hardly qualified as a moral victory.

It was the awareness by the Phnom Penh authorities of the political consequences of some international aid schemes which explains their reluctance or refusal to concur in some of them. However, it must be recognized that international aid also contributed to the rebuilding of an administration in Cambodia under the Heng Samrin Government. Donated rice was distributed as salary for several months to civil servants, and thus had a political impact. The rebuilding of a minimal administration inside Cambodia, even for aid to be distributed, can be defended as an unavoidable necessity. However, the rebuilding of Pol Pot's oppressive machine cannot be ascribed to any material necessity. The political consequences of international food aid might have been unavoidable in the first months of what was defined as an emergency situation. Obviously, there was a real but limited emergency in 1979 and a bigger one in prospect for 1980. By early 1981, however, the food emergency — that is, the danger that any sizeable number of people would die because of lack of food — had ceased. The 1980–1 crop was good, and although the 1981–2 crop will not be as good, there is still time and room to cope when in the second half of 1982 the food situation may prove difficult. A Cambodian administration is in charge and should be left to take care of the most basic food requirements. If, in fact, a real rice shortage is anticipated in 1982, there are measures which should be taken now, and which are within the competence of the Cambodian Government. It is clear that the free sale of cooked rice in the numerous small markets and restaurants of Phnom Penh can easily lead to wastage, and it might be well to institute strict rice rationing now.

If an emergency, *stricto sensu*, ended months ago, international help is continuing, partly because of its own momentum (large sums of money have been raised for Cambodia and part of it is still unspent) and partly because many other basic needs, other than minimal food, still remain to be fulfilled. However, the major donor nations have decreed that the money cannot be used for development purposes, as it was not raised for that goal. Especially in the case of using money raised in the US, the aid agencies are bound by the policy of the US Government that this money can only be used for humanitarian relief, not for development.

In fact, it would be very difficult to evolve any programme now in Cambodia which might correctly be called developmental. The rehabilitation of the rubber plantations and the rebuilding of the rubber processing plant might be one. But this is obviously to be left to bilateral government agreements and it is probable that no NGO would be allowed to touch it.

Cambodia before the war was a slowly developing country which enjoyed a fair amount of international aid. In the situation today no real development can be conceived because the very basic requirements for it are not met. If we call development any project which generates a surplus, freely made available for either further investment or any other use, then it should be understood that the amount of destruction since 1970 is such that no economic input is apt to generate such a surplus because any possible profit would be eaten away by the side costs of maintenance, supply, power, and so on, which become extremely expensive in the absence of a normal infrastructure. These side costs include lack of transport, of power, of skilled personnel, of administrative and clerical experience, of supplies, of spare parts. The effect of these lacks is to make everything very costly. Any economic endeavour in this context has near zero profitability and is undertaken more because of social utility than because there would be the prospect of generating a surplus that could be used for further investments. Thus, before there is any rational prospect of development, the **basic need of the country is a return to normalcy: this is the wider meaning of ending the emergency**. A "normal" situation in Cambodia is somehow a return to what the economic infrastructure was before the war, with a comparable population and without taking into account those surpluses which were formerly exported and which could now be used either for consumption or investment.

Within these limits, several economic sectors should be taken into consideration since they are obvious bottlenecks in the return to normalcy.

Communication networks, harbours and waterways are quite usable. Barges and other boats are lacking. They could do much to alleviate road transport. Roads are in a very bad condition. If nothing is done now, rehabilitation will become increasingly difficult. Most of the repair work could and should be done by labour and the input of heavy equipment should be kept at a minimal level. Tar is badly needed. More rational ox carts could perhaps be devised to enhance local transport capabilities. Telecommunications badly need rehabilitation.

Water and power distribution networks both badly need rehabilitation work. Tools, supplies and some engineering costs would probably be offset by the reduction of waste. Power generation might be seen as a larger problem but here also there is an obvious need of rehabilitation.

In the area of learning, general education (secondary and higher) has yet to be fully reorganized. But the production of teaching material should be considered as most important, especially so since Khmer is the medium of instruction and no material may be imported. The most urgent need is probably in the field of basic technical learning: mechanics, agriculture, hydraulics, public works are sectors where skilled workers and technicians who have survived are the most needed, but there are not many of them, they need retraining, and new people should be taught these trades. In the medical field, results are being achieved and though the situation seems rather poor, it may be approaching what it was before the war, particularly in the rural areas. It means there is still room for a really large improvement. A very pervasive problem is the general lack of records and reference works, as most of the administrative archives, books and technical records have vanished. Cambodia is a place where reference material, on almost any subject, is just unavailable. Although it has something to do with traditional attitudes towards written culture, the need still exists and is felt in every field.

There is the special case of the Angkorian temples. The huge task of maintaining, restoring, and studying these treasures of world art is something that Cambodia cannot do alone and in fact never did. Some form of international co-operation should be established. The salvage operations led by UNESCO in Aswan and Borobudur should now be repeated at Angkor. This is an emergency in its own right. No serious maintenance work has been done for more than ten years, and none of the basic documents are to be found in Cambodia any longer. Duplicates of a great many of them are fortunately to be found in Paris.

Other fields of concentration in a plan for return to normalcy will reflect the priorities of the people and the authorities. For instance, rural housing is of very poor quality in comparison with the past. Large local efforts should be made to provide the wood and the tiles necessary for rebuilding proper and healthy housing in the villages. That will come along with the rebirth of local economy and markets.

When normalcy is restored, in the sense of getting essential components in the economic infrastructure rehabilitated, such as the systems for communication, transportation, water and power supply in the cities, education and health more ambitious development projects may become a primary focus. By that time, it is possible that the administration will have a more established doctrine and ability to cope with bigger projects. If one considers the amount of trade, investment, loans and other economic activities provided by Western governments and firms in the Soviet Union, China and Eastern Europe, one sees no reason why this source of investment could not be used as well in Cambodia, unless somehow it is decided by political circles to punish the Cambodians for faults that were imposed on them.

The Present Cambodian Regime

For those of us who have closely observed Indochinese developments over some decades, predictions of future developments can be made only with many qualifications. No more than it was possible to foresee a Peking-Washington axis in the early sixties is it possible to foresee what Vietnamese-style socialism will be in the next twenty years. Obviously Vietnam's economic record since 1975 is very weak, and Vietnamese officials are the first to offer that judgement. The generation in power has been leading the Party since the thirties and is not yet disappearing. A new generation might set a different course. All these policies and economic practices we see now should be considered as provisional in the long perspective. But one thing shall remain: Vietnam's concern for its own security. No government, whatever its political complexion, could have passively accepted the murderous raids launched by Pol Pot's armed forces from early 1977. Saigon is 50 miles away from the nearest Cambodian border post. It is quite clear that any Cambodian government has to demonstrate that it harbours no threat to Vietnam. If that is achieved, Vietnam's flexibility might be quite considerable.

So, when international conferences meet in New York or elsewhere to "solve the Cambodian question", the debate seems rather unreal: the Cambodian question is already solved. There is a government sitting in Phnom Penh, in charge of administering the near-totality of the Cambodian population, probably close to seven million. It owes its protection from external military pressure to the Vietnamese army and there is no reason to believe the Vietnamese troops will pull out before this regime, including its future variations, is able to maintain its own security. The Pol Pot, Son Sann and Sihanouk groups have not much appeal inside the country and draw their main resources from foreign aid. Their future is most probably comparable to that of the Communist Party of Malaya, still fighting in remote forested border areas, 30 years after its basic defeat. The truth is that there is no political unity in Cambodia, probably not even a single majority trend. No politician has any deep spontaneous popularity. The Heng Samrin regime is, so far, the least authoritarian regime Cambodia has ever had (which is of course no guarantee for the future). The most vital aspect of the "Cambodian problem" is the rebuilding of the country. So far this regime, whatever its political attractiveness, has coped rather well with extremely limited means.

The top level of leadership in the present regime consists first of all of a very small group of communists who began fighting against the French in the 1940s and 1950s in close co-operation with Vietnam. Many of them spent 1954–70 in

Vietnam and returned to fight against Lon Nol, only to find that they were considered dangerous enemies by the Pol Pot faction, which was responsible for the deaths of hundreds of their comrades. The goal of this group is socialism of the Vietnamese type and co-operation with Vietnam. There are also a certain number of younger revolutionaries who began their career in the Pol Pot organization but then rejected its policies at various dates after 1970.

Below this very thin topmost layer, the administration is staffed mainly by former officials, technicians and intellectuals of the Sihanouk and Lon Nol regimes, who, although they were often in opposition to the policies of those regimes, never formulated a consistent opposition strategy, and were probably unsympathetic to socialism. In their opposition days before 1975, they generally hoped for a liberal, democratic regime which, in contrast to the Sihanouk-Lon Nol governments, would be run honestly and efficiently. As a whole their group was bourgeois and nationalistic and would probably have been unsympathetic to some of the goals of the present regime.

Since most of the highest-ranking, and the majority of the most competent, of the pre-war technicians and administrators either disappeared during the Pol Pot period or have emigrated abroad, an interesting feature of the present administration is that many people are holding posts of a much higher rank than anything to which they might have aspired before 1975.

Not all the loss in trained personnel can be ascribed to the Pol Pot regime. For example, of the 450 or so physicians in pre-war Cambodia, only 50–55 were found alive here in 1979, but over 200 are alive abroad, having fled the country before 1975. And of those left here in 1979, one-third to one-half have fled across to the refugee camps in Thailand, attracted by that channel to life in the West. There has also been a considerable loss of teachers via the refugee camps.

Some Economic Issues

Parallel with the dual background of the present administrative class is the paradox that the regime is socialist in name but economically liberal in fact. Nothing markedly socialist has been attempted yet. Markets are totally free, no regulation seems to be applied, and the only restriction is that they have not been authorized to set up in the former central markets in the cities, as it is expected that someday State-run markets should set up there.[3] Goods traded include local foodstuffs and handicrafts as well as consumption goods smuggled from both Thailand and Vietnam. The administration has set up no obstacles to the smuggling and does not seem so far to plan to hinder this totally free trade, which includes some amount of Cambodian exports, such as dried fish to Thailand. These exports will have to grow as the amount of unearthed gold available for trade diminishes, since foreign currencies available on the black market will remain a very small source of exchange.

The free market had a very important role in the first two years in providing essential elementary goods to households in the process of reconstitution after the breakdown of totally collectivized life. But very soon, it implied also the import of less obviously necessary goods, such as motorbikes which fetch very high prices. A small new trading class is thus being formed and it includes, for the first time, quite a sizeable number of Khmers. Nevertheless, the traditional role of the Chinese traders may be observed and they are surely in the better position to dominate the market, because of their experience and their connections with the Chinese traders on the Thai side and, probably, on the Saigon-Cholon side. It seems that the authorities are quite undecided about the policy they should follow. The idea of a State-run market might look quite good on paper. But in practice there is some danger that such a market might degenerate into a private business for officials and become a boost to corruption. And a State market would probably have to get most of its supplies from the free market itself, having little chance of success in competition with the free retail trade. As long as the State does not have a large production of its own, be it in the form of State farms and plants, or compulsory food and produce deliveries from local production units, the most likely alternative is either to enter into competition with the free trade and then suffer defeat and indirectly subsidize the latter or to shut down the free market altogether. The Vietnamese who attempted the latter course found it counterproductive, as it lowers living standards and creates political disaffection, and they seem to advise the Cambodians against such a move. Anyway, these issues are very far from being solved yet and many developments are to be expected in the coming months and years.

Another area of uncertainty is the organization of agricultural production. Right now, 80 to 85 per cent of the population is still rural. It is loosely organized in *krom samakki*, "solidarity groups", with a system by which labour days per family unit are counted and rewarded according to their number when the crop is harvested and shared. This, in the usual socialist thinking, starting back in early Soviet policy and transmitted to the Chinese and Vietnamese economic doctrine, is the first phase of agricultural collectivization. Subsequent stages include the formation of co-operatives by gathering these groups into larger units, gradually dissolving the link between reward and what the peasant brought to the co-operative in the form of land, tools, draught animals, and ultimately, work. The top of the system is the State farm where everything belongs to the State and the labourers receive a fixed salary. Private plots are usually maintained. Although the economic efficiency of this system is extremely low, no alternative concept has ever been evolved because this system provides for other important goals: (1) the prevention of the resurgence of inequalities among peasants or the formation of an agricultural entrepreneurial class which would control production and keep the State at its mercy; (2) political control over peasants considered as naturally disinclined to support socialism; (3) control over surpluses; and (4) a pattern which could more easily absorb rationalization and modern industrialization (that is, if the State is able to provide the industrial implements). It is obviously the course which is being taken by the Cambodian Government. But this first phase might be quite long and any attempt to gear the *samakki* group into the second phase of low-level co-operatives may prove difficult and is certainly now premature.

The main reason is the peasants' reluctance to lose their grip, as they would, on their private means of production. Although the land is nominally State property — and that certainly had a political counterproductive effect in 1979 as most farmers obviously expected to regain their private property — the *samakki* formula does offer ways to conceal a private reappropriation of the land, by regularly assigning certain plots and certain tasks to certain families. In groups of ten to fifteen families, such arrangements might well amount to customary distribution of land. Under the surface, the restructuring of peasant society along former lines is a distinct possibility. And there are many reasons to believe that those who were poor before the war are poor again, those who were affluent are now better off than the rest and so on. There was a political rationale at first, since the poorest sections were those who were given prominent positions under Pol Pot, and were then the object of either revenge after Pol Pot's downfall, or at least they were suspect and had no way to claim any of the spoils which were redistributed as private property: tools, animals, carts, housing, etc. Even now, whatever potential political support Pol Pot has would lie first with these people who, relatively speaking, suffered much less from his regime and sometimes enjoyed a fair amount of local power.

It is thus quite possible that the old society pattern will covertly subdue the *samakki* system, if not cause it to disintegrate completely. In those countries which have attempted to collectivize agriculture, such a trend is usually offset by government pressures and even harsh measures to promote higher level co-operatives, in which local peasants have a lesser say and party cadres and administrators have a bigger role. But in Cambodia, the party is very far from having enough personnel to go down to the village level, and administrators are totally unprepared for this kind of task. Thus a race is set between the State's ability to work downward to manipulate the local rural society and the upward trend to restore growing inequality and private control.

The establishment of State industries is another central feature of socialist regimes. In the present situation, the first task is to restore the capability of facilities which were already State-run before. It would be logical to think that whatever increase occurs in the industrial sector will be brought about with Soviet and Eastern European aid. No real planning for the future has been made for a significant enlargement of industrial capacities.The most rational course would certainly be to serve agriculture first, supply tools, implements, pumps, multipurpose motors, and so on. But meeting consumption needs in the countryside is equally important in order to provide incentives to produce surpluses. This is an extremely important question which remains unsolved in China and Vietnam. The smuggling in of these items cannot be considered as a long-term solution. There is no risk in saying that Khmer peasants might be content to live in a subsistence family economy, with almost no surplus, if they are not somehow lured into buying materials, bicycles, radio sets and so on.

The building of industries immediately raises the question of the market and of the size of the economic sphere in which these products are to be sold or exchanged. Cambodia is obviously a tiny economic space, a fact which precludes industrial goods being turned out in quantities large enough to bring the prices down to a low enough level. But Cambodia is also part of a larger geographical entity, which includes Thailand and Vietnam. It is often alleged that Vietnam intends to establish an Indochina Federation under its hegemony. Whether or not Vietnam has such intentions, an Indochina Federation makes economic and political sense. First, countries as small as Cambodia and Laos cannot exist in the modern world in total independence, and the hegemony of some larger power, overt or covert, is inevitable, particularly in the case of Cambodia which has been so badly damaged over the past ten years. As a separate economy, living on its own means, Cambodia could probably never rise above medium peasant prosperity. It is too small to establish its own industries, either to provide necessary consumer and production goods or to absorb population from agriculture. Integrated with Vietnam, Cambodia could provide food surpluses in exchange for industrial products and alleviate some of the foreign exchange problems faced by both economies. The rationality of Indochina was of course apparent to the West so long as it was controlled by a Western power, and only became undesirable once these Asian countries had become independent.

Furthermore, the inclusion of Thailand — and Burma — in a single economic sphere would make even more sense but such a possibility appears for the time being so politically remote that no serious consideration is required.

The aid that might come from the Soviet Union to increase industrial capacities in Cambodia might have several side effects. First, economic projects from the Eastern block will have precedence over any other venture, be it Western government projects or NGO or international aid programmes, for obvious political reasons, whatever the economic rationalities involved. The role of the Eastern European communist advisers and technicians will also be given prominence by the higher authorities, although at lower administrative and technical levels this role might be resented for political and psychological reasons. It should be added that Soviet and Eastern advisory and technical activities in other underdeveloped countries do not fare much better than Western ones and usually commit the same kinds of psychological and technical errors, whereas the Cubans (and Chinese) generally prove more flexible and adaptable.

Although useful in many ways, Soviet aid might contribute somewhat to the isolation of Cambodia from the world market. The country cannot possibly repay that aid and will therefore have to direct most of its raw material exports toward the Soviet Union as a partial reimbursement. The records of Cuba, Egypt and other countries show that the Soviets are then in a position to set their price and may well resell those commodities they get in exchange for their help at world market prices and then pocket a profit which could have accrued to the aided country if it had had the oppotunity to sell directly. Thus Cambodian rubber, by far the most promising currency earner, might become victim of a captive market, leaving Cambodia with few other items with which to procure other goods that the Eastern European countries would not or could not provide. This creates a pattern of dependency with long-term consequences. It should be added that the Vietnamese do not seem to favour increasing the involvement of the Soviet Union and Eastern Europe in Cambodia. Any future role that Western governments and business would like to play should fit into this pattern and be rather unambitious. Although actual socialism in this country is still a very long way off, it is more than likely that the authorities will keep that option open and that any circumstances that do seem presently to further economic liberalism will be conceived as mostly provisional.

Since socialism will have almost no appeal in most parts of the society — partly because of the ghastly legacy of the Pol Pot regime, or the fear that the present regime would later turn out to use the same methods — the authorities have to find ways to mobilize the labour force. The level of wages, ranging from 100 to 200 riels in the administration, that is from 6 to 12 US $ a month at the black market rate — is an open provocation to graft, theft and absenteeism. If normal adequate salaries are not paid, the whole economic machine will be perverted by the private interests of those officials who will use any power they have to make a living for their families and themselves.

A significant pay rise may have important inflationary effects, which are difficult to evaluate as the local monetary system works in a somewhat mysterious way. The money, reintroduced by mid-1980, is of course based on no reserve at all. It might be understood that it is guaranteed by the ability of the State to provide for some essential services and for food in case of necessity. The fact that the value of the riel has stabilized, in a way comparable to the Vietnamese *dông*, shows that the government policy so far enjoys a certain amount of credibility. Until now, the government has moved with caution. Even more caution should be applied in the years to come since the recovery itself makes economic problems more complex. The Khmer leadership has a very short experience in terms of economic management and may sometimes be tempted to react according to the book. The best the Vietnamese advisers can do is to preach caution and flexibility. It is of course easier to preach than to act accordingly, as the Vietnamese well know.

A very cold view of Cambodia's economic potential would indicate after this period of recovery, a rather long one of stagnation, along with some form of internal reorganization. Only in the very long term, if opportunities have been carefully fostered, is there a prospect for a slow development and the entry of Cambodia, for better and worse, into the modern world economy.

6

The Pattern of Cambodian Politics

It might seem paradoxical to consider the evolution of modern Cambodian politics as a continuous and at times repetitive process, because it appears mainly as a succession of brutal changes, involving merciless replacements of ruling élites. Successive regimes abhorred the preceding ones and tried to stamp out any left-over influence. But these total and abrupt changes, sometimes labelled revolutions, occurred in a distinctively Khmer way that calls for some reflection on what Cambodian politics is really about. The most crucial question for Cambodia is not so much its international position as its ability to rebuild a political system of its own.

When King Sisowath of Cambodia first visited France, at the beginning of this century, he provoked quite a sensation in Paris. *La belle époque* was already fond of exoticism, but the display of Oriental luxury surrounding the king, his royal ornaments, his retinue, and his ballet — which amounted more or less to his harem — sparked a cultural shock. Rodin drew sketches of the lovely Khmer dancers. This shock recurred later, in 1930, with the *Exposition coloniale,* the biggest colonial exhibition in France, at which a huge cardboard rendering of Angkor Wat struck the fantasies of a whole generation. In these fantasies, Cambodia would always be a beautiful and graceful country, shrouded in Oriental mystery and ruled by a divine king, flanked by dancing *apsaras.* No attention was paid to the fact that the bill for the show was footed by the colonial administration and that the king was pretty much its servant.

This illusion had its local counterpart in Cambodia itself. The French intrusion into the country had also been a cultural shock, triggering a violent insurrection in 1886–7, after the colonial authorities had at gunpoint secured the allegiance of King Norodom (Sisowath's half-brother and predecessor) to their own particular concept of "protection". Although the French had several able administrators who could quickly grasp and analyse the basic functioning of the Khmer kingdom (see, for instance, the works of Leclère and Moura), colonial authorities were for the most part unable to understand, much less adapt to, the basic working concepts of the Khmer political system. The repeated and fruitless efforts to build up a system of private land ownership, based on notions of Roman law, bears interesting witness to this enduring misunderstanding. The Khmers, for their part, ensconced in their own culture, naturally made few efforts even to grasp the rules of the new political game. They stuck very much to their traditional leaders and ways of exercising a power that was now under the control of a foreign administration. In some ways, they behaved with the deep lack of realism that has up to now been a permanent factor in Cambodian politics. For a long time, they somehow pretended that the French went about their own business, and this business was unrelated to the real power struggle. That struggle mainly consisted of obtaining honorary positions, along with titles bestowed by the king — titles which the French, using a word out of its original context, likened to those of mandarins. There was in fact nothing in Cambodia like the Chinese mandarins, civil servants climbing up sheerly by dint of their literary knowledge and managerial abilities.

The more appropriate reference here is the tradition of the Theravada Pali Buddhist states of Southeast Asia, where literate men, until the last century and to a degree still now, were usually elected to join the *sangha* (monks' community). They did not join the civilian or military upper administration, which was reserved for the sons of the aristocracy or, up to a point, those of the merchant class.

Politically, Cambodia should be first understood as part of a cultural world that makes it foreign to both Western values and Chinese (or Sinicized) political and administrative traditions. Just ask the Vietnamese. This bitter lesson in cultural difference was first brought home to them in the decade of the 1830s, when Emperor Minh Mang had to withdraw his protectorate after a complete failure to change the nature of politics in Cambodia.[1] The same may be expected today, as soon as the military situation stabilizes and brings the question of political reorganization to the forefront. This is only prevented now by the continuous turmoil at the border, which is almost completely fuelled from abroad.

To grasp fully the present situation [in 1982], we have to go back to the nineteenth century. To simplify greatly, I would say that Cambodia was then a part of the Siamese political system. Being "a part of" should be understood not as what it means today (a region included in a state, as in the case of Sicily being "part of" Italy), but as what it meant at the time: an area under a local ruler — a country, a kingdom, whatever its official name — having a specific relation to another that is considered by both parties as the centre, and which is ruled by a paramount king to whom some kind of personal and renewable loyalty is owed by the local ruler. This local ruler maintains a court, an army, a corvée labour force in much the same manner as the paramount king but on a less grand scale. I would hesitate to call this arrangement feudalism because that might confuse rather than clarify the issue. Yet there is something of feudalism here: the personal bond of loyalty, usually referred to as the "drinking of allegiance water". Tribute was paid, but this was not the same as the tributary system of the classical Chinese empire, where tribute was first and foremost an economic affair. It was perhaps more like the Aztec federation, the way the Spaniards found it, with Cortes playing the periphery against the centre.

The Siamese kingdoms of Ayuthaya and Bangkok were so constructed as to include peripheral states, which were ever poised to seize upon the opportunity of a weakened central influence in order to set themselves free from that influence and attempt to establish themselves as competing centres. These peripheral states at times included culturally related areas like the Chiang Mai kingdom in the north or the Laotian principalities in the Mekong valley, as well as foreign entities, such as the Malay sultanates in the South, large slices of Khmer-speaking areas of the former Angkorian empire, and the kingdom of Cambodia itself, the *srok khmer*. A detailed analysis of these polities and their roots in Buddhist conceptions of religion and kingship, particularly in the Indian empire of Ashoka, is to be found in S. J. Tambiah's book.[2] He calls the system a "galactic policy", which seems suggestive enough. This also is the backdrop for the feeling shared by most Thais that Cambodia should somehow belong to a Thai sphere of influence. At the first opportunity, for example the submission of the French Vichy regime to the Axis powers, the Thais managed to seize several western provinces of Cambodia, which Thailand had to give back after the downfall of its Japanese protector. Again, in 1970, in the wake of the March coup, the Thai military intervened as the Lon Nol policy was opening a new opportunity. And nowadays the Khmer resistance groups, the Khmer Rouge included, are under the complete control of the Thai military.[3] Thai politicians are quite reluctant to accept the idea of an independent Cambodia because it challenges their own "legitimate" claim to some kind of overlordship.

For reasons that probably have more to do with the shifting of international trade routes than the exhaustion of the soil or Siamese military attacks, the Angkorian empire fell into oblivion. By the eighteenth century, for all practical purposes, Siamese influence dominated every area of political life, including administration, court rituals, education, kinship alliances and royal chronicles. But the kings in Oudong, the royal capital before the coming of the French, had a much smaller economic base and were relatively poor. The basic Theravada conception of the ruler was that of the *dharmaraja*: the righteous ruler, embodiment of the *dharma,* maintainer and supporter of the *sasana* (religion), benefactor of his people, and source of the moral law. Closely connected was the notion of *chakravartin* or world ruler (with the palace representing the centre of the world), as a necessary link between the several levels of cosmic existence, animals, nature, mankind, gods, and so on. The divine nature of kingship, inherited from a very early Hindu influence, was not altogether stamped out by Theravada Buddhism, as can be seen by the role played, up until 1970 in Cambodia and still today in the Thai court, of Brahmin families attached to the royal cult. In a way, all this removed the king from the direct management of affairs, which was entrusted to powerful ministers and their wives, not to mention royal wives and consorts, thus precluding the establishment of fixed rules of succession and leaving the door open to much internal fighting among princes and other royal offspring. Siamese, Burmese and Khmer history is replete with internecine struggles for succession and long periods of decline due to political instability.

The colonial impact completely changed the way this system operated, but it did not suppress it altogether, at least not in Thailand, Cambodia or Laos. In Burma and Ceylon, the system was decapitated with the disappearance of the monarchy, but its background in the local culture has not yet disappeared.[4] Politics in Theravada societies is supposed to be chiefly concerned with the morality of the leaders and the welfare brought by their action. Righteous leadership and mass welfare are the basic requirements for the growth of religion, which allows individuals to accumulate merit through donations and good deeds. Power is supposed to reward a good karmic "credit" for past merits, accrued from former lives. Legitimacy stems mostly from the *sangha,* which is in turn honoured and protected by the power holder. Sihanouk became king on the basis of this mental framework, though he was selected and put on the throne by the French. Since the death of King Norodom (1904), the French had favoured the Sisowath branch of the royal family, which they deemed more pliable to French interests. Palace intrigues to win the governor general's favour replaced open struggle by contending families. Colonial interference thus brought swift successions, but old cliques and factions were still playing very much the same game as before, even though the power of a Cambodian king was more apparent than real.

It has been said that French colonial authorities enhanced and refurbished the status of kingship in Cambodia. There is some truth in this, but the French closely watched and always controlled the administration. Nevertheless, this added prestige caused more competition among "powerful" families, some of commoner origin, to fill court and local administrative positions. The role of family links seems to be highly contradictory in this respect. Although the concept of the extended family, well established throughout Asia, is not unknown in Cambodia, genealogical ties are remembered only in some families, when they have some link to the royalty.[5] Solidarity is far from being automatically deducible from kinship relations. There are many examples of ordinary people, before the war, trying to take advantage of their claim to kinship solidarity and being mistrusted or rebuffed by those to whom this claim was addressed. There is a tendency to model kinship ties on the patron-client pattern and to use them to fulfil individual ambitions.

What the French had in mind was to *conserve* kingship. Calling the king powerless may not imply a great departure from traditional realities. In the last century, he was surrounded by powerful lords, like the *obareach* (pali *uparaja*, "underking"), who shared part of his political and religious privileges, and other royalty who had control over large provinces and could "eat" them, that is, collect taxes and revenues. Although his religious role made him unique, the king was far from being an absolute monarch; his will was often checked and rebellion was always waiting in the wings. Rebels would often seek foreign help in order to win power. With French dominance came administrative interference and tax control. But for a long time, the Khmer élite could conveniently ignore it, as modern administration did not attract much interest. No Khmer king had really thought of attempting reforms in the way King Chulalongkorn had in neighbouring Siam. So the Protectorate's *bureaux* (the administration's offices) were conveniently filled with trained Vietnamese freshly imported from Saigon.

The introduction of a parliamentary democracy in the aftermath of World War II provided an entirely new political arena. Old courtiers and traditional administrators had now to compete with wealthy business people and young French-educated intellectuals, who heralded the emergence of a still tiny local middle class. The new political game had rules that were entirely foreign and directly derived from the French Third and Fourth Republics. But there was nothing like the big, established sociopolitical blocs that shared power in the French Assemblies. The nationalist movement in Cambodia, born in the late 1930s, was torn apart by diverging loyalties toward its prime leaders, like Son Ngoc Thanh, or the king, or the Viet Minh. It largely disintegrated and could not build a regular electoral constituency despite its rather broad base of public support. Other parties had only a narrow social base, if any. It was thus only normal to see parliamentary life as a new opportunity for factional and individualistic power contests. Naked self-interest was the rule for a host of small leaders and chieftains.

We know of course of other fissiparous polities, working along the same lines, in Thailand for instance, or even in Japan. There, however, some kind of political device ensures the overall unity of the system. In Cambodia, as in Thailand, this role obviously fell to the monarchy as the sole embodiment of all values that could tie the people together. The modern concept of nation had not yet reached the outer fringes of village life, although, of course, the feeling of Khmer cultural identity was firmly established. The idea of nation as a mould for unity and action was slowly trickling down, along with educational progress, but it was still a rather new and somewhat puzzling concept in the countryside before the war in 1970. The nationalist "bourgeois revolution" which erupted in the urban popula-tion, and mainly among students, after Sihanouk's overthrow in March 1970, was largely confined to the main cities. In many places, it provoked an angry rejection by large segments of the rural populace, which rallied to the older concept of kingship, even though it implied at the time the acceptance of foreign (Vietnam-ese) troops as allies. In the l950s, Sihanouk, as king, was confronted with a difficult choice. He could remain a constitutional monarch, the paramount symbol of unity, his actions mainly directed to ritual observance of an elabourate religious protection of the kingdom, in much the same role as the kings of Thailand after the 1932 "revolution"; or he could spring into action and make political use of his charismatic appeal to further his own policies. Feeling it impossible to expose the throne to the hazards of daily politics, he stepped down and had his father, an obscure and shadowy figure, replace him. This arrangement did not really work because, with characteristic megalomania, Sihanouk wanted to have his cake and eat it too.[6] Although formally relinquishing the regalia to his father Suramarit, he nevertheless retained as many royal trappings as possible, and there was no question for the population as to who the real king was. Entering politics, he moved quickly to build his own party, soon to become the only one in the country. Factional struggles thus took place right at the heart of the party, and the tradi-tional pattern of individual squabbling petty leaders, including princes and other aristocrats, could go on unimpeded. The victim was not so much Sihanouk as politician — he was successful for a rather long time — but rather kingship itself. After Suramarit's death in 1960, Sihanouk, drifting toward a sterner autocracy, did not dare have a successor appointed. A new king would have drawn support that he, Sihanouk, needed and commanded. Such a change would have destroyed an ambiguity that was very profitable to him because it allowed his mistakes to be hidden by the magical aura he drew from his position as former king and lord protector of the *sangha*.

The French parliamentary tradition thus had no chance to graft itself on to the Khmer body politic, except for a short period between 1945 and 1955 with the rise of the Democrat party, which was aborted when Sihanouk stepped down. He was the perfect "Oriental" ruler, with harem politics, secret police, widespread corruption, costly festivals, and even a touch of buffoonery in the shape of his absurd dabbling in singing and movie-making. (Even in 1982, while attending the UN session in New York, Sihanouk could not refrain from offering lavish parties and jumping on the stage to sing for his guests. He had a Khmer band specially flown in from Paris. As a Khmer singer, he is indeed not bad.) But when, under the pressure of the outside world, the internal crisis got out of hand and Sihanouk's ubiquitous demonstrations failed, the whole system broke down. The coup of 18 March 1970 created a gap between politics, concentrated in the towns, and kingship, abolished by law but still a central point of reference for most of the peasantry. Republican politics, without a democratic tradition to lean on, could not fare much better and was very soon heading back to the old pattern of squabbling petty leaders. Prominent among them was Lon Nol's own brother. As is classical in a case such as this, these leaders tried to improve their hand by relying on foreign influence and money. Thus American, Thai, South Vietnamese, French, and even Russian help was solicited and sometimes given. These contending politicians appeared typically as patrons commanding a more or less important retinue of clients whom they had to pay off with gifts and posts. They had to control resources and redistribute wealth as a mean of keeping and enlarging their crowd of clients. These resources could come from illegal business through Chinese middlemen, gross corruption, or foreign aid. The pattern did not look very different from that of the old days; only the economic opportunities and environment had changed.

By cutting all ties with kingship, even allowing the queen mother, Kossomak, to join her son Sihanouk in Peking, the republican regime lost its chance, not only to unify the country, but to gain legitimacy, even among the mass of urban dwellers. The sangha was deeply divided and could not fill the gap. Lon Nol's personal mystique, though strange, appeared as a dull and unattractive compound since he was never invested with any recognized supernatural power, as kings "naturally" are. His appeals for struggle against the Thmil (the Tamils, non-believers) could not match Sihanouk's appeal for struggle against the "rebels".

In his Peking exile, Sihanouk did not feel he should change his political demeanour. Still surrounded by his court, though on a somewhat reduced scale, he tried to muster as much personal allegiance as he could. The Sihanoukist and communist groups in Peking lived in completely separate quarters and had almost no contact with each other. Usually Chinese officials would act as intermediaries. For the communists, Peking was a training ground and many students were being prepared for the honour of going back to fight inside their country. They were thus set in the classical party life, which applied to sympathetic non-party members as well. Obviously there was no possible reconciliation between traditional and communist ways of thinking and acting politically. This situation gave rise to Sihanouk's widely reported remark that, after victory, the communists would spit him out, "comme un noyau de cerise" (like a cherry stone).

Interestingly enough, the communists after they came to power were more cautious than the would-be Jacobins of 1970 had been in not disposing entirely of kingship. They kept Sihanouk under a rather liberal house-arrest, in spite of the boiling hatred that most Khmer Rouge veterans harboured toward him. He was allowed to celebrate Queen Kossomak's funeral in the palace in September 1975, some months after she had died in Peking. He was several times allowed to travel in the countryside and shown off to startled tillers. All in all, he got better treatment than the last of the Sons of Heaven in China, mainly because the Pol Pot regime thought his royal appeal should be kept as a potential asset, and they used it when they saw that their policy toward Vietnam was growing sour. This regime, possibly the most radical eraser of "old-regime" politics, thus held on to a chance to manipulate royal symbols (the Angkorian past, the Sihanouk charisma) that had proved so useful during the 1970–5 war. It was to be useful again, as the establishment in July 1982 of an unnatural coalition cabinet in exile was to prove. This all goes a long way to showing how influential the traditional political pattern still is and why no other political tradition, whether communistic as represented by both Pol Pot and Heng Samrin, or Western democratic, as heralded by Son Sann, has been able to establish a stronger foothold in the country. The obvious caution demonstrated by the Vietnamese regarding the person of Sihanouk is another illustration of this point.

It is clear for most observers that, whether they like it or not (and I do not), Sihanouk still has a large appeal to broad sections of the Khmer population. But it would be mistaken to assume that this appeal is an approval of the prince, his person or his politics, as was shown by the rather cool reception he got in Khao-I-Dang in July 1982. The older people have many causes of resentment for his past mistakes and the younger people, say under twenty, know nothing about him. His strength is thus much less due to his own debatable skill as a politician than it is to his charisma as former king, the embodiment of *dharmaraja* and of the unity of the *srok khmer*. His resumption of power would mean — in the realm of Buddhist ideology — the re-establishment of the kind of harmony between nature and world that has been so badly shattered for the last 15 years.

What are the means whereby Sihanouk or his successors can claim legitimacy while an empty throne is denying them its religious sanction? The nationalist credo is not very efficient because its basic tenet has not yet permeated the entire society. Chauvinistic appeals to the preservation of Khmer "race" or "blood", successively launched by Sihanouk, Lon Nol and Pol Pot, failed to transcend the boundaries of the educated class. The related manipulation of the image of the "hereditary foe", the Vietnamese, also failed to produce spontaneous action or commitment. Measures against the Vietnamese civilian population settled in Cambodia were taken by, again, Sihanouk, Lon Nol, and Pol Pot, but they never aroused any visible public passion. Seen from the village level, the peaceful coexistence and co-dwelling of local Khmer and Vietnamese peasants and fisher-men is a too ancient fact, both in the Mekong Delta and in Cambodia proper, to stir up homicidal feelings. The dirty job of massacring Vietnamese civilians was carried out under military orders by the troops alone (Lon Nol, 1970; Pol Pot, 1977–8). The Khmers are not given to pogroms, no matter what officials may say about the Khmers hating the Vietnamese.[7]

It is fairly logical, I think, to relate the question of the Cambodian borders to these attempts to raise nationalist feelings and to promote the legitimacy of successive regimes. The most fascinating feature of this question is how these regimes exactly repeat each other's posture. The basic legal fact is that Cambodia has no border freely agreed upon with its neighbours. Frontiers with Vietnam, Laos and Thailand were drawn by the French, and only with Thailand was the line defined in an international treaty signed by both sides — the French acting as "protector" of Cambodia. This situation is far from being unique in the aftermath of the colonial era. But what is striking is the refusal of the successive Cambodian regimes to commit themselves to any precise boundary. The most clearly articu-lated definition was reached by Sihanouk when, in 1968–9, he appealed for international recognition of Cambodia "inside its present borders" ("à l'intérieur de ses frontières actuelles").

This vague formula can be understood as an implicit renunciation of former Khmer territories lost in the course of past centuries to the expansion of the Thai and Vietnamese states, and an implicit acceptance of the Brévié administrative line as an international boundary.[8] This contradicted earlier claims made by Sihanouk at the time of the Geneva Conference to the effect that the lost territories, now in southern Vietnam, had never been formally renounced by any Khmer king and that, on the contrary, actions taken by the French to subsume Khmer territory under Cochinchina colonial administration had always drawn angry protests from the Khmer sovereigns. He knew well, of course, that Cambodia would never regain these provinces, now heavily populated with ethnic Vietnamese, but he thought this non-recognition gave him some leverage with Saigon.

There is also a wide body of evidence from refugees that Pol Pot troops, when they were launched across the border in murderous raids in 1977–8, were told by their commanders that these operations were aimed at regaining lost provinces "as far as the *thnot* (sugar palm trees) grow", this being a sign of Khmer land occupancy. Sihanouk reported the same thing from his conversations with Democratic Kampuchea officials while he was in Phnom Penh. Unbelievable as it might seem in retrospect, this territorial ambition should be taken as a fact. It reflects the survival of the concept of a "galactic" state with no fixed border line, whose influence extends as far as it can go without meeting a force of equal strength emanating from another central polity, like Bangkok or Huê in former times.

Of course, though they may be unrecognized by treaty, borders do exist. In practice, only a few tiny spots still seem litigious along the land border; the problem of delimitation is somewhat more complex at sea. Old principles concerning territorial waters were swept aside when technical advance permitted offshore exploration for, and exploitation of, oil. The Gulf of Siam has quite a considerable potential for oil and gas. The concept of a 200-mile exclusive economic zone has further sharpened conflicts between neighbouring countries. The Lon Nol and Nguyên Van Thieu Governments entered into negotiations to define an acceptable border line dividing the continental shelf, but they failed to agree and succeeded only in establishing respective sea-patrolling areas. The Khmer called the Vietnamese claims abusive, and the student opposition in Phnom Penh voiced strident protests against the very idea of an agreement with Saigon. Later, in April 1976, the newly installed Pol Pot Government abruptly broke off a round of talks with the newly unified Vietnamese government, claiming they would not even discuss border delimitation. The main bone of contention was again the sea line. In July 1982 the Heng Samrin Government held talks with

Hanoi. Although it seemed that prevailing political conditions would ensure a quick outcome, the two delegations were unable to reach a settlement on the sharing of the continental shelf. Details have been agreed upon that are very similar to those in the Thieu-Lon Nol arrangement. According to the official statement, the question of sovereignty was to be solved "later". No further details were given.

It seems, then, that no Khmer Government, whatever its political stance or degree of independence, has been able to reach the point of no return, that is, the establishment of a clear border line that would mean the relinquishing of any potential claim on land or waters that were once under undisputed Khmer sovereignty. It is to be noted, for instance, that, to my knowledge, neither the Khmers Rouges nor Sihanouk criticized at the time the Heng Samrin-Hanoi agreement. In view of the particular situation of Cambodia, it might thus be said that an essential attribute of legitimacy is the refusal to sign any agreement recognizing that lost territories are, effectively, lost forever. This is of course purely symbolic, since borders actually exist, but the fact that this symbol has appeared necessary to all successive Khmer governments since the beginning of the colonial era is all the more significant.[9]

Equally indicative may be that the most learned and articulate exponent of the Khmer border case, Sarin Chhak, who had strong ties with Prince Sihanouk and had worked with the Pol Pot regime, although he was far from being a communist himself, is now detained in secret by the Vietnamese. He was apprehended when Phnom Penh fell to the Vietnamese in January 1979 and allegedly refused to co-operate with the Heng Samrin Government. As he is known to have had no part in the Khmer Rouge atrocities, it seems likely that only his expertise in the border question has prompted his continued detention and "re-education" in a camp where he is reported to be in extremely poor condition.[10]

What we know of the life of Khmer Rouge élite in 1975–8 provides some glimpses into something commonplace in Cambodian politics: nepotism and corruption. This is particularly striking when compared with official ideology and with the treatment of the population and average party members. Everyone was supposed to relinquish family ties and feelings for relatives. Children were taken care of by the organization and parents were supposed to transfer their love to the party and the country. It is thus all the more remarkable that Pol Pot himself, who had no children, saw to it that several of his nephews and nieces had good careers, particularly in the Foreign Affairs Ministry, run by another uncle, Pol Pot's brother-in-law, and in the Central Committee offices he personally controlled. One of these nephews, called Hong, " Ieng Sary's right arm, Pol Pot's nephew and special commissar for Phnom Penh" could travel abroad with Ieng Sary.[11] Hong managed to get a sister of his late wife appointed head of the office for general affairs of the ministry. This lady was known to have a private flat and to live entirely out of the community system; to maintain her status, she later married a highland tribesman, which in Phnom Penh at the time was seen as a final proof of unconditional loyalty to the party. Khieu Samphân is also said to have married a tribesgirl and to have had his son Kroch ferried about in a Mercedes limousine.[12]

Ieng Sary had several children, in their teens at the time. His eldest daughter was appointed director of the former Calmette hospital and the second one director of the Pasteur Institute, although neither had finished her secondary education. The third and youngest daughter was a military officer. His son had the privilege of going to China for a pilot training course usually reserved for poor peasants' sons. His nephew (the son of another Khieu woman, sister to Madame Ieng Sary and Madame Pol Pot), strangely named Noeu (stupid), was one of the rare Moscow students to survive; he was even authorized to leave Peking and join the guerrillas before 1975 (where he married a tribesgirl). He was later made president of the Civil Aviation Company. His sister, Da, was employed as an English translator and a news reporter for the radio, although she was notoriously ill-equipped for these duties. Their mother was receiving, with each bi-monthly plane from Peking, fruit, vegetables, and fabrics from China. All these relatives enjoyed privileges in lodging, food allowances, and even some luxuries. Along with Nuon Chea's nieces, they were part of the tiny crowd that appeared at every offical party for foreign guests.

Until February 1977, the Foreign Ministry was colonized bv another powerful family. The head of the Office for Trade in the Ministry of Industry, Doeun, had his wife, Roeun, nominated head of the Diplomatic Shop, a profitable business in any communist regime. Since the shop was also connected with the Foreign Affairs Ministry, Roeun could expand her influence there through a nephew named Roun, who had extensive access, and through a niece, Moeun, married to a petty official called Pich Chheang. Roeun won the intense struggle that followed the decision to reopen some embassies abroad by having her niece and her husband nominated for the Peking embassy, the most desirable position. She later introduced another niece, Noeun, as head of the Ministry's children's section, and other relatives took control of the removal section (in charge of controlling and emptying houses and properties in Phnom Penh), the manual work section, the sewing section, and the kitchen section. These posts were particularly important at a time when offices were rather understaffed and real power mostly lay in the control of food and other basic necessities. Such people with such posts were thus not only in control of other people's material needs, but they could enjoy private banquets with the best food, servants, and so on. The whole family, including children, with the exception of the Peking couple, was later purged and executed.

Because the facts are well known, I shall only make passing mention here of the family nexus composed of Ieng Sary and his wife Khieu Thirith, sister of Pol Pot's wife, and the lesser family of Son Sen and his wife Yun Yat, also both ministers. Son Sen (or possibly his wife) had a younger brother (or half-brother) named Kon, who had a military position until he went to the Foreign Affairs Ministry, soon becoming chief of protocol. (He is the Kan described in Y Phandara's book.) Upon the fall of Phnom Penh, he returned to military duty and is now one of the most prominent field commanders in the Phnom Malai area, near the Thai border. [This is still true in 1992.] Kon, or Nikon, came into the limelight because he was implicated in the murder of Malcolm Caldwell by the "confession" extracted from "the contemptible Chhaan", apparently a member of the murderers' gang. This document comes from the Tuol Sleng interrogation centre. It is not known if Kon was actually part of this plot or if this confession was fabricated in order to implicate Son Sen and bring about his removal. Kon was probably involved in some kind of factional activity.[13] Son Sen was the obvious target of the next high-level purge planned by the Security to purify the party and eliminate the "traitors" hidden at the top. In the ensuing controversies in the Western press, the fact that Kon is a relative of Son Sen has usually been overlooked.

Among other families who had played a role in Cambodian politics under previous regimes, we should mention some who were also present in the upper strata of the DK regime, such as Nuon Chea's relatives, and the Thiounn family, who managed to survive rather well, or the Thouch and Pok families, who did not do so well.

It should be remembered that this "family strategy" was far from being systematic. Relatives could be judged as useless or even nonentities by powerful figures. It was said in Phnom Penh that Ieng Sary refused, in late 1978, to meet a brother of his who had come from Preah Vihear province to Phnom Penh for medical treatment. In 1981, the *Vietnamese Courier* carried an interview with an elder half-brother of Pol Pot who explained that a large part of Pol Pot's most direct relatives were just ignored and suffered the common fate of ordinary people.

It seems again that kinship solidarity was far from being automatic but was used as a convenient way to reach for more power. Y Phandara made the following observation regarding Ieng Sary and the formation of a new committee in the Boeung Trabek camp in late 1978: "He did not want husband and wife to sit in the same committee, but a couple could take part in two different committees." The reference was to his leading the Foreign Affairs Ministry while his wife Ieng Thirith led the Social Affairs Ministry. He offered an indirect justification, saying that "if a high-ranking cadre gives important tasks to members of his family, the reason is that he cannot find other people whom he can trust". Y Phandara was led to the following conclusion: "Norodom Sihanouk and Lon Nol have been accused of giving privileges to their relatives. But the Khmer Rouge, under the cover of principled ideas, did the same."[14]

As for corruption, refugees' testimonies show that it was very common, the most favoured currency being not money but food. Pin Yathai provides an excellent description of this traffic with a wealth of detail reminiscent of the living conditions and ways to buy off guards in the German concentration camps of World War II.[15] All these details, for all their triviality, can help us understand some aspects of the tragedy that took place in the DK period. The fact that removing or purging an individual cadre meant that the same fate was met by his relatives, often his close associates, and sometimes most, if not all, of the people under his authority had some root in social reality. People tended to look for a patron who would help them and promote them. Among the motivations of most young educated people who returned to Cambodia after 17 April 1975, the craving for power was certainly foremost. Peasant motivations in joining the Khmer Rouge are not well known, but individual ambition certainly ranks quite high. This would echo similar motives in Viet Cong recruitment in South Vietnam, which have been more thoroughly explored by the Rand Corporation.[16]

But in such a context, one does not compete all alone; the best chance is found with a powerful leader who can provide protection (and the Security Service was a deadly threat to anyone) and promotion. These bonds of loyalty, however, were not absolute; they could be switched to another, more powerful patron. But it would be quite normal for a cadre, when replacing another who had been purged, to bring along his own dependants and clients, thus leaving few chances for the clients of the former boss to fit into the new network of personal affinities, for lack of "trust". The likely outcome for the follower of a losing patron was that he would share his patron's fate. In this highly collectivized society, no one could survive outside a strongly hierarchical group.

Along with other authors, I once argued that the CPK was a loose federation, composed mainly of three contending trends with diverging political affiliations.[17] After more research and more discussions with Khmer participants in this period, I would now tend very much to downplay the role of ideology as a divisive factor. Take, for example, the fall of the Eastern Zone command in April–May 1978: I see much less evidence of an ideological split between So Phim's politics and those of the Centre. I believe that the Eastern Zone had been basically loyal to the party line throughout. But the urge to take possession of this quite autonomous "fortress" was strong enough, I think, to prompt a coalition of Pol Pot (Centre), Ta Mok (Southwest), and Pok (North) forces to smash what had been one of the oldest strongholds of the party. Party loyalties there were oriented toward So Phim, an old veteran, and in order to reorient these loyalties toward the sole legitimate power, the Centre, So Phim and the whole party chain of command of the zone, together with a large chunk of the local population, had to be removed.[18]

The Heng Samrin regime is certainly not immune to this kind of problem. Its ruling layer is composed of very diverse groups: Khmer Viet Minh returnees, former local Khmer Rouge, and former Sihanouk and Lon Nol military and civil servants. But there are other sides to it. I would suggest that the removal of Secretary General Pen Sovan in early December 1981 is a case in point. From random conversations with various officials in Phnom Penh six months later, I got the feeling that Pen Sovan was rather isolated, or perhaps was isolating himself, and that he had "his" people. He had been placed in the top position in the new party because he was a choice for the future. The bulk of the party, at least of its surviving members, had followed Pol Pot in his retreat to the Thai border. A new party had, in the Vietnamese view, to be rebuilt, as a safeguard for the future, out of the remnants of several generations of activists, former Khmer Viet Minh, former Khmer Rouge who had followed Pol Pot or some other local leader, and even left-leaning intellectuals and administrators of Sihanouk and Lon Nol vintages. An experienced and able leadership is the key to the development of the party and, again in the Vietnamese view, the sole guarantee that the Khmer party would not fall again into criminal errors. But no obvious personality was available for this crucial task. The most trusted elements being already quite old, the Vietnamese probably settled for the younger Pen Sovan, who would slowly mature, over maybe ten years, into a suitable and efficient secretary general. In the meantime, the task of reorganizing and expanding the party would fall to older, more experienced hands, like Bou Thong and Say Phuthang.

What probably went wrong was that Pen Sovan was unable or unwilling to be just a learner. He apparently started to play politics and build up a faction of his own followers, exactly the opposite of what was expected of a secretary general, whose main task is to hold the party together, continually reinforcing unity. If he was not a unifier, then he was not suited for the job. I think this fits well with the comments of some Vietnamese diplomats who expressed their "disappointment" with Pen Sovan's performance in his job. Speculation about his playing the Russians against the Vietnamese does not have much substance and is in fact must less to the point than the very crucial question of the party's reconstruction. The Vietnamese were reacting not so much to his political alignment as to the fact that he was apparently trying to create a political faction. One may surmise that the Vietnamese, who belong to the only party in power that has so far avoided schisms and bloody purges, are particularly sensitive to any trend in the new Khmer party that might lead to a renewal of the factional struggles that so strongly undermined the party under Pol Pot's leadership and finally wrecked the DK regime.[19]

Factionalism is not a Khmer monopoly, of course, but it is a choice specialty in the local political tradition. Nepotism, corruption and factionalism, as means of governing, are too well documented for the Sihanouk and Lon Nol periods to deserve more comment here. The same can be said about the present situation on the border. The bloody fighting among petty warlords in 1979–80 has been widely reported in the press, although sometimes in a rather unclear way. Now the surviving warlords have gained a respectable cover by allying themselves to some prominent politicians. But, all the same, corruption, nepotism, and killings are still prevalent in most camps outside the Khmer Rouge areas. The last such killing prompted the return of Son Sann fron the United Nations and the demotion of General Dien Diel from his KPNLF military command. So wide is the gap between the politicians and the civilian administration of the camps on the one hand, and the warlords turned military leaders who control the border markets on the other, that only very strong Thai pressure can prevent a complete disintegration of the camps. There, in this unstable set-up, it is clear that nothing has been learned from the past and nothing credible is proposed for the future.

Southeast Asian Theravada societies never had an institutional framework of hierarchical relations, like the Hindu caste system, but they had other means for building up pyramidal relations, namely, patronage and slavery, which complemented each other. The very elaborate system of slavery has been formally abolished by the colonial authority, but it has left a deep historical imprint. It is fascinating to consider how quick and easy it was to turn Khmer society into a system having so much in common with the old slavery, with its hierarchical layers of slaves. Such very oppressive regimes always had a very low economic productivity, contrary to what some ignorant ideologists expect. But my point here is concerned mainly with the political system and its continuities, as they persisted through a series of different regimes. I think it is fair to say that factionalism is the most recurrent tendency. It is the modernized version of the old patronage system. What we call nepotism, favouritism, graft, are just the means and ends by which this system is expressed and fed with people, money, and other required resources. There is no judgement here. This political pattern obviously caters to social needs. Khmer society, compared with others, appears loosely structured. Before the war, the presence of the State was far from being felt everywhere. In other words, political integration had not been completely achieved. The same can be said for Cambodia today, with the State appearing even weaker than it used to be, the Vietnamese presence notwithstanding.

These continuities should be the basis of any projection of a political future for the country. They are certainly internal boundaries within which a political reorganization is thinkable. Any proposal going beyond them, calling for some kind of modern representative system, had better be forgotten as unrealistic and probably dangerous. It is a time now in Cambodia when, having gone through the most excruciating experimental reforms, the people can think only of one thing: the past, how good it was, how peaceful, how unmurderous. The criticisms of this past may not be forgotten, but they are hardly relevant. The Khmers dream of the advent of a dharmaraja, maybe without the name, but a just and righteous ruler, a messianic figure they call nak mien bon, a source of harmony, a fountain of merit. The only candidate for such a wishful dream would be a king. This is not a matter of any particular person; nobody is looking for another politician. On that level, they are all bankrupt. But let us for one moment entertain a sociological dream, and picture the royal palace with a great festival going on for the crowning of a young descendant of Ang Duong, the royal barges on the river, the monks chanting, the villages rejoicing, the dawn of a new era...

The decision makers in our world do not usually indulge in dreams, even if they are sociological. But who cares for the dreams of the Khmers?[20]

7

Cambodia 1987: Time for Talk

Many talented diplomatic correspondents have already analysed in detail the multiple signals of an impending period of negotiations about Cambodia. I shall not duplicate their subtle comments but I wish to draw attention to the Cambodian side of the question and the long-term consequences that any kind of international agreement may have on this dismembered country. This paper is not dealing with the complexities of the negotiations to come but with the prospects **after** the settlement. From this point, feedback will concern the content of the negotiation and touch on its phasing.

First, it should be clear to anyone that the present division into four so-called "factions" in which Cambodian political forces are regrouped may not be representative at all of the actual political feelings among Cambodians at large. In fact, Cambodians inside the country or in Thailand have no choice about their political affiliation. It is determined by the locality of their permanent or temporary residence. Persons who wish to switch their allegiance from one group to another have to change their place of residence, something which can be done only with an amount of money sufficient to bribe one's way out and into a new abode. Otherwise, the displacement is risky and, at times, may prove dangerous or even lethal. The vast movements of populations which have been observed since January 1979 have many motivations, primarily the availability of food and family regrouping. Political affiliation has ranked rather low and has been very often superseded by other more immediate needs. Typical of this would be the many cases of former civil servants or professionals who left the country, while professing nationalistic or militant views, to build a new life of their own in a third country, losing thereby any possibility of exercising political weight in the politics of their country.

I will not take into account here the quite considerable number of exiles who have resettled abroad. Whatever the reality of their achievements in the third countries, these people will not come back to their native land because, even with an amiable political solution, the country will remain very poor for a very long time and will not provide amenities even remotely comparable to those which the exiles now routinely enjoy. Moreover, in the safety of exile, they have developed an amazing number of political or cultural-political organizations which are mostly squabbling with each other. Their function is mainly to procure prestige for petty leaders and their potential contribution to the future of Cambodia seems quite negligible.

In the PRK area of control, which includes most of what the French geographers called "le Cambodge utile", that is, the populated wet-rice growing core of the country, political choices are limited to one party, namely the People's Revolutionary Party under a shadowy National Union Front for the Salvation of Kampuchea, founded 2 December 1978 and renamed Solidarity Front for the Construction and Defence of the Motherland of Kampuchea by the end of 1981. This PRP is obviously, from the point of view of historical legitimation, the inheritor of the old Communist Party of Kampuchea, founded in 1951 under the very same name. Later on, apparently in September 1966, the name was changed to Communist Party of Kampuchea and its birthdate was altered to 1960 by its then Secretary General, Mr Saloth Sar, alias Pol Pot. This party proclaimed its own dissolution in 1981, though in reality it is the very backbone of the Khmer Rouge faction, still very much in existence. In order to strengthen the legitimacy of their intervention and stress the closeness of their relationship with the brotherly Cambodian party, the Vietnamese, days before the fall of Phnom Penh, marshalled a congress of the PRP, so that it could appear as a legitimate child of the old Indochinese Communist Party, as against Pol Pot's bastard one.

The attempt to rebuild the Cambodian party from scratch would be the subject of a fascinating story in which I am not going to indulge here. Enough will be said if we consider that there was in the PRP a massive influx of non-communist personalities, most of whom had no political commitment in the past while some had a minor role in the administrations of the Sihanouk and Lon Nol periods. Obviously these persons had no revolutionary experience and were inducted into the Party only on the basis of their administrative competence — a rare commodity at the time — or just their willingness to play a role in the rebuilding of the State under Vietnamese supervision. Since there was no way to transform these people into militants, the alternative was to teach them socialism in classrooms. Hence the endless "seminars" and "conferences" that so many people in Cambodia had to endure. These courses, sometimes held in Vietnam for higher ranking officials, generated mostly boredom. Every former teacher in Cambodia, like me, has experienced at times the very strong passive resistance of minds who protect their inner thoughts by learning by rote. Intellectual escapism and passivity are two protective weapons that are widely used by Khmers when they refuse to enter into a challenge they have not chosen. Anyway, classroom communists cannot be counted as real.

The result is that more and more non-communists have a function in the Phnom Penh administration, both in the Party and in the government, and even at ministerial level. Some observers have been struck by the fact that replacements for veteran regroupees who had spent the years 1954–70 in Vietnam were often former Khmer Rouge junior local leaders, thus branding the Heng Samrin administration as "a continuation of the Khmer Rouge". But this is a partial, if not partisan, view. Notwithstanding the very minor role these people had played in the DK period, the complete picture should allow for the even wider entry of former non-communists into the power circle. This is paralleled by the very unique type of economy now enjoyed by Cambodia, a "socialism" without a large State intervention and connected by a wide open channel to the world market. At one time, it was the land border trade with Thailand. Nowadays this huge traffic is mostly maritime. Boats are shuttling between Kompong Som, or Koh Kong, and the Thai coastal harbours. This trade is not well known but involves certainly several million baht daily.

This long development leads me to believe that political uniformity is not so clearly established under the PRP as appearance would have it. This party is obviously far from being homogeneous and its non-communist component is itself both wide and diverse. Socialism in Cambodia got a very bad name after it was "practised" by Pol Pot and claimed by the Vietnamese and their allies. In a situation of political opening, of competition among parties, the PRP would have to revise its programme drastically in order not to shrink, maybe to the point of adopting a reformist social-democrat line, which after all was the case with the old Pracheachon Party. It could have been a very significant force in Cambodia, had not the king of the time altered the rules of the game, not to mention imposed a somewhat ferocious repression.[1]

The French people, who have undergone quite a number of revolutions and insurrectional periods in their recent history, are also known to have a remarkable stability when it come to elections, even across more than a century. Parties wax and wane but political sensibilities mostly remain stable. This feature has been thoroughly researched by historians. I want to submit here the hypothesis that

Cambodia also possesses this kind of stability, with this caveat, that free elections are almost completely unknown there. In the past, actual political feelings have had to be surmised through indirect means. But there is more to that.

The Border Situation

In terms of real numbers, the border population, compared with the population inside the country is very small indeed, around 250,000 people as against seven million. These figures are not definitive, of course, they just show the proportions. It would then seem that, in the hypothesis of a political settlement being achieved, these border people being back home would not carry big political weight. But the real question is not in the numbers, it lies in the potential attraction of political parties as they evolved on the border since 1979. They might be allowed to settle in the country in order to compete in an electoral process.

Several interesting phenomena must be underlined. First, although there was a situation of theoretical freedom in which parties could have developed their own personality, the border situation has been closely scrutinized and in fact drastically controlled by the Thai authorities, with a predominance of the Thai military point of view. This resulted in an almost complete absence of political freedom of choice. In that respect, it is quite comparable to the PRK side. Consider, for instance, the almost complete impossibility for the Sihanoukists to organize themselves during the first years. Some tiny groups were tolerated — on the Khmer side of the border — but pressure was constantly on them. The prince himself was far from being welcomed in the Kingdom of Thailand. It was only after Prince Sihanouk reluctantly gave his approval to the Coalition Government formula that he was allowed into the country and his partisans permitted to get organized.

But even then political choices available to the Khmer border population remained severely limited. It is, then, not so astonishing to see that no new political force was able to emerge. Basically, the three options offered to the military and civilian people at the border are representatives of the three last political regimes which have ruled Cambodia in the last twenty years, chronologically the Sihanoukist, the Lon Nolist and the Khmer Rouge regimes. It is quite probable that, on the one hand, quite a number of people would like to have new alternatives since all of these three regimes ended in dismal failure and, on the other hand, many people suffered personally or through their kin, under one, or two, or possibly all three of these regimes. Expectations generated by the remnants of these ruling classes cannot be seen as running very high. This is the basic fact which was entirely disregarded by those who, for the sake of their own diplomatic goals, installed the so-called Coalition Government, which was in reality totally repugnant in at least two of its components, for different reasons, to most of the grass-roots supporters of the three movements. Even before coming into its shadowy existence, the Coalition Government was a dead horse, as far as Cambodia's political future was concerned. Continuous flogging failed to get it into motion.

Let us take them one by one. First the Khmer Rouge. The solid veil of secrecy which surrounded most of the history of the Communist Party of Kampuchea is still intact, with the added protection extended by the Thai military who act as a rampart between the Khmer Rouge encampments and Western "humanitarian" activities. In almost all cases, UN or NGO personnel are not allowed into, and sometimes not even near, the camps. Their activities take place at some point two or three kilometres from the camps, and in most cases they have no activities at all, for lack of permission. Goods and food for the civilian population are given to the Thai Army which is supposed to supply the camps. This is an effective way to shelter these camps from Western opinion. Neither the New York-based Lawyers Committee for Human Rights nor Amnesty International has been able to document the situation in these camps, although bits of information and rumours available at the border point to a systematic coercion.

Disobedience of orders is not usually sanctioned by summary execution but by hard labour or assignment to dangerous missions. Manpower, carriers and fighters are recruited in the same old authoritarian way as before. The cadres exercise the same dictatorial power as in the DK. The power structure which binds the whole together being the same, it has not been conceivable to change significantly the relations between the apparatus — the Angkar — and the civilian population. The big difference from the 1975–80 period is that the majority of the people under Khmer Rouge control managed to escape at one time or another. By September 1979, at the time when they had to cross over into Thailand, the Khmer Rouge had around 300,000 to 400,000 people under their sway. This figure (just an indication of magnitude) has dwindled to less than 100,000 people. There is limited access to some camps, in particular Site 8 which is the Khmer Rouge showcase. Information coming from Site 8 shows a great tension between the mass of the civilians and the Khmer Rouge administration. In early 1987 the Khmer Rouge had to shell the camp to prevent unrest and demands for transfer to other places, like Site 2.

Internal sources say that, if given a chance, three-quarters of the population would leave at once. This shows how far the "change" in the behaviour of the Khmer Rouge has gone.

What should be remembered here is the role of secrecy as a tool, as a means of political action. See, for instance, what the number 2 of the Party, Nuon Chea, said on this issue in 1978: "Now [in full DK glory] we struggle openly and in secret with secret struggle as the basis of our struggle.[...] Secret work is fundamental in all what we do.[...] Only through secrecy can we be masters of the situation and win victory over the enemy who cannot find who is who." And further he adds: "The leadership apparatus must be defended at any price. If we lose members but retain the leadership, we can continue to win victories. Defending the leadership of the party is strategic. As long as the leadership is there, the party will not die. There can bo no comparison between losing 2 to 3 leading cadres and 200–300 members."[2] Note that the party leadership is still intact.

Let us now turn to the KPNLF side. Any simple talk with ordinary refugees shows that people in KPNLF camps, that is, mostly Site 2, are deeply unconcerned by the quarrels among leaders which are intermittently splashed in the Bangkok press. In a very traditional way, people "belong" to one camp which is said to follow one or another "chief". This does not give much room for political choice, as "dissidents" have been in many instances beaten up or imprisoned in camp gaols if they voiced too strident criticism of the leaders. As usual in Cambodia, people tend to accept passively their self-appointed leaders. In the KPNLF, leaders are of two kinds: warlords and returnees. Warlords are the products of the complex situation prevailing at the Khmer–Thai border since the 1960s when smuggling developed into a quite large and profitable industry, due to the nationalization of foreign trade. With ups and downs this situation remained, even during the Pol Pot period, but was further complicated from 1975 onwards by the arrival of refugees from inside Cambodia. They were not always welcomed and some looked towards "uncontrolled elements" for protection. Smugglers often turned into bandits to protect their trade and were in a favourable position to control the enormous resources put into the border area by the international response to the 1979 emergency.[3]

The huge influx of refugees gave the opportunity to the smugglers turned into bandits to emerge as warlords, complete with private armies, enormous cash incomes and close relations, though conflict ridden, with the Thai military. Then came the returnees, mostly former military officers from the Lon Nol army establishment. They had been refugees, often resettled in the United States.

Although their military record was usually quite poor, they tried to establish themselves as "natural" leaders of a would-be resistance, by virtue of their former training and status. For a long time, their power was more apparent than real; their overlordship was recognized by the warlords as long as it fitted their interests and provided a shield to their struggling business. Former politicians, also returned from exile in Western countries, provided a blanket of political respectability. Their attempts to uproot the border trade triggered many skirmishes but they never really got the upper hand. Among all these people claiming leader's status, the competition for resource control and actual power developed in a series of small-scale conflicts, rife with killings, corruption and even bombings of refugee camps. The strongest pressures put up by the Thai military failed to resolve the conflicts; at best, they were sometimes patched up by some kind of formal reconciliation but the composite nature of the KPNLF system, the isolation of the self-appointed leaders and the restricted freedom of their followers are the continuing causes of further strife.

The interesting point is that underneath these competing leaders, one can find a layer of competent cadres and administrators, people endowed with drive and skills who manage the camp situation quite well, given the circumstances. These people are quite close to the refugees, they know their plight and, given the opportunity, could provide a quite competent leadership. But their "junior" status prevents them from playing any role in a much needed reform of the KPNLF system.

It seems that the question of democracy never arises in the thinking of the KPNLF élite. The word is used just for external consumption, as the Front is supposed to uphold Western political values, but the idea of starting to apply democratic principles inside the working of the Front itself seems entirely ludicrous to all concerned. Democracy is not for now, it is argued, it would weaken our struggle against the enemy. There is obviously not the slightest confidence in the democratic process as a source of political strength. What looked in 1970 on the surface to be a process of destroying the *ancien régime* in Phnom Penh and replacing it by a bourgeois revolution, with democracy as a new base and source of legitimacy, is entirely forgotten. The political working of the KPNLF is very much a return to the old traditional pattern of Cambodian politics, with its powerful leaders, surrounded by the retinue of their clients, fighting each other for higher status and looking for foreign support. It smacks of conservatism in the full meaning of the word.

It is difficult to assess how Khmers inside Cambodia view this group. Whatever support it gets now is probably related to the problem of the presence of the

Vietnamese. But so far the Front has been unable to develop an image of a new Cambodia that could be politically attractive for the future. Moreover, its leaders are either unknown or discredited for their corruption or brutality. The only chance for the KPNLF to survive into a peace process period is to give prominence to younger and more skilled administrators and to initiate a democratic process which would be a real novelty in Khmer political history.

The growing success in the past few years of the Sihanoukist group stems mostly from the failure of the two other border groups to attract spontaneous support. This was demonstrated by the fact that it was led for several years in Thailand by a well-known political figure, prominent during both the Sihanouk and the Lon Nol periods, Mr In Tam. In April 1975, he fled to Thailand with an intact military force. Only in 1983 was he replaced as leader in the field by Prince Norodom Ranariddh. Leadership conflicts occurred there too, but the authority of Prince Sihanouk prevented their spreading and it is no surprise that the Sihanoukist group seems both better organized and more efficient. It was the only group which put up a real fight when the Vietnamese troops attacked the border camps in 1985.

It has no political programme to speak of. Royal charisma is more than enough. In all his speeches and writings, Prince Sihanouk staunchly defends his past policies, he sees no faults in them and he considers criticism as a veiled attack against him.[4] His enemies of yesterday are his enemies of today and he did not come out with any really new proposal. It has to be assumed that he is in favour of a regime as similar to his past one as circumstances might permit. But it may also be presumed that most of his present followers, some of them having taken quite serious risks to join his group, have been attracted by the protective nature of his royal figure more than the political perspectives he is offering; they are still very much shrouded into mystery. It would be entirely out of the question for the people concerned to do anything else, on the political level, than to approve of decisions taken by Samdech Euv, to use the paternal appellation the prince likes best.

Needs and Prospects

Nobody should be surprised by the conclusion that traditional forms of politics are extremely prevalent among Cambodians, whatever their allegiances, because, basically, the country has not yet experienced real social and economic modernization, as a by-product of intensified exploitation of resources, both human and natural, by a highly intense and massive capital. With its old exports of rice and rubber, and its very low agricultural productivity, Cambodia was and still is a poor country, even if Cambodians tend to believe the opposite. A peaceful settlement, whenever it comes, might, or might not, according to circumstances, bring with it the economic input for a reconstruction and a modernization of production. For the sake of political stability and to allow such an economic process, it would seem safer to look for a new political system which should include a relative modernization of access to, of exercise and sharing of power.

At this stage, preliminary thinking should be the task of Cambodians themselves. They know too well the defects of the regimes under which they have lived. Some new institutions and a new political spirit should be conceived to accommodate, not only the several existing parties, or factions, but also those which could emerge if a free choice is given to the Khmers at large. The most probable thing is that present political groups will either explode or be severely diminished in an open competition. Others might grow out of proportion with their real ability to solve the country's problems. There is a great need to have these new institutions designed by Khmers themselves, to cater for the very specific requirements of Cambodian politics. Otherwise, if there is no agreement between the present factions, the institutional pattern will be designed by foreign patrons who will try to ensure their ability to intervene in the internal affairs of the country. It will come naturally to the mind of all of them.

This thinking, this search for a new formula should take place **before** the diplomatic settlement which otherwise will include a framework into which Cambodia will have to be remoulded. And there is one very good reason why it should take place **now**.

A date has been given by Hanoi for the withdrawal of its military forces: 1990. Most probably this date was chosen as the earliest time by which a credible Cambodian army may be raised in the bosom of the Heng Samrin regime. Obviously the Vietnamese want an ally in Cambodia, a force strong enough to guarantee that the security of Vietnam will not be threatened from Cambodia. On the other hand, the proposals for negotiations put up by Hanoi, whatever their acceptability, show that the famous sentence by Pham Van Dông, "The situation is irreversible", should be qualified. As shown in many different ways, the Vietnamese never believed Cambodia was ripe for a socialist regime; this was a bone of contention between them and the CPK from the mid-sixties. And they did not push for collectivization in Cambodia; they even let channels open to the world market. And of course they did not commit the stupidity of trying to "Vietnamize" Cambodian society, as a mediocre war propaganda campaign would like us to believe. They control security, which has far-reaching and sometimes damaging consequences, but is altogether an entirely different enterprise. Idle talk about "ethnocide" is quite irresponsible and out of context. Such talk comes from one-sided minds which are out of touch with the complex realities of the country. The Vietnamese communists know Cambodia well and they have already withdrawn on two occasions, in 1954 and 1975. They entered Cambodia because they had every reason to believe that if they did not, others would have done so, directly or indirectly, and would have attacked them. All this is established fact.

If the Vietnamese have repeatedly committed themselves to a date for withdrawal, both to their own population (and the war is quite unpopular at home, mostly in the South) and to their own Cambodian allies, it means they have considered the alternative outcomes: either there is an international settlement by 1990 or there is not. If there is one, it would include some kind of provision to guarantee Vietnam's security. Cambodia will then be a kind of neutral country with a non-socialist economy and will include, among its political forces, people whose power and influence will derive from their alliance with Vietnam. But the other situation — no international agreement — is possible too. Some commentators — a minority of experts, I believe — claim that the Vietnamese will not withdraw in this case. But if this were so, the Vietnamese would not have committed themselves so adamantly. Transgressing their own promise would involve a loss of face, an increased international condemnation and a further delay for economic take-off, more unrest in Southern Vietnam and more trouble in Cambodia, all things that seem quite undesirable from the Hanoi point of view.[5]

We then have to face what would happen if the Vietnamese withdraw **before** there is an international agreement. Hanoi thinking could only envisage one thing: spreading chaos in Cambodia. Whatever the military growth of the Heng Samrin armed forces, it will not be able to suppress the Khmer Rouge. The fight for ultimate power will intensify, not only between the Khmer Rouge and the Phnom Penh armies, but also between the Khmer Rouge and the other components of the Coalition Government. The most logical prospect is even a tacit alliance between these components and the Phnom Penh forces in order to stop the Khmer Rouge, bent on destroying all of them. But the fortunes of war are quite unpredictable, at this stage at least, and Pol Pot's army taking Phnom Penh again is a distinct possibility. In that case, two or three million people would flee to Vietnam, the only open road for escape. The Vietnamese army would intervene again but this time with wide support, as the international community is not prepared to accept Pol Pot again. The political future of Cambodia would be extremely grim, whatever the military outcome of such chaos, which would become a permanent feature of this wretched country. It would then be possible to speak of the destruction of Cambodia as an entity.

I insist that this horrendous scenario, chaos in Cambodia, is based on facts. It belongs to the realm of concrete possibilities. Think of Beirut. It makes an agreement all the more necessary. But it implies also that the maximalist position of ASEAN — negotiation **after** the withdrawal of the Vietnamese troops — should be abandoned for a more realistic approach — negotiations **along with** a withdrawal. It underlines also the need for a negotiation among the Khmer parties which should be distinct from the one among the concerned powers. Saying this does not support Hanoi's fiction that the Cambodian question should be solved by Cambodians only and that Hanoi is not concerned. The Cambodian question in its essence is double: one part is international because Cambodia is a battleground where big powers settle their quarrels, as Lebanon and other places can be; and the other one is a very old unresolved problem: what kind of state can be built that would be representative enough to maintain a peaceful development of the country? Historians can reasonably assert this problem is open for debate for two centuries…

Nobody denies the right of Cambodians to have a political body of their own. Since 1979, the ongoing war has not brought profit to anyone. The positions of both sides are now not very far from each other. The only serious disagreement concerns the Chinese position on the Khmer Rouge and its refusal of disarmament of the factions. A compromise may be sought which could provide, for instance, an integration of most of the Khmer Rouge together with the exile of some leaders, like Pol Pot and Ta Mok. Western and ASEAN powers could clearly tell their Chinese friends that the present Khmer Rouge leadership is unacceptable on the basis of common law — and common sense. To pave the way, the most useful process is to start a negotiation among Khmers now to try to reach an agreement on a new political system in Cambodia. Those who harbour friendly feelings about Cambodia should help them to succeed. And fast.

7 July 1987

Addendum: The Afghan Model

The calculated risk of a long-term chaotic civil war just on the other side of the border has been carefully taken. The Soviets are withdrawing their troops from

Afghanistan although they could not reach a political settlement. They know they have enough friends and influence in this war-torn country to keep the conflict going on for years, the factions bleeding each other white. Whatever the outcome, the resulting regime will reign over a wasted land and will owe something to the Soviets for the establishment of peace and for reconstruction.

This, I believe, gives a strong credence to the chaos hypothesis in Cambodia. Intense diplomatic activities, since September 1987, have achieved much to bring us closer to an international settlement. In particular, there have been several sessions between the Soviets and the Chinese entirely devoted to the question of Cambodia. Everybody can see the key is there, in a Sino-Soviet agreement, but so far no complete account of the talks has been made available. In Cambodia, Vietnamese troops left the border areas and a sizeable number of troops, including the high command, has been withdrawn. This did not trigger an increase of insecurity. Obviously, the Khmer Rouge satisfy themselves in stockpiling weapons, food and other implements and keep a rather low military profile in order to be in a position to play their cards after the complete withdrawal of the Vietnamese troops, probably by the end of 1989 or the beginning of 1990.[6]

All of a sudden, the West, mostly the United States on the one hand, and the ASEAN countries on the other, awoke to the real possibility of an agreement which would lead to a military and political comeback of the Khmer Rouge. The Americans realized at the Reagan-Gorbachev meeting in Washington that something was happening, that their policy of letting the Chinese run the show was outdated and dangerous. Which American President would like to be held responsible for the return of Pol Pot to Phnom Penh? They scrambled for re-evaluation. Part of Prince Sihanouk's gestures was designed to ring precisely this bell: what would his return to Cambodia as Head of State mean without an insurance against a new take-over by the Pol Pot-Ieng Sary group? All available information from defectors, including a recently acquired document from inside the Ta Mok group (North and Central Cambodia) point to a strong continuity with the Communist Party of Kampuchea (CPK) line. Its final objective is to regain total control by the elimination of other political groups. In the case of negotiation leading to a settlement, the Khmer Rouge will probably resort to their old tactics, namely splitting formally between a politically "acceptable" party, led by some characters like Son Sen and Khieu Samphân, and a "refusal" guerrilla group including the real CPK core, Pol Pot, Ta Mok and Nuon Chea, which will remain in the forest, living on accumulated reserves of food, gold and weapons, and refusing to bow even to the Chinese "wishes", confident that they will be able in the long run to undermine any real attempt to reconstruct a Cambodian state. In order to resist this military sabotage, a new Cambodian state, whatever its political colour, will need to be strong and will require a sizeable amount of support from abroad, in order to contain the Khmer Rouge deep in the forest and to wait for their natural decline, as happened with the Malayan CP, this being possible only if Thailand accepts the cutting of all its links with them.

As a diplomatic problem, Cambodia is on the road towards a settlement. But as a social problem, we have seen no progress at all. In spite of several conferences, symposia, papers, talks of every denomination, no serious proposal has been advanced to build a new political system which would bind the Cambodians together and give them a sense of a common destiny. Every faction, or subfaction, is clinging to its own dogmatic and unrealistic point of view. Paradoxically, the most flexible seem to be the people in power in Phnom Penh, probably because they do face reality. But we are still far away from a real solution. In its stead, we are contemplating rivalries, old feuds, struggling ambitions, spiced with the the most deadly Cambodian specialty, the dream of power. There is not now a single reason to be optimistic for the post-settlement future

4 October 1988

8

Indochinese Refugees in France:
Solidarity and its Limits

France's relationship with the countries which comprised its colonial "Indochine française" stretches from the beginning of the nineteenth century, with its intervention in favour of the Nguyên Dynasty, its occupation of the Saigon area in 1852, and its protectorates system established in the 1860s–80s, to the 1954 Geneva Conference. Although the colonial era ended in the dismal failure of Dien Bien Phu, French politics maintained a committed interest in Indochina; its apex was de Gaulle's 1966 speech in Phnom Penh in which he advocated a neutralization of the Indochinese States as the only way to avoid the catastrophic consequences of a conflict that no foreign power could win for its own profit, and to establish a political balance. This stance was still more or less visible ten years later when, in the last moments of the war, the French made frantic efforts, with the last-minute approval of Washington, to reintroduce Sihanouk in Phnom Penh and General "Big" Minh in Saigon in April 1975. But the war was over[1] and the communist parties were strong enough to capture all power in the three States of the former French Indochina.

The fall of Phnom Penh and Saigon was considered in France to be the expected result of a "wrong" policy led by the Americans who never "understood" Indochina, meaning that they had not shared French views and had not helped in the application of the Geneva Agreements which they did not endorse. The flight of 150,000 refugees from Southern Vietnam in April 1975 was considered an American affair and not many of them went to France. It was only later when the boat people movement started, particularly with the *Hai Hong* affair in October 1978, that French public opinion became emotionally involved. A solidarity movement developed across traditional political lines and its momentum accelerated one year later when large masses of starving refugees were allowed to cross the Thai border by their Khmer Rouge herdsmen.

These developments triggered bitter political debates on the French political scene — which are not our concern here[2] — but a feeling of solidarity and a desire to help these victims of the war and its aftermath became a pervasive feature of both government and private action. Pressure was put on the government to facilitate and organize the reception of the refugees. Particular rules were laid down to ease the processing of the Indochinese refugees and to provide them quickly with a status that other refugees would take a long time to achieve, if at all. This was done on the assumption that citizens of those three countries had formerly been French subjects and as such deserved special attention. This is why priority was given first to the persons who had worked for the French civilian or military authorities and secondly to those who had a working knowledge of the French language, and of course their families.

In France the status of political refugee is legally based on the Geneva Convention (1951) and on the Foreword of the 1958 Constitution where it is said that "any person who is persecuted because of his action in favour of freedom has a right of asylum in the territories of the Republic". In practice, this right has to be recognized by a special office called OFPRA (Office Français de Protection des Réfugiés et Apatrides). This office, acting upon refugee files and other information, is free to grant or deny asylum to those who submit requests. OFPRA's policy is a reflection of the government's political judgement on situations and has accordingly known several variations. For instance, Polish refugees very easily obtained political-refugee status in the early 1980s but Sri Lankan Tamil separatist refugees are now mostly rejected. Only 11 per cent out of 14,000 such people have so far been granted asylum. They have to prove that they have been tortured or gaoled in their native country, and this, of course, is not always the case. Concerning Indochinese refugees, however, clear indications were given in 1975 by the highest authorities that they would be granted political asylum even before their departure for France. A special organization was set up, the CNE (Comité National d'Entraide), which sent delegates to Thailand to select from the refugees those who would be accepted in France. In other countries, such as Malaysia, consular offices were responsible for the selection. Furthermore, it was decided that Indochinese refugees could apply for French citizenship soon after their arrival, with no probation period (*Circulaire du Ministère du Travail*, 18 Sept. 1975).

The following numbers of refugees from Indochina were admitted into France:

1975	=	9,183	1981	=	12,303
1976	=	12,035	1982	=	9,154
1977	=	12,026	1983	=	8,690
1978	=	12,402	1984	=	5,195
1979	=	15,397	1985	=	2,951
1980	=	11,981	1986	=	2,764

(*Source*: Croix-Rouge française)

To this official total of 114,081 persons should be added an unknown number of clandestine refugees which is variously estimated between 20,000 and 30,000 people, who bought false ID papers in Bangkok, were taken to Europe and ferried through the border to Paris where they gave back their ID papers to their guides. A number of them were later registered but there is no threat of deportation or, for that matter, of any sanction.

The Refugee Processing Mechanism

The first contact was usually established in the camps. The members of the French mission were military personnel and most of them had had an experience in the French Indochina war. It might be useful to note that old Indochina hands, former military and business people, exerted a strong influence in the CNE and in the ministries at the time of the emergency, from 1975 onwards. President Giscard himself belongs to a family known for its long connection with major colonial and overseas interests. As I have said, selection criteria were at first family links already in France, former employment in the French administration or army, and knowledge of the French language. More and more, with the drying up of the two last categories, the selection criteria narrowed and focused on family links. As defined by the Red Cross (March 1987 interview), the criteria are: nuclear family regroupment, for instance a mother with young children to be reunited with her husband; exceptional cases, that is people who speak French well; humanitarian cases, concerning either isolated children or people suffering a physical handicap. The latest edition of the *Guide pratique du réfugié* (June 1985) has these explicit restrictions:

Only certain members of the family are allowed to come to France: people whose husband or wife is already in France; children whose nearest direct parent is in France; the nearest direct parents of a child already in France; adults having one of their direct parents in France; adults having a member of the nearest following generation arrived in France before Sept. 1st, 1984. Example: a refugee who lives in a camp has a grandson already in France. But he has a son in Thailand. He cannot come to France since his nearest generation progeny, his son, is in Thailand. Whereas if his son is in France and his grandson in Thailand, he will be authorized to come to France.

The official guidelines used by the French Embassy refugee section in Bangkok in mid-1987 run as follows:

1. Reception for family reason: — husband and wife being apart
                                  — direct kinship (parents–children)
Those who request the coming of their parents must have settled in France before September 1st, 1984.
2. Reception for individual reason: it will be considered case by case.
    Particular consideration will be given to: — prominent services to France
                                           — humanitarian reasons.

This first contact with French officials is a cause of fear and anxiety for the refugees who want to emigrate. Although there was no complaint by the refugees, some French press reports suggest that these military officers were not the best ambassadors of traditional French courtesy. Cicumstances explain part of the dilemma: refugees have no papers and their declarations about their family status must be taken at its face value. But the files sometimes become so contradictory and riddled with fake identities that solutions become difficult.

There have been several attempts to give minimal preparation to those who have obtained an establishment visa in France during the several months they remain in the camps before their actual departure. In the early 1980s, a small NGO called Écoles Sans Frontières established a little school in Phanat Nikom Transit Camp but it lacked funds and its survival remained an unsolved problem. It also wanted to establish schools in other camps of Khmer refugees but the promises made by the French Cabinet to Prince Sihanouk were never made good. Since January 1986, another NGO called SIPAR has provided courses, three hours a day, for six months, about French life and language, to prepare the minds to the cultural shock. The results, so far, are seen as quite positive by those who, back in Paris, accommodate the refugees when they arrive.

Upon their arrival at Paris airport, refugees are taken care of and registered by the French Red Cross. They are then, with the exception of isolated youngsters, transported to a transit centre. Several such centres have been active but with the reduction in the number of arrivals, only the Créteil Centre, in a southeastern suburb of Paris, is still open. Since 1975, it has accommodated more than 40,000 people. This centre is administered by an NGO called France Terre d'Asile (FTA) with public funds. Isolated youngsters remain in the care of the Red Cross and are sent to a special centre in the town of Sens where they stay for two or three months. After that time, during which the children's needs and capabilities are assessed, they go to school or a vocational training centre.

The refugees remain in the transit centre for about two weeks; they receive medical examinations, further explanations about their future life in France and they establish contact with whatever family they have in the country. Those who are not then taken into a family are directed toward a CPH (Centre Provisoire d'Hébergement) which is always in a provincial city, where they will stay for several months, normally six months, before jumping into real life. Lodging, food and clothing are free, as are courses in French language and about everyday life necessities. These centres are administered by local private associations, under the supervision of FTA, and receive a public allowance. They help the refugees to look for housing and job. In case of need, the stay may be extended by several months, rarely more than four. The situation may differ considerably from one centre to another, according to the availability of jobs and other social services in the region around the centre. The refugees are free to leave these places whenever they feel secure enough and they may go to other centres closer to their kin.

All in all, the system seems quite flexible, as most of its action is outside the big bureaucratic machine. Although this is a very difficult period for the refugees because they are stepping into an entirely new world, it seems that this transitory period, away from the stress which characterizes the time in the camps, softens the psychological problems which arise in the adaptive process. Real problems do come later; it very often takes two years for the new exiles to go around full circle and neatly grasp the surrounding reality, to assess rationally the difference between their past expectations and their present condition. More often than not, the balance is tipped. The refugee realizes that he will not regain his former social status but, if he has children, he is supported by the idea that they might, with effort and luck, do so.

All sociological surveys agree on at least one point: a massive professional dequalification awaits the refugees. Either because their diplomas are not fully recognized or because their skills are not adapted to the new environment, professionals start their new life at a much lower level than the one they enjoyed in their previous life. A very large number of people who have had white collar jobs at home are now doing manual work. Former skilled workers lack the required basic knowledge and start as unskilled workers. Former peasants just cannot adapt to industrial work and rely on their wives who manage with sewing machines. The level of education of the refugees now arriving from Indochina is lower than that of earlier refugees. The best educated probably had better connections and could emigrate earlier. These newly arrived refugees are also more destitute, even though their physical condition is somewhat improved, because of the better organization of medical facilities in the camps. Only former petty traders find easy opportunities to resume trading. They mostly belong to the Chinese community, with its own internal rules for solidarity and money-lending.

The number of refugees of Chinese origin is not known since they are registered as citizens of one the three States. But they benefit from the long-established presence of a Chinese community in France, to which they bring a new dynamism. Cultural assimilation is rather superficial as the community tends to be inward oriented. There is a possibility of tension with the authorities who do not see with favour the formation of a strong and rich community. Recently, Jacques Toubon, who is No. 2 in the RPR (Gaullist party whose No. 1, Jacques Chirac, is both Prime Minister and Mayor of Paris), said more Chinese should apply for French citizenship and that he wished the Chinese community would contribute more to social action programmes. The press regularly complains about the "secretiveness" of the Chinese, who avoid resorting to the police or the courts to settle their internal problems, and whose businesses may sometimes stand on the fringe of the law. The pressure to enforce a deeper social and cultural integration is likely to grow in the future, whatever the trend of French politics.

The Vietnamese refugees are also doing quite well. Although the younger generation did not speak French, the level of education of at least the first waves of post-1975 refugees allowed a rather quick integration. The school achievements of the younger ones have been amazing. The Vietnamese have massively entered technical professions, particularly in the computer field, where an incomplete mastery of the local language does not constitute a barrier. Computer techniques have their own simplified language which makes access easier. The process of cultural assimilation is deeper among the Vietnamese because the family structure had already been shattered by the war period and also because the older generation had been strongly influenced by French education in the colonial period. Solidarity bonds are still strong but modern individualism generated by the economic development in France, and in Europe, is pervading the old family concept. Refugees can see the example of second generation Vietnamese, born in France and who have incorporated most French values, for whom Vietnam is an underdeveloped country, the culture of which is attractive but complicated and foreign. This triggers a fear of losing one's identity and of experiencing a slow distortion of family bonds with the next generation.

Less well known is the case of the Laotians, both ethnic Laos and Hmongs. Former members of the Laotian élite could easily slip into French society, as their education had been very French. But people of peasant origin or Hmongs and other minority people from the highlands could find only menial jobs and remain rather poor. A young Laotian girl wrote, in a paper presented for a final examination at school, that the refugees

> have already gone through the drama of the war and now they believed that with their departure they would find peace and happiness. But all this does not last. One cannot get rid easily of one's past and even less of one's status as a refugee. Moreover, if in the exile one finds only contempt, one is submerged by despair and hate, which only reinforce suffering, the nostalgia of home and regret over the past.... Of course, there are nice people who help us and understand us but their number is too small to drag us away from our misfortune."[3]

Among the Laotian refugees, the proportion of youngsters is particularly high. But the older children leave school early (at 16) to find jobs in order to support the family. Very often, adults do not find work.

There was at one time a lot of press coverage of an original solution for Hmong refugees: two sites were opened for them in 1976 in French Guyana, in South America, a tropical land, thickly forested. Land was given to start vegetable cultivation. Around 1,200 Hmong refugees, along with French missionaries who worked among them in Laos, were settled in two villages. This project raised some protests from the local population and authorities who feared an "invasion". The economic results are satisfactory though not impressive, as the market for vegetables is rather limited. Anyway, the prospects of a rapid take-off of the territory have faded away. The planning was unrealistic and there is no further project to settle more Indochinese refugees in Guyana where, moreover, 6,000 people took refuge, fleeing civil war in neighbouring Surinam. The main problem in the Hmong settlement seems to come from the French priests which want to protect at all cost the Hmong cultural "identity", thus creating a conflict with the younger generation which is ready enough to enjoy the so-called "modern culture", its music and its values, far remote, it is true, from the traditional Hmong ones. It is not the least paradoxical to see the foreign helpers acting as a conservative force opposing the refugees' ability to adapt to their new environment.

The Cambodians certainly had the heaviest share of the tragedy. The war in 1970–5 killed around 600,000 persons in a population of over seven million. There is a general agreement on the magnitude of this figure which in itself is a ghastly result of the war, with far-reaching consequences. The style of the Pol Pot regime was mostly shaped by the war period. It is difficult to gauge the depth of human losses which were provoked by the inhuman policies of the Cambodian Communist Party between 1975 and 1979 but a million deaths seems a minimal estimate.

In the wake of the swift defeat of the DK in early January 1979, the retreating Khmer Rouge forces took with them into the forest an estimated 600,000 people. Malnutrition and exhaustion killed again, as the Khmer Rouge leaders forbade these people to cross the border until September 1979. Since then, the number of Khmer displaced persons has dwindled to around 250,000. Only a very small number of them are considered refugees in the legal sense.

Between 100 and 150 Cambodian refugees arrive in France each month from Thailand. It seems there is some disagreement between the Thai authorities, who would like to see DK peasants go first and refugees holding FC and RC [official registration] cards go next, and the French authorities who favour people with family connections already established in France; this is rarely the case with people of rural origin. Officials and volunteers in the humanitarian agencies who take care of them when they arrive in France have become rather pessimistic about the chances of a new start. The figures are grim. More than half of the Cambodian refugees who came in 1986 did not find jobs. In some provincial cities with a bad employment record, less than 10 per cent of these refugees could find regular work. As they cannot stay for ever in the provisional holding centres, they move to stay with distant relatives or friends because they cannot afford to pay rent. They survive on monies given to the jobless or for the children. Those who have no children may experience very hard times.

For the last four or five years, the situation has been getting worse. The first refugees had a higher level of education and could speak French. They could adapt, at the price of lower social status. For instance, former teachers or military officers could become taxi-drivers or night watchmen. But the people of peasant origin do not have this kind of opportunity and tend to stay at home, if they have one. In some instances, pieces of land were given to peasant refugees so that they could grow vegetables but weather and soils are too different and these attempts failed. They are not attracted by the countryside where problems and manners are strange and entirely different from Khmer village life. How do you heat a house when you know nothing about cold? All refugees, including those of peasant stock, are attracted by urban life and, given the choice, they will go to the bigger city. There, they may find a Chinese boss who might give work to their wives. And the women are trapped, because they speak even less French than their husbands; but they react, they grow more independent, they deny the sometimes brutal authority of their husbands, and as a consequence many marriages break down. This is also the case in the Vietnamese community, where divorce is much more frequent than in the home country.

Children also have problems, mostly at school with language. It appeared that the children raised during the Khmer Rouge regime, who were removed from the family unit and "organized" by cadres, had developed a much greater adaptability than children raised in the traditional way. But those who were born later, in the non-stimulating environment of the camps, are not so forward. Until 1982–3, children usually refused to speak Khmer. But growing up into their teens, a number of youngsters start to look for their roots. They are split between a desire to assimilate with the French way of life and the desire to find out their own identity. But this does not bring them back to *sasana*, the traditional religion. The younger generation does not attend the dozen or so Khmer pagodas in France. There are no young monks, no teaching of Pali or even of Khmer language in the *wat*. There is some affluence for festivals and ceremonies for the dead. But it is more practice than real faith. Some want to become Christian: "Since we are in France, we should take the religion of the French people". This attitude maybe stems from a feeling that somehow Buddhism has failed to protect the Cambodians.

Politics attract people more than religion. We find a fast growing number of political groups and cultural associations with a distinctive political aspect. But the old tendency to split into competing groups led by individuals who see themselves as rivals is still quite strong. Most groups are anticommunist, of course, but even the pro-Heng Samrin group is split into three or four factions. There is no prospect of curing this disease of Khmer political life and, in this respect, nothing has been learned from recent history. In fact, many people would like to go back to Cambodia, if conditions allowed for their return. But this is just one more illusion.

Chantal Blandin wrote an accurate report on the Khmer refugees in *Le Monde* (13–14 Oct. 1985):

> Very few are the Khmers who live in the Paris "Chinatown" area. You have to look for them in the most miserable corners of the capital or in the remote suburbs, lost among other immigrants from other countries. Formerly they were peasants or petty officials, and they disapprove of illegal work. Those who have a job in a French enterprise can make it with difficulty. As for the others, public money for the children is often the only resource. Idleness and loneliness are dramatic. To kill time, many play cards, lose their meagre income and start drinking. Older people are mostly unable to adapt.... They all feel bitter in the face of the success achieved by the Sino-Khmers, and the two communities despise each other.... Going back to their native country, all Khmers want it badly, even if they know this hope is empty.

Perspectives in France

The overall economic perspective in France is not really bad. The most difficult problem lies with the sustained rhythm of technical change in the production process. Industries quickly become obsolete and, in order to survive and adapt, they resort to new technologies and lay off large sections of their work-force. The level of unemployment has thus regularly risen to around 12 per cent now, which represents around three million people, out of which one million have been out of work for more than one year. This is nothing compared to the Great Depression of 1929 but poverty is on the increase and the various welfare systems have entered a new era of financial troubles.

In this context, the influx of foreign workers was much reduced, if not stopped, in the early 1980s. Around four million foreigners live in France and there is a general feeling that this number should be stabilized. On the far right of the political spectrum, a new movement has even campaigned on the theme of a gradual expulsion of foreign workers, described as taking jobs away from nationals. Although this theme has been strongly opposed, a feeling of resentment against foreign workers has made inroads into the political debate, and there is considerable pressure against allowing more foreigners to settle in the country. This also affects the situation of refugees, and even more so since the acuteness of an emergency is no longer there to influence public opinion. Quotas have been regularly reduced since 1982 and there is no immediate prospect of seeing them increased again, unless some political shockwave triggers a new feeling of emergency. The case of the Sri Lankan Tamils is quite significant: they are perceived as and mostly treated like economic migrants, although the political nature of their plight is quite obvious. But French public opinion is not emotionally involved and develops no interest in the civil war that plagues the island.

Moreover the question of cultural assimilation does arise in this case. The traditional policy in France is quite clear: foreigners have been welcome as long as they showed a willingness to assimilate and become, at least by the second or the third generation, fully French. This has happened, in this century, with Italians, Russians, Poles, Central European Jews, and others, escaping misery and political oppression. The children went to school and became fully French citizens, in most cases forgetting their parents' language, joining the army and fighting for their new motherland during the war. This means there is no ethnic community with political weight: this would not be acceptable. Ethnic communities may exist as cultural, economic or religious entities but, by an unwritten rule, should leave politics aside. In the French view, citizenship is above ethnicity and encompasses it. A heavily centralized government is supposed to provide equally for all.

All this has been quite visible as far as Indochinese refugees are concerned. State Secretary for Family and Migrant Workers Affairs, Mrs Georgina Dufoix (Socialist Party), said in 1984: "Of all the waves of immigration, the one from Southeast Asia has best merged into French society." But she also warned: "I do not favour the formation of specific urban areas, which would pretty soon look like ghettoes, neither for North African people nor for Asians. It may become dangerous." Difficulties were already visible: "The reception of new arrivals becomes more and more difficult and delicate because of growing tensions in the employment market." In the last three years, these difficulties have only increased.

There is no political force in France that would now increase the quotas. More and more, only humanitarian cases will be allowed. The welfare systems are slowly coming into a major crisis. Solidarity has been a growing concept in recent years in France, both as a new dimension of politics and as a network of new enterprises, dubbed "charity business".[4] After the Cambodian emergency in 1979–80, the Ethiopian famine in 1984–5 triggered an emotional upsurge which materialized into huge amounts of money and a flurry of new NGOs. Although from many quarters attempts were made to play on these feelings of solidarity to further political aims, the general result was rather disappointing for the would-be manipulators. Public opinion is very dependent on images provided by TV but does not look for political rationality. It wants swift action but is not concerned by the root causes of the larger problems (for instance, hunger in Africa). The limits of solidarity are then defined by the short term. Action is bound to stop after several months because new causes or new problems arise which attract public opinion in new directions. The money collected may be used over a longer period through institutional channels but the funding tends to be more and more limited to govermental souces. And with lessening public interest, public money is also less and less available. The case of Indochina, which is mostly the case of Cambodia, is seen in France as a good case for negotiation.

For a better use of available resources, the only thing that can be done is to increase education inside the camps, if the Thai authorities are willing to allow such a move. The present situation is quite bad. Thousands of children cannot enter primary school. Thousands more have already achieved a mediocre primary schooling and are in need of a secondary school, not to mention higher-level teaching which is not available. Whatever the future of the refugees now in Thailand, whether going into exile, returning to their country, or fighting as some kind of guerrilla, they need education. The problem is complex because the political situation of the refugees is not settled, but nevertheless any future solution would benefit from a concerted effort by all concerned nations. It has often been said that Thailand was possibly preparing a new Palestinian syndrome with the Khmer refugees, meaning that in a distant future warlike activities may get out of control. Although this might be a pessimistic view, the need to think about the future is obvious. It is clear that most of the 250,000 or so Cambodian refugees will not go to a third country. Their value as a military asset has not yet been proved in a conclusive manner after eight years of protracted war. But their political value would increase if the younger generation was better educated. In this context, France has a long experience of public education in Indochina which can still be tapped. Through voluntary agencies and government money, the French could contribute in a way which would gather public support and bring a renewed contribution to the plight of Indochinese refugees

When I started to collect data for this paper, I first met with Father Ponchaud, the well-known author of *Cambodia: Year Zero*. He has worked with Khmer refugees since 1975. His views were clearcut:

All this is a failure. At the July 1979 Geneva Conference, no one dared to talk politics. Bringing in the refugees is a failure. The first human right is to live at home. The regime in Phnom Penh should take the refugees back. But I am afraid whatever the regime in Phnom Penh, this will not happen. Even Sihanouk would not take them back. Departure is definitive.

Moreover, says Father Ponchaud, most of the élite of the country has been transferred elsewhere, and this reinforces the Vietnamese influence in the country. When one considers the global results of resettlement into industrial societies, the failure for a large proportion of the refugees, particularly those of rural or poor urban origin, is obvious. A lot has been said on the "pull" factor since the famous articles published by the *Far Eastern Economic Review* in 1981. As noted by Giao, there is no significant difference between the number of Vietnamese refugees and the number of migrant workers leaving other Asian countries, like the Philippines, South Korea and even Thailand or Singapore during the same period.[5] An internal UNHCR document estimated in 1981 that refugees were leaving Vietnam mostly for economic reasons (55 per cent), while 25 per cent were leaving to avoid the draft and only 8 per cent for political reasons.[6] There is every reason to believe that this proportion is still roughly the same now. The cases of Cambodians and Laotians are somewhat different, but economic reasons are doubtless also prevalent.

In the meantime, asylum policies are threatened by the steady rise of unemployment in Europe. In Switzerland, a governmental bill restricting the access to political asylum was approved by a referendum on 5 April 1987. Belgium has withdrawn by law its liberal policy of allowing UNHCR to grant the status of political refugee, the situation of whom has seriously deteriorated in recent years (see *Le Monde*, 4 April 1987). In France, a campaign launched by 170 associations in favour of the right of asylum ended in October 1986 in a pessimistic mood:

It would be difficult to choose a worse time to defend the refugees. In this period of unemployment, would they not look like hidden job-seekers? After the last wave of terrorist attacks, they are often seen as dangerous people, potential terrorists, able to bring in their luggage some of the violence they are escaping from. If refugees in France have always been perceived in a more positive manner than migrant workers, their image has been eroding in the past years. Today, individual victims seem to look more and more like a troop of unwanted persons. There is less talk about the quality of reception than about the size of the "invasion".[7]

As a matter of fact, the size of the refugee population is not impressive: refugees comprise only 4.5 per cent of the total foreign population in France, and Europe at large accommodates only 6 per cent of the twelve million refugees in the world.

The alternative solution to the problem of Indochinese refugees is obviously a political one. The peaceful settlement of what I called several years ago the Third Indochina War[8] would bring back home most of the Khmer border displaced persons and considerably lower the outgoing flow of refugees from Vietnam and Laos. In the case of the Cambodian border refugees, we should remind ourselves how they were made refugees. More than anything they are hostages of war. They are needed as the Big Rear of this frontless war, providing manpower and family R and R to the guerrillas. Humanitarian aid is providing food and goods to these same guerrillas and acts as a blanket for political designs. A coalition has been forced upon refugees who would never have spontaneously reunited the murderers and their victims.

But the time is coming for negotiations. On the international level, talks are already on the way to try to remove some of the blockages. Some steps have been made by big regional powers which narrow the gaps between them. Never since 1979 has the prospect of a settlement been so close, though some progress is still needed to reach this decisive point. In the meantime, Hanoi has decided to withdraw its troops from Cambodia in 1990, whatever happens, and has committed itself repeatedly, not only in front of its people and its local allies, but also in the international arena. Apparently the calculation made in Hanoi runs like this: **if there is an agreement**, then it will provide for the security of Vietnam and the existence of a credible ally of Vietnam inside the Cambodian body politic, as a guarantee. The burden of the war being lifted, energies may then focus on development. **If not**, if no agreement can be reached and if Vietnamese troops withdraw, then Cambodia will fall prey to a new bloody civil war, with four or more factions reaching for each other's throat. There will be chaos. It is difficult to predict who might win but neither the Vietnamese nor the West will allow the Khmer Rouge to emerge on top. Chaos would affect negatively the interests of the West, of ASEAN and ultimately of China. But the risk is there. And those who do not really want to have two or three more million Khmer refugees should think about it as a matter of urgency.

9

Genocide as a Political Commodity

In memoriam Allard K. Lowenstein,
of early Namibian commitment

Just after the signature of the so-called Peace Agreements on Cambodia, in Paris, on avenue Kléber where the 1973 Agreements on Vietnam were also signed, Roland Dumas, the French Foreign Minister, held a press conference, together with Prince Sihanouk and Mr Perez de Cuellar, the UN Secretary General. A nasty journalist, quoting directly from the UN Convention on the Prevention and Punishment of the Crime of Genocide, a treaty to which France like a majority of other States is party, reminded the audience that, in the absence of an established *ad hoc* international court, each state was duty bound to act against the perpetrators of such a heinous crime. It was clear from the text that the French Government was bound to place Khieu Samphân and Son Sen, the Khmer Rouge signatories, under arrest and to charge them with the crime of genocide under international law.

The reply was what could be expected from a true statesman: he shrugged and laughed. "Do not worry", he said to the nasty journalist. "We have very good lawyers. [He is a famous lawyer himself.] It does not matter what documents we give them, they'll always come up with the solution [we want]." He was expressing the absolute cynicism of power: treaties are worth no more than the paper they are written on when they contradict the policy of the day. Referring to the law is just idle talk.

As I write this, sitting in a garden facing the Royal Palace in Phnom Penh, the second Supreme National Council meeting is taking place inside. Seated there is the same Khieu Samphân, representative of what is left of the Pol Pot regime, overthrown in early 1979 by Vietnamese troops. He rode into the Palace protected by a strong military escort; there is not much love for him in town. In the plane bringing him from Bangkok, he complained to an American correspondent, Nate Thayer, that some governments in the West are attempting to derail the "peace process" by their reluctance to allow the Khmer Rouge to play their full role in it. There is a grain of truth in what he said.

As James Baker III was delivering his speech at the Paris Conference, he said casually that his government had no objection to a trial of those responsible for past horrors in Cambodia, with whom he was about to sign the Agreements giving them a legal share of the future power in Cambodia. It was the first time a high-ranking US official had publicly considered such an idea.[1]

Monsieur Dumas escaped this contradiction by laughing. But Mr Baker does not even seem to know how to smile. He wants to have it both ways: to sign an agreement that jacks the Khmer Rouge up into a legitimate position and also to distance himself from them on moral and legal grounds: his right hand ignores what his left hand is doing. If Monsieur Dumas scoffed at the notion of international law binding sovereign states, Mr Baker was more subtle. He implied that, although denying it now, his government could, in the future, give its approval to an application of the law if others, Cambodians for instance, choose to take such action. Seen from Pol Pot's point of view, this could be seen as an obvious duplicity.

In the following weeks, there has been a lot of speculation in the Western press, feeding on comments it extracted from Cambodian leaders, on the circumstances which could lead to a trial for genocide of the Khmer Rouge. But nobody so far has considered taking action and Prince Sihanouk, speaking in the Royal Palace on 16 November aptly said that, before being brought to the dock, Pol Pot must first be found. He suggested that one might ask "the prestigious general Suchinda Kraprayoon, chief of the Royal Thai Army, who told me recently he just had a most agreeable conversation with Pol Pot". In addition, an obviously embarrassed Sihanouk said he would not visit the Tuol Sleng "Genocide Museum".

Everyone knows that for the last dozen years Pol Pot has been quietly sitting in his compound near the Thai town named Trat, enjoying Chinese money, Royal Thai Army protection and inconspicuous support from what could be called the CIA border network. There he is able to direct the Khmer Rouge political and military campaign in Cambodia and hold long seminars to train his local commanders and appraise them of the new line.[2] Though he has dropped out of public life on the advice of the Chinese who found that his name was embarrassing in the West, he obviously does not feel at risk. If a move is later undertaken to bring him to court, it will mean the Khmer Rouge's usefulness as a weapon against communist Vietnam has dwindled into insignificance. By then, of course, the moral strength of the case against them will have diminished correspondingly.

These considerations remain valid regardless of which words — with their varying legal implications — we use to describe the huge human losses which occurred in Cambodia under Communist Party rule, with Pol Pot as the highest authority. I shall discuss the use of the word "genocide" later, but let us first look at the facts.

Ben Kiernan has provided information on those limited surveys, conducted in the years immediately following the DK's demise, which are available to us.[3] They were mostly carried out by individuals doing research on the border. No institution attempted to do a global survey; only the CIA provided an estimate based on several explicit hypotheses, which raised a number of questions.[4] It should be very clear that we do not know the real figures and it is also probable we shall never have them because the "killing fields" were operated with very few written documents. Of those that have been found, many are still inaccessible. Moreover, the killers are still at large in the jungle. The documents lack precise figures about the size of the population when the war started in 1970, when it stopped in 1975, when Pol Pot fled in 1979, and even now. These have not been destroyed: they never existed. Moreover, Khmers are not always registered and change their name at will.

Based on these few surveys and my own interviews, I fully accept an estimate between one million and 1.5 million deaths. We must keep in mind that these figures have been constructed by asking individuals to collect the number of family members thought as being dead or missing. Some of the missing persons may of course be alive, somewhere else. The Red Cross tracing system and Khmer newspapers and television still carry requests for information on missing or lost persons, with obviously some results. But the number of people thus accounted for is probably not very high.

On the other hand, Khmers would include in their "family" count a sizeable amount of non-kin people, like sworn friends, adopted children, neighbours, who, for all practical purposes, are family members. But these people would also be claimed by other families as their kin relatives, leading to double counting. I consider that the proportion of double counts is probably high in the early border surveys and would fully account for the three million figure produced by the PRK, if this is based on any serious work, which I doubt.

There were three main causes of violent deaths.

First was **the killing of identified Lon Nol regime personnel,** heavy at the beginning, following the 17 April 1975 collapse. There was obviously a central decision to eliminate these people, as an extension of the death promised to the seven "supertraitors" who led the ousted regime. Possibly between 100,000 and 200,000, including relatives, were executed under this blanket order, which was, though, not applied everywhere in the same way. The thinking was probably to eliminate all those who had been invested with some form of power in the old society and could then be a germ for growing again a power hostile to the revolution.

Then there were **the intra-Party purges**. The need for the Party Centre to establish itself as the sole source of authority led to the destruction of individuals, group or zonal commands, including their relatives, former subordinates and associated non-Party people who were deemed by the Pol Pot group as having either intellectual origins or political affiliations that were not 100 per cent inspired by the Centre. They called it the "purification" of the Party, and each new wave of purges increased the "level of purity". Several tens of thousands of people were thus disposed of, a lot of them after "confessing" imaginary treasons. The figure may be as high as 200,000 people if we include the destruction of non-Party civilians in the Eastern zone in 1978.

Finally there were **assertive killings**. Local cadres, mostly uneducated peasants, or half-educated teachers, had risen to power because they had been good petty military leaders in the war. They compensated for their lack of legitimacy, their incompetence and their lack of grasp of social mechanisms in an extremely authoritarian way, even to the extent of killing anyone not showing the mask of passive acceptance. It is impossible to estimate the number of those killings — which did not derive from central orders but from the psychological requirements of youngsters in need of asserting an undue authority, but, by any count, it was massive.

Attention should be paid to this phenomenon as its dynamic is still active in today's society, and even more threatening with the planned demobilization of 70 per cent of the troops. The weakness, or the outright lack of institutional links among individuals may lead someone in authority, facing any form of challenge, to resort to immediate and violent retaliation. This is probably a result of the traditional basic education, handed down from the ancient times when a majority of the people were slaves of the rulers, which insists that authority should never, and cannot be, challenged — for any reason whatsoever.[5]

One way or another, these three categories of mass killings had the same purpose: to establish an entirely new type of power, based on an entirely new type of people, drawn from social layers from which no one had ever dreamed of climbing to the top. It was, in a nutshell, a revolution, although it was produced by not much more than the power of the gun. We know of violent political changes which are not revolutions and of revolutions which are not bloody. I shall leave that to philosophers, but it could be useful to remember that the old regime, until 1970, treated its opponents in a very rough way which included the use of systematic violence, claimed as a legitimate response to opponents of bad faith. Sihanouk's regime pushed the future revolutionaries into the forested wilderness whence they emerged in 1975 to gather power like a ripe fruit.

This may lead us to a more thorough examination of the problems.

What Were the Social, Political and Economic Pre-conditions for Genocide in Cambodia?

The most obvious answer is the war, which produced a political vacuum in Phnom Penh in 1975. In the wake of the 18 March 1970, coup, the war apparently started as a continuation of the American war against the Vietnamese communists. But it immediately cracked wide open Khmer society with, very broadly speaking, on the one hand the urban bourgeoisie thirsty for dollars and Western consumption goods and, on the other hand, the more traditionalist peasantry, almost untouched by the modern economy. The Republican regime quickly dissipated any hope of reform and immediately lost the war. Then the war went on as a massive destruction of the countryside by air power. The most important political change to come was the provision inserted by the US into the Paris Agreements in 1973 which obliged the VC/NVA to evacuate Cambodia in a naive attempt to revive the Lon Nol regime. As a result, the Vietnamese handed over the administration of the countryside to Pol Pot who started immediately to eliminate, one by one, his allies in the "Front" and the "impure" elements, namely all those who had not been directly forged by him, inside the Communist Party. Under the heaviest bombings ever launched so far on a country, radicalization was accelerated and in some areas an authoritarian policy was implemented which was to become standard after April 1975. Without the war which, in a bitter paradox, the Americans needed to prepare their orderly withdrawal from Vietnam, Pol Pot's tiny Communist Party would certainly have met the same fate as its equivalents in Malaysia, Thailand and Burma — a marginal insurrection partly fed by China, doomed to slow extinction.

The conditions of this war permitted the progressive elimination of all moderates or less-than extremists, with the exception of the person of Sihanouk, carefully kept as a symbol in Peking. A small secretive clique arose, entirely devoid of experience in organizing economics or manœuvring social forces. Their narrow nationalism led them to believe that Cambodia was now able alone to solve problems which were still unresolved elsewhere. If things failed, if the Cambodian revolution quickly turned into a bloody mess, it was mainly for intellectual and cultural reasons. These "thinkers" never suspected the complexity and the contradictory nature of social evolution. They did not master the meaning of the ideas they were using and, unable to convince, they either hid their views or resorted to terror and passive acceptance.[6] Stalin, at least, was a realist. Pol Pot, a much watered-down imitation of a faded Chinese copy of Uncle Joe, was and still is an unimaginative idealist, a forest monk, lost in dreams. The tragedy came when an imported war gave him hosts of uneducated wild youngsters toting guns to translate the dreams into a deadly reality. As this war drags into its twenty-second year, the man is still there, still preaching the same bad news.

What Were the Aims and Methods of the Khmer Rouge Movement?

The aim was to establish, for the first time since the almost mythological period of Angkor, an independent state, without any foreign interference or influence (the Chinese role went unacknowledged), more or less autarchic. Destroying the towns, the bourgeois class and even religion (also seen as foreign) was deemed to be necessary to rediscover the "Original Khmer", which happens to be the name Pol Pot used in his first known article, written in Paris in 1952.[7] These ideas of a pre-Hindu, pre-urban, pre-State "original" Khmer society, ideally organized in a kind of basic village democracy, later adulterated by every successive form of state power establishing oppressive authority on the basis of doctrinal ideas borrowed from outside (India, China, Europe), were elaborated by a brilliant young Khmer intellectual, Keng Vannsak, probably the most influential figure in the Khmer intelligentsia in the middle of this century. Although not a Marxist himself, he blended a Marxist view of history with a Rousseauist concept of a primitive form of democracy based on a "contract", adapted to the tentative reconstruction of Khmer history by French orientalist historians. Although by no means supported by hard facts, this interpretation had the advantage of putting the blame for all evils on the kingship and of channelling energies to fight the puppet king and the French colonial authorities who were using him in such a blatant way.

This struck at the very heart of a controversy which raged among colonial historians at the beginning of this century concerning the nature of these Southeast Asian societies which during the last 2,000 years had developed statecraft along the lines of successive Indian patterns, sometimes called "Hindu-ized kingdoms". George Cœdès, who coined this expression, wrote: "The Cambodian is a hinduized Phnong",[8] referring to the Khmer word for the "savages" living a tribal life in the mountains, out of the royal realm, and speaking dialects different from but related to the Khmer lowland language. Military expeditions sometimes brought back *phnongs* as slaves who then became Khmer through integration into a state and a culture imported from India. This is the process alluded to by Cœdès in a sentence which raised the question of the real depth of this acculturation and of what was left of the non-Indian origins in the true culture of Cambodia.

In Paris, Saloth Sar (the future Pol Pot) and Keng Vannsak became close friends and though Vannsak did not join the French CP, they worked together, agitating against Sihanouk and his rotten alliance with the French. That was student politics, in those times, but when he came back to Phnom Penh and chose to fight within the ranks of the Democrat Party, trying to renovate its leadership and radicalize its opposition to Sihanouk, who was tied by his subservience to the colonial masters, Vannsak enlisted the help of Pol Pot, by then a full-time member of the communist Phnom Penh leadership, to reorganize the party and prepare for the elections. Sihanouk, using the most undemocratic means, forced an electoral rout on both the Democrat Party and the Pracheachon (the legal arm of the communists) and Pol Pot, promoted as Secretary General after the killing of the previous one, Tou Samouth, by the secret police, decided to go into hiding in the forest. When he left Phnom Penh in 1963, the man who took him on the ship upstream to Krauchmar, where he was to exfiltrate from public life, was none other than Keng Vannsak.

After some time passed in Base 100, a Viet Cong logistical area in the northestern province of Rattanakiri, Pol Pot moved to live among the *phnongs*, (the "savages"), away from the Vietnamese. There he discovered the tribal life of these "original" Khmers and learned to hold these people in deep appreciation, later giving them as examples of "purity", meaning they had not been spoiled by royalty, Buddhism, money or any other foreign imported ideas and instruments of domination. He used them as bodygards and encouraged cadres to marry tribal women. He transferred the "primitive democracy" that Vannsak had put in a time framework (the "origin") into a space category by which purity on the periphery would come to encircle the soiled heartland of the country and, in a Maoist graphical way, conquer it. This highly debatable view of the Khmer past[9] thus left a recognizable imprint on Pol Pot's mind and limited historical knowledge; this Utopian vision of a "democratic village state", buried in the past, led to the curious unorthodox appellation of the new State: literally, "Kampuchea Democracy", more usually translated as "Democratic Kampuchea" (DK).

As for the methods used to achieve this desperate nationalistic vision of a country returning to its obfuscated roots, they were classical Asian communist ones, learned from the Vietnamese and Chinese professional organizers, but learned as Cambodians do learn, by rote, more accustomed to reproducing the form than to catching the spirit. These methods included the passive indoctrination of the youth (considered as naturally "pure") with a crypto-Buddhist morality emphasizing modesty and obedience, and the use of terror instead of political persuasion, a sophisticated technique to which Cambodians, unlike other Asian communists, rarely resorted.

Terror spread gradually, giving birth to specialized organs which, as they did in other communist revolutions, outgrew their objectives and set about destroying the very cradle from which they grew. If we compare the short Pol Pot era with the beginnings of communist state power in the Soviet Union, Mongolia, China, Albania, Yugoslavia, to take examples of indigenous movements taking over, and even Korea, the Cambodian case is comparable in the scope of destruction brought about by the requirements of establishing a completely new social order. The difference lies in the direct American involvement in the chaos conducive to this great destruction and the presence of television crews at the border in the heat of events. Also, the sudden fall deprived Pol Pot of the time to "normalize". There were indications that he was moving in that direction. Who remembers clearly the early purges led by Choibalsan or Kim Il Sung or Enver Hodja?

What Were the Results? Who Were the Victims? How Many Were There?

I have already addressed these questions in part. However, I should add, concerning the case of the minority Chams, that I believe there is no evidence at all for a persecution based on "race" or ethnicity but that they were victims of an attempt to eradicate religion, as a matter of general policy, exemplified by the razing of the Catholic cathedral in Phnom Penh, undertaken early after the victory, and the general suppression of Buddhism. Chams were (and still are) the core and the majority of the Muslim community in Cambodia. If there was more resistance among the Muslims, and then more repression, it is because Islam as a cement was stronger than other religious beliefs. Anyway, the use of words like "national minorities", introduced into the political language of Cambodia by the Vietnamese, after the Soviet and Chinese models, is entirely misleading and does not describe at all the traditional status of small religious or linguistic groups in the country. This complicated issue would require lengthy treatment which I shall not pursue here. But, generally speaking, people were persecuted under DK because of what they believed, or were supposed by security organs to believe, and because of family links with those suspected of harbouring wrong beliefs or thoughts detrimental to the State. Killings based on racist hatred involved only the small number of Vietnamese residents left after the May 1975 evacuation and the wanton murdering of Vietnamese farmers in the raids across the border in 1977–8. The practice of systematically killing Vietnamese civilians is still the policy of the Khmer Rouge. Chinese and Sino-Khmers were killed not as Chinese but as traders and capitalists, in the greatest need of "reformation", mostly by hard labour. From the point of view of the Genocide Convention, destroying an ethnic group or destroying a religious group is the same crime. But looking for a "racist" motive in the persecution of the Chams seems to stem from an unconscious desire to equate the Chams with the Jews and Pol Pot with Hitler (the same operation as with the Kurds in the case of Saddam Hussein), which might be good propaganda but is poor history.

Besides the killings motivated by politics, the big majority of those who perished during the DK era died of hunger, deprivation and diseases related to malnourishment and exhaustion. The greatest part of the human losses must be ascribed to the *economic* policy of the Communist Party of Kampuchea. The whole population sent back to the rice fields was organized into large units called co-operatives, although they were nothing more than State farms with slave manpower. The Centre decreed quotas of rice to be delivered to the State and, emulating the Chinese communes, set quite unrealistic quotas for a country with one of the lowest levels of rice productivity in the world. Very soon, although varying according to local conditions,[10] the co-operatives could not deliver the requested quantities other than by taking them from the food reserves set aside for the workers. The co-operative leaders understood that failure to meet the quotas was tantamount to treason, a crime they would pay for with their lives. Although they obviously also used food to discriminate between friends and foes, thus leaving most of the burden due to the lack of food on the shoulders of the former urban population, they could not dispute the targets imposed on them from above. In fact many of them were later killed when the southwest cadres, more trusted by the Centre, came and took over, after information about the disastrous situation had started to filter up and reach Pol Pot's offices. The bad news was ascribed to treason anyway and purges were launched on a wide scale. But in general the southwest cadres, under Ta Mok, were even more ruthless than their predecessors because they had very good reasons to see that the failure to meet these unrevised quotas was an urgent matter of life and death. Everyone had to suffer to ensure the survival of the tormentors. But if the leadership had not been so unrealistic, the system could have worked without starving the workers, as some improvements in productivity were introduced in some places, at least for a while.

What Were the Effects on the Survivors? On Neighbouring Countries?

Survivors, in early 1979, were left with a totally disrupted social and economic life. Families were scattered and eveyone was scavenging for food. It was worse than any war because the tragedy affected everyone everywhere in the country. The word "rebuilding" never had such a full meaning. Whereas people slowly started to settle down and reunite with whoever of the family had survived, a considerable part of the surviving élite decided Cambodia was to be written off, that it was not worth rebuilding it under the Vietnamese saviours, and then made the individual choice of rushing to the border to reach the "dreamland" of abundance, a third country in the West. Coming from people who professed a nationalist fervour before the catastrophe, and after it in the safety of exile, this exodus shows how conventional and superficial the attachment to the idea of nation had been in the educated élite. They abandoned the sinking ship at a time when their lives were no longer threatened, and their flight heavily handicapped the redevelopment of the country for at least one or two generations. The flight of the trained teachers or their refusal to go back to the schools, in particular, has produced the nightmarish situation of education we can see in today's Cambodia.

The psychological effects of these years of terror and suffering are certainly very deep but have not been studied at all. The resumption of medical services was entirely in the field of physical health and, up to this day, there is no psychological therapy available other than the rather efficient one provided by the traditional healers, the *kru khmaer*. Some limited clinical observations suggest that damage has been widespread, particularly for women, and that a great many people still suffer from their traumatic experiences. This field is still wide open for analysis and action.

Another set of consequences has been a kind of political freeze due to the Vietnamese military and political presence for ten years. The threat of a return of the Khmer Rouge cooled the people into a passive acceptance of a regime in which they had much to object to, although it was quite efficient in the use of the small resources it could muster. Even the Paris Agreements provided a system ensuring the military factions — ghosts coming down from the past — a political role that Cambodians would probably not choose if they had a chance to freely express their will.[11]

Among the consequences, we should include the systematic elimination of critical minds. Cambodian culture certainly emphasizes submission, but if most people keep their inner thoughts to themselves, a small number of people develop highly organized critical views and provide the only channel by which the power learns anything about public opinion. The absence of most of these people in Cambodia after the DK period made very difficult the correction of the political course set by the new regime. Moreover, many survivors hide the shame of having been silent slaves. Very often, they had not been able to maintain moral standards and this, in itself, may be the cause of recurrent depression.

For **neighbouring countries**, the effect of the rise and demise of the DK was to attract them into a new cycle of conflicts. Thailand, after swallowing some bloody Khmer Rouge incursions in border villages, quickly reached an agreement with the new masters in Phnom Penh through which a small barter border trade was resumed and rather friendly relations were obtained. The Thai military, closing their eyes to Pol Pot's dealings with the Thai communists, saw the new regime as escaping Hanoi influence and thereby reopening this buffer area for later Thai potential influence. This was a calculated strategic advance after the disastrous end of the Vietnam war. This paved the way for the January 1979 decision to accept the Chinese proposal of a tripartite alliance between the Thai military, the battered Khmer Rouge and Chinese logistics to provide Pol Pot with military equipment and money, under the cloak of a silent US approval. The Khmer Rouge were to act as a battering ram in the ongoing Western war with Vietnam, in the best interests of a China bent on pressuring the Vietnamese into "normal" tributary submission.

The only country deeply affected was Vietnam. The communists had withdrawn their forces from Cambodia in early 1973, leaving behind only storage facilities in the remote northeast border area. But within days of the fall of Phnom Penh, the Khmer Rouge attacked the large island of Phu Quoc and several incidents occurred at sea. Then, in the process of the evacuation of towns, all remaining ethnic Vietnamese, many of them born in Cambodia, were expelled. Uneasy peaceful relations were restored and lasted until about the end of 1976. The death of Mao and the crisis which followed in Peking somehow triggered some waves in Phnom Penh and the beginning of the high-level purges. It was probably at that time that preparations for the first transborder raids were made. The year 1977 saw several dozen incidents typically involving two or three hundred Khmer soldiers attacking a Vietnamese village, slaughtering the peasants, including women and children, looting the cattle and burning down the place entirely. Local militias could not stop these well-armed infiltrations. Provincial authorities evacuated between one and two million persons from the border. Hanoi kept the losses secret while still hoping for a diplomatic solution to this undeclared border war. This proved later to be a costly mistake because it prevented Hanoi from showing that it was reacting in defence when its armies struck at the centre of Pol Pot's battle order.

The motivations of Pol Pot's policy of attacking Vietnam are not, to this day, very clear. We may rule out local initiatives and must ascribe this decision to the Party Centre which later claimed it had determined much earlier, in secrecy, that the Vietnamese were the "acute enemy". Although this policy of aggression may seem to us silly and self-defeating, we must remember that most certainly the Party Centre thought the Vietnamese were weak, even cowards, as shown by the fact that they had agreed to negotiate and sign the 1973 Paris Agreements. Most probably Pol Pot believed he had single handedly defeated US imperialism; the proof of it was that the fall of Saigon occurred *after* the fall of Phnom Penh.

Although the DK never officially claimed such a policy, there are indications that local commanders told their troops that they were going to reconquer Kampuchea Krom, the lost provinces absorbed by Vietnam two centuries ago. Successive royal Khmer governments, including Sihanouk's, always maintained that, even though they did not request an alteration of the maps, they had never fully recognized the successive transfers of sovereignty accomplished by the Annamese emperors or the French colonial government. In a rather atypical way, Ieng Sary's foreign ministry gave a slightly privileged status to Cambodia's only legal expert on the border question, Sarin Chhak who, though not a communist, was left quietly working on historical documents and providing the CP leadership with information, notes and explanations on these complicated issues.[12] Though Sarin Chhak disappeared at the hands of the Vietnamese troops on 7 January 1979, his papers have survived and are now in private hands in Phnom Penh, a testimony to the deep attention Pol Pot paid to the question of the lost provinces and the claims the Cambodian State could still eventually lay to them.

The consequences are well known. Hanoi reacted to the threat against its southern provinces by a mixture of diplomatic, political and military moves which have been well described by Nayan Chanda, and my own research fully concurs with his findings.[13] Pol Pot paid for his miscalculation with the destruction of his regime. Had he refrained from going over the border, he most probably would still be in power, the killings would have subsided and we would have another North Korea, another "hermit kingdom" of silent slaves, on which our information would be very sketchy, and our indignation slight.

What Problems Arise in Defining "Genocide"?

It is certainly appropriate to sit here, in the Yale Law School, in a Raphael Lemkin Symposium, and now discuss the problem of defining "genocide" because the very word was coined exactly fifty years ago by a New York Polish Jewish publicist called Raphael Lemkin. A zealous Zionist, he warned of the impending destruction of European Jewry at the hands of the Nazis and drew argument from the persecution — inventing a word to name the killing of a race — to reassert the necessity to create a Jewish state, to which all the Jews of the world would migrate and thus suppress the existence of any "Jewish question".[14] He wanted to impress his readers with the idea that the forcible disappearance of the Jews from the face of the earth would be, among nations, comparable with suppressing a person from among fellow humans. He spent three years lobbying in the newly established United Nations before he succeeded in having his draft Convention voted by the General Assembly in December 1948. Then followed a long fight for ratification. Successive American administrations attempted to get a ratification because they basically saw in it a potential anti-Soviet weapon but they had to face a very determined opposition from the American Bar Association which saw contradictions in the text with US constitutional principles. We must be reminded that up to now, nobody, and certainly not the Nazis, has ever been brought to court to face the charge of genocide, with the ridiculous exception of Ceaucescu in the mock trial before his summary execution.[15] Does the fact that this crime has never been tested in court mean that it has never been committed since the time it was registered in international law? Or does it mean it is an unusable category, legally flawed, that prosecutors discard because they would rather rely on more solidly established criminal charges?

Lemkin's neologism lingered for a long time. The notion was a curiosity and was not much picked up. After World War II, the standard word for what happened to the Jews in the Eastern territories was "extermination". Technically, there was no need for a new word. The UN in 1948 was merely a diplomatic firing-ground for East–West ideological fights, with Lemkin himself the expected Cold Warrior. Mass murders, massacres, suppression of aborigines or minorities fill the pages of history books and there is, unfortunately, "nothing new under the sun". George Orwell was writing books to show what consequences were implied by changes in the meaning of words. By the end of the war, the Allied powers had decided to try the Axis leaders in an attempt to use guilt to destroy in advance any attempt to revive a national spirit, both in Germany and Japan. In order to achieve this, the Allies created a special military court, with special rules, and invented a new category of crime, said to be "crime against humanity". It was to be applied in a retroactive way, which, we should recall, is prohibited by the Declaration of Human Rights. Any lawyer knows that, in normal times if it were submitted to any Appellate Court, the Nuremberg trial would be annulled. But these times were not quite normal. There was of course no legal need for this innovation. The sheer application of German law would have provided straightforward condemnations, but there was the political need of a device to destroy morally an already vanquished nation, to go beyond a mere military defeat. That failed in Japan but succeeded well in Germany, where Christianity provided a ready acceptance of guilt. But nobody picked up the invention of Lemkin and it seems the word, as a legal tool, cannot be found in the 42 volumes of the proceedings of the International Military Tribunal.

Maybe the word, and the idea, have a built-in weakness. The idea was to describe the killing (-*cide*) of a people. But instead of using the Greek roots for people (*demos*) or nation (*ethnos*), or more simply the Latin root for people (*populus*), Lemkin had used the word for "race", or "group related by blood and kin", which includes the notion of shared heredity that appears in the word *gene*tics. As did most people, including scientists, in the first half of this century, Lemkin, educated in Lvov and Heidelberg, thought that mankind was divided into "races". Classifications varied according to authors (Caucasian, Nordic, Black, Mongoloid, Semitic and what not). Many Jewish authors spoke also of a "Jewish race". It was only later, when the advance of biological sciences showed that although individuals may vary genetically, these variations had little significance and there is no such a thing as "race" inside the global human population, that the concept of biological racism began to decay.

The notion of "killing a race" (the original meaning of the word "genocide") might have been embarrassing for the big powers with the dismal record shown in the recent past by the United States and its treatment of the native Amerindians, by the USSR and its deportation of populations collectively accused of "collaboration" with the Germans, by the Allied colonial powers, like France and Great Britain, still using race as a political basis for their supremacy, and so on. To further explain why genocide was never an influential concept, we may refer to a French lawyer, Bernard Jouanneau, who wrote for the Socialist Party the bill that became a law in France, in July 1990, making it a crime to dissent publicly from the verdict of the Nuremberg Trial.[16] In a radio programme, he explained that they had wanted to find a way to punish those who deny the Nazis perpetrated the act of genocide against the Jews. But when we tried to define what genocide was, he said in substance, we found out the past was full of events which could be described as such, like the slave trade, wars of destruction, the Spanish *conquista* of America, and even some ugly episodes of the French Revolution, and that there existed controversies about the nature of these events. Since it looked impossible to rule by law what historians could or could not say about all past events but one, the lawyer turned legislator resorted to the legal enforcement of respect for the Nuremberg verdict, which, however, does not speak of genocide.

So, if jurists, politicians, historians (with the exception of Cold War diplomats) found this notion too vague to handle with any amount of practical usefulness, a reality demonstrated by the fact that in fifty years no one has ever been indicted on this count in a fair trial, how come that it has crept into such general use?

For a long time, the word was used in only one connection, the one for which Lemkin had coined it. The trial of Adolf Eichmann in 1960 triggered the slow evolution of Western understanding of World War II: as the real reasons for the war receded into the past, being obscured by a new world order born with the victory, the relative importance of the Nazi persecution of the Jews was given a growing prominence until, a generation later, many people believe that the fate of the Jews lay at the core of the war. It is a little bit as if, in one or two generations from now, writers and historians were to try to have us believe that the whole Pol Pot enterprise was centred on the will to exterminate the Chams. In an Islamic view of things (already more or less prevalent, for instance, in the Malaysian perception of Pol Pot), this could be perfectly understandable, and supported by a careful selection of the facts.

From the 1960s onward, Israel's growing needs for Western support, money, weapons and general protection shifted the moral grounds of its requests more and more on to what the Nazis had done. No more massive Jewish immigration was anticipated and the enormous military requirements, which at one point pushed the Israeli share of US world-wide aid to almost half, led to a considerable effort in propaganda to spread the Israeli point of view across Western public opinion. The vocabulary itself testifies to the spread of the word "genocide", the explosion of the word "holocaust" (with a completely distorted meaning), the appearance of the word "shoah" and the near disappearance of words like "destruction", "extermination", etc. An analysis of book titles together with their date of first printing would reveal a lot about our changing ideological view of things past and present.

If, for a long time, the notion of genocide was restricted to one event, which happened once in history to one people, the political benefit it provided to the State of Israel could only attract attention and lead to emulation. The next to adopt it as a political instrument were the Armenian nationalists. The Israeli example of the "rebirth" of a State which had disappeared since ancient times could not but appeal to radical Armenian nationalists who were eager, not only to revive a state — they had one under communist rule in the Soviet Union — but to claim its former political space, now the northeastern corner of Turkey, where "historical Armenia" was once to be found, and from where all Armenians had been forcibly expelled in 1915. By all sorts of means, including terror, Armenian nationalists tried to obtain from Western governments an official pronouncement that what had been known all along as the 1915 "Armenian massacres" and deportation had really been "genocide", possibly the first in our time. Only this word, internationally recognized, would pave the way for a process of dismantling Turkish territory. It was precisely for that reason that Western governments, put under pressure, nevertheless refused to include it in official statements, not out of lack of sympathy for the Armenian cause, but for fear of creating an unmanageable conflict with a valuable ally.[17] A wise decision when one sees the war that has been going on for the past two or three years between the former Soviet republics of Armenia and Azerbaijan for the control of Upper Karabagh, a small district inhabited mostly by Armenians.

The most violent Armenian militants, requesting recognition of "genocide", belonged to the ASALA movement, born in Beirut among youngsters who had been under strong Palestinian influence. Those Palestinians were under the spell of the Israeli success in attracting international support and were prone to imitate Israeli moves, including the use of the notion of genocide (victims of which would be the Palestinian people).

Recently, Serbia justified its attacks on Croatia by calling the mass murders which occurred in the region during the last world war genocide. Every mass killing is becoming an act of genocide when its memory is being used as grounds for national expansion, war against neighbours, or any form of violence which is difficult to legitimize. The usual inflation of political vocabulary led also to a growing misappropriation of the word. We currently hear that the road accidents of the weekend are causing a genocide, that a mad killer shot eleven people in an act of genocide, that AIDS is a potential genocide, and so on. Examples may be culled from any media.

The concept of "ethnocide", launched in 1968 to describe the cultural destruction of native tribes, in places like Brazil or Guatemala, never really took off and, instead, "cultural genocide" (implying the death of a culture, and not the physical destruction of the people) has been widely used to describe, for instance, the near total annihilation of cultural places and goods in Tibet by the Chinese so-called Cultural Revolution.[18]

Does the Cambodian Case Fit the Requirements of the Genocide Convention?

If we understand genocide, as most people do, as the killing of people purely on ethnic grounds, or the attempt to do so, then Cambodia does not fit in. Even cases of indiscriminate killings based on purely ethnic, or tribal discrimination, as we have seen taking place, for instance, in Burundi, or elsewhere in Africa, Sabra and Chatila, the Sumgait pogrom against Armenians, the killings of Tibetans in Eastern Tibet, the destruction of a third of the population of East Timor by the Indonesian army, the destruction of Brazilian or other Amerindian tribes, and many other similar massacres which have taken place since the Genocide Convention has been "active" (1951), show that the international community cannot handle this notion because too many of its members are or have been guilty of barbaric acts of this kind. Big powers not only close their eyes when it is committed by one of their allies but they usually help them to commit and cover up the crime.[19] The press and the judicial powers are usually accomplices, either by silently approving or by directing selective blame on the enemy's misdeeds.

Amid growing speculation in the West on these questions concerning Cambodia, few writers address the Cambodian reaction. The concept of genocide is of course a complete novelty in this country. But in general Khmer ideas about law may look rather confused. It would take a long time to try to show that two entirely diffrent schools of thought — the first one inherited from Theravada Buddhism mixed with traditional wisdom, the second one painstakingly brought into the country by the colonial administration — lived side by side without really blending together. The Cambodian Codes were mostly a matter of oral tradition and justice was administered by political authorities on the basis of wise judgement rather than on any fixed set of abstract principles, even if some crimes had established penalties.[20] Colonial administration needed a body of logically related notions as a framework into which its power and activities, entirely new in the country, could be regulated. The Cambodians could not care less and the new legal system remained largely restricted to the French sphere of action. For instance, there were repeated attempts, from the start, to involve the Cambodians in establishing a land ownership system — which they found entirely alien.[21] Later, notions of Roman law were incorporated in state laws. There were written laws, voted by an elected Assembly, a system of courts and even a Faculty of Law. But this alien system affected the population only slightly and never put down intellectual roots in it. The arbitrary decisions of a mostly corrupt administration, the violence of the state power and the unlimited greed of the commercial class anyway made a mockery of any pretence of a rule of law.

In this *ancien régime* mentality, there is no justice to be expected from a system entirely devoted to the interests of the mighty and the wealthy. This does not mean Cambodia is a lawless society. On the contrary. A complicated set of implicit moral rules regulates everyday life and very clear standards of good conduct are taught to the young. If circumstances of war, famine and political crises allow massive ruptures and if the necessities of survival throw individuals beyond the normal rules, they reappear afterwards. But they are not, in themselves, strong enough to impose order on what we could be tempted to call the "natural anarchy" of the Khmers. So far, only some form of terror has succeeded in doing this because the law is not deeply rooted in the peoples' consciences.

The concept of a particularly defined concept of "genocide" and of the trial of a political chief would seem rather ludicrous to most Cambodians. Revenge is understandable but retribution belongs to future lives. Trust in an independent judiciary just does not exist, and for good reason. A trial held by foreigners would be just one more piece of foreigners' business. With the exception of a tiny number of intellectuals and politicians acquainted with Western mores, everyone would see in the complicated procedures of a court the useless prelude to a retaliatory killing. And, anyway, such a trial has taken place already. In the summer of 1979, an international tribunal was convened in Phnom Penh to try Pol Pot and Ieng Sary *in absentia*. Documents, testimonies, witnesses were produced. I believe that around 1,000 pages of documentation were presented. A summary was later published.[22] As it was obviously organized by the Vietnamese, the Western press ignored it. Ten years passed before this same press started toying with the idea of a genocide trial, while Cambodia had all along been submitted to an economic embargo the criminal nature of which could also be tested in court. May I submit this idea to our interested lawyers?

Pol Pot is no longer a real person in Cambodia. It has become a common word: "Twelve pol pot entered village so and so." It certainly focuses feelings of hatred and resentment. (The word Pol Pot is never used in Khmer Rouge usage, where the man is usually referred to as "number 87".) Any form of violence would seem legitimate. When a crowd surrounded the house of Khieu Samphân in Phnom Penh in November 1991, the rumour was that "Pol Pot" was there. And even more than blood, what the people wanted to see was the *face* of the man, a face they have never seen, a face they probably thought of as inhuman. The man never really exposed himself and his name is nothing but a symbol.

We must start from the fact that Cambodians were never in a position to know the reasons for this bloody mess. In these ill-clad wild boys, they could only recognize the naked figure of power, doing what power has always done in this country: humiliate or eliminate. (This goes a long way towards explaining what some would describe as suicidal tendencies, in individuals as well as in society.) Renouncement is the only narrow escape from the alternative but this time even monks and hermits were trapped. Would then a trial be a great educational move, providing at last an opportunity for the new generation to reconcile remembrance and understanding? It probably could. Although historians usually pass severe judgement on this kind of great political trial, these staged dramas may have a cathartic effect, reorder collective thought and provide new bridges for the legitimization of emerging powers. But we should remain lucid: the law is built with concepts and politics with symbols. A political trial is a hybrid exercise where lawyers do their intellectual trick while the audience at large watches a symbolic play.[23]

Today, Cambodians both remember and forget. The pains they suffered, as individuals, as members of crushed families, are deeply ingrained and the wounds will probably never heal. But the catastrophe seems to remain cicumscribed in personal history. Paradoxically, this period of totally collective life developed into an individualistic struggle for life, aimed at surviving and, later, at re-establishing some normalcy. The global dimension was just an added burden and, for many, the sense of a collective drama seems to be waning.

In the West, the paradigm of genocide is still very much centred on Auschwitz. So true is this that, in an effort to attract part of the sinister charisma of Auschwitz, the masters of the new Cambodian regime, in early 1979, commissioned some

Vietnamese experts, trained in Poland, to refurbish the interrogation centre called Tuol Sleng.[24] Very few people saw it in its original state. But this paradigm plays also in another field, called in a vague manner: "memory". As opposed to "history" (reconstruction of the past based on documents and material evidence), "memory" would be a tale of the past based on personal remembrance, subjective feelings, nostalgic attachment to "roots". Some even think that "memory" has more truth in it than the cold reasoning of "history". Genocide and the "memory" of it (basically, a reconstruction made by the **descendants** of the survivors) are linked with a refusal to mourn (and an acceptance of the passing away) of those who died an unnatural death. Psychoanalysis has a lot to say about this.[25] Jews and Khmers do not mourn and bury the dead in the same way and there is the risk that our Western concept of "memory" could be entirely irrelevant to the Khmers who obviously have their own. I wish we may not succumb to the temptation to force our views on them, as we already do in so many other fields.

When we compare the Cambodian experience with the legacy of fascism — and we have no doubt as to the legitimacy of this comparison — we should note that, in the case of Europe, there was a struggle against it. Later, people could identify with that struggle, whatever had been the reality of their own commitment, and build a memory, somewhat selective, around these notions of refusal, the struggle of Good against Evil, and victory. But in Cambodia, there was no such struggle. The level of terror was too high. There was not even a victory since Mr Pol Pot is still alive and kicking. Foreigners did the struggle and, with them, a handful of Khmers who were later largely rewarded by the gift of exclusive state power. So, Cambodians have nothing positive to rely on, except an association with a foreign power that most of them would not want. If there is a political memory, it is a rather shameful one of abject submission, fear, passivity, inability to protect one's own family, of helpless dying children, of stealing bits of despicable food. It is difficult to build even hatred on these bases. And when the government, in the 1980s, organized a yearly Day of Hatred, which would have delighted Orwell's sarcastic mind, people performed it casually.

When the crowd rioted in the front of Khieu Samphân's house, an old lady came with her kitchen knife in order to chop the guy into pieces.[26] The striking fact was she was alone of her kind. When the people saw the event on television and watched this white-haired man with blood dripping down his face, there was a general feeling of disapproval, a fear, stronger than anger, that bringing back this memory would endanger the present. There is a will to forget. The idea that the

Khmer Rouge have changed, which they try so hard to disseminate, could come as an anxiety-killer pill for many people.

Because the government established by the Vietnamese made large use of a rather simplified view of the recent past to justify its policies and its temporary dependence on foreign troops, it was perceived as government propaganda and, as such, it obliterated the survivors' ability to build up their own retrospective understanding. On the Coalition side, it was worse. The victims were coerced into working closely with their killers. Echoing Father Ponchaud, they had to fabricate the myth that the Vietnamese were even more "genocidal" than the DK. Even now Pol Pot refers constantly to the "genocidal and aggressive *yuon* enemy". And Sihanouk went to great lengths, on American television, to explain that the Khmer Rouge were "no more criminals".

If we understand genocide in a broad sense as meaning unjustified mass murder, then Cambodia, as well as many other states, is a case, and its leaders may be brought to an international court — which, by the way, does not currently exist. If, on the other hand, we consider the notion has a very specific meaning, then we have to expand its significance considerably in order to include Cambodia. This is what I tried to convey, many years ago, when I wrote that "if words have a meaning, there was certainly no genocide in Cambodia".[27] I understand that some Cambodians took exception to this sentence, but then is not their use of the word a kind of substitute for a victory over Pol Pot they could not win in the battlefield, and even less by being his political ally?

If we could catch Pol Pot and give him a fair trial, he would certainly claim he was not the worst killer in Cambodia[28]: he would point out that many victims of starvation suffered the consequences of the aerial destructions of the Cambodian countryside. He would remind us that Messrs Nixon and Kissinger concentrated US air power on his country and destroyed around 600,000 lives in the process. Would they sit in the same dock? Would they also face the charge of genocide in Cambodia, for having killed Khmer peasants "as such"?

Who fought for months and months to include in the future Peace Agreement on Cambodia a reference to the "genocidal practices of the past", in order to provide a ground for the political elimination of the Pol Pot group, at the risk of jeopardizing the whole diplomatic process? It was the Phnom Penh government, led by people who had been very junior leaders in the Khmer Rouge movement and knew, better than most, its true nature. And what happened? The American government gave its full support to the Chinese scrapping of this infamous label.

The final version of the Agreements does not mention genocide at all and this is in order to reincorporate the Khmer Rouge into Cambodian public life, very much against the will of the huge majority of the people here. The hypocrisy of American officials explaining that they did everything possible to prevent the return of Pol Pot to Phnom Penh is revolting, particularly when one remembers that at the UN Geneva Conference, in 1981, they voted down the ASEAN proposal to look for a political solution based on a disarmament of the Khmer Rouge.

In fact, there are two entirely different concepts of genocide: the one we all know and use on occasions, as a kind of historical category, and the one used by the lawyers, based on the widely unread UN Convention, which could make the murder of two people fall technically into the "genocide" category, according to the motive for this crime. The discrepancy between the two is so wide that confusion is unavoidable.

The reality is that genocide, massacres, wiping out entire peoples or cultures, and other inhuman atrocities, torture, massive corruption, and so on, are part and parcel of government policies, most usually applied to foreign countries. There is no other law than the law of the jungle. If we want to change this situation, we must reform our own laws first, strip the authorities of their political immunity, abolish the "Reason of State" and the system of official secrecy which covers up all these crimes. If we could reach a stage in which any official would be tried according to the same rules that apply to you and me, to any other ordinary human being, we would not need all these extraordinary concepts because common law is quite enough.

Just after the Algerian war, the French government passed a law of amnesty: the thousands of crimes committed by the troops in this seven-year long conflict were abolished. They reputedly never existed. Nobody was punished and nobody may publicly be named in connection with those crimes. As for the USA, checking the name of the village My Lai in a Viet Cong list of villages wiped out by the US ground forces, I found out it was one among several hundreds, recorded long before My Lai became a public affair. Was there any enquiry into the destruction of those villages? Were even those responsible for the slaughter in My Lai really punished? Who are we to give moral lessons to others?

I of course fully agree that Pol Pot should be prevented by any means from returning to power. I find it a bit paradoxical that so much blame was poured on the Vietnamese, who did just that, prevent Pol Pot from coming back, by people who did so much to promote the same Pol Pot and insisted he kept his seat in the

United Nations. I am also fully in favour of a trial of Pol Pot and of his accomplices and his foreign associates, including American, Thai and Chinese officials who conspired to support him when he was in power and after his fall. I suggest the application of the ordinary Cambodian law for events which took place in Cambodia.

Genocide is nothing else but a political label aiming at the exclusion of a political leader or party beyond the bonds of humanity. It leads us to believe we are good, that we have nothing to do with these monsters. This is entirely misleading. Pol Pot has been produced by our political world, is part of it, is using it and is getting strong from it. Before saying he is dirty — which is what he is without a doubt — we should clean our own house first[29].

10

Cambodia 1992: United Nations Traditional Apathy in Cambodia

I landed in Pochentong in November 1991, on Sihanouk's heels. Phnom Penh was somewhat feverish. After almost two decades of austerity, rich people had begun to reappear in 1989. Through the border trade, Cambodia was plugged into the world market but the changing of the political line had somehow authorized people to become rich, or to show they were. Consumption of luxuries was no longer hidden. People had some savings from the time when there were not so many goods on the market, except gold. Traders and civil servants started to buy cars (many of them stolen in Bangkok) while ordinary people started a buying spree on Japanese motorbikes. All the used motorbikes in Southeast Asia, it seems, were shipped to Cambodia, whence many of them continued their trip to southern Vietnam. The motorization of life soared, after twenty years of manual work, to what it was under Lon Nol.

Intense real estate speculation accompanied and fuelled the boom. In 1979, the repopulation of Phnom Penh had been gradual and planned. The Vietnamese, at first, did not allow people to flock into towns where food and services were unavailable. They wanted first to reconstruct the basis of a State administration. Selecting people with some experience, they gave housing to them first, in the middle of the town. For most of these people, it was a fantastic upward social movement. For a long time, this was not very important since the housing belonged to the State and civil servants had a very low income anyway. But by 1989, property rights were given to tenants, whatever the origin of their occupancy, from civil servants assigned housing by the State to squatters who had arrived later. Ownership gave a value to real estate since it could then be bought and sold. And the value started to rise quickly, all transactions being made in gold *damlang* (small ingots). High level civil servants managed to have more than one

186

house. And as foreigners started to pour in, the value of housing climbed to quite irrational heights. In the process, many people were evicted from their houses, either because they could not claim ownership or because they were on the losing side of speculation.

Money was again displayed, particularly in town, because the countryside naturally did not benefit from this speculative enrichment. But there too, appropriation started. Farmers could claim the land they were tilling but within rules decreed by law. The village headman had a key role in organizing the distribution. For instance, land was to be kept aside for soldiers and given to them after future demobilization. Although not the object of complete ownership as in Roman law, land could then be bought and sold. Social inequalities started to develop and the weakest elements started to lose their land altogether. Moreover, rich townspeople started to buy land in the surrounding areas. With incredible speed the whole society, it seemed, was evolving toward the same pattern that had been abolished by the war and its Khmer Rouge aftermath. When the Alliance française reopened in 1990, young pupils of affluent families literally flocked to learn French, which had been in the old society a sure sign of belonging to the élite.

One absence struck me. Russians were gone or were going. The last remnants of their presence were some fading photographs of cosmonauts still displayed in a corner of the airport. What a strange idea it was to glamorize the Soviet Union with cosmonauts in a country where even draught animals were scarce! The Soviets had made a real effort to maintain the country's food supply in 1979 and rehabilitate its technical structures. Thousands of expatriates, some of them speaking quite fluent Khmer, had come over the years. The cost for Moscow had been considerable. Gorbachev had paved the way for a global negotiation by alleviating Chinese anxieties; he had despatched Foreign Affairs Vice-Minister Igor Rogachev to move the discussions forward, up to the Paris Agreement. But Washington, when an agreement was made to provide Russia with food aid in 1991, had imposed the condition that all Soviet technical experts, in some 44 underdeveloped countries, should go home immediately. You can't help anyone if you need help yourself, the Russians were told. As a consequence, all the Russian technicians had to leave Cambodia within four weeks. The Technological Institute and the Faculty of Agriculture, for instance, instantly lost all their teachers. All the accumulated expertise was thrown overboard. Some individual scientists and technicians managed to stay and tried to get employment with the UN but, as a whole, it was a sure testimony of the way the West was brutally sweeping the place clean to install its own trusted personnel, many of whom came from the border network, co-ordinated since 1979 by the US, under several successive disguises. Who says Cambodia should be independent?

Thousands of small incidents struck me as I watched this attempt to reconstruct an old social order which had failed and plunged the country into its worst misery. Most of the actors had changed, but the old power games, black money and traffic were there again, generating the same disgust in the population, or the same moral reaction among poorly educated intellectuals. The students demonstrated, not so much against the corruption, as a naive or prejudiced international press wrote, but because they wanted to have their share of it. How could they protest against corruption since they had bought their entry into university? And most were studying only because they anticipated the illegal profits they would draw from their future jobs. Studies were not determined by individual taste but by the price of entry into university, varying according to the faculty. The richest students take medicine and the poorest archaeology.

I watched most of the demonstrations from very close by. It was the first time since 1973 that demonstrators had taken to the streets in Cambodia. Nobody knew what a demonstration was. The first one occurred when Pol Pot's representative, Khieu Samphân, came back to Phnom Penh to take his seat at the newly established Supreme National Council.

It could have been the same story as the week before, when Son Sen, the Khmer Rouge Defence Minister arrived in Phnom Penh, thanks to the Paris Agreements: arrival at Pochentong airport, with the regular early morning flight from Bangkok, mobbing by the press, and then a crazy motorcade through Phnom Penh, speeding along the former Boulevard Norodom (now Tou Samouth), and the Khmer Rouge leader closeting himself in a government house. That could have been it. The only change was that Khieu Samphân, upon his arrival, on 27 November 1991, was going to settle in a modern concrete villa, bought two days before by his SNC colleague, Son Sen, who was so happy to be "back home" and had told a journalist: "People here are so nice, they call me uncle."

The day before, students had been called to take to the streets to demonstrate that they were not prepared to accept this avuncular pretence. They had banners, in Khmer but also in European languages they do not usually speak, castigating the authors of the massacres. Photographs of Khieu Samphân had been distributed and angrily crossed with black or red pens.

Exile, civil war and diplomatic tasks have whitened his hair, and somewhat fattened his jaws. On the tarmac, he flashed a broad smile and just said: "I am happy", presumably to be back home. Maybe in the plane he had recalled how he, together with Pol Pot and other communist leaders, had had to escape in a panic towards the mountains. In early January 1979, the swift attack of the Vietnamese troops took them by surprise. They had intoxicated themselves into believing that the famished yuon army was vastly inferior to their "pure" Khmer one. The lightning attack came as a shock. They fled in disorder, leaving behind suitcases, archives and hot meals, by trucks and trains, rushing for the bush, the Vietnamese *bodoi* on their heels.

So he was back, thanks only to the Chinese whose face everyone in power in the West wanted to save. After all, Nuremberg had been good only for those bloody Germans and nothing of the sort could be relevant for the small ally of Big China. We, Khmer Rouge, have committed no crimes, only "mistakes".

The students were back in the morning, at some points reducing the width of the road from the airport so as to make sure the Red leader would drive through a crowd chanting "Down with Pol Pot". But the man in the limousine stared ahead and did not seem to notice. These youngsters he did not see had all lost part of their family during the Pol Pot era and never knew exactly why. Khieu Samphân was aware he could not provide any clear explanation. He had dodged questions so often in the last 13 years. They had done everything well, according to the rules, and the structure had crumbled down. Did he fully understand himself why it had finished in a disaster, why the uncontested Communist Party power had been so easily swept away by the arch-enemies, the former "brothers"?

Of course, at the beginning, and for a long time he had been just a figurehead, behind whom Pol Pot and his group could conveniently remain hidden. But he had climbed the ladder and obtained the trust of Brother No. One. He had become executive secretary of Pol Pot's office 870, the supreme direction. They knew it in the West since American Cambodia scholar Steve Heder, combing the archives, produced evidence of this.[1] He had at last entered the inner circle. Other figures in the Party had power too but the Party had to be remoulded, with only one thought and one leader, and they had to be destroyed. He was safe in the shadow of the Centre, he was immune and could order purges. And these devious Vietnamese who came and destroyed the magnificent architecture built up by Pol Pot... And then all these years in exile, observing Chinese admonitions, bowing to prince Sihanouk and licking his feet...

Now he was back in Phnom Penh, a town which had liked him in the sixties, when he came back from Paris with a title of Doctor in Economics. He had published a newspaper called L'Observateur. He drew glory from being incorruptible, a rare commodity in Cambodian politics. Sihanouk, who enjoyed manipulating people, had tried to bribe him by offering a Mercedes but he had kept riding his old bicycle, even as a member of Parliament. So enraged had the prince been that he had had him caught in the street, stripped of his pants and beaten up by his roughies.

Sihanouk had paid for that, much later. When he was a virtual prisoner in the Royal Palace, in 1976–8, Khieu Samphân would sometimes come amd take him for a ride in the countryside, showing him happy crowds digging canals, in a black Mercedes. What a revenge! The prince was then so humble, worried about his diminishing stocks of champagne, *foie gras* and other such amenities.

Samphân had seen the boss, Pol Pot, the other day, in his Thai compound, a few miles from the border with Cambodia. The guideline was clear: stick to the Prince, play the game, do everything to maintain an opening into the Phnom Penh system, whereas we, in the forest, shall maintain our forces, be ready to filter in and destroy the enemy grip from within.

He and his ten-man retinue soon arrived in the villa and started unpacking. There were some curious onlookers in front of the villa and a dozen cops. Security had been guaranteed by the Interior Vice-Minister who talked with Son Sen. Passers-by stopped. The journalists hesitated. Was the day over? Some decided to stay for a while, maybe waiting for the students who, not knowing where he was staying, took to the Cambodiana Hotel, in the opposite direction. The crowd thickened. In front were young chaps who were probably earning their living with their hands. Some shouted. Feelings of hostility and memories of past sufferings swept through the little crowd. Some hundreds of people were then looking at the blind windows. A stone was thrown. The noise of broken glass triggered more stone throwing. It was a convenient message and the crowd approved. A hail of stones soon destroyed all the glass panels, leaving the windows only protected by their iron grilles.

Then a young man threw himself against the gate and soon opened it. The police rushed to close it again but the demonstrators approached the railings. The cops softly pushed them away but they were back immediately and started to shake the iron bars. The crowd had thickened and tension was rising. Wave after wave, the assailants tried to tear the railings down. Some helmeted cops appeared but, mixed with the demonstrators, they did not try to fight them off. They were soon submerged and demonstrators invaded the courtyard and climbed the external stairs. Then things started to fly on to the street, mattresses, papers, suitcases, cooking utensils. A fire was lit. The fire brigade was already on the spot, with two or three enormous Russian watertank trucks, parked nearby. The cops were mixed with the invading crowd, pushing some softly away, while more were coming in. The door was kicked open and some youngsters rushed in, while nobody knew what the bodyguards inside would do. Were they prepared to put up a fight and shoot?

The rumour said there were Chinese armed men inside. But no shot was fired and more people, cops and demonstrators mixed, packed into the house as more things, smashed furniture, radio sets and clothing were thrown outside, piled up on the bonfire and set alight. A huge red firetruck moved into position and doused the fire, just enough to put the flames down but it kept burning, emitting toxic fumes. The small transmitters of the plainclothes Security men were chattering away. Nobody cared and youngsters were dancing. Many Western journalists believed that Khieu Samphân was no longer in the house, that he had been somehow spirited away. In the crowd it was said Pol Pot was in the house and people badly wanted him to come out of hiding. They wanted to see him, they wanted him to expose his secretive figure to the light of the day, as if that would be enough to dissolve his demoniac figure together with the nightmares of the past, which still too often haunt the present.

In a house across the boulevard, the Prime Minister appeared at a balcony and addressed the crowd with a powerful loudspeaker. He said that he understood, he shared the feelings of revolt of the crowd, but he had been obliged to sign the Paris Agreements, that people should quieten down. Not everyone was listening. Everybody was gazing at this enigmatic villa. They all wanted to see the inside of the house. The words of the Prime Minister could not break their obsessive expectation. Only a small minority was assaulting the house. The crowd cheered when objects were seen flying from it, but was otherwise quite silent and watchful. The Prime Minister, Mr Hun Sen, spoke in bursts, interrupting his speech with conversations over the radio. Security people were there, in and near the house, with their tiny transmitters.

As time passed, more people milled around in the house, sweating, shouting, elbowing, smashing everything into small pieces. Two or three guys had brought along hatchets to acheive a better result. Then monsters appeared. Two pairs of armoured cars arrived. Russian armoured vehicles, with machine guns carefully wrapped with a dirty cloth, the drivers wearing leather helmets of World War II vintage. They stopped nearby. Nobody was frightened. The cops and the soldiers were very casual and there was no indication of fighting in the air.

On the other hand, the tension inside the house was great, firstly because the crowd was so thick. Young green photographers had thrown themselves into it while older, more experienced journalists remained outside, smelling the lust for blood, and feeling it was the right time for a Molotov cocktail or a hand grenade, if someone wanted this event to splash blood on the front page of the world press.

The pandemonium continued inside, until a cop opened the door of a small bedroom upstairs. There was a rush, and then everybody stopped for several seconds. Khieu Samphân was there, standing stiff against the wall. The crowd looked at him, suddenly not sure of what it really wanted. Then in a brief spasm the reputedly North Korea trained bodyguards were overpowered, one of them lying on the floor, another standing against the wall, sticks at their throats. Cupboards were searched. An AK submachine-gun promptly disappeared. And then someone hit Samphân on the head with an iron rod. He sat on the floor, blood running down his face. Some photographers and Security men surrounded him. Some people tried to kick him. But this blood was enough, maybe. Samphân suddenly appeared very old and tired. The smiling mask had been broken.

But meanwhile the rumour was spreading outside that he had been badly injured, trampled underfoot. A Japanese photographer, coming out the house, just said: "Still live." Press corps members hotly debated the matter: "This rascal should be hanged anyway", said one. "Something should be done" said another. "It's a lynching. Can't accept that." Then the armoured cars started their engines and took position, presenting their rears to the entrance. Suddenly the cops became active and organized. They started to evacuate people from the house, slowly pushing them away, and keeping the entrance clear. Journalists grumbled at this new attitude.

Then I felt a hand on my shoulder. A young man was standing behind me: "The Prime Minister wants to see you. Bring AFP along." I spotted the young lady reporter. She had been inside and had come out white, exhausted, soaking, obviously off balance. I called her and we ploughed through the crowd to get to the opposite house where the Prime Minister and his team had improvised their headquarters. When we arrived he was talking on a radio telephone. She was so lost she could not recognize him or take down notes. He said he had repeatedly warned that this kind of thing was inevitable, that there was not much he could do, without resorting to violence.

Of course, it would be finished in ten minutes if I were to use force. But can I shoot my own people? I understand their feelings. It shows there is no safe place in Cambodia for this kind of person. I contacted Mr Son Sen by telephone, asking him to propose Mr Khieu Samphân go back Bangkok, but Mr Samphân refused to see him for one hour. And then he delayed his answer for more than another hour. Now he has accepted and we are going to drive him to the airport, if we still can save him.

"But you could have found a safe place for him, in a military barracks, for instance", I said.

"No, it could not be kept secret, and the crowd would find him, and everything would start again."

"What does that mean for the peace process?"

"I do not know yet. I have always requested the absence of these people. We know the mind of the Cambodians. We'll have to see."

At the moment, the crowd roared. The Khmer Rouge chief, the blood cleaned from his face, was stepping out of the house. He was helped to climb aboard the armoured car under a hail of sticks and stones. A tree on which too many spectators had climbed slowly fell down, crushing some motorbikes.

"You see, nobody wants them here", said Hun Sen, who looked tired and quite nervous. He had certainly had a hard time controlling the situation. Of course the events had matched his prediction of the week before so well that he could be thought of as having more or less engineered the whole show. He insisted it was spontaneous. Maybe so, but the cops never took any measure to contain the crowd or to clear the area surrounding the house. They even participated in the rampage inside the house. "Let's go to Pochentong" (the airport), he said. But he wanted to make a last phone call. The man with the radio telephone was not at hand. "Bring it now", shouted the Prime Minister, with an outburst of temper that is rare for him. Everybody then sped away to Pochentong.

It was all over.

At the airport, Khieu Samphân had a long phone conversation with the prince. Everybody was very nervous. On the way to the plane, he shook some hands but avoided Hun Sen's. He did not appreciate the trap into which he had so quickly fallen. Two Soviet pilots had been hastily summoned and the special plane took off at ten past four. This short day in Phnom Penh had lasted less than eight hours.

A little later, the week starting Sunday 16 December 1991 was agitated. Workers in several State firms had protested against the rush of some administrators to sell buildings to unknown Sino-foreign buyers. It was not clear on what authority the sales had proceeded. If it was an administrative decision, it had not been made public. If it was a private one, then the property had been misappropriated. Maybe the Party was just trying to amass money for the upcoming elections or, maybe, it was just embezzlement for personal profit, or a mixture of both.

Whatever the truth, the clear result was that workers were laid off. And their protest spread like wildfire. On Friday 21st, a house was burned down by demonstrating workers near the Stadium market. The police waited until a truck with a loudspeaker came and blared out a recorded speech by the Prime Minister who said he would intervene. In the following hours, he sacked the Transportation Minister. This in itself was a rare feat. Hun Sen considered the man to be incompetent and corrupt, and for a year had requested his demotion. But this Transportation Minister appeared to be some kind of nephew of Chea Sim, the Party strong man, and president of the National Assembly. You cannot touch a member of the clan without dangerously affecting the balance of forces inside the government. Hun Sen had boldly seized the opportunity and he was immediately suspected of having fomented the demonstrations himself. Fearing for his life, the Minister took up residence in Chea Sim's home in the evening.

The background is interesting as it provides a glimpse of what Khmer politics is about. This Chea Sim's nephew (the word may have no real kinship content) had replaced Ung Phon in the autumn of 1990. This Ung Phon was a close friend of Hun Sen, by now Prime Minister. They had belonged to the same military outfit during the Pol Pot period, in the Eastern zone. They were together when Hun Sen, a low-level regimental commander, rebelled and took to the forest, probably towards the end of 1977. It was a hard time: running away from Pol Pot's army, they hesitated for several months before crossing over to the Vietnamese. They were not sure what the Vietnamese reaction would be. They had taken part in the early 1977 attacks against Vietnam... This kind of situation forged mighty bonds of loyalty between several young officers who had led this daring enterprise. Ung Phon is a bold strong-willed man with tremendous drive. He felt the Party was heading nowhere and started to gather some disaffected members and other people, agitating for the creation of a new political party, in order to be prepared to inherit power from the dying communist parties. This kind of thing had occurred in Eastern Europe. Chea Sim could not see this internal threat without reacting. His point was that, in the middle of the delicate process of negotiations, the Party had to stick together. In ruling Party circles, Hun Sen was seen with suspicion. He was needed as the only politician with the ability to carry on the negotiations and relations with the foreigners' world. But his reformist views were dangerous for the people in power, because their political system was destabilized by the very process of negotiation and opening towards an unknown political future.

Chea Sim prevailed upon Hun Sen and had Ung Phon and a dozen others arrested. Ung Phon, as a high-ranking Party member and a Minister, was secluded in a house but the others were thrown in jail, and remained several months incommunicado. Many other high-ranking officials were known to have been approached by Ung Phon's group. They were quietly discarded or demoted. In Chea Sim's view, the manœuvre had its origin in Hun Sen's group of technicians, who could be curbed but not removed. The problem was reopened several months later when at the Party Congress in 1991 Hun Sen described the choice open to the Party: it must either agree to reform itself radically and fight elections with a fair chance of securing a large share of the resulting power, or stick to its old communist practice. If it took the latter course, he, Hun Sen, would split away, with his friends, to build a new party with a reformist platform.[2] By a massive majority it was decided to follow the first path but the antagonism between the factions remained. In the autumn of 1991, as a consequence of the Paris Agreements, Ung Phon and his followers were freed. Later, in February 1992, after he had again indicated his intention to launch a new "liberal" party, he was shot by three unknown gunmen. He had the incredible luck to survive and Hun Sen took him from the hospital into his own home as a measure of protection. Suspicions concentrated on the special police loyal to Chea Sim. Hun Sen was deeply shocked and acknowledged he was the ultimate target of this terrorist attack. So, it is hard to avoid the feeling that the Transportation Ministry had retained some kind of symbolic value in the internal struggle for power.

The following morning, Saturday 22nd, Khieu Samphân was supposed to come back from Bangkok after his first ill-fated attempt. We later learned, from Sihanouk himself, that in the night the prince had called Samphân in Bangkok and advised him not to come because of the "fever" in town. Probably feeling the recent bruises on his skull, Samphân had quickly concurred. Not knowing this, students had lined up again on the road from the airport. But the only visible demonstration was a handwritten inscription on one of the giant portraits of the prince recalling that Sihanouk had been waging war on his opponents since 1963 and that he was responsible for the subsequent massacres. Apparently, not everyone had forgotten.

In the meantime, workers had been demonstrating in front of the town hall, the former seat of the Catholic archbishop. Students at the nearby Faculty of Medicine had come and were talking to the workers. The police certainly wanted to avoid this kind of potentially explosive combination. A brutal intervention followed. One man, beaten on the head, was taken away to the Calmette hospital. He died soon afterwards. The rumour spread among the students that some of them had been abducted by the cops. They marched on the nearby police station, where in fact nobody was detained, and the police immediately fired in the air to disperse the crowd. A crazy day had started. Students gathered in several faculties, leaflets were produced requesting "respect for human rights", calling the UN into action, as if massive arrests had occurred. Some unknown characters toured the schools calling on schoolboys to take to the streets. In the afternoon, a demonstration took place in front of the National Assembly. A spokesman tried to calm down the crowd by saying that arrested persons had already been released but this was not enough. A house sold by a school director was burned down. At the end of the afternoon, a crowd surrounded two police stations near the New Market. Street kids were more numerous than students, most of whom had gone home. There was no organization, and no slogans, but stones started to fly at the entrenched police and they requested orders. Someone who listened to their radio exchanges later told me that the Ministry of Interior had replied: "Make do with what you have."

It was a blank order. They started to shoot into the air, rushing out of their dugout. The crowd backed way, but did not disperse. Night was falling and soldiers appeared to take over from the frightened police. They had AKs and machine-guns. These young soldiers shouted and the demonstrators shouted back, dancing in the street in defiance. Instead of firing into the air, the soldiers started to aim at the pavement or at the façades of buildings. Ricocheting bullets took their toll on the excited youngsters. A team of plainclothes police, with some very young kids, and equipped with truncheons and handguns arrived, tried to catch some demonstrators and then disappeared. At one point in the evening a mysterious person repeatedly threw small stones at the soldiers from the top of a long building. Enraged soldiers sprayed the building with long bursts of machine-gun fire. Later, the government explained that "bad elements" had fired on the troops from the roofs, a pure invention. One man, looking for his son, tried to come and talk to the soldiers. He was shot down in cold blood by a soldier. I watched it happen from 10 metres away. It looked like civil war, with soldiers firing like mad and the demonstrators chanting and throwing stones. At least eight people, possibly twelve, were thus killed during this long day. Then armoured cars arrived and a curfew was decreed.[3]

Watching the frenzy, sometimes lying low because of the hazardous sprays of bullets, I felt I could see in action the process by which the Khmer Rouge had reached their sinister fame. Take a young Khmer, probably a shy and slender teenager, and give him a gun and some authority. The first act of derision makes him immediately go berserk: he shoots to suppress any opposition. He has only one alternative, either to obtain total submission or pull the trigger in an act of suppression. But looking at the demonstrators, it was clear to my mind that if they had reached the police, they would have killed them on the spot, with stones or with their bare hands. No measure, no compromise. An open conflict has no other end than killing. One has to realize that in the expression "Khmer Rouge" — "Rouge" meaning the dogmatic Stalinist brand of communism — is only one half of the equation. There is also "Khmer" — meaning a way to resort immediately to maximum violence, not so much to **resolve** a conflict as to **suppress** its root cause. This aspect of the Khmer personality has been touched upon but not yet fully studied.[4]

Around mid-February 1992, Chea Sim invited for lunch the main civil servants of the Health Ministry. "I am sorry I have not been able to meet you earlier, but I have been very busy for the past ten years", he said.[5] He inquired why some people were absent and was told their wives were just having babies. He begged the audience not to be angry with the government. Only one demonstrator had been killed, he insisted, adding that no one had been detained. He said the event had been provoked by enemies. He also said that anyone talking about the sale of government properties would be put into prison. He promised each of his listeners 50 kg of rice, four bars of Soviet soap and possibly four metres of fabric if there was any left. The guests had their finger and toe prints registered, and had to sign a text condemning the demonstrators and supporting the Party.

Politics could be seen as another theatrical show. Typical of Phnom Penh rumours is the story I heard when I arrived: the urn in the Independence Monument had been opened in anticipation of Prince Sihanouk's return (I guess this means the anonymous remains of some Vietnamese soldier had been removed as a sign of transition into another period), and three black owls flew out. (Leaving aside the magical transformation of the corpse's ashes into these sinister birds, the main point is that they flew away and disappeared.) This story alludes, in a condensed way, to the end of a political era, but the most interesting aspect is the symbolic images in which the meaning is couched. Politics everywhere has to do with symbols and theatricals but Cambodia has its own brand of performance and language.

The return of Prince Sihanouk, as the first step in the implementation of the Paris Agreements also marked the return of Cambodia to the international scene. The country and its government, which had been installed by the Vietnamese 12 years earlier, had been boycotted by the international community. Although the

Government controlled more than 90 per cent of the territory, was stable and did run its internal affairs in a rather efficient way, the old Cold War system of exclusion had been imposed by an American fiat. The Indochina war was not finished. The majority of the US political establishment wanted revenge which could be obtained only by the demise of communist power in Hanoi and, as a consequence, in Vientiane and Phnom Penh. Among non-communist countries, only India had established ties with Cambodia.

The return of the prince was the symbolic end of this isolation. It was no mean victory for the Chea Sim-Hun Sen regime to be thus recognized as the (main) component of the new structure. The pressure to dissolve that government had been very strong and only its grip on Cambodian realities had enabled it to avoid disappearance, as had happened in Eastern Germany, Czechoslovakia or the Soviet Union. For a long time, Hun Sen had tried to convince Sihanouk that he should distance himself from the Khmer Rouge and strike a deal with those who had the real power inside the country. Several times, notwithstanding the very pro-Chinese sympathies of his wife Monique, the prince had been tempted to endorse this view, which he shared. Only strong Chinese pressures had prevented him, until after the Paris Agreements when the Chinese had to relent. The signing of the Agreements had been for them a partial whitewashing of the repression of the Tien An Men demonstrators.

So, at least, the prince came back with his hands free. But empty. Festivities were highly organized. Hundreds of thousands of people lined the roads, clapping their hands and waving small flags. Workers and pupils had come in organized squads. It looked as if they had been organized by himself. Observers could not detect any spontaneous bursts of enthusiasm, but rather a sympathetic curiosity. After all, most Cambodians knew nothing about him, except that he was the former king and he had been supporting Pol Pot for many years. The subtleties of all his serpentine moves were ignored. But somehow the crowd understood his return heralded a new era which could make peace real. And peace meant money, a better life. The people of Phnom Penh had been largely unaware of the war, except at the time when many workers were sent, in 1986–8, to build a quite useless " Bamboo Wall" at the border, suffering great hardships. The weight of the war is felt by peasants in several provinces. But in town it remains an abstraction.

Sihanouk was housed in the Royal Palace compound. The French Government, always eager to remind Cambodians it had been the generous overlord, had paid for a rapid rehabilitation of several pavilions. The painters were putting the last coat on the outer wall.

The prince was not happy at all. He dislikes the Palace, where he was under his mother's sway during his youth and was detained as a virtual prisoner between October 1975 and January 1979 by the Khmer Rouge. There he had suffered from anguish as he had never done before. Several times he was about to run out of food, and this drove him crazy. He has spoken a lot about the food situation in his memoirs and in many interviews. And he wanted to go back to Chamcar Mon, the place he had built for himself when he ruled the country. But Chamcar Mon was used by the Government. And Sihanouk did not dare to go beyond saying he wanted to live elsewhere. The Palace, with its heavy symbolism, mixing Hindu and Chinese forms of organizing sacred space, belongs to the age of kings.[6] And Sihanouk did not like being king because that meant having no real power. The behind-the-scenes influence is not for him. He wants to be centre stage, performing the lead role in the play. This leaves room for backstage influence, always more important than frontstage power itself. That he left to women, his mother when he was ruling the country, and now his wife whose secret wish is to become a queen and act as a Chinese empress, from behind the yellow curtain.

Although many rumours concern her real origins, the official version is that Monique Izzi was born in Saigon to a Khmer woman, Mrs Pom Peang, and an Italian expatriate who did not want to recognize her and her sister Nanette. In Phnom Penh, she lived in the household of Sirik Matak who introduced her when she was still quite young to his cousin Sihanouk. She was then a mistress among many others. But she somehow succeeded in beating the competition and the prince converted to official monogamy although there was never any public wedding. A king could only marry a princess and one could only be a princess by birth. Although she was called *moneang* in Khmer, a traditional way of designating third-rank concubines, the prince imposed on the Western press the use of the word "princess" (and for himself the word "prince" whereas in Khmer his title is "former king" or Samdech, which means "lord"). The interesting thing is that the prince wrote a letter to all ambassadors in April 1992 saying that Monique had been made a princess. The affirmation is so ludicrous, since it is quite impossible to change someone's birth in the Cambodian social order, that the "decision" was not made public to the Khmers.

The prince's letter came weeks before a trial was held in May 1992 in Paris. A journalist had written in a December 1991 issue of a women's magazine, *Elle*, that Monique was not a princess, that she was not even married to Sihanouk and that she had used her power to protect greedy crooks.[7] She sued the magazine for damage. Although these facts are quite familiar to any Khmer or anyone having known Phnom Penh before the war, the use of a court in far-away Paris was meant to intimidate the press and keep it from investigating this period. The "princess" has great ambitions, she is quite sure she will outlive the prince, as she is much younger, and she wants a new political virginity and an image of legitimacy. The prince's letter thus gave her a status she could not have proven in a French court if it had bothered to inquire into her background. This is the resumption of court politics, exactly as it had stopped in 1970. The intrigues, the struggles among the courtiers and the royal children seem to be taken out of a sixteenth-century Florentine princely court and provide readers with all the elements of a best-selling novel, or a Shakespearian play, including cloak and dagger assassinations, bed-chamber intrigues, betrayals, corruption, jewels, infidelity, suitcases filled with cash, and so on. The only trouble is that these stories are real; they are not unrelated to the causes of the dismal tragedy that befell the Cambodian people. And to see them resume again, weeks after the return of the prince is not funny at all. This revival triggered the departure of a longtime close adviser to the prince, Julio Jeldres, a Chilean-born admirer of Sihanouk, who left, completely disgusted, within three months.

Soon after his arrival, the prince gave several press conferences. He affirmed again that he wanted only a figurehead role as President of Cambodia, like Albert Lebrun, the Third Republic French President, or Vincent Auriol (Fourth Republic), both powerless figures. He was also the only Khmer politician to say: "I recognized in front of the whole world that the Cambodian people and myself would have died, without the Vietnamese intervention" (Royal Palace, 16 November 1991). When he tried to explain to his compatriots why he had had to stay out of the country so long and support the Khmer Rouge, he made this quite frank admission: "Only the Chinese were ready to support me at the time. They give me $ 300,000 a year and I have to live on that." The implication was that this money was barely sufficient for survival. He did not mention that, from time to time, his friends Kim Il Sung or Mitterrand gave him a suitcase full of dollars. Even back in Cambodia, he is living on Chinese money and he made it clear there was a political price, although he did not elaborate on this point. In the Palace he was to be surrounded by freshly imported Chinese maids and cooks, and North Korean bodyguards. He has, as always, foreign advisers (a Thai general, a French diplomat) and very few Khmers around him.

Some weeks after his return, he sent three letters to the other factions requesting them to recognize that **he** was and always had been Head of State. Politely, the Khmer Rouge and the Phnom Penh regime immediately complied. The Son Sann people abstained as if the mail had not reached them. Then Sihanouk gave another press conference, endlessly insisting he had come back only to clear his name of all the insults and base calumnies which had been spread by the small evil clique of those who toppled him in March 1970. He wanted to settle this 21-year-old score once and for all. He had no strong enough words to condemn the Lon Nols and Sirik Mataks, both dead for many years, who had dared to trample on his majesty. Few Khmers could remember who Lon Nol and Sirik Matak were. But for the prince, it was as if the crime had been committed the day before. This recognition of his having been Head of State all along was a denial of the very existence of his long-forgotten enemies. The acceptance by all factions, with the notable silence of Lon Nol's political inheritors, was purely political. The Paris Agreements had no provision for this question. The nomination of a Head of State, it was thought at the time, would depend on the next constitution.

Of course the press corps bought the story. But it was historically false. At the press conference, I reminded the prince that we have in our archives the photocopy of the letter he wrote in April 1976 resigning from his formal position as Head of State under Pol Pot. He has elaborated on this in his memoirs.[8] Moreover, when he was leading the Coalition, he gave himself several different titles, resigning many times, and at times calling himself "Norodom Sihanouk of Cambodia", which did not mean much. He replied evasively. He did not mind rewriting history. He only wanted to rejoice over his old enemies' corpses, telling them he was alive and kicking, Head of State again while they, stinking rebels, had lost and were dead, desolate wandering souls. It was a pathetic cry of victory and my awkward questions were best pushed aside. The following day, we had another press conference where Hor Namhong, the Phnom Penh Foreign Minister had the embarrassing task of explaining that while recognizing Sihanouk as Head of State of the whole of Cambodia, his regime was maintaining Heng Samrin as Head of the State of Cambodia — the Phnom Penh regime. Legal subtleties were flying low that afternoon and nobody could clearly make out what it all meant. Some months later, as Heng Samrin was officially declared in poor health, Chea Sim had a law passed providing for the president of the National Assembly (himself) to take over the function of President if the need should arise. Khmers make good warriors but poor lawyers.

Then, bit by bit, the United Nations arrived. First, the forward team, called UNAMIC, occupied the old Russian Cultural Centre. When called into action, they insisted their role was only to observe. They were in town only to prepare the way for the much more subtantial UNTAC. In New York, there were delays. I visited some of the people involved in New York, in early 1992, and was amazed by the enormous amount of bureaucratic machinery involved. The UN machine is made up of so many committees, subcommittees, subsubcommittees and meetings, where people from every corner of the world have a say, each one producing a steady flow of papers, that nobody can drive it. It is worse than Moscow and Washington put together. With few individual exceptions, the people I met had a purely abstract view of Cambodia and were totally immersed in their bureaucratic procedures, their experience of petty office struggles and diplomatic red tape. You got the feeling the UN was taking Cambodia as an experiment in what world politics should be after the fall of the Soviet Empire. The Gulf War on the one hand, covered but not led by the UN, the big stick firmly grasped by the US as an international mercenary force, and, on the other hand, the UN itself as the only organizer of peace and settlement of the most complicated problems inherited from the Cold War. Cambodia was one of the most interesting left-overs from that period, with Ethiopia, Angola, Guatemala. Afghanistan was abandoned to its own vultures because the situation there was intractable.

The Paris Agreements on Cambodia had been written by people who wanted to forget about this poor wretched country and recover it in order to put it back into the Western fold. The Chinese had a central role. All the Cambodian factions were in fact controlled by big powers. No decisive victory had been won on the battlefield, so the situation was deemed ripe for a settlement. Of course, out of deference to the Chinese, the Khmer Rouge had to be inserted into the political framework. This was a bit touchy, morally speaking, but *Realpolitik* was the order of the day. The Agreements were signed after a long battle in which the Phnom Penh regime, which really controlled the country, made many concessions but finally won the main point, that it would not be dismantled and the country left to anarchy.

I watched the signing from a video room next to where the diplomats were scratching the documents. Sihanouk was happy and his wife Monique put her hand on his shoulder when he signed, as if giving him approval after much resistance. Khieu Samphân was grim. Mitterrand had come ro reap the benefit of an action which had cost him nothing. Dumas, the French Foreign Minister, had his speech typed in enormous letters, maybe because he cannot read. Baker was as unsmiling as ever. Shevarnadze had just been replaced by an unknown Russian. Asian diplomats looked very much like Asian diplomats. Perez de Cuellar smiled at the idea of retirement. I had mixed feelings.

The Agreements had some good points. The international community was coming back to Cambodia and some money would be spent to rehabilitate the country, a very great need indeed and a just compensation for what this very international community had done to the country by isolating it so cruelly after the dark age of Pol Pot. The level of warfare would diminish. Just before the signing of the Agreements, there had been a small conference in Paris on the "return to democracy" in Cambodia, where some politicians mixed with scholars and journalists. I was disgusted by this attempt to provide a clean conscience and the cynical use of the human rights theme, no account being taken of the reality. From the floor, I objected and said there was only one basic problem in Cambodia, a condition for any progress toward a political settlement, and that was the military crushing of the Khmer Rouge. Nothing serious could be done if that condition was not fulfilled. The pedlars of democracy protested but everyone had felt my point was crucial.

Now watching the signing of the Agreements, it was clear that this condition was not only **not** fulfilled but its implementation was entirely discarded. The Khmer Rouge were now signatories and could come back to Phnom Penh and take part in deliberations in the so-called Supreme National Council where Khmer independence and sovereignty were to be provisionaly embedded, until elections generated a new Constitution and a new government. Morally, it was outrageous. In my view morality was not a mere abstract character painted on a scheme. If it was not incorporated into these Agreements, they would not be workable. You were not dealing with communist bureaucrats convinced in their inner thought that they had to reform their system because they were lacking the means to modernize it, but with isolated forest guerrillas, convinced that, whatever their past horrors, they had always been perfect. What the Vietnamese army had not done, destroying the military base of the Khmer Rouge, the Paris Agreements could do even less. The idea that Pol Pot would agree to do it by himself was just a sweet dream that could occur only in some diplomatic heads. Experience had taught him that he could only win by being more extreme than any other contender. The logic of his position is to eliminate all other forces one by one.

But the process which was initiated could have some partial results in reintegrating some kind of reformed government into the international community. It is clear that nobody else is going to fight the Khmer Rouge. Not the UN. Only Khmers can do it. If not now, then later. The only acceptable future for the Khmer Rouge is what happened to the Malayan Communist Party: a slow depletion caused by age in the most remote parts of the forest, an extinction by oblivion. The Paris Agreements were about as realistic as if, after World War II, the Allies had imposed on Germany a coalition between the Nazis, the Communists, the Social Democrats and the Christian Democrats. A political monster. Not only can it not survive, it cannot even come to life.

Watching Cambodia then meant watching the return of Sihanouk, the arrival of the UN, the comeback of the Khmer Rouge and the evolution of the Phnom Penh regime under these various pressures. After so many years of paralysis, everything started to move again. The failure of the UN was quite predictable. As some of their staff explained time and time again, the UN had only one weapon: to withdraw, if one party was seen to be deliberately sabotaging the Agreements, and denounce it as the culprit. Not the kind of threat to worry Pol Pot too much. The UN, it was said, was not coming to wage war, its role was only to help people who had already reached an agreement among themselves. If they did not respect the agreement, the UN would simply desist from playing its role. That is the theory. In reality, being the instrument of several member states, the UN behaves just like any other state and eventually alters its course. We can see this in Angola where, after years of negotiations, an agreement was reached. But when he lost the elections, Savimbi started the war again. Instead of leaving, the UN sticks to the place, just to be there, without any chance of achieving anything, as they have in Korea, in Cyprus, in Lebanon, and so on. Its uselessness is even more tragic in Yugoslavia or Somalia...

I fully agree that the UN should not be another fighting force, adding one more agressive army to a complicated military chessboard. But the "weapon" of the UN seemed to be a one-shot gun. As long as you do not shoot, it is a supposed deterrent. But you cannot use it, because if you do, your are left naked. The Paris Agreements failed in mid-June 1992 when, after some procrastination, UNTAC decreed the beginning of Phase 2, that is regroupment, cantonment and disarmament of the military forces of the four factions (two of them being almost non-existent in the field). The Khmer Rouge did not co-operate and started to produce a steady stream of worn-out arguments which they had already used in the preliminaries of the Paris Agreements and which led nowhere. They repeatedly alleged that the Vietnamese army was still in Cambodia and that "two million" Vietnamese settlers were in Cambodia on Hanoi's order to "Vietnamize" the country. The Khmer Rouge's point of view is exactly the same as the Serbian policy known as "ethnic cleansing": the use of every means, including massacre, to expel or destroy people with a different ethnic background. This has been said in a very explicit manner and repeated by Khieu Samphân in 1992. It seems that the Son Sannists and to some extent the Sihanoukists fully concur. The UN so far has rejected this view which is apparently repugnant to most of world opinion.

But one has to keep in mind that it is very probably the view of the majority of Khmers.

Neither this Vietnamese phantom army nor the two million disguised soldiers could be found, of course. But a flow of poor Vietnamese looking for jobs was quite visible. This might create a real social problem. Whereas the Paris Agreements very clearly indicate that any long-lasting problem should be dealt with by the elected government, the Khmer Rouge argue that it should be done in advance by the UN under a Supreme National Council (SNC) acting as a real government. One just wonders why UNTAC did not, as the Khmer Rouge insist, declare a verification of the departure of foreign troops, as the Agreements provide. The UN observers know pefectly well that the Vietnamese army is gone. This procrastination probably originates in political differences inside the circle of the Permanent Five.

But the UN, although it could see by the end of June 1992 that the process was blocked, did not, as I fully expected, fire its one-shot gun. How could the UN, after it had claimed it was launching the biggest UN operation ever, requesting US $ 1.7 billion to cover its cost, bluntly say, "OK, this is a failure, we were badly mistaken, let's go home and wait for another time"? Instead, we had a series of useless talks between the Thais, the Japanese (who invested a lot in this "Operation Return"), the French, the Indonesians and Pol Pot's emissaries. Pol Pot himself was visited by a Chinese vice-minister. To no avail, of course. What diplomats cannot fully grasp is the fact that the Khmer Rouge leaders are obsessed with Geneva.

Geneva, in 1954, was the settlement which ended the first Indochina war. A lot has been said about this historical arrangement and some very good books are available.[9] But, to throw some light on the present situation, one has to see it from the point of view of people like Pol Pot. He had found his way into the Viet Minh held areas in August 1953. He was then groomed by the Vietnamese local communists to become not a fighter, but a political leader. When the Geneva Agreement was signed one year later, the whole military structure of the guerrillas was to be dismantled. Many cadres were evacuated to North Vietnam. Pol Pot returned to Phnom Penh in order to prepare for the 1955 elections.[10] When these occurred, massive manipulation and fraud deprived the communists of even a small representation, and Sihanouk's police chased them and their suspected allies. In a matter of four or five years, the whole left wing movement was almost totally annihilated by a combination of all sorts of legal and illegal means. Pol Pot and Ieng Sary have repeated to cadres in seminars and to visitors that they do not want to see this kind of thing happen again. They want to "protect their rank and file". The Khmer Rouge machine is entirely militaristic. Although some years ago Pol Pot appealed to his cadres to devote their energy to political efforts, they are caught in a dilemma. If they turn to political propaganda in the villages, they have to conceal their weapons, act as propagandists and relinquish their status as military commanders, leaving their troops exposed. This they cannot do. Junior and female cadres may try to assume this newly defined role but they lack the charisma and the experience. Besides, they do not have access to the core of the village network, their safety being linked to the proximity of the troops. The survival of Pol Pot and the Khmer Communist Party (dissolved only in name) is entirely dependent on the continuation of the military structure. It would be unthinkable for them to give anybody free access to their zones. "Avoid a new Geneva" is the main objective.

Then why, candid Western observers would ask, did the Khmer Rouge sign Agreements making disarmament an obligation if they were not willing to disarm? Because war is always a dual effort, with a military side and a political one. The military side is decisive only when political conditions are ripe. Sun Tze wrote about this 2,000 years ago. The Paris Agreements give the Pol Pot communists the enormous advantage of being able to come back on to the open political scene, to have their people in Phnom Penh and to open new channels in international politics. Pol Pot was never under any illusion about the elections. He never thought he would get a major share of the vote. But somehow the Agreements guarantee he will be part of the process and each concession he makes to maintain the process has its price in more access and more control through the mechanism of the Agreements. The Khmer Rouge are now claiming that almost any activity, from money printing to logging, and so on, should be controlled by the SNC, considered to be a government, in which they have a statutory role and a veto. With the ability to block any State activities, they should be able to undermine State control over the economy and the rural population, weaken and freeze the Phnom Penh armed forces, obtain from the elections a weak parliament and a powerless government, remove Cambodia from the international agenda and create a situation of powerlessness where their military force, having maintained its discipline in isolation, could draw from its huge stockpiles of weapons and start to reconquer village after village in the heart of the country, once again isolating the towns and their corrupt political élite, to finally come back and vindicate their thirty, forty, or fifty years of struggle. The calculation is sound: buying time until a better opportunity arises which could allow them to emerge from of the forest and retake power. The Vietnamese are gone and are not in a position to come back. The road is free on one condition: do not allow anyone, be it UNTAC or anybody else, to destroy the military machine which is the essence of the Party and the only guarantee for the future.

The mandate of the UN is limited, its ability to interfere in military matters is nil, its political will is weak and divided between many players with conflicting interests. The best example is the question of the mines. It was not treated in the Paris documents. Only after UNAMIC had settled in Cambodia was it realized that mines were an enormous problem, for many reasons. Most of the arable land that could be given to the refugees was not occupied because it was mined. Transportation of the refugees was in itself a problem because many roads were mined. The military concentrations of each faction were protected with mines which made access, for the purpose of regroupment and cantonment, difficult if they were co-operative and an impossibility if they were not, access being possible only by air in the best of cases. It soon appeared that Khmer Rouge offensives, mostly in the Kompong Thom region, included the mining of access roads. UNTAC troops were paralysed and could not accomplish their interposition role. Some hasty thinking was done in New York in February and a demining component was added to the UN action. But as it is a dangerous job, political reasons prevailed and a general agreement was reached according to which the UN **would not demine**, whatever obstacles mines presented to its projects. Blue helmets are not supposed to die and some governments sent troops on the implicit condition that they would not suffer losses. Instead, some UN contingents would open de-mining schools and train Cambodians to do the job. Wages would be local, meaning quite low, in the region of $ 50 a month. Some private corporations would be hired, like the British company Helo Trust, to de mine specific areas requested for civilian use. As for the military situation, UNTAC would simply expect those Cambodian troops which had laid the mines to remove them. No reliable maps could be made available. The most ridiculous idea was incorporated in a "Mine Awareness Programme" through which farmers would receive little flags in order to gently mark minefields. But who would have the guts to laugh?[11]

The refusal by UNTAC to demine by itself is impairing its ability to move in a decisive way. In press conferences, I have repeatedly asked the UN Secretary General, Mr Boutros-Ghali, and the UNTAC heads, Mr Akashi and General Sanderson, why the UN was not taking the responsibility for demining, as it was obvious no Cambodian faction could do it, or was even willing to do it. Each time I received replies which gave monetary figures and referred to the training of deminers, which looked very nice on paper. But in my view, they were entirely irrelevant. We saw on television a French sapper battalion which had demined the beaches of Kuwait City, so that the fat spouses of the Emirs could safely sit on the sand, and the same sappers, present in Cambodia, do not even have the money to organize a training centre, not to speak of acting themselves. I believe this is scandalous, as several thousands of children get blown up every year, and will continue to get blown up for a long time to come. In fact, since the impact of UNTAC on demining will, at best, be restricted to some limited areas, the problem will remain with the farmers. Dire economic necessities will push them to try to recover mined fields and increase the area available for the gathering of wood, for selling or for their own use. A simple rational calculation will result in the younger children being sent into the most dangerous areas. Their loss would impair the household's economic potential less than the loss of adults. This may seem more cruel but it is quite logical and the guilt lies with the international community which alone has the means to solve the problem, at least partially. In Vietnam, no aid was given and new victims of mines and unexploded ordnance are still being added every year, whereas in Kuwait mine clearing has been done swiftly with minimal losses. For the UN, it is a self-defeating lapse in the thinking of the peace process.

The best that the UN Security Council can think of, as the Secretary General is urging, is to go on with the electoral process and decree an economic blockade of the Khmer Rouge border zones. We have seen that elections have a secondary role in the Khmer Rouge strategy. As for economic asphyxiation, for a long time they had to face the possibility of a cut in Chinese supplies. They knew the Chinese are capable of betraying their best allies if the situation requires it: they did it with the Thai and Burmese communists. Pol Pot is not stupid. The alternative was to spread their economic interests in Thailand itself, to mix with the Sino-Thai commercial and banking networks, to join in economic ventures with the Thai military (gemstones, logging, banking, weapons traffic) and make them financially dependent on an alliance with the Khmer Rouge, since they get a big cut in all these illegal businesses. *The Economist* said on 5 October 1991, that the income of the Khmer Rouge could be estimated at US $ 100 million per year. When the military were in power in Bangkok, the Khmer Rouge could expand their share of Thai economic interests and General Suchinda clearly supported them. When the Thai big brass lost its nerve and machine-gunned citizens in the streets of Bangkok, in May 1992, they had to relax their grip on political power somewhat. But this made them even more dependent on the Khmer Rouge's ability to give them access to hidden resources. And they clearly said an embargo was not feasible. The Secretary General of the Thai National Security Council, Gen. Charan Kullanijaya has been quoted as saying that Thailand should ask for a lump sum of money to cover the cost of sealing the border, in the event of sanctions, adding that the best way to persuade the Khmer Rouge to join the peace process was to provide them with basic necessities and structural aid (*The Nation*, 10 November 1992).

It would require enormous pressure, such as that exerted on Iraq, to see the Thais really cut their links with the Khmer Rouge zones. We may anticipate all the evasive tactics from a Bangkok government which has made opportunism a golden rule. The Thai army will not relinquish the border as it has been an enormous source of enrichment for the generals, a subject which is even more taboo in the Thai press than the royal family itself. Or we may envisage a change, in the distant future, in the military balance that would swing back to Phnom Penh the control of the rich mining area of Pailin, and the big northern forests. This cannot be done under the UN now, but it points the way to a new period of warfare to wrest control from Pol Pot and stop the export and the huge waste of the natural resources of the country. Whichever way you look at it, the military solution has to come first. Politics is meaningless in a state of terror or threat.

As I write, only an embargo on the supply of petroleum products and logging in the Khmer Rouge zones has been decreed by the Security Council. It is a first step, tentative, ineffectual, but going in the right direction. The key to the Cambodian tangle is, for the moment, in the middle of the UN Security Council. Recent development shows the UN has become an unpredictable entity. Already the Gulf War has displayed some alarming distortions of the world body's legal authority. But the US intervention in Somalia effectively destroyed the UN Charter as the General Assembly backed up one unnamed member State (the US) intervening of its own will in another sovereign member State's affairs (Somalia). Resolution 794 explicitly says the intervention should facilitate a "political settlement". This has been generally overlooked by the press. But all political analysts agreed this was a break with usual practice. The UN has also unilaterally changed the border between Iraq and Kuwait, including in the Emirate's territory the harbour and naval base of Umm Kasr, Iraq's only maritime outlet. This shows that sovereignty, the respect of which is the basis of the Charter, has been practically abolished.

As far as Cambodia is concerned, it means there is no longer a legal basis or guidelines for regulating UN intervention. Everything is possible, including big power direct intervention, such as that which looms over former Yugoslavia. With the fall of the Berlin Wall, we entered a very chaotic world. When to this is added the chaos Cambodians have been able to spread by themselves in their own country, the results might lead to new nightmares.

Appendices

Appendix 1

The Moral Reaction

[During 1976, many stories came from refugees who managed to escape from Pol Pot's Cambodia to the border and then to Thailand. Missionaries, reporters from Bangkok, spooks and others, started to visit the border area and reported refugee stories. Watching Cambodia, at the time, was not an easy task, while we had to disentangle a lot of stories, many of which came from incompetent or highly biased sources (government agents, CIA-sponsored journalists, and so on). Still, the conviction that something horrible was taking place inside Cambodia, where almost nobody could go from outside, grew slowly as I tried to check and find the kernel of truth in the stories allegedly reported to journalists (none of whom could speak Khmer). The opportunity to speak out was given, I thought, with the publication of two books I reviewed for the French daily *Libération*. This triggered a long struggle among the editorial staff and strong opposition from the "specialist" in charge, Sabatier, but finally the article was published on March 7 1977.

As my attempts to analyse some aspects of the Pol Pot era have led some dogmatic minds to label me as "pro-Pol Pot", I wish to put the record straight. This was the first piece I wrote dealing with Cambodia after the Khmer Rouge had taken over in Phnom Penh.]

Cambodia, the Organization and Barbarity

Is there a Cambodian revolution? Yes, one social organization is replacing another.

Do we have to judge this revolution? Of course, like any other political phenomenon.

What do we know about it? We know that the country is in the hands of a revolutionary anonymous organization (*Angkar*), that the economy seems to be based on total collectivization, that more than half of the population has been chased from the cities and is treated like a slavish mass, exploited without limits, hungry and terrorized, that the Organization is systematically destroying all those who, one way or the other, had anything to do with the former regime.

After Hitler, Stalin, Nixon and Suharto

Are we able to judge this regime? Certainly, even from far away, even without knowing the country very well, even if all the testimonies are not equally valid. The authorities have not allowed anyone to come and see what is happening. Without even referring to humanistic views, no revolutionary morality known to this day could approve of this kind of blind massacre where, guilty or not, victims fall in the tens, or possibly hundreds, of thousands. Doubts are unfortunately not possible. After Hitler, Stalin, Suharto, Nixon, the Revolutionary Organization of Cambodia is in the process of reaching one of the best "scores" of our modern barbarity.

The most simple solidarity should compel us to stand with the victims of this bizarre forest bureaucracy, even if we come across strange bedfellows. The right wing is crying over Cambodia, which it viewed with dryer eyes when this country was agonizing under the 500,000 tons of bombs dropped by American warplanes. Good souls who used to wander in Phnom Penh when it was ruled by a weak-minded paranoid called Lon Nol wake up now to explain to us a revolution which they ignored at the time and which they saw only from very far away. From the bunch of recent books, one can take two: François Debré, *Cambodge, la Révolution de la forêt*, Flammarion, 261 pp., and François Ponchaud, *Cambodge, annnée zéro*, Julliard, 250 pp., because they contain documents, testimonies and analyses which are not without interest. Debré, for instance, has the story of an old guerrilla who fought along with the Viet Minh and documents about the last attempt of Sihanouk to come back to Phnom Penh [in April 1975] through an arrangement between the French, the Chinese and the Americans[1] while Ponchaud has interesting analyses of the new vocabulary used by the Cambodian authorities. It seems Ponchaud, as a missionary, knows the Khmer language well. These two books, in spite of many factual errors (for instance, Debré's confusion between Seoul and Pyong Yang, p. 252), are worth reading because there is something to be learned from them. But there is one important drawback: neither of the authors understands much about politics, and particularly about the politics of Indochinese revolutionaries. Condemning a policy should not mean sparing the effort to understand it. This is perhaps the most compelling task.

The Laziness of Fatalistic Thinking

"The Cambodian revolution was ineluctable", writes Debré (p. 36) and Ponchaud seems to share the idea. It is one of these serious mistakes generated by the laziness of fatalistic thinking. Reality is entirely different. Until the overthrow of Sihanouk in 1970, the Cambodian revolutionary activists' influence on the Khmer society was practically nil. Their number ran into the hundreds only, most of them hidden in the forests, like the usual outlaws who had always haunted the fringes of the rice-growing areas.

Villagers were poor and victims of the usurers and agents of the central power. But it was tradition: under pressure, the individual could just go away and live somewhere else, because land used to be available. In spite of some peasant rebellions, which were not asking for social innovation, there was no sign of a real social crisis. It was in the towns that political power was confronted by the business class. This showed very clearly in March 1970 when Sihanouk [in Peking] called an insurrection against the newly instituted republic; the peasants massively answered the call. They did not escape to the *maquis,* they became the *maquis* itself because they remained inside the [traditional] legitimacy. The towns were the place where a bourgeois revolution was taking place. It was also the time when the Cambodian communist cadres sprang out of hiding and, protected by the Vietnamese NLF troops, started to organize resistance [in the countryside].

Radicalism and *Chouannerie*

Until then, even when they were hunted down, the communists suported Sihanouk, although they thought his regime was "feudal" and corrupt, because his neutralism was providing a huge tactical advantage for the struggle in Vietnam, where the decisive confrontation with imperialism was taking place. If the communists, after 1970, persisted in putting the Sihanouk label on their propaganda, if they stopped doing so around 1973–4 because their feared a peace compromise, if they evacuated the cities immediately after their military victory, it was precisely because Sihanouk and all his conservative weight still had a very powerful impact in Phnom Penh and in the countryside. Neither the peasants nor the suburban poor felt by themselves the need to make a revolutionary move. The *maquis*, in 1972, with its Buddhist monks and its peasant cadres, looked rather like a *chouannerie*.[2]

Radical views belong only to a handful of ideologists, probably born in the countryside but with a smear of education acquired in the pagoda or State village schools. Their power comes from the control they have on the military machine; they make themselves acceptable by an extreme nationalism which certainly meets a deep popular aspiration. Nevertheless, it is obvious the regime is politically very weak: this weakness explains the use of the concentration camps method. Contradictory to what it claims, this revolution is led from above.

Moving Backward to the Time Before Classes

When the Swedish ambassador Kaj Bjork, one of the very few Western visitors allowed into the new Kampuchea, says that "the Khmer revolution is much more radical than the Chinese and the Russian ones", his implicit thinking needs to be turned upside down. In Russia and China, class struggles brought about revolutions, but these struggles have been going on under different forms. If in Cambodia there is no longer a class struggle, it is because the old ruling class is physically annihilated. It is thus a way to come "radically" back to the situation which existed before the emergence of classes. The authorities say that the country is led by "the workers, the poor peasants, the lower strata middle peasants and the other layers of country and town workers who constitute more than 95 per cent of the whole Kampuchean nation". Is this not a picture of a *radically disappeared past*?

The Eyes of the Pineapple

Ponchaud, Debré, and many others believe, in their naive vision of historical progress, that Cambodia is a place where a modern revolution is happening, a "Marxist" one, bent on creating the nightmare of the New Man. They speculate heavily on the personality of the leaders and the splits between them.[3] Debré believes that the division of tasks among the militants proves the existence of these splits. By isolating the Cambodian problem from its Indochinese context, they both condemn themselves to a kind of new kremlinology which in the end will mire in the fertile rice fields of their imagination.

If we had to qualify these leaders politically, it would probably be best to refer to good old Stalinism. Schooled by the French Communist Party in the 1950s or by the Vietnamese who did not always resist the Stalinist temptation, these Cambodian leaders use old recipes: absolute discipline, the pervasive power of the organization, surrounded by an imposed cult. As a former revolutionary says [in an unwitting tribute to George Orwell]: "The *Angkar* has got eyes like a pineapple and it sees everything" (Ponchaud, p. 131).

One may ask who is responsible for this bloody mess: the revolutionary leaders who want to change history by force? The Vietnamese communists who know and keep quiet? The former leaders of the Lon Nol regime whose stupid greed and sordid selfishness have thrown the country into this atrocious chaos? They all share a part of the burden. But the main people responsible, those who, against the advice of their diplomats and their intelligence services, launched this country into a chilling war, for some mean electoral profits, Mr Nixon and Mr Kissinger, can rove around today, free and honoured, their hanging for war crimes being most improbable. Talking about the American intervention in Cambodia, Mr Kissinger quietly said: "I may lack imagination, but I do not see where the moral problem is."

Appendix 2

Sex on a Tiger Skin

Being a review of *The Quality of Mercy: Cambodia, Holocaust and Modern Conscience*, by William Shawcross, published by André Deutsch, in London, 1984, 464 pp. Paper edition by Fontana, 1985, with a supplementary chapter dealing with Ethiopia.

The subtitle of this book is more revealing than the title. It stresses the ethical aim: an understanding of Cambodia, an evocation of the Holocaust and the evaluation of contemporary reactions to man-made disasters. Drawing parallels between the Cambodian and Nazi tragedies was commonplace, in both the Western and Soviet presses during 1979 and 1980. The Pol Pot-Ieng Sary trial in Phnom Penh in August 1979 was modelled on Nuremberg. The Tuol Sleng Museum, with its horrors of Pol Pot's repression, is a conscious attempt to emulate the Polish displays in the museum at Auschwitz. But for William Shawcross there are also family reasons why he indulges in historical analogies: he happens to be the son of Sir Heartley (now Lord) Shawcross, the chief British prosecutor at Nuremberg. The son quite openly equates his father's experience there with his own in Cambodia. Both of them, of course, saw nothing. They only made inquiries after the events, but both claimed to speak with historical authencity, something belied by a reading of Sir Heartley's speeches at Nuremberg. The trials there were highly political, the final episodes of the propaganda of war,[1] and they were at the centre of political calculations designed to lay the cornerstone for the new post-war order in Europe. Historians and judges are two separate species, and are better kept apart. As for the mainstream journalists, their task is to protect and expand the ideological implications of the established political order. Seen in this way, the achievements of Shawcross father and son are indeed very similar, and quite remarkable.

218

As was the case with his earlier *Sideshow*, this book is not *on* Cambodia, but about issues *around* Cambodia, or more precisely on Western policies *vis-à-vis* Cambodia. William Shawcross has undertaken to describe and assess the Western humanitarian response to the Cambodian Emergency which aroused world opinion in late 1979. He concentrates mainly on the UN system, with its host of specialized agencies, and curiously omits most of the voluntary agencies which have been swarming around the Thai–Cambodian border. The story is actually rather dull. Seen from this bureaucratic point of view, it is a predictable tale of organizational clumsiness, individual performances, political wariness and governmental pressures. It was, at the time, the biggest relief operation ever mounted (Ethiopia is now bigger), and the book cannot tell us how all this money (which now stands at around $1.5 billion) was really spent. It would have been a very interesting book if it could, but Shawcross did not push very hard to find out. There is no systematic evaluation of the waste, or of the incredible amount of money the Thai military were allowed to pocket (certainly hundreds of millions of dollars). Nor is there any analysis of the political activities and ambitions of the powers involved. The changes in Thai government policy regarding the Khmers refugees are mentioned but not explained. Chinese political considerations are only alluded to, while those of Europe and Japan are hardly mentioned. A description of American policy is limited to the personal reactions of Morton Abramowitz, the then US ambassador. We are told that he was a Jew and a liberal and that he did all he could to help the refugees. At times, it seems almost to be a fairy tale, with the complete absence of the CIA, and no American military roving along the border.

As for political judgements, it is better, the book makes out, if we stand in the middle of the road. Everyone was a bit right and a bit wrong. Even the Vietnamese were to blame for the state of Cambodia in early 1979. Political judgements such as these are made to comfort both the author and the reader, for there is no attempt to explain how and why the situation had become so disastrous by 1979. Pol Pot was bad, of course, but then so were the Vietnamese, by their very nature. So there is no need to explain precisely what all these bad guys did, although quite a number of studies, well known to Shawcross, have been devoted to these questions. But then, Cambodian politics is not a subject which creates best-sellers.

"There were two sources of information: the border and Phnom Penh", says the author (p. 200). He mentions "a handful of relief officials" in Phnom Penh, disregarding journalists who went there and, of course, local authorities who could not be considered as "sources". "Far more information was coming from the border. And much of that news came through the US government." Despite this candid admission he is still struggling with the fact that his reporting was so wrong, particularly at the end of 1979, when he described Cambodia as threatened by famine, when in fact it was not. This was the time for the main rice harvest, and, little as it was, there was something to eat, at least for some of the time. But the US government and the press were bent on demonstrating the unwillingness of the Vietnamese to accept Western relief food. And Shawcross, who played his part in this campaign, still wonders why he got it so wrong. Like everyone else in the press, he judged the situation inside the country from the mass of starving Khmers crossing into Thailand, prodded by the Khmer Rouge who had left them dying near the border for six months until they had the green light from the Americans to cross over, regroup and replenish the Khmer Rouge militia. All this was clear enough from Paris or London, but Shawcross could not see it.

Cambodia was a myth in the making, and Shawcross and his like were not perceptive enough to see the parts they played as myth-makers.[2] One Oxfam official told him that Cambodia "had everything. Temples, starving brown babies and an Asian Hitler figure — it was like sex on a tiger skin" (p. 423). Shawcross's universal insistence on Holocaust rhetoric is one aspect of his approach — imposing on a new and complicated situation the interpretative grid of an old and well-known one. At one point he decides that the Nazi comparison is rather counterproductive, and suggests instead the Lubyanka model — though it would have been more appropriate to make a comparison with the Chinese system of State repression. But the Chinese have lately become "good guys" and their sins have been forgotten. And in any case they have never been very well known.

The use of Nuremberg to interpret Cambodian realities is not only irrelevant, it is simplistic — a view tailored for the victor only. The highest intensity of the Holocaust rhetorical barrage was reached when Israel invaded Lebanon in 1982. This invasion was not subjected to the same standards as the Vietnamese one of Cambodia in 1979.

In a general way this book might appear as an apology for the shortcomings and mistakes of the press. But it contains no real self-criticism. We are told that journalists are right when they are wrong. Their values are beyond reproach. All they wanted to do was to raise emotions and save lives. The inefficiencies of the relief organizations are simply human failings. There is no real solution. The additional chapter in the paperback edition repeats the same themes in relation to Ethiopia; nothing new is really added. However, there is something which could be the start of a solution. That is to identify the next country in which William

Shawcross and his colleagues are going to set foot, to analyse, to study deeply, delve into its detailed history, its social and cultural depths, and try to understand. After that a lot of mistakes and stupidities, both in press coverage and in humanitarian action, could be avoided. This would be a serious undertaking, though — not just spending a week flying over the beautiful parched mountains of Ethiopia.[3]

Appendix 3

About Tou Samouth

Being an open letter to Prince Sisowath Thomico.

In your last text, "Norodom Sihanouk and the Khmer Factions", published in Singapore in issue No. 9 of *Indochina Report*, you raise a point in a way I believe to be erroneous. It needs clarification, also, because the same point was made by Roger Pic in a recent television programme on Cambodia, called *Allez-retours*. It concerns the disappearance of the former Secretary General of the Cambodian Communist Party, Tou Samouth. You say, and Pic says, and some others too, that Pol Pot is guilty of it; he would have thus started his career as a political murderer. This rumour is spreading and by repeating it with a host of details, you give it some credence. The question is not unimportant for those who want to understand what happened in a political group, very tiny at the time, the group of the Cambodian communists, but everyone knows the crucial role they later played and the horrible deviation they imposed on the fate of the Khmer people.

I must first insist on the fact that **we do not know precisely how Tou Samouth disappeared**. We have no documentation on this subject. Even the fact of his disappearance has for long remained doubtful. In a book published in 1971, I could write he was still alive, quoting from an article published in the *Far Eastern Economic Review* (6 August 1970), which drew from official [republican] sources in Phnom Penh. He was described as the "president of the Communist Party" supposed to be operating in the eastern zone.

Lon Nol himself had used the same words in *Le Sangkum* in November 1969. But this information was wrong. Tou Samouth, a man of culture, had received a strong traditional education and had formerly been known as *achar* Sok. [An *achar* (from a Sanskrit word) is a man well versed in traditional knowledge, able to read the Pali texts, usually a former monk.] He had played an important role in the Issarak movement, in the fraction of it which had come under Viet Minh guidance. He was among the most important leaders of the "Revolutionary Party of the Cambodian people" — the first version of the Communist Party — whose Secretary General was Sieu Heng who later defected to the [Sihanouk] regime around 1958–9, at a time when the Party was losing ground in the countryside. The network of urban cadres fared a bit better; it was led by Tou Samouth whose personal secretary was then Saloth Sar, later known as Pol Pot.

In September 1960, at the famous congress which was held [clandestinely] in the Phnom Penh railway station, and which later has been described by the Pol Potists as the real founding congress of the CPK, Tou Samouth was elected Secretary General. Prince Sisowath Thomico says Tou Samouth was arrested in 1960 or in 1961 together with Non Suon but this is not true. In fact, there was no arrest in the legal meaning of the word, as there was for the Pracheachon people, particularly at the beginning of 1962. Tou Samouth disappeared on 20 July 1962. The Communist Party, in several later documents, gave this date, adding he had been abducted and killed by Sihanouk's secret police.[1]

The rumour of the possible involvement of Pol Pot, who had filled Tou Samouth's position one year later, arose much later, in 1978, when Pol Pot started to rewrite the history of the Party to justify his policy and the purges which went along with it. More and more he erased any reference to his predecessor, implying by this means that Tou Samouth was now considered as a traitor because he had been too close to the Vietnamese communists. This, which was at this stage only a falsification of history, was then used as an innuendo, after the fall of Phnom Penh in January 1979. The first to give credence to this rumour was my late friend Wilfred Burchett who was sometimes prone to echo Hanoi's propaganda [which at the time was quite heavy]. But the Vietnamese did not go as far as saying it themselves, to my knowledge. My friend Ben Kiernan reports in his book *How Pol Pot Came to Power* the existence of a Khmer secret security service report, dated the beginning of 1978, involving in the death of Tou Samouth a man named Som Chea, who was at the time a courier of the Central Committee, and another man called Ros Mau, as well as Sieu Heng [the predecessor of Tou Samouth who had defected to Sihanouk]. Kiernan notes that the government of Sihanouk is not named but that does not exclude the possibility that Tou Samouth may have been sold.

In August 1981, I asked the Minister of Justice of the Phnom Penh Government, Mr Ouk Boun Chhoeun, a former eastern-zone cadre about this matter. He told me that what was known in the Party was that a courier had sold Tou Samouth to the secret police and that he had been executed after April 1975. In the document quoted by Kiernan, Som Chea, who was killed in March 1977, was secretary of the Party in the Kandal region. Nothing in what we know leads to a clear conclusion. But, on the other hand, nothing involves Pol Pot in the murder. Besides, it would not fit very well with the political atmosphere of the time because political positions were not so clearcut before the departure of Pol Pot to the safety of the countryside and his decisive trip to China — which took place in 1965.

The future of Cambodia will be better served by honestly establishing facts. I would agree that this is sometimes difficult but it is most certainly in confronting testimonies and discussing them among historians that we may find the light.

Appendix 4

Cambodians and Vietnamese: Not the Same Tune

The difference between Cambodians and Vietnamese is obvious at first sight. Appearance, body structure, language, religion, housing, food, it seems that everything distinguishes and even separates these two close neighbours. Moreover, history teaches that large portions of the former Khmer empire have been conquered and populated in the last three centuries by the Vietnamese, in the Mekong Delta area. Incidentally, the Thais did the same in the northern and western provinces of the Cambodian realm. It is enough for most foreigners to assume there is an ancestral hatred between the Khmers, or Cambodians, and the Vietnamese. Some believe this is the main key with which to unravel the tormented past of Southern Indochina.

But history tells otherwise. They have the same origin, as is demonstrated by comparative linguistics. But these two human groups have entirely lost the memory of their common Stone and Bronze Age ancestry because they developed state-craft along two different lines. In the north, a millennium of Chinese colonial rule, ending in the tenth century, failed to transform the local populace into proper Chinese but left the Vietnamese State and society basically organized along Chinese lines. During the same period in the south, Indian commercial, intellectual and religious expansion slowly permeated local Mon, Khmer amd Cham societies, leading to social rearrangements through the use of Indian technical and political concepts. The split between these two different worldviews made conflicts unavoidable.

The Vietnamese had a bureaucratic state while the Cambodians lived under an aristocracy. The Vietnamese had a strong village organization, which duly registered land, people and taxes, while Cambodians had no other institution than the family and loose links to the nearest pagoda. Land in Vietnam was always scarce while it was free and available in Cambodia. When, by the seventeenth century, Vietnamese demographic pressure (and military expansion) reached the southern expanses of the Mekong Delta, large tracts of land were found unexploited and soon included in a state-controlled network of Vietnamese villages, surrounding scattered Khmer settlements. The Cambodian State, unable to retrieve a substantial part of the revenues levied by the aristocrats' tax collectors, was too poor to resist. Though it may have been painful, this situation did not erupt, as far as we know from the few available records, into ethnic friction. When dissatisfied with local conditions, Khmer farmers, who do not bury their ancestors in the ground, could easily dismantle their house, load it on to an oxcart and move elsewhere.

French colonial power repeatedly failed to establish a land ownership system in the countryside. Since there was no competition for land, Khmers were reluctant to work for wages. Trade was in the hands of Chinese. In order to develop towns, administration and industry, workers were imported from Vietnam. There again there was no real competition and no ethnic problem. Many Vietnamese settled down and intermarriage occurred quite frequently in town. We can say that, in the past, although their cultures made them foreign to each other, Khmers and Vietnamese were quite accustomed to living side by side, complementing each other more than competing, both in Vietnam and Cambodia. Collective violence was completely unknown. And in the revolts against colonial rule, in 1885–90 and 1946–54, rebel groups were almost always mixed bands of Vietnamese and Khmers.

Nationalism was born very late in Cambodia, compared with its neighbours, because the slackness of the economy prevented the emergence of a Khmer bourgeoisie until the 1940s and 1950s. Until then, trade was in the hands of the Chinese and some French companies, and wage workers were mostly Vietnamese. Phnom Penh was a colonial town with only half of the population being ethnic Khmer. When the local bourgeoisie emerged, produced by the French schools, it had power only through access to bureaucracy and rarely entered business.

Because of the ambiguous nature of the monarchy, the Cambodian élite split on the question of how to attain independence. There was no clear-cut class division. Two ways were open: to side with the Viet Minh as the main opponent to the French presence, or with the king, as the embodiment of legitimacy, notwithstanding his rather passive posture. Under Viet Minh pressure, the French chose to give independence in 1953 to the king, who saw the Cambodian allies of the Viet

Minh as a threat to his own power. From then on, anti-Vietnamese rhetoric became a classic theme among Cambodian politicians wishing to establish their nationalistic credentials. Hammering the idea of the "lost Kampuchea *krom*" (southern territories now in Vietnam), exalting the quality of the Khmer "blood", and sometimes falling into crude racism, the competitors, trying to top each other, were Sihanouk, Lon Nol and Pol Pot, displaying an astonishing continuity of thought, from an alleged Angkor "grandeur" to the massacre of Vietnamese civilians and a dream of winning back Kampuchea *krom*. It is probably because the idea of "nation" has remained all along rather foreign to the traditionalist peasant masses that the urban élite, only partially Khmer,[1] developed an aggressive chauvinism to counter the weakness of its appeal and of its ability to draw support from those peasant masses who knew at least one thing: the Vietnamese are not Khmer.

In the countryside, Vietnamese were generally not in competition with Khmer rice growers. They had other occupations. Their presence was a fact of everyday life. During the first Indochina war, many guerrilla units were either Vietnamese or mixed, Khmero-Vietnamese. After the 1970 coup, VC and NVA units were quite accepted by the Khmer peasants who had followed the call of Sihanouk to fight the Americans. Of America, these farmers knew only the planes and the bombs.

The Vietnamese Side

On the whole, what prevails in Vietnam is a complete and definitive ignorance of everything Khmer, or for that matter, of all the other previous inhabitants of present-day Vietnam. Vietnamese at large share the traditional Chinese prejudice against "brown" people, hardly distinguishing between the *moi* (savages), supposed to live naked in the forested highlands, and the Chams and Khmers, inheritors of a high Hinduized culture. All these "dark" people are thought of as inferiors because they ignore the grand "manners" for which the Imperial Chinese court has always been the model. It does not take long in any random conversation with Vietnamese to dig out racist stereotypes about those people being "black, lazy, lascivious" and so on. Respect can be found only for religious monuments left by these former kingdoms, in which the Vietnamese common folk recognize altars dedicated to the spirits, possessors of the land, and, as such, requiring honour and offerings. Stone age agrarian cults do thus survive, transmitted from one population to another.[2] But, generally speaking, Vietnamese arrogance is not a myth.

Communist ideology always opposed this ingrained racism, quite unsuccessfully, but at the same time treated the highland people with a heavy-handed paternalism. Habits do not die easily. One should probably ascribe to a serious education and control of its troops quartered in Cambodia the low incidence of troubles between them and the local populace.

The End Result

The result of decades of propaganda, centred on the conscious manipulation of anti-Vietnamese feelings, in Cambodia has been a success in the towns and a mitigated failure in the countryside. In purely historical terms, the grudges against neighbours' territorial appetites would have been better addressed to Thailand which never really accepted the loss of Battambang and northern Cambodia, due to French pressure. It is interesting to note that Sihanouk encouraged the brilliant young scholar Sarin Chhak to publish his analysis of the border problem with Vietnam — in a well-known book — and restrained him from publishing his study of the Khmero-Thai border problem.

In 1979, the Vietnamese, having swept away the Pol Pot regime — which they had perceived as a Chinese threat — found a country stricken by famine, with no administration, a total chaos. They started to rebuild a state, recruiting any available talent left. That was not much; a large part of the surviving élite, forgetting its fierce nationalism, chose to run away, to find in the West the affluent society that Cambodia could not become in any case. As the years passed, the role of the Vietnamese in restoring some basic economic functions, in rebuilding a state, an army and a Party, as the key to the whole structure, became somewhat heavy, and, for that reason, more and more resented. Khmers have their own ways of dealing with problems and the Vietnamese have others. But the fact that they had succeeded in establishing a genuinely Cambodian political system was proven when it did not collapse after the 1989 Vietnamese withdrawal.

The border camps have produced the myth of the "one million Vietnamese settlers" and, up to now, the Khmer Rouge propaganda is centred on the Vietnamese presence, occasionally leading to the wanton killing of ethnic Vietnamese workers or farmers. Lon Nol also entertained this self-delusion.

There are Vietnamese in Cambodia; it seems they are less numerous than before 1970. But Cambodia, with its institutional smuggling of Western goods, provides a rare opportunity for many, in Saigon, who are looking for jobs, trade and profits. They keep a low profile as they know the situation is far from stable. The local policemen know how to take advantage of this.

The Vietnamese have several times during this century controlled most of Cambodia and they contributed much to its rebirth. But now Cambodia is again standing alone and gratefulness is not a political virtue. The future Cambodian State will have to redefine its relationship with its powerful southern neighbour.

Appendix 5

On Some Cambodian Words

The Word *Yuon*

In 1978, Pol Pot wrote in the *Black Paper*: "Yuon is the name given by Kampuchea's people to the Vietnamese since the epoch of Angkor and it means 'savage'. The words 'Vietnam' and 'Vietnamese' are very recent and not often used by Kampuchea's people".

This is not a futile exercise in semantics. In the spring of 1992, the United Nations authorities (UNTAC) realized the Khmer Rouge radio was launching frantic attacks against the Vietnamese immigrants. There was the distinct possibility that the Khmer Rouge were trying to spark pogroms in furtherance of their political aims. In a letter of 14 August, Mr Akashi, head of UNTAC, strongly objected to the propagandist use of racist crudities and of the "derogatory" word *yuon*. Khieu Samphân (in a telegram of 20 August) brushed aside the remark and advised Mr Akashi "to do more complete and more responsible research on the origins of the words '*yuon*' and '*Vietnam*'". He added that under Vietnamese occupation, the use of the word *yuon* could be punished by two years in jail, which is a pure invention. He then suggested that the UN, by forbidding the use of the word, was condoning the supposed Vietnamese "strategy of Indochinese Federation". This typical Khmer Rouge paranoia is shared by many non-communist Khmer politicians and intellectuals.

All press commentators, without exception, have adopted this assertion that the ordinary name used by the Khmers to refer to their neighbours is pejorative. This fits perfectly with the assertion, also repeated a thousand times, of the hereditary antagonism that divides them. Not very convinced, I questioned various Cambodians. Apart from the word "Viet" which is a foreign word (like "Kazakh" or "Apache" in English), there is no other word besides "yuon" in the old Khmer language to refer to the Vietnamese. Moreover, no one finds the word pejorative **in itself**; it designates in a neutral way — but the connotation is obviously the reflection of the sentiments of the speakers towards the Vietnamese. And with things as they are now, a large array of feelings may be observed.

This view is confirmed by a Khmer writer who cannot be suspected of pro-Khmer Rouge leaning, Mr Hann So, editor of the California-based nonpartisan bulletin called *Sampajann Khmaer — Khmer Conscience*. In his Summer 1992 issue (VI, 3), he writes:

> When the Khmer call the Vietnamese "yuon", it is not pejorative at all. From one generation to another, the word "yuon" is the only term known by the Khmer. They were never told of using any other word. For them, "yuon" means a native of Vietnam. They never knew that it meant something else. The foreign press was the one that raised this issue that a Khmer is not aware of at all. It is the same thing with the use of *Siam* when [Khmers are] speaking of the Thai, or *akeang* [for] the Americans. All these words become so common in parlance that nobody pays attention (p. 8).

Nevertheless, it could be of interest to address Mr Samphân's demand and, for the benefit of many others, look into the origins of the word *yuon*. All we know is that the word is quite old. Though I do not know if it is mentioned in the Angkor inscriptions (Cambodia and Vietnam did not have a common border then since Champa was between them), the antiquity of the term can be accepted. It exists in Thai, in Burmese, and in Cham. Edward Schafer, in *The Vermilion Bird*, writes:

> In a few villages of Binh Thuan in southern Vietnam, no longer in touch with their former Chinese neighbours, are the remnants of the once rich and powerful Chams, now trifling enclaves among the Vietnamese, whom they contemptuously style *yu'o'n* — that is, Yavana (to use the Sanskrit original), or, ultimately, "Ionians" — a term suggesting subnormal, devilish men.

These inhabitants of Iona, or Ionaka (that is, Ionia, the eastern Aegean coast of Greece), appeared rather abruptly on the borders of the Indus, brought there by Alexander the Great in 326 B.C. The commotion was felt in the rest of the subcontinent, although there was more negotiation than warfare. We know that Alexander finally decided to turn back and return to Babylon, where he soon after died from a bout of malaria. These intruders were not your ordinary barbarians; they came with an organized army, a script and a government, not to mention the arts which produced the magnificent Gandara sculptures. Alexander had left but the Greeks remained and organized Greek-style kingdoms in what is now Afghanistan and part of Pakistan. They were well known by the Indian rulers and there are several mentions of the Yona in the oldest historical text of India, the Edicts of Ashoka, carved in Pali on rocks and stone pillars (third century B.C.). Yona came to mean "foreigners" in Indian usage, or, more precisely, non-Indian foreigners. We also know that the word expanded to southern India, far from the northwestern area where Greeks were, for a time, a familiar sight.[1] Indian cultural influence in Indochina mostly came from southern India.

My *Dictionnaire de la civilisation indienne*, by Louis Frédéric, does not support Schafer's assertion that Yavanas are devilish. It only says the word applied to all foreigners in northwest India and mention a king Yavandhipa in the *Mahabharata*. It mentions also "yavani" as a militia of female foreign slaves in charge of policing the lords' palaces and harems, until the sixteenth century, when eunuchs were put in charge.

Transplanted on to the Indochina coast, where they "civilized" what the Chinese called "the naked tattooed savages", the pilgrims and merchants from India quickly realized that to the north lay a threat to their trading posts and settlements, the threat of an organized force equipped with an army, a script, a government, a technology, a body of art, and so on. The term Yona fitted them like a glove. The first Indianized people, the Mons and the Chams, used it.

In Champa, it designated the Chinese colony of Giao Chi before it freed itself to become Vietnam, around the tenth century A.D. We know that the Chinese army made many incursions in response to Cham attacks. In the common cultural flux of Hinduization, the Cambodians most probably borrowed it from the Mons — living in what is now the central plain of Thailand — and adopted the term which was already detached from the area to which it originally referred. The ignorant writer of the *Black Paper,* absorbed in his desire to show that the Cambodians have hated the Vietnamese from time immemorial, could certainly not have known that he was repeating a term historically marked by ambiguity, that is, both admiration and fear, and born out of the clash of two civilizations that were different but equally full of themselves.

But we may go further. The word *Iôn* seems, in early antiquity, to have meant the whole of Greece, at least before the Ionians moved to the eastern shore of the Aegean sea from their original abode in the north of Peloponnese, according to tradition. The "Ionian islands" (Corfu, etc.) are on the *west* of continental Greece (Hellas). Greek traditions that modern historians see no reason to reject say that Ionians (the supposed descendants of a common ancestor called Iôn) lived in the north of Peloponnesian peninsula, then moved to Attica, where the city of Athens was to rise, and finally crossed the sea to establish 12 new cities, which rose to fame because of their trade and the birth of philosophy — Ephesus, Miletus, Phocaea, Priene, etc. Other Mediterranean people then adopted the habit of calling the Greek-speaking people "Ionians". The Persians called Greece *Yauna* and Hebrews *Yawân* (sometimes written *Ja'van*, cf. Gen., X, 2). In the Bible, *Yawân* is expanded to include all Greek-speaking populations, and even all the pagan people (Dan., 8, 21; 10, 20; Zac., 9, 13). In other Semitic languages, the same word is present, usually in the plural form, *yonanawi*, as in Arabic, Syriac (Aramean) and Ge'ez, the Ethiopian Church's language (see Dillman's *Lexikon*, col. 1422).

This has gone on to this day since the Turks, though they chased the Greeks from Ionia in 1922, after the Graeco-Turkish war, still call Greece (without Ionia) *Yunanistan.*

In a further irony, the old Greek legends (see Strabo, 383) attribute to Iôn, the eponymous ancestor of the Ionians, the Utopian division of society into four classes, the fourth of which is made up of "guardians" (*phylakes*), of which Pol Pot offered an impressive realization.

In a reciprocal way, the Greeks of the time of Alexander the Great borrowed from the Persians the name of the river (and province) which stood at the eastern border of the Persian Empire. They thus named *Hindu* (Persian pronunciation) what the Indians called *Sindhu* (the river Indus), or *Hind*, and later *India*, what is still locally known as *Sindh*. But of course Indians never used this name for themselves, except under British influence. It took 25 centuries to convince the Indians that Alexander knew better what to call them...

The final irony is to be found in the fact that the Khmers themselves were called *yuon*. We find in the classic Burmese chronicle *Hmannan Yazawin*, known as the "Glass Palace Chronicle of the Kings of Burma" a note on the attack carried out by Khmer troops against the Mon city of Pegu some time before 1050 A.D. and the successful intervention of Burmese troops, under General Kyanzittha. The defeated Khmer warriors were later resettled in Lower Burma. In the chronicle they are called *gywan*, this being an attempt to translate into English the old Mon or Burmese word, obviously our *yuon.*[2]

In order to give Khieu Samphân a complete reply, it should be added that the word "Viêt" is an old Chinese word meaning, at the beginning of Chinese history, "beyond", used to name the tribes living "beyond, across the Yang Tse Kiang", probably first the fishing communities living in what is now the area of Shanghai,

Greece and Ionia

and later those along the coast of Fukien. Tradition says that some of these tribes later migrated to Tonkin. The local populations, before the advent of Chinese colonization, 2,000 years ago, were known as Au-Lac, again Chinese words. "Nam" is the Chinese *nan*, the south. But the original meaning of the word has long been forgotten and "Viêt" is now understood by the Viêts themselves as the name of the people. In olden times, they often used the word *kinh*, which means the capital, the seat of power, and hence the subjects of this power. (This is the same word as in Pe*king*, Nan*king*, Japanese *kyo*, as in To*kyo*.)

But the fact is that the word "Viêt" is now part and parcel of the Khmer vocabulary and may be used as a normal ethnonym. Khmers generally ignore the fact that the word *yuon* just meant "foreigner". It is only because of recent history that this word is now tainted with anguish and despised. The defence of Khieu Samphân is not innocent and any propaganda based on hatred is sure to produce results which may be catastrophic to everybody.

Yona Art

We tried to explain the origins of the word *yuon*. The word has been borrowed by several cultures of mainland Southeast Asia from India, where it designated the Greeks of antiquity, *Yona*, meaning "Ionia", a region of Greece, on the Asian side of the Mediterranean sea. The name of a parcel had become the name of the whole, as is often the case.

The Greeks came directly in contact with India after Alexander the Great had subdued the powerful Empire of Persia in 331 B.C., that is 2,323 years ago. The political and military genius of Alexander was his capacity to blend Greek and Oriental (Persian) ideas, people, soldiers. His enterprise lasted for centuries after him precisely because of this capacity to mix and merge together ideas coming from several traditions.

One of the most interesting results is, under the influence of the Indian king Ashoka, the spead of Buddhism in the Graeco-Persian kingdoms bordering India. Ashoka had a systematic policy of sending out missionaries. He had held the third Buddhist Council and wanted to expand Buddhism in the west of India. In what are now the valleys of Afghanistan, Buddhist preachers were well accepted. But local converts, deeply impressed by Greek culture and art, started to do something entirely new in the realm of Buddhism: they created statues. A mixture of Greek and Indian aesthetic rules produced what is now called the Gandhara art, which flowed back to India, creating a tradition of carving Buddha images and a set of conventions by which they could be recognized. These conventions later spread across the whole Buddhist world, to China and Japan in one direction, and to Sri Lanka and Southeast Asia in another. Now, Buddhist devotees praying in front of a Buddha image in a pagoda should spare a grateful thought for those *yuon*, meaning ancient Greeks, who provided them with this graceful embodiment of their faith.

The Words *Kambuja*, Khmer, Champa

An old tradition explains the word *Kambuja* as the country of a venerable sage called Kambu, who is supposed to be the originator (*mula*) of the Khmer royal race. This is written down in the Angkorian Baksei Chamkrong inscription, dated 947 A.D.[3] The descendants of Kambu were supposed to unite a "solar" race and a "lunar" one, maybe a coded way to describe the ruling families of Chen La and Fou Nan, two Hinduized kingdoms occupying, at the beginning of our era, the lower course of the Mekong. The story is obviously related to the kings' need to establish the legitimacy of their rule over what was at the time of the inscription, Kambuja, which was the successor state after the disappearance of both Chan La and Fou Nan.

Kambu is given as a descendant of the founders of Fou Nan, an Indian brahmin called Kaundinya and the daughter of the king of the Nâgas (water spirits with snake bodies), a quite interesting union indeed. The trouble with the Khmer story is that it also appears in Cham inscriptions. It seems to be a local adaptation of an Indian legend, given as explaining the obviously mythological origins of the powerful Pallava dynasty of south India (fifth to eighth centuries). But Cœdès thought this legend was created before the first century A.D., at the beginning of Indianization. The myth was perhaps an explanation of it.

There is nothing to support the existence of a historical character called Kambu, a word which does not look very Khmer either. Col. Gerini, in his famous work on Ptolemy's *Geography* asserts that *kambu* means in Sanskrit "a thief, a plunderer". According to him, Ptolemy is naming the coast of Cambodia and Western Cochinchina the country of the *Lestai*, which means "robbers" or "pirates". He concludes with the following hypothesis:

> The coasts of this region have, up to quite recent times, been noted for piracy, and it is therefore possible that the name of their inhabitants, *Kambujas*, originated from this fact, and was afterwards made to look more decent by a slight alteration of the vowel *u* into *o*, thus making it identical with the classical name of a people in Northern India" (pp. 156–7).

Whatever the origin, there was later the tale of a man named Kambu but the myth should be overturned. From the name Kambuja, the name of a man Kambu was invented. At the time countries were often called by the name, or the title, of the rulers. Hence the need to give a meaning to the word *Kambuja* that Khmers could not understand, thus providing a political etymology.

But no Kambu is known in Indian literature whereas *Kambuja* or *Kamboja* are well attested, and a long time before Indians set foot on the shores of Indochina (an area which was neither Indian nor Chinese before the second or the first centuries B.C.).

Kambuja is not a Khmer word but it obviously comes from Sanskrit. In fact Khmers do not use this word in a casual, non-political way very much at all. They rather speak of "*srok khmer*", the land, the territory inhabited by Khmers. The Arab navigators who sailed in this area a long time ago used to call the country *Kumar,* an obvious rendering of *Khmer* and not of *Kambuja.*

As for the word *Khmer*, there is no certain origin. Another Mon-Khmer speaking people, living in northern Laos in an area quite close to the residence of the ancestors of the Khmers, call themselves the Khmu, which means in their language "the men".[4] It is quite possible the *Khmer* also means "the men". But it is not proven.

On the other hand, Kambuja is the name of a people known in Indian texts, for instance in the Edicts of Ashoka (third century B.C.). Curiously enough, it seems to belong to the same area as the Yona. The fifth Rock Edict mentions them together. The king says he is sending his emissaries of the Law (*dhamma-mahamatta*) to "yona kamboja ghandaranam...". The French Indianist Alfred Foucher said that the Kohistan, a mountainous area near Kabul might be the land of the Kambojas, of which we know very little, except that they were more Iranian than Indian and raised fine horses. It seems from some inscriptions that they were a royal clan of the Sakas — better known under the Greek name of Scyths.[5]

Historians tend to believe the Kambojas were in fact an Iranian tribe. (Old Iranian and old Sanskrit are closely related languages. All these people called themselves Aryan, from which comes the name Iran.) Pânini, the Indian genius of grammar, observed[6] that the word *kamboja* meant at the same time the tribe and its king. Later historians identified the same word in the name of several great Persian kings, Cambyse (Greek version) or *Kambujiya* (in Persian).[7] Cambyse the Second is famous for his conquest of Egypt (525 B.C.) and the havoc he wrought upon this country.

It seems, ironically enough, that the Yonas and Kambujas lived quite close to each other in the Kabul area (although some authors would place them further north in Kashmir), in a cold mountainous country, using furs and wool garments, living, as a lot of Afghans still do today, from agriculture, horse trading and the manufacture of weapons.[8]

But, seen from the point of view of orthodox Brahmanists, these people were not acting properly. The Buddha himself is reported as saying[9] that among the Yonas and Kambojas there was no caste, or only two, masters and slaves. Slaves could become masters and vice versa, which was anathema to the Indian social thought of the time. And the *Jataka* say the Kambojas have savage and horrible customs.[10] La Vallée-Poussin concludes from what Panini says: "These are people who do not observe the laws regulating food and marriage."[11] Pânini also says the Kambojas and Yonas shave their heads, which seems a bit odd. But who knows the fashions of the time?

It would be proper here add to our file the word *Champa*. This is not a local, Indonesian, word but an Indian one. It is the name of the central city of an important tribe (*samgha*, which means clan, before it designates the religious community), in the country of the Angas whose name has become Bengal. Champa is today in the vicinity of Bhagalpur, on the Ganges, downstream from Patna. Bengal, at the time, and even now, is the most eastern point in the Aryan push, the cultural process of transforming local populations into Brahmanical (or Buddhist) societies. Assam and the northeastern part of India are only half Indianized even today. There has obviously been strong resistance to the cultural change brought by the Vedic invaders coming from the west or northwest.

Georges Maspero, at the beginning of his book on the Kingdom of Champa refers to the Sanskrit origin of the word and adds that the word is used in Sanskrit for a tree and its white flowers, with a strong scent (*Michelia Champaca* L.). The old Chinese chronicles provide a transcription of the name as Tchan(-tcheng). But what is much less known is that the Chinese also used the word in connection with a Mekong valley chiefdom, which fell under Mongol domination for some time. And Tatsuo Hochino, who establishes the fact, reports a tradition according to which Laos was once called Champa Lao.[12] We know, in southern Laos, a town called Champasak. And there is not much reason to believe that coastal Champa ever ruled these areas. The conclusion would then be that the word Champa, borrowed from Bengal, has been applied to several regions at different times. Let us add that there was also a Yonaka in northern Thailand, and Michael Vickery in his thesis has shown that "Kamboja" has been used by the Burmese and the Thai chronicles to name regions which were not at all in the Khmer realm.[13]

So why were all these words, used in reference to existing populations of the subcontinent, transported to Indochina? The most likely explanation lies in the fact that, when Indians came into contact with local populations, the Brahmans or traders dug out from their geographical memories the names of populations (whose real name they probably ignored) who, in their view, were similarly marginal and remote. All these people were only partially, if at all, observing the Brahmanical rules which, to the Indian view, were the most superior and the most desirable. Local people had no castes, no proper food observances, had other rules for marriage. Under Indian influence, their élite was learning these rules, so they should not be treated as *dasyu*, or savages, like some groups in India who resisted and refused the new social model. If somehow Champa meant "half-Hinduized", Kamboja "casteless" and Yona "non-Hindu foreigner", then these verbal categories could fit the situation Indians encountered when they mixed with the local Southeast Asian rulers and reorganized the political and economic structures. Early Hindu settlers used their own mental categories and imposed them on the natives, as we see from the documents. It is not astonishing, then, that they also imposed the names of these new entities, if only because Sanskrit was the vehicle of this cultural transformation. These words had no ethnic content but were, with all due qualifications, political. They said something, which is unfortunately not very clear to us, from the point of view of classical Indian culture.

But we also see that somehow the local population maintained its own language, traditions and even its own (popular) religion. Neither the Chams nor the Khmers have become proper Indians. But they have accepted Indian names, forgetting in the process the alien origin of these words and using these new concepts to name new political entities.

The Word *Barang*

In Cambodia, Westerners are usually called *barang*. Some have understood the word to mean specifically "French", but in fact it means a foreigner with a Caucasian complexion. Khmers have a local adaptation, "fransay" when they want to be more specific.

The word is not Khmer. It has a long history.

First of all, the word may be found in several unconnected languages in the area. The Thais say *farang* (or sometimes *falang*) when the Khmers say *barang*. It is because there is no sound "F" in the Khmer language. And "B" is a tentative rendering of "F". In Vietnamese, where Westerners are usually called *tay* (which means west), the word *pha-rang* or *pha-lang-xa* is also known, if fallen into disuse. It was probably a mixed attempt to blend *farang* and *français*. At the time of the Nguyên dynasty (nineteenth century), the word for Europe was usually *Hoa-lang*, "being a Vietnamization of the Siamese word for white men, *farang*".[14]

Vietnamese as well as Chinese speakers tried to make the best out of this sound "FA", which they heard from foreign travellers, and which seemed to concern the French, which used the sound "FRA" (as in France) in their name for themselves. But this is an impossible sound in Chinese or Vietnamese. "FA" was available instead, but already had a meaning: "law, justice". And in order to write a sound, the ideographic script uses a word with approximately the same sound. France was then written *fa-guo* in Chinese and *phap-quoc* in Vietnamese, meaning, in a double sense, France or "country of law, or justice". The French colonial enterprise took stock of it. Let us only add that the Vietnamese pronunciation is quite close to the ancient way of pronouncing Chinese that one can hear in Cantonese today, which is more conservative than the Mandarin (northern) pronunciation.

But nothing of the sort occurred in Khmer. The word was just new, when it was acquired from the Muslim traders coming from Malaysia, India and the Gulf region. The Malays who probably got the word earlier have no sound "F". Unlike the Khmers who rendered "F" with "B", they used "P". And when they heard Arab seafarers say "frandji", they uttered *perantjis*. This is still the word for French.

It is clear now that *barang* is just one form of a word which has been adapted from India — where it is also found with several spellings — to China, borrowed from the Muslim, often Arab traders, known in Asia for many centuries. They circulated along the shores of Africa and India the word *farandji* in order to name the people from Europe, to distinguish them from the *Rumi*, the "Romans", in fact the Greeks from Byzantium which was the successor of Rome. It means "Franks" and was the word the Crusaders used for themselves. They had established a "frankish" kingdom in Jerusalem which had lasted about one century (1099– 1187; the last stronghold, Acre, fell in 1291). Some Christian Arab families have taken the word as a name; for instance, a president of Lebanon was called Suleiman Frandjié. The word has travelled since: from Arabic *faranji*, it has spread to Ethiopia, on the way to India: "*Ferendj, faranj, farangi* is the usual word in the Ge'ez [medieval] chronicles used to name the Europeans."[15]

The first Crusades were led by the kings and the military aristocracy of northern Europe, mostly Germans, Flemish, British, French and Normans. In this vast area, the word "Frank" had a long political history.

The Franks, when we hear of them in the earliest historical records, are a group of unorganized Germanic tribes living to the west of the Rhine. (This record calls them *Pranci*, but later *Franci* prevailed.) They started to cross the Rhine in the third century A.D. They controlled an important ford to which their name is still attached (Frank*furt*). During the fifth century, the Salian Franks expanded and, taking advantage of the growing weakness of the Roman empire, they established Frankish kingdoms in the north of France, Belgium and on the left bank of the Rhine. They were warriors, spoke their own Germanic language and had their own laws. In the following centuries, they expanded their area of control over most of northern Europe, destroying in the process other Germanic kingdoms in Spain, Italy, and so on. They inherited the title of Emperor in the ninth century. The name of *Francia* was given to the north of France where the most important Frankish kingdom was established.

In the process, they had become Christian and more and more assimilated into Roman culture. Some maintained their Germanic language but others, on the territory of the former Roman empire, started to speak "Roman". The word "Frank" meant less and less a tribal origin and more and more a common belonging to the class of warriors who had become big landowners by right of conquest. At the time of the Crusades, it was still used as a political word encompassing a great number of these new States, born out of the disappearance of the Roman empire. Many French kings have the name Louis, an evolution of the Germanic name Hludwig, or, as the chronicles said, Clovis, considered the first French king (around 486 A.D.) On the other hand, Francia, at first a small part of northern Roman Gaul,[16] expanded southward and its inhabitants were called "Français", although very few of them had Germanic ancestry. They spoke a rather rotten form of Latin, called "Roman", and later "French".

So, to put it in a nutshell, when Thais say *farang* or Khmers say *barang*, they unwittingly use the name of a bunch of tribes who used to live in central Germany about 2,000 years ago, a word of which nobody knows the original meaning. It is lost in the dark forests of the past. It has been said that the word originally meant "free". (Thais also entertain the myth that the word *Thai* means "free", a pure invention.) An earlier source (*Historia Francorum*) says in 660 A.D. that it means "ferocious"; but both are late mythological rationalizations; it came to mean "free" much later, because of the privileges of power.

Is not the history of words sometimes strange?

Notes

Introduction

¹   See Deac, "Chenla II: Prelude to Disaster". General Creighton Abrahams, Jr., the US commander in Saigon, said: "They've opened a front 40 miles long and two feet wide."

²   *The Political Economy of Human Rights II: After the Cataclysm*, Chapter 6.

³   The full text of Hu Nim's "confessions" was later published in Chandler, Kiernan and Boua, *Pol Pot Plans the Future*, pp. 233–317.

⁴   The results of this small conference were edited by David Chandler and Ben Kiernan, and published at Yale. See Bibliography. My contribution is reproduced here as Chapter 4. It deals with the idea of revolution which, I think, was badly perverted by Pol Pot and his associates.

⁵   After several "wars of the Cambodian succession", as Woodside calls them, the Nguyên dynasty established a protectorate over Cambodia at the beginning of the nineteenth century. See Chandler, 1973, and Woodside, 1988, pp. 246–261.

Cambodia 1972: Within the Khmer Rouge

¹   *Réalités cambodgiennes*, 23 April 1971, p. 8.

²   It is only in the international press that the regime recognizes the existence of 15,000 Khmer Rouge. For local consumption, it speaks of NVN and VC — North Vietnamese and Viet Cong.

[1992 Addition] When I returned to the same region in 1981, I was told by a petty cadre who had attended meetings where I had been travelling that a special unit was sent ahead of me to chase away any Vietnamese troops that might be stationed in the area.

³   [1992 Note] Two months after this article was published in *Le Monde*, I received a detailed request to write a paper on the subject for the *Washington Post*. Among other things, the paper wanted a specific comment on the North Vietnam-

ese / Viet Cong presence in Cambodia. I wrote this: "To the question of foreign aid, the Cambodian guerrillas answer they rely only on themselves; in any case, what I saw proves they really do think along this line. In 1954, they learned that autonomy alone gives a right to be part of political settlements. They did not forget this lesson. Moreover, the internal components of the Cambodian situation are at a considerable variance with neighboring countries. Most probably, it will become clear later on that the Khmer insurgents' political independence is particularly large. But for the time being, first comes the war." (11 May 1972). After several rounds of negotiation, the *Washington Post* pulled out. The article, another wartime casualty, was never published.

The Agrarian Question in Indochina

[1]   Mao Tse-tung, in Edgar Snow, *The Other Side of the River*, p. 70.

[2]   Vû Can, "Les luttes populaires contre le régime US-Diêm de 1954 à 1960", p. 83.

[3]   We have only dealt with this problem in Vietnam and Cambodia, because we could observe it there. A complete analysis of the problem in its Indochinese context would have to include Laos and Thailand, with their very different socio-economic systems. Also, one would have to look at Burma.

[4]   Pierre Gourou, *La terre et l'homme en Extrême-Orient*, p. 24.

[5]   [1992 Note] Many people, and some very considerable authors, hold the above view that the Angkorian irrigation system collapsed because it silted up and the soil fertility decreased. I no longer share this view because any irrigation system needs maintenance and maintenance was done in Angkor for more than five centuries. It was thus possible, I now think, that the political, social and intellectual (religious) system somehow broke down, making maintenance is impossible. But this is another story.

[6]   Nguyên Thanh-Nha, *Tableau économique du Vietnam aux dix-septième et dix~huitième siècles*, p. 58.

[7]   Nguyên Thanh-Nha, *op. cit.,* p. 60.

[8]   A term used in an "Order" handed down to the Censors' Council in 1719, quoted in Nguyên Thanh-Nha, *op. cit.*, p. 67.

[9]   [1992 Note] We now have the first results of interesting research carried out on early nineteenth-century land registries in Tonkin. See Bibliography under Ngô Kim Chung, with a very useful introduction by Georges Boudarel. Research

on early nineteenth-century land registries in the Mekong Delta is being carried out by the well-known historian Nguyên Dinh Dau.

[10]   R. Bienvenue, *Régime de la propriété foncière en Annam*, p. 29.

[11]   Antoine Baffelœuf, *Les Impôts en Annam*, p. 44.

[12]   Nguyên Thanh-Nha, *op. cit.*, pp. 70–71.

[13]   Often Chams, or non-Vietnamese mountain tribespeople.

[14]   The revenues from these provinces were their property. These rights were abolished in 1905. On slavery in Cambodia, see J. Moura, *Le Royaume du Cambodge*, I, pp. 329–33.

[15]   From the beginning of the eighteenth century, the principle of priority of expenditures (to which revenue has to be tailored) prevailed in the budget of the Vietnamese government, but in Cambodia budgetary expenditures remained subject to variation, which restricted the possibilities for modernization.

[16]   Jean Imbert, *Histoire des institutions khmères*, p. 71.

[17]   Cf. Jean Imbert, *op. cit.,* p. 84. See also Etienne Aymonier, *Le Cambodge*, I, *Le Royaume actuel.*

[18]   The problem was an important one for the colonial power, anxious to set up its own state property. Most authors insist that the sovereign was the *owner* of the soil. This seems true enough of Cambodia, and in fact was clearly attested to in the medieval era. (Cf. George Cœdès, *Inscriptions du Cambodge*, II, p. l07.) Nevertheless the problem demands a complete study. As for Vietnam, it is apparent that the first colonial authors applied their notions of Roman law to a situation which in fact bore no relation to it. Because the same error has been committed in relation to China, one might usefully consult the excellent work by Henri Maspéro ("Les termes désignant la propriété foncière en Chine"), where he shows that this conception of private property has never enjoyed *legal* sanction. It has more to do with a philosophical concept according to which the land belongs "to everybody". "When the interests of everybody are at stake, the emperor is there to represent the common interest, and he does so not through legal action, but by dint of his authority; and he speaks not as the owner, which he is not, but as sovereign; he decrees the extent of the rights of each rank of the hierarchy to appropriate the land which belongs to all" (in *Études historiques*, Paris, 1950, p. 206). Marx, referring to feudal property, recalls this French dictum: "Nulle terre sans maître" (No land without a master), which, he says, "expresses the confusion of sovereignty and landed property". (In *Ébauche d'une critique de l'économie politique*, 1844, *Œuvres*, II, p. 51.)

[19]   K. A. Wittfogel, *Das erwachende China*, p. 161. Cf. Max Weber, *Konfuzianismus und Taoismus*, in Part I of *Gesammelte Aufsätze zur Religionssoziologie*, Tübingen, 1920 (*The Religion of China*). Wittfogel's book, as well as his important *Wirtschaft und Gesellschaft Chinas*, has neither been republished nor translated because of the author's opposition to it, in denial of his earlier Marxism.

[20]   "La Naissance du capitalisme en Chine", in *La Bureaucratie céleste*, pp. 290–312.

[21]   Camille Lejeune, *Régime de la propriété foncière en pays annamite*, p. 89.

[22]   *Ibid.*, p. 61. It is a law of classical economics: "The ordinary market price of land, it is to be observed, depends everywhere upon the ordinary market rate of interest... and if the rent of land should fall short of the interest of money by a greater difference, nobody would buy land, which would soon reduce its ordinary price" (Adam Smith, *The Wealth of Nations*, p. 458).

[23]   Pierre Gourou, *op. cit.*, pp. 64, 66.

[24]   Camille Lejeune, *op. cit.*, p. 122.

[25]   *Ibid.*, p. 111. Cf. the detailed study of this question in Milton E. Osborne, *The French Presence in Cochinchina and Cambodia*.

[26]   Ordinance of 11 July.

[27]   Circulaire of the Résidence Supérieure, 29 December.

[28]   Cited by André Roux, "L'acquisition de la propriété par la possession en droit foncier cambodgien", *Annales de la Faculté de Droit de Phnom Penh*, vol. IV, pp. 191–192.

[29]   A. Boudillon, *Le Régime de la propriété foncière en Indochine* (rapport au ministre des Colonies).

[30]   In December 1898, several hundred peasants assembled and travelled secretly to Hanoi, convinced that the spirits, when summoned, would get rid of the French. But the army got wind of this, and trounced them in an ambush. A colonist, questioning the first honorary president of the Court of Appeal in Hanoi, asked if the rebels should be termed "bandits, political dissidents, or vulgar thieves". "Only taxpayers", came the reply with a smile. (Joleaud-Duval, *La Colonisation française en Annam et au Tonkin*, p. 188.)

[31]   Paul Collard, *Cambodge et Cambodgiens*, pp. 152–3.

[32]   The land registry, as recommended by M. Boudillon, was only instituted in Cochinchina in 1929. By 1939, "77,793 land titles had been issued. 340,320 remained to be considered" (Pierre Naville, *La Guerre du Vietnam*, p. 63).

[33]   Charles Robequain, *l'Evolution économique de l'Indochine françaiss*e, p. 211. Cf. also Camille Lejeune, *op. cit.,* p. 137.

[34]   Yves Henri, *Économie agricole de l'Indochine*, p. 224.

[35]   Charles Robequain, *op. cit.,* p. 243.

[36]   *Ibid.,* p. 205.

[37]   On the formation of this new class in Western Cochinchina, see Pierre Brocheux, "Les grands *diên chu* de la Cochinchine occidentale pendant la période coloniale", in *Tradition et révolution au Vietnam,* ed. by J. Chesneaux, G. Boudarel and D. Hémery.

[38]   J. Bourgoin, "Données et perspectives indochinoises", *Revue de la Défense nationale,* November 1946, cited by Pierre Naville, *op. cit.,* pp. 72–3.

[39]   "To struggle for the abolition of the vestiges of feudalism and for the *liquidation of precapitalist forms of exploitation* in order to bring about radical agrarian reform" (our italics). This principle is a curious one in that it proposed the elimination of capitalism, in its early form, at the very stage when it was starting to play its role in the development of the productive forces in the rural areas. Cited in Lê Chau, *La Révolution paysanne du Sud Vietnam,* p. 53.

[40]   Hô Chi-Minh, *Écrits,* p. 108.

[41]   "Un siècle de luttes nationales, 1847–1945", *Études Vietnamiennes,* No. 24, Hanoi, 1970, p. l20.

[42]   Hô Chi-Minh, *op. cit.,* p. 108.

[43]   Paul Mus and John McAlister, Jr., *Les Viêtnamiens et leur révolution,* p. 35. It is worthwhile to mention here, if only for the record, the existence of particular movements through which certain rural regions demonstrated the strength of their local feelings. These movements were prophetic and syncretic, such as the Cao Dai, founded in 1926, or the Hoa Hao sect, whose beginnings date from 1939. Probably as a reaction to colonialism, Buddhist sects, spiritualist groups and secret societies sprang up all over Cochinchina from the beginning of the twentieth century. The Cao Dai sect, which grew up amongst petty officials, soon spread rapidly in the countryside. From 500,000 members in 1930, its faithful grew to a million and a half in 1967, despite factionalism in the Cao Dai church. (Cf. Nguyên Tran Huan, "Histoire d'une secte religieuse au Vietnam: le caodaïsme", in *Tradition et révolution au Vietnam, op. cit.,* pp. 189–214). And as the war raged on year after year, it continued to spread in the countryside as well as in the suburbs of Saigon. The Hoa Hao movement was exclusively rural and completely dominated a province of the western delta, Long Xuyen, which is in fact a political and religious island. Finally, this phenomenon should be compared with

other forms of messianism (in the Congo, South Africa, Melanesia, and so on) and the evident relationship between the local agrarian social structure and the ideological reaction that it provokes should be analysed.

44   "It can be seen that [in China] very much depends on the legal definition of large landlord, rich peasant, middle peasant, poor peasant —these expressions one can easily recognise as transcriptions of the Russian words *kulak, bedniak,* etc. " (Etienne Balazs, *op. cit.,* p. l63).

45   Referred to by Nhu Phong, "Intellectuals, Writers, and Artists", *The China Quarterly*, 1962, p. 54.

46   Lê Chau, *op. cit.,* p. 58.

47   In *Hoc Tap* (Studies), January 1960; cited by Nguyên Khac Viên, *Expériences vietnamiennes*, pp. 82–3.

48   "One day we were able to discuss the question of landlord exploitation with a tenant. We asked, 'The landlord collects half the produce as rent at harvest time; is this exploitation?' The tenant replied, 'You can't really call it exploitation. I don't own any land, so I am lucky that he rents it to me. I can farm, and he owns land, so of course it is just that each of us get half the harvest.'" Truong Chinh and Vô Nguyên Giap, *The Peasant Question*. [Translator's note.]

49   For its description of a village and the workings of the village social structure, see the classic work of Gerald C. Hickey, *Village in Vietnam* (preface by Paul Mus).

50   In Japan, Korea, and Taiwan, the limit was from three to five hectares.

51   *Land Reform in Vietnam*, Summary Volume, p. l3. The same report gave a figure of 60 per cent for 1967 as well (table, p. 43). Half of the *landowners* shared 10 per cent of the land. It must be noted that these figures were theoretical. Many large estates were in the hands of the tenants in the zones controlled by the guerrillas.

52   And by 1962, land transfers stemming from Ordinance 57 had become virtually negligible.

53   A study of the policy of regrouping villagers into "strategic hamlets", "agrovilles", "New Life Hamlets", and so on, would be particularly interesting. Cf. Milton E. Osborne, *Strategic Hamlets in South Vietnam*.

54   *Land Reform in Vietnam*, III: *The Viet Cong, op. cit.,* p. 53.

55   *Ibid.,* p. 59.

56   "Land for South Viet Nam's Peasants", *Time*, 11 July 1969.

57   [1992 Note] I shall not pursue here a study of communist land policies in Vietnam, which underwent so many changes, since the bloody revolt in 1956 in

Nghê An, that a large volume would hardly be enough. Nowadays, the "liberalization" of the rural economy has produced a considerable increase in agricultural production. I studied the American attempts to achieve a land reform in "Les Réformes agraires d'inspiration américaines au Sud Viêt-Nam", in *Histoire de l'Asie du Sud-Est, révoltes, réformes, révolutions*, ed. by Pierre Brocheux, pp. 125–38.

58   Yearly statistics of the UN, 1966.

59   Yves Henri, *op. cit.,* p. 211.

60   Jean Delvert, *Le Paysan cambodgien*, Paris, p. 495.

61   Hu Nim (later Minister of Information with the Khmer Rouge, purged under Pol Pot), *Les Services publics économiques au Cambodge*, p. 86.

62   Rémy Prud'homme, *L'Économie du Cambodge*, p. 72. See his discussion of the figures used here, pp. 71–3.

63   In 1952, a study of the Office of Crédit estimated that three-quarters of peasant owner cultivators were in debt. See J. Delvert, "La paysannerie cambodgienne dans la tempête", *Le Figaro*, 2 July 1970, p. 5 [translator's note].

64   [1992 Note] This information, current at the time (1972) is entirely inaccurate. Khieu Samphân was only a figurehead, as he is now, acting as a representative of Pol Pot in the Supreme National Council in Phnom Penh (1992). It reflects the deep secrecy surrounding the real Khmer Rouge leadership. It took us a long time to understand its true nature.

65   Khieu Samphân, *L'Économie du Cambodge et ses problèmes d'industrialisation*, p. 48.

66   Cf. Mau Say, "Les Institutions cambodgiennes de crédit", pp. 219–51.

67   For a description of the latter, see Wilfred Burchett, *La seconde résistance*.

68   Programme of FUNK. (French acronym for the National United Front of Kampuchea), *Nouvelles du Cambodge*, Paris, No. 3, 11 May 1970.

69   Paul Mus, *Viêt-Nam: sociologie d'une guerre*, p. 14.

The Ingratitude of the Crocodiles: The 1978 Cambodian *Black Paper*

1   There are several editions of the *Black Paper:*

(a) Phnom Penh edition, in French, roneo, September 1978, 116 pages; its title is: *Livre noir, faits et preuves des actes d'agression et d'annexion du Viêt-Nam contre le Kampuchea.*

(b) Paris edition, in French, printed, January 1979, Editions du Centenaire E-100, 87 pages. Contrary to what it claims, this edition **is not** "the complete reproduction" of the first. Several phrases were omitted or truncated. The revisions were made in Phnom Penh. A special courier brought them to Paris.

(c) English-language edition: *Black Paper: Facts and Evidences of the Acts of Aggression and Annexation of Vietnam Against Kampuchea,* New York, reprint [sic], Foreign Affairs of Democratic Kampuchea, September 1978. It does not seem there ever was an English version produced in Phnom Penh.

² [1992 Note] However, visiting, some months ago, the Museum of History in Saigon (Bao Tàng Lich su' Viêt Nam, TP Hô Chi Minh), where the former "Société des Études indochinoises" was located, I was surprised to see several typical Khmer carvings, found in Vietnam, described only as "Mekong delta culture, X–XIIth centuries". The word "Khmer" was carefully omitted. Moreover, the ethnic maps showing the location of "national minorities" gives to the Delta Khmers an imaginary coastal settlement, as far away as possible from the Cambodian border. All this points toward a deliberate falsification of the Khmer history in the area. The worst enemy of historical knowledge is, as always, modern nationalism.

³ *The Vermilion Bird, Tang Images of the South,* 1967.

⁴ [1992 Note] On the Chams, see Lafont and Po Dharma, *Bibliographie Campa et Cam.* On Hà-Tiên, we now have an interesting account of *The Princes of Hà-Tiên (1682–1867),* by an American, Nicholas Sellers, 186 pp. Note the subtitle: *The last of the philosopher-princes and the prelude to the French conquest of Indochina: a study of the independent rule of the Mac dynasty in the principality of Hà-Tiên, and the establishment of the empire of Viêtnam.*

⁵ [1992 Note] The "Ethnohistory" of the (now) Vietnamese Central Highlands, and the complicated way the French incorporated these territories into Vietnam is superbly told by Gerald Cannon Hickey (see Bibliography). This is a most valuable book.

⁶ An account of the origins of this old Cambodian legend can be found in Thai Van Khiem, "La Plaine aux cerfs et la Princesse de jade". The arrival of the Vietnamese in the Saigon area dates to about forty years later. According to the Khmer chronicles, the young woman's name was Nang Cu.

⁷ *Relatione della nuova missione delle P. P. dela compagna di Giesu al regno della Cocincina,* translated into French at Lille in 1631, cited by Léonard Aurousseau, "Sur le nom de Cochinchine".

⁸ Cited by Father Bouillevaux, "Ma visite aux ruines cambodgiennes en 1850", p. 11.

⁹ Michael Vickery, *Cambodia after Angkor,* p. 375. [Note that the former capital of Thailand, called Ayuthaya, took its name from the Gangetic city of

Ayodhya, now called Audh, the supposed bithplace of Rama—and of the *Ramayana*. The place hit world headlines when a Hindu crowd rioted and destroyed the Babur mosque built on a former Hindu temple (Dec. 1992).]

[10] Edward Shafer, *op. cit.,* p. 11. The author refers to the Cham-French dictionary of Aymonier and Cabaton, Paris, 1906, p. 401.

[11] [1992 Note] See below, Appendix 5.

[12] [1992 Note] Although we had many reasons to suspect it, we later got confirmation that the author was none other than Pol Pot himself. This was the understanding of the person who typed the Phnom Penh version, Laurence Picq, working at the time at the Foreign ministry, under Pol Pot's brother-in-law Ieng Sary. She later wrote a very interesting account of this period under the title *Au delà du ciel, cinq ans chez les Khmers rouges.*

[13] "The General Situation", document captured, translated and published by the Americans in Saigon, in *The Vietcong's March–April, 1970, Plans for Expanding Control in Cambodia,* Vietnam Documents and Research Notes, No. 88, p. 67.

[14] [1992 Note] The unconscious irony of this sentence could be appreciated only later, when it was learned that, at the time of the Vietnamese invasion, the Chinese were putting the final touches to an enormous military airbase in the centre of Cambodia, about thirty kilometres northwest of Kompong Chhnang. Comprising a gigantic concrete runway, well protected behind the Phnom Aural, and installations carved into the hills, this base, built by the Chinese, could accommodate a modern fleet of warplanes, half an hour's flight from Saigon. In order to avoid further antagonizing the Chinese, the Vietnamese did not publicize this Pharaonic enterprise. No photographs were ever published. In the following years, the place was quietly looted bare by the local inhabitants. But it is still an impressive achievement, though desolate and useless.

[15] Colonel Maurice Laurent, *L'Armée au Cambodge,* p. 47.

[16] See references to Comintern directives in Robert F. Turner, *Vietnamese Communism,* pp. 15–19.

[17] Text in *Etudes vietnamiennes,* Hanoi, No. 24, 1970, p. 208. [In the English edition of *Political Theses of the Indochina Communist Party,* October 1930, p. 193, point number 6, the language seems to vary slightly. It says: "Indochina to be completely independent; national self-determination to be recognized". Translator's note.]

[18] [1992 Note] We now have a detailed study of this period, based on a wealth of documents and interviews, including Nguyên Thanh Son's, in Ben Kiernan's *How Pol Pot Came to Power.*

¹⁹   The English-language version of the *Black Paper* has "many" instead of "several".

²⁰   [1992 Note] There are even some naive propagandists to deny it, like the well-known Hanoi historian and psychologist Nguyên Khac Viên who dared to say to Françoise Corrèze: "From 1954 to 1970 the Sihanouk government could maintain its independence and neutrality; there were no Vietnamese troops in Cambodia", *Choses vues au Cambodge*, 1980, p. 187.

²¹   [1992 Note] We now know that Pol Pot, when he left Phnom Penh in 1963, proceeded to the northeastern province of Rattanakiri and stayed for about two years in a Viet Cong base. There was no organized Khmer *maquis* at the time. Interestingly, the book written by Wilfred Burchett, after his early visit in the NLF zones (*J'ai visité les zones libérées du Sud-Vietnam*), published in Hanoi in 1965 (note the date) carries an author's cover photograph depicting, against a jungle background, Nguyên Huu Tho, the president of the NLF and a massive man, easily recognizable as Nuon Chea, the right hand of Pol Pot, although he is not identified. Steve Heder drew my attention to this picture.

²²   Timothy Michael Carney, *Communist Party Power in Kampuchea*, p. 56.

²³   [1992 Note] I have touched on this subject in a letter to a Khmer monthly published in France, "À propos de Tou Samouth", *Srok Khmer*, published below in Appendices.

²⁴   For a report on this *Reader's Digest* book, see Tørben Retbøll, "Kampuchea and the 'Reader's Digest'".

²⁵   Serge Thion, "The Social Classification of Peasants in Vietnam", pp. 328–38.

²⁶   [1992 Note] The reader should be reminded that, at the time of the writing of this paper, in mid-1979, few internal documents were known and the archives of Tuol Sleng, the interrogation centre of the Pol Pot regime, had not yet been studied at any great length. We must now categorically state that nothing in the archives shows any trace of foreign involvement, be it American or Vietnamese. Such admissions were only the product of torture but may have produced a huge self-delusion in the higher ranks of the organization. Nowadays, Khmer Rouge cadres still believe in the dogma of the "Vietnamese agents" as imaginary culprits of the main bloody deviations of the revolution.

²⁷   [1992 Note] I believe this basic thought is of particular relevance now, in the context of the UN operation in Cambodia. While the agreements are based on the presumption of a permanent ceasefire and demobilization of troops, the Khmer Rouge cannot exist if they do not fight. The Party is nothing else than its military

force. They knew this already in 1965. This fact stems from the impossibility of stating openly the communistic aims of the struggle and **convincing** the Cambodians to take part. See Chapter 4 below.

28   *Le Monde,* 13–14 May 1979.

29   An account of her life is now available (see Bibliography). She died in August 1992.

30   This phrase is missing in the English version of the *Black Paper.*

31   [1992 Note] There is not a word about this in the Tuol Sleng documents I know: two so-called confessions, of 4 March 1977. There may be others, yet to be compiled.

32   Kenneth M. Quinn, "Political Change in Wartime. The Khmer Krahom Revolution in Southern Cambodia, 1970–74", p. 10.

33   *Sideshow*, pp. 266–7.

34   See Sarin Chhak, *Les Frontières du Cambodge.*

35   *Dossier Kampuchea*, I, Hanoi, 1978, pp. 56, 122 and 123. Document of the Ministry of Foreign Affairs entitled, "La Vérité sur le problème frontalier vietnamo-khmer", 7 April 1978, pp. 119–44.

36   See these documents in *Bulletin of Concerned Asian Scholars,* 11, No. 1, 1979, p. 24.

The Cambodian Idea of Revolution

1   In his BBC lectures published as Max Gluckman, *Custom and Conflict in Africa*, pp. 43–4. Also see his more elaborate *Order and Rebellion in Tribal Africa.*

2   Gluckman, *Custom and Conflict*, p. 48.

3   *Ibid.,* p. 45.

4   Maurice Comte, *Économie, idéologie et pouvoir: la société cambodgienne (1863–1886)*, p. 237.

5   David P. Chandler, *Cambodia Before the French*, p. 39.

6   See Franz Michael, *The Tai Ping Rebellion, History and Documents.*

7   On the early colonial period, see Comte, *op. cit.*, on the later period, see Alain Forest, *Cambodge. histoire d'une colonisation sans heurt*, and Roland Thomas, *L'Évolution économique du Cambodge.*

8   Paul Collard, *Cambodge et Cambodgiens*, pp. 115–16.

9   Gabrielle Martel, *Lovea, village des environs d'Angkor.* She mentions the crucial problem of cash money: "Cet argent après lequel tous les villageois

soupirent à défaut de courir" (p. 192). (Villagers dream of having money instead of going to earn it, outside their home village.)

[10] René Lefèbvre, *L'Économie agricole du royaume du Cambodge*, p. 279.

[11] Milton E. Osborne, *The French Presence in Cochinchina and Cambodia*, p. 203.

[12] Pol Pot, "Monarchy or Democracy?", in Thion and Kiernan, *Khmers rouges!*, p. 357.

[13] See the excellent study by Alexandre Bennigsen and Chantal Quelquejay, *Les mouvements nationaux chez les musulmans de Russie*.

[14] Harold Isaacs, *The Tragedy of the Chinese Revolution*; Pierre Broué, ed., *La Question chinoise dans l'Internationale communiste (1926–1927)*; Y. V. Chudodeyev, ed., *Soviet Volunteers in China*.

[15] Chalmers A. Johnson, *Peasant Nationalism and Communist Power*.

[16] [1992 Note] We have recently learned from the press of the arrest in Lima of Abimael Guzman, "Chairman Gonzalo", the leader of the *Sendero Luminoso*, the Shining Path Maoist guerrilla movement of Peru. Several authors have compared this movement with the Khmer Rouge. This comparison is well justified, in my view.

[17] See such a classification in an unpublished paper by Laura Summers, "Co-operatives in Democratic Kampuchea". Also François Ponchaud, "Viet-Nam–Cambodge, 'une solidarité militante fragile'", pp. 1250–1.

[18] See Daniel Hémery, *Révolutionnaires vietnamiens et pouvoir colonial en Indochine*.

[19] [1992 Note] At the beginning of 1935, the Long March columns, trapped in Western Szechuan, escaped into the territory of a non-Han hostile population, known as Lolo. They are now officially called Yi. The relationship of the Communists with these aborigines smacked of colonial trickery. Later, in the 1950s, the Yi revolted.

[20] *Asiaweek*, 8 December 1978.

[21] Roland Lew, *1949, Mao prend le pouvoir.*

[22] [1992 Note] At the end of 1988, in a speech to delegates of the Union of Women, Pol Pot explained to the cadres that they have to do precisely that kind of work, adding in an aside that the Party had so far perhaps relied too much on sheer force. Such a turnabout is unlikely to be achieved and anyway comes too late. A detailed analysis of the "new course" has been made by Christophe Peschoux (see Bibliography).

[23] The French anthropologist, Marie A. Martin, has observed such councils in the Cardamom mountains and in Khmer-speaking areas on the Thai side of the border (personal communication).

[24] It was also rumoured in the Party, towards the end of 1978, that a traitor was sitting at the top of the Party, which was generally understood to be putting Nuon Chea, the Party's assistant secretary general, as the next high-level target. Son Sen and Nuon Chea still sit in the DK government, whereas Deuch, the notorious director of the Tuol Sleng interrogation centre, after having spent several months in Sakeo, in Thailand, is still at large, probably hiding in the forest. Among the Khmer Rouge, the psychological pressures, if somewhat relaxed in 1980–1, are still in existence. The tiny political élite which is representing the DK in its relations with foreigners on the Thai border and abroad, is far from being able to impose a real relaxation in the hard core apparatus ruling the army and the civilians in the field.

Cambodia 1981: Background and Issues

[1] [1992 Note] The Khmer State deeply influenced the lowlands and produced a relatively homogeneous society. But on the periphery, old Mon-Khmer (Austroasiatic) languages and social organizations were less affected. Many inhabitants of the forested north of Cambodia, including a large proportion of "Cambodians" living in Thailand, are Kuys. Kuy is quite distinct from Khmer and these people are usually bilingual. In the west, many people are Samré or Pear and speak these unwritten languages to a greater or lesser extent. These people are officially considered Khmers, different as a whole from the *Khmer loeu*, or tribal montane people who speak other Mon-Khmer languages. *Loeu* means "above", hence "further north". To complicate matters a bit more, Kuys of Thailand also call themselves *Khmer loeu*.

In the late 1940s, Sihanouk made a film called *Tarzan among the Kuys*, fortunately lost and now forgotten. But the title shows the type of prejudice against not fully Khmerized minorities which was then prevalent among the Phnom Penh social élite. (S.T.)

[2] See Pierre L. Lamant, *L'Affaire Yukanthor.*

[3] [1992 Note] In 1983–4, central markets were progressively reopened. Concessions were first given to the wives of civil servants and military officers, as a means to provide income to poorly paid high ranking administrators. Vietnamese officers' wives were quite active too. But in the following years more and more Chinese traders came back into business and progressively took over. Now Chinese gold traders dominate the scene. Back to square one (S.T.).

The Pattern of Cambodian Politics

[1]   See Alexander B. Woodside, *Vietnam and the Chinese Model*, Chapter 5.

[2]   S. J. Tambiah, *World Conqueror and World Renouncer.*
[1992 Addition] Another view of the traditional Thai political systems has been provided by Georges Condominas in *L'Espace social* in two articles, translated into English in *From Lawa to Mon*. See the review by Michael Vickery in the *Thai-Yunnan Project Newsletter.*

[3]   Thailand's view of Cambodia as a buffer zone, which should be open to some form of Thai influence, is well presented by Khien Theeravit, a professor at Chulalongkorn University and adviser to Premier Prem, in a paper presented to the pro-Democratic Kampuchea Tokyo Conference in June 1981, "Thailand's Response to the Vietnamese Aggression in Kampuchea".

[4]   See Tambiah, *op. cit.*, and Immanuel Sarkisyanz, *The Buddhist Background of the Burmese Revolution.*

[5]   The Salot family of Pol Pot, for instance. See Thion and Kiernan. *Khmers rouges!,* p. 367. [Also David Chandler's *Brother Number One,* a biography of Pol Pot.]

[6]   [1992 Note] On megalomania, see *Sihanouk reminisces*, by himself.

[7]   [1992 Note] In 1992, in the middle of the peace process, the Khmer Rouge, the Son Sannists and the Sihanoukists led by Prince Norodom Ranariddh are all competing in strident anti-Vietnamese propaganda. It seems they have no more urgent proposal for the future of Cambodia than to uproot the Vietnamese settlers entirely, in a dream that is strongly reminiscent of the "ethnic cleansing", now destroying Yugoslavia. Even the Phnom Penh side is not immune to bursts of hatred. Racist behaviour is on the rise, as more and more Vietnamese workers, traders and prostitutes flock to Cambodia in order to take a share of the sudden influx of money in Phnom Penh.

My understanding is that active anti-Vietnamese feelings have deeply penetrated social strata which, in the olden times, were only passive or indifferent. Violence now and then occurs, and the future may see more of it.

[8]   The Brévié line was established in January 1939 to allocate to Cambodia and Cochinchina islets and islands on the coast of the Gulf of Siam, for administrative purposes only: "The matter of territorial dependence of these islands remains entirely reserved". The Khmer governments have insisted on saying that the present border was established mostly by the French colonial authorities.

without proper and free acceptance by Cambodian authorities, to the advantage of Cochinchina, which at the time, as a colony, was French territory. Sarin Chhak, *Les Frontières du Cambodge,* contains all the documents, including the Brévié letter, together with maps and the Khmer legal point of view.

⁹   [1992 Note] In 1992, in their effort to procrastinate, Khieu Samphân and Son Sann again raised the border question, making its solution a condition for implementing the Paris Agreement, which contains no provision of the sort. In this futile attempt to manipulate UN Authority, one can see a way to claim legitimacy before elections could confirm or deny it. "The territorial integrity of Cambodia must be restored before the election date", writes Son Sann (letter to the Supreme National Council (SNC), 24 Aug. 1992). The treaties "of July 7, 1982, November 12, 1982 and July 20, 1983" are null and void, said Khieu Samphân to the SNC the same day. But the texts of these treaties have not been made fully available. Khmer Rouge and KPNLF policies having no real content, their leaders are thus content to toy with symbols.

¹⁰   [1992 Note] These lines were writtten in 1982. Since then, ten years have elapsed and we have never received any solid information on Sarin Chhak's fate. Incontrovertible testimonies of his arrest by Vietnamese troops after the fall of Phnom Penh in early January 1979 are the latest information. He had missed the last-minute evacuation of the Foreign Ministry personnel. He was a perfectly respectable scholar and diplomat.

The new Vietnamese Foreign Affairs Minister, Nguyên Manh Càm, visited Cambodia for three days and gave a press conference in Phnom Penh on 26 February 1992. I took this opportunity to request information about the fate of Sarin Chhak, insisting that it was an obligation of the Vietnamese authorities to give this. The minister replied that he knew nothing about this affair. Three months later, in Saigon, I asked the same question to Ngô Diên, ambassador to Cambodia until the return of Sihanouk. He recommended that I ask in Hanoi, implying that he had not the authority to speak.

I also asked Mr Càm about the Heng Samrin-Hanoi border treaty and its provision for "further negotiation". He professed to have no knowledge of the question, adding that any problem should be "peacefully resolved" by negotiation. The Vietnamese have obviously a lot to say about Cambodia but it is still too early.

¹¹   Y Phandara, *Retour à Phnom Penh,* p. 176.

¹²   *Ibid.,* p. 102.

[13]   [1992 Note] "Responses of the contemptible Chhaan", Tuol Sleng document translated by Steve Heder. The responsibility for the murder is clearly ascribed, in this document, to Son Sen (noted by his alias "Khieu"), allegedly in a bid to undermine the credibility of the Party's leadership. Son Sen is now a member of the Supreme National Council, representing the Khmer Rouge. He regularly and faithfully reports to "Ta 87", the codename of Pol Pot.

[14]   *Op. cit.*, pp. 149–50.

[15]   See, for instance, Pin Yathai, *L'Utopie meurtrière,* pp. 169–71 and *passim.*

[16]   See under Henderson in the Bibliography (a study of 2,400 interviews with prisoners and defectors).

[17]   See Thion and Kiernan, *Khmers rouges!*

[18]   Ben Kiernan provides the most detailed description of the Eastern Zone crisis in his essay "Wild Chickens…", in Chandler and Kiernan, eds., *Revolution and Its Aftermath in Kampuchea,* and his later *Cambodia: The Eastern Zone Massacre.*

[19]   [1992 Note] I met Pen Sovan in Takeo in April 1992, shortly after his return from a ten-year exile in Hanoi. He came back with an axe to grind. The interview confirmed he has a strong authoritarian and uncompromising personality. He does not provide any credible explanation for his 1981 demise. Party sources in Saigon confirm my theory that he was just not fit for the job because of his tendency to factionalism.

[20]   I would like to thank Donald Nicholson Smith for his help in revising the text.

[1992 Note] I believe I attended such a moment of grace when Sihanouk, upon his return from a long exile, in November 1991, attended the Water Festival, for the first time in 22 years, amidst popular rejoicing. At a Moon evening ceremony, at the entrance of the Throne Hall, in the Royal Palace, wearing a dark traditional garment, he presided over the dancing of the reconstituted Ballet, the chanting of the monks, while the *achars* read the future of the crops in the wax of candles. It was harmonious, beautiful, peaceful. Heng Samrin sat by Sihanouk, a poor shy farmer, suddenly elected to represent the peasants in this royal pomp.

But the next day, this transient image of the past vanished into thin air and power politics was again the order of the day. The prince made very clear that he did not intend to re-ascend the throne. The clever former king resumed his intrigues, through which he expects to regain one day the substance of power, not being satisfied with having recovered only its trappings.

Cambodia 1987: Time for Talk

[1]   [1992 Note] Four years later, the Party, having dropped all reference to socialism, changed its name to Pracheachon (People) Party. But the strong man, the secretary general Chea Sim, remained firmly in control and has even strengthened his grip on the organization.

[2]   "Statement of the CPK to the CWP of Denmark, July 1978", as introduced by Laura Summers, *The Journal of Communist Studies* (see s.v. Nuon Chea).

[3]   See L. Mason and R. Brown, *Rice, Rivalry and Politics*, for the basic facts; a much better book than the Shawcross one [reviewed here, in the Appendices], by the way.

[4]   [1992 Note] Upon reception of this paper, the prince had my name scrapped from the mailing list of his monthly bulletin. See also my "Despote à vendre", *Les Temps Modernes.*

[5]   [1992 Note] I would not mind receiving some apologies from some analysts who spilled tons of ink to demonstrate that the Vietnamese would never leave Cambodia and called me a Hanoi stooge because I thought the balance of evidence indicated they were wrong.

[6]   [1992 Note] They left in August 1989. A small number of élite troops and military advisers were left behind. It seems all of them left by the summer of 1991, before the signing of the Paris Agreements. A number of deserters were left behind. Some sort of intelligence network is probably still active.

Indochinese Refugees in France: Solidarity and its Limits

[1]   I described the end in a contribution to *Ho-Tschi-Minh Statd, Die Stunde Null,* edited by my sadly missed friend, Börries Gallasch, pp. 125–34.

[2]   I touched upon them in "Le Cambodge, la presse…", pp. 95–111.

[3]   Savitry Sorasinh, p.14.

[4]   Cf. Bernard Kouchner, *Charité Business*, written by a renowned specialist in the humanitarian field.

[5]   Nguyên Ngoc Giao, in *Vietnam,* No. 4.

[6]   *Le Monde*, 8 July 1981.

[7]   *Le Monde,* 19–20 October 1986.

[8]   In *Cornell Review*, 1979.

Genocide as a Political Commodity

[1]   "Cambodia and the United States are both signatories to the Genocide Convention, and we will support efforts to bring to justice those responsible for the mass murders of the 1970s if the new Cambodian government chooses to pursue this path." The US ratified the Convention in 1986, long after Cambodia.

[2]   See Christophe Peschoux, *Les "nouveaux" Khmers rouges.*

[3]   "An Overview of the Cambodian Genocide", a paper prepared for the Yale Cambodia Conference (February 1992). Kiernan's and Heder's surveys have not been published.

[4]   *Cambodia, a Demographic Catastrophe,* which I reviewed in *Libération,* Paris, 17 Sept.1980. Michael Vickery discussed it in the *Bulletin of Concerned Asian Scholars.*

[5]   On traditional wisdom, see the texts edited and translated by Saveros Pou, *Guirlande de Cpap'.*

[6]   Pol Pot would agree. In December 1988, he said in a speech to his Women's Association cadres: "Our troops previously did not know how to conduct popular work because the concrete fact was that they did not yet have any faith in the people and instead relied exclusively on bullets and other material things", an interesting comment coming from the man who has been in charge of a guerrilla movement for 25 years.

[7]   Translated in Thion and Kiernan, *Khmers rouges!*, pp. 358-61.

[8]   *Les États hindouisés...,* Introduction, p. 3.

[9]   See Keng Vannsak, *Recherche d'un fonds culturel khmer,* unpublished thesis.

[10]   A good analysis of regional and local variations is to be found in Michael Vickery, *Cambodia, 1975–1982*, Chapter 3.

[11]   See above, Chapter 7.

[12]   See Sarin Chhak, *Les Frontières du Cambodge.* See above, Chapter 6, note 6.

[13]   See Nayan Chanda, *Brother Enemy.*

[14]   See Raphael Lemkin, *Axis Rule in Occupied Europe.* Lemkin had been a technician of law in the Polish civil service until 1939. He then went to Sweden and in 1941 to the US. He died in 1959. The concept of genocide occupies a rather limited space in the book. In his view, it included cultural assimilation, as a

weapon to destroy one's identity: for instance, the Germans, he said, were imposing a genocide on the Poles because they were pushing pornography and gambling, thus destroying Polish culture. Today, such an extensive use of the word is generally rejected. The 1948 Convention still cites "mental harm" against a group as a crime.

[15]   Gregory Stanton informs us that the former president of (formerly Spanish) Equatorial Guinea, Francisco Macias Nguema, a very bloody dictator indeed, has been condemned for genocide. I still believe some more obvious candidates could be found, excluding new regimes putting on trial their predecessors. On the circumstances surrounding Macias coming to power, see Donato Ndongo Bidyogo, *Historia y tragedia de Guinea Ecuatorial*, 1977.

[16]   "Will be punished [up to three years in jail] those who will have contested [through the press] one or several crimes against humanity as they have been defined by Article 6 of the statute of the international military tribunal annexed to the London Agreement of Aug. 8, 1945." (Art. 9, Loi du 13 juillet 1990). This law is an obvious violation of basic constitutional rights but, in France, citizens cannot appeal to the Constitutional Council, which is usually stacked with former politicians.

[17]   The very political nature of the wording is fully recognized in the *1991 Annual Report of the Cambodia Documentation Commission*, headed by David Hawk in New York when it says, p. 5: "At the 1989 Paris Conference on Cambodia, the Khmer Rouge, China and Singapore insisted on the removal of the reference to genocide." Then a footnote adds: "The point is not a legal technicality. The use or non-use of the word 'genocide' (a crime under international law) was **diplomatic code language** for the present and future role of the top Khmer Rouge leaders. The substitution of the more vague formulation 'past policies and practices' for the word 'genocide' was the signal that top Khmer Rouge leaders such as Pol Pot, Ieng Sary, Nuon Chea, Khieu Samphan, Son Sen, Ta Mok et al. would not be barred from potential and actual, *de jure* and *de facto*, leadership roles in Cambodia's future."

[18]   In a list of publications provided by *Cultural Survival Quarterly* (Cambridge, Mass.), 14, 3, p. 55, out of 46 titles, three refer to "ethnocide" and three to "genocide", to describe quite similar situations of threatened indigenous peoples. It does not seem any legal action is implied.

[19]   The case of Indonesia, for instance, is heavily loaded, with the massacre of more than 500,000 communist affiliates in 1965, the violent oppression exercised in Irian Jaya since 1969 when the international community approved the forceful

take-over of Western New Guinea, and the invasion of Portuguese Timor in 1975, followed by massacres equalling those of Pol Pot. But Indonesia is a trustful ally of the West which generously provides the weapons to carry out the mass murders. In which press would it be possible to call Suharto "perpetrator of genocide"? On Irian Jaya, see Robin Osborne, *Indonesia's Secret War.*

[20] See Adhémar Leclère, *Recherches sur le droit public des Cambodgiens.*

[21] See A. Boudillon, *La Réforme du régime...*; Roger Kleinpeter, *Le Problème foncier au Cambodge.* See above, Chapter 2.

[22] *People's Revolutionary Tribunal...*, Phnom Penh, 1988, 311 pp.

[23] For an Asian context, see Paul Mus, "'Cosmodrame' et politique en Asie du Sud-Est", reprinted in *L'Angle de l'Asie.*

[24] The analogy is always tempting. See, for instance, what a distinguished Khmer senior economist with the Asian Development Bank, Mr Someth Suos, said recently in Penang: "The killing field was a world major historical event that surpassed Hitler's killing of the Jews." (*Workshop on Reconstruction and Development*, p. 37). He later adds: "The Khmer Rouge cadre should be accorded a role in the society." The parallel with Nazi Germany is nothing but laziness of thought.

[25] See the numerous references to "Mourning" in *The Complete Psychological Works* of Sigmund Freud and, in particular, "Mourning and Melancholia" and "Thoughts for the Times on War and Death" (written in 1915), in vol. 14, Standard Edition. For the Cambodian context, see James K. Boehlein, "Clinical Relevance of Grief and Mourning among Cambodian Refugees". I am grateful to Lane Gerber who provided me with a copy of this article.

[26] See below, Appendices.

[27] Introduction, p. 35 in Thion and Kiernan.

[28] Ieng Sary recently answered this question in a talk with two journalists (*Le Nouvel Observateur*, 17–23 Nov. 1991): Genocide? "A lie.... I am human. I never thought I committed acts of genocide, I shall never recognize that." Any regrets? "Yes, I regret I could not efficiently oppose erroneous points of views which prevailed at certain times, I regret I had not the courage ... to directly oppose some people.... Maybe I could not have stayed alive until now."

[29] I wish to thank Helen Jarvis and David Chandler for their useful suggestions when reading previous drafts of this paper.

Cambodia 1992: United Nations Traditional Apathy in Cambodia

[1] Stephen Heder, *Pol Pot and Khieu Samphan.*

[2]   Interview with Prime Minister Hun Sen, Phnom Penh, 21 January 1992.

[3]   Amnesty International published a report on these demonstrations in early 1992.

[4]   For a first approach by a Khmer psychologist, see Seanglim Bit, *The Warrior Heritage*. He has recently returned from the United States to launch a new political party. Some consideration of this subject may be found here in Chapter 9.

Outside Cambodia, a certain amount of confusion is visible. For instance, the more principled, or dogmatic faction inside the French ecologists' Green Party is dubbed "green Khmers" by its adversaries and the press.

[5]   It is exactly the same sentence as was used by Pol Pot when he had Sihanouk brought in front of him on 5 January 1979, after having kept him as a virtual prisoner for three years. See Sihanouk, *Prisonnier des Khmers rouges*, p. 317.

[6]   See Jacques Népote's thesis.

[7]   The status of Sihanouk's wife may seem unimportant as long as the prince is alive. He says in his memoirs that a king's marriage is in essence the event's inscription in the Palace's book. He adds that a king cannot squat on a mat beside a woman of common birth (*une roturière*), meaning he cannot marry her. In 1949, he thus offered a mock marriage, without the inscription in the Palace's book, to his Laotian mistress, Manivan. At the ceremony, he was represented by his royal clothing (*Souvenirs doux et amers*, p. 188). Manivan bore him two daughters, one of whom married one of Sirik Matak's sons.

He says elsewhere (p. 82) that just after his abdication from the throne in 1955, he took the opportunity of his mother being busy with the preparation of her own and her husband's coronation, to marry twice in 24 hours, first his aunt's daughter, Princess Norodom Norleak, and then Monique. But since he was no longer king, it is not clear where these marriages were registered, if they were. It does not seem there was any public announcement.

The political question is: what will happen if the prince is survived by his wife, whose status is so widely disputed?

[8]   A copy of the manuscript letter in French is in the author's possession. See Sihanouk's own account in *Prisonnier des Khmers Rouges*, pp. 85–105, on the circumstances of his resignation. Another book by the prince,*Chronique de guerre*, carries a photograph of the prince reading his message announcing his resignation and Khmer Rouge Chhorn Hay recording it in the Palace (2 April 1976).

⁹ See in English R.F. Randle and, in French, F. Joyaux.
¹⁰ See Pol Pot's biography by David Chandler, *Brother Number One*.
¹¹ See *Land Mines in Cambodia* for a general survey.

Appendix 1

¹ [1992 Note] The American emissary was George Bush.
² [1992 Note] This is a reference to an episode of the French revolution, in western France (Vendée, Bretagne) where peasants rose in several successive rebellions, together with their priests and some aristocrats, against the urban-oriented and bourgeois revolution. The bibliography is enormous. But see, for a historical analysis, Paul Bois, *Paysans de l'Ouest*, Paris, 1960, Mouton, and, for a contemporary judgement, Gracchus Babeuf (the so-called "father of communism"), *La guerre de Vendée et le système de dépopulation*, edited by Reynald Secher (author of several controversial books on the subject) and J.J. Brégeon, Paris, 1987, Tallandier. Repression turned into bloodbath and some authors, like Secher, now call it "genocide".
³ (1992 Note) For instance, Debré speculates that under the alias "Pol Pot" one finds a member of the old Parisian group called Rath Samoeun (p.78) and describes him as the wildest Communist leader. In fact this brilliant man played no role under Pol Pot (Saloth Sar).

Appendix 2

¹ See Michael Balfour, *Propaganda in War*.
² [1992 Note] Of course, all the records in myth-making were later broken with the war over Iraq. The purely propagandistic nature of our so-called "free press" reached new unthought heights. Even the information provided by all the Western military intelligence services, pointing to the inability of the Iraqis to launch air chemical attacks was completely disregarded by the press.
³ [1992 Note] I realize this review is not very specific. Names other than Shawcross's could easily come to mind. And places other than Cambodia. Just take Iraq, Somalia, Serbia, Bosnia, Azerbaijan, and so on... The media show and describe less and less, and produce instead more and more ready-made judgements. Images replace understanding.

Appendix 3

[1]   In an interview given in Phnom Penh in April 1978 to an American Maoist journalist, Dan Burstein, Ieng Sary said: "the police assassinated the Secretary of the CPK in February of 1963" (*Kampuchea Today*, p. 42). Although he was speaking with the help of notes (p. 47), Ieng Sary is not known for his reliability. In some quarters, he is even held to be a compulsive liar.

Appendix 4

[1]   Except for peasants, most people in town, before the war, had some Chinese ancestry. People of mixed descent are usually called Sino-Khmers. Among them, those who maintain the Chinese language at home are considered Chinese, and those who speak Khmer inside the familily are viewed as Khmers. As a cultural and social category, the Sino-Khmers cannot have a clear definition, as all shades of cultural variations may be observed. As a whole, Cambodian society, and particularly its urban component, has been more influenced by China than by any other culture.

The repopulation of Phnom Penh after 1979 has much increased the "Khmerization" of the city. But Chinese and Sino-Khmers are again strongly present in the city élite. The films shown in the numerous video shops are 90 per cent Chinese.

[2]   See for instance Nguyên Thê Anh, "Thiên-Y-A-Na..."

Appendix 5

[1]   See Pierre Meile, *Les Yavanas dans l'Inde tamoule*, p. 80.

[2]   See the translation by Pe Maung Tin, p. 92. Some details on this event may be found in Khin Myo Chit, *Anawrhata of Burma*, pp. 84–86 and D.G.E. Hall, pp. 159–60.

[3]   George Cœdès, *Inscriptions du Cambodge*, II, p. 10, p. 155.

[4]   Michel Ferlus, *"Les langues du groupe austroasiatique-nord"*, p. 47.

[5]   See Foucher, *La Vieille route de l'Inde*, p. 271; see also Rock Edict 13, 30 (see Bloch).

[6]   Pânini's Grammar, IV, 1, 175; see Vasu.

[7]   See La Vallée-Poussin, *L'Inde aux temps des Mauryas*, pp. 15 and 40.

[8]   All information about the ancient Kambojas has been culled by B.-C. Law, *Kshatriya Tribes of Ancient India*.

[9]   In *Majjhima*, II, p. 149, London, Pali Text Society.

[10]   VI, p. 208. See Étienne Lamotte, *Histoire du bouddhisme indien*, p. 110.

[11]   *Op. cit.*, p. 42.

[12]   *Pour une histoire...*, pp. 5 and 170.

[13]   *Cambodia after Angkor...*, p. 375.

[14]   Alexander B. Woodside, *Vietnam and the Chinese Model*, p. 246. Woodside quotes, on *farang*, a book I have not yet seen, Chula Chakrabongse, *Lords of Life: The Paternal Monarchy of Bangkok, 1782–1932*, London, 1960, p. 36.

[15]   Manfred Kropp, "'Grecs' et Européens. Note de lexicographie éthiopienne", *Semitica*, p. 128. For a complete study of the use of the word in the Middle Eastern languages, the author refers to E. Littmann, "Fränkisch" in *Aufsätze zur Kultur und Sprachgeschichte vornehmlich des Orient*, Breslau, 1916, and "Weiteres über Fränkisch" in *Zeitschrift für Semitistik*, 4, 1926, pp. 262–5.

[16]   This meaning has remained: the small region where Paris is located is called "Ile de France". The Charles de Gaulle international airport north of Paris is located in a village named Roissy-en-France, referring to the limited early geographical extension of the word.

Credits

Each article has been revised but only in order to improve its readability and to ensure a measure of consistency within the present volume. Only minor stylistic or lexical changes have been introduced. The substance has not been altered. Some footnotes have been added, clearly identified: "1992 Note".

Within the Khmer Rouge, the first chapter, was first published in *Le Monde*, in April 1972 and translated into English by Laura Summers in *Indochina Chronicle*, 17, July 1972. Here is a complete version.

The Agrarian Question in Indochina was first published in *Cahiers Internationaux de Sociologie*, No. 54, January–June 1973, and it was later translated by Ben Kiernan.

The Ingratitude of the Crocodiles was first published in *Les Temps Modernes*, No. 402, January 1980, and translated by William Mahder in the *Bulletin of Concerned Asian Scholars*, 12, 4, October–December 1980.

The Cambodian Idea of Revolution was presented at an SSRC Conference in Chiang Mai in August 1981 and later published in *Revolution and its Aftermaths in Kampuchea: Eight Essays*, edited by David P. Chandler and Ben Kiernan, Yale University Southeast Asia Studies Monograph Series, 1983.

Cambodia Background and Issues was written in collaboration with Michael Vickery and published in Phnom Penh by Church World Service in September 1981. In early 1982, the pamphlet was confiscated by the Cambodian police.

The Pattern of Cambodian Politics was first presented at the Princeton Cambodia Conference, in November 1982 and was published in *The Cambodian Agony* by David A. Ablin and Marlowe Hood, Sharpe, New York, 1987.

Time for Talk was first circulated in the summer of 1987 and this revised version appeared in Cologne, in *Internationales Asienforum*, 19, 3–4, in 1988.

Indochinese Refugees in France was first a paper presented at an International Workshop, held in Bangkok and Prachinburi in May 1987, organized by the Institute of Asian Studies, Chulalongkorn University, and published in *Indochinese Refugees: Asylum and Resettlement*, edited by Supang Chantavanich and E. Bruce Reynolds, Bangkok, 1988.

Genocide as a Political Commodity was a paper presented at a Raphael Lemkin Symposium, organized by the Schell Center for International Human Rights at Yale Law School, in February 1992.

Chapter 10 includes a description of the demonstration against Khieu Samphân of which a shorter version was published in the *Asian Wall Street Journal*, New York, on 16 December 1991.

The pieces which form the Appendices, were published under somewhat different titles, *The Moral Reaction* in *Libération,* a Paris daily, on 7 March 1977; *Sex on a Tiger Skin*, in *Inside Asia*, London, No. 8, April–May 1986; *About Tou Samouth,* in *Srok Khmer*, a Khmer monthly published in Sarcelles, near Paris, in May 1987; *Cambodians and Vietnamese*, in the *Asian Wall Street Journal Weekly*, 20 January 1992; *On Some Cambodian Words* appeared in several issues of the *Phnom Penh Post* in January and February 1993.

Bibliography

Ajchenbaum, Y., Chandelier, G., Ponchaud, F., *Le dispositif d'accueil des réfugiés du Sud-Est asiatique*, Paris, 1979, Adres.

Aurousseau, Léonard, "Sur le nom de Cochinchine", *Bulletin de l'École Française d'Extrême-Orient*, Hanoi, 1924, pp. 563–79.

Aymonier, Etienne, *Le Cambodge*, Paris, 1900.

Babeuf, Gracchus, *La Guerre de Vendée et le système de dépopulation*, ed. R. Secher and J. J. Brégeon, Paris, 1987, Tallandier.

Baffeleuf, Antoine, *Les Impôts en Annam*, thèse de droit, Paris, 1910.

Balazs, Etienne, *La Bureaucratie céleste*, Paris, 1968, Gallimard.

Balfour, Michael, *Propaganda in War*, London, 1979, Routledge and Kegan Paul.

Bastié, Jean, ed., *Les Réfugiés du Sud-Est asiatique dans le XIIIème arrondissement de Paris*, Paris, Sorbonne, UER de Géographie, 1981.

Bennigsen, Alexandre and Quelquejay, Chantal, *Les Mouvements nationaux chez les musulmans de Russie*, Paris and the Hague, 1977, Mouton.

Benveniste, Émile, *Le Vocabulaire des institutions indo-européennes*, Paris, 1969, Minuit, 2 vol.

Bienvenue, R., *Régime de la propriété foncière en Annam,* Thèse de droit, Rennes, 1911.

Blandin, Chantal, "Les galettes et le riz de l'exil", *Le Monde*, 13–14 Oct. 1985.

Bloch, Jules, *Les Inscriptions d'Asoka*, Paris, 1950, Les Belles Lettres.

Boehlein, James K., "Clinical Relevance of Grief and Mourning among Cambodian Refugees", *Soc. Sci. Med.*, 25, 7, pp. 765–72.

Bois, Paul, *Paysans de l'Ouest*, Paris, 1960, Mouton.

Bonvin, François, Ponchaud, François, *Réfugiés du Sud-Est asiatique. Leur insertion en région parisienne*, Paris, 1980, Fondation pour la recherche sociale.

Boua, Chanthou, see Chandler.

Boudarel, G., see Chesneaux; Ngô Kim Chung.

Boudillon, A., *Le Régime de la propriété foncière en Indochine*, Paris, 1915.

—— *La Réforme du régime de la propriété foncière en Indochine. Rapport au Gouverneur Général*, Hanoi, 1927.

Bouillevaux, Charles Emile, Father, "Ma visite aux ruines cambodgiennes en 1850", *Mémoires de la Société académique indochinoise*, I, 1874.

Boyer, Agnès, "La polygamie chez les réfugiés d'Asie du Sud-Est", *Migrants-Formation*, 54, Oct. 1983.

Brégeon, J. J., see Babeuf.

Brocheux, Pierre, ed., *Histoire de l'Asie du Sud-Est, Révoltes, réformes, révolutions*, Lille, 1981, Presses universitaires de Lille.

See also Chesneaux.

Broué, Pierre, ed., *La Question chinoise dans l'Internationale communiste (1926–1927)*, Paris, 1965, Études et Documentation internationales.

Brown, R., see Mason.

Burchett, Wilfred, *J'ai visité les zones libérées du Sud-Vietnam*, Hanoi, 1965.

—— *La seconde résistance*, Paris, 1966, Maspero.

Cambodia, a Demographic Catastrophe, Central Intelligence Agency, Washington, Government Printer. (CG80-100190).

Carney, Timothy Michael, *Communist Party Power in Kampuchea (Cambodia): Documents and Discussion*, Ithaca, 1977, Cornell University Southeast Asia Program Data Papers No. 106.

Chanda, Nayan, *Brother Enemy*, New York, 1986, Harcourt Brace Jovanovich.

Chandelier, G., see Ajchenbaum.

Chandler, David P., *Cambodia Before the French: Politics in a Tributary Kingdom, 1794–1848*, Ph.D., University of Michigan, 1973.

—— *The Tragedy of Cambodian History*, New Haven, Yale University Press, 1991.

—— *Brother Number One*, Boulder, 1992.

Chandler, David P. and Kiernan, Ben, eds., *Revolution and its Aftermaths in Kampuchea*, New Haven, 1983, Yale University Southeast Asia Monograph.

Chandler, David P., Kiernan, Ben and Boua Chanthou, *Pol Pot Plans the Future. Confidential Leadership Documents from Democratic Kampuchea, 1976-1977*, New Haven, 1988, Yale University, South East Asia Studies Monograph No. 33.

Chesneaux, J., Boudarel, G., Hémery, D., eds., *Tradition et révolution au Vietnam*, Paris, 1971, Anthropos.

Childers, Robert Cæsar, *A Dictionary of the Pali Language*, London, 1909, Kegan, Trench & Trübner.

Chomsky, Noam and Herman, Edward S., *The Political Economy of Human Rights II: After the Cataclysm, Postwar Indochina and the Reconstruction of Imperial Ideology*, Boston, 1979, South End Press.

Chopin-Roussel, M.D., *Les Modalités d'adaptation à la vie française des réfugiés du Sud-Est asiatique*, Thèse 3ᵉ cycle, Sciences de l'Education, Paris V, 1983, 2 vol.

Chudodeyev, Y.V., ed., *Soviet Volunteers in China. 1926–1945. Articles and Reminiscences*, Moscow, 1980, Progress Publishers.

Ciavaldini, Pierre, *Situation des réfugiés du Sud-Est asiatique dans le Midi de la France*, Montpellier, Thèse de médecine, Nov. 1977.

Cœdès, George, *Inscriptions du Cambodge*, tome II.

—— *Les États hindouisés d'Indochine et d'Indonésie*, Paris, 1948, De Boccard.

Collard, Paul, *Cambodge et Cambodgiens; métamorphose du royaume khmer par une méthode française de protectorat*, Paris, 1925.

Comte, Maurice, *Économie, idéologie et pouvoir: la société cambodgienne (1863-1886)*, Doctoral Thesis in Economics, Lyon II, 1980.

Condominas, Georges, *L'Espace social; A propos de l'Asie du Sud-Est*, Paris, 1980, Flammarion.

—— *From Lawa to Mon, from Saa' to Thai, historical and anthropological aspects of Southeast Asian social spaces*, ed. Gehan Wijeyewardene, Canberra, 1990, Australian National University.

Condominas, Georges and Pottier, Richard, eds., *Les Réfugiés originaires de l'Asie du Sud-Est*, Paris, 1982-1984, La Documentation française, 2 vol.

Corrèze, Françoise (aka Juliette. Baccot), *Choses vues au Cambodge*, Paris, 1980, Editeurs français réunis.

Deac, Wilfred P., "Chenla II: Prelude to Disaster", *Vietnam* (Leesburg, VA), 5, 1, June 1992, pp. 42–48.

Debré, François, *Cambodge, la Révolution de la forêt*, Paris, 1976, Flammarion.

Delvert, Jean, *Le Paysan cambodgien*, Paris, 1961, Mouton.

Djilas, Milovan, *Wartime*, New York, 1977, Harcourt Brace Jovanovich.

Elliott, Mai V., see Nguyên Thi Dinh.

Estramon, B., *Exil et psychopathologie*, Limoges, mémoire de psychiatrie, 1981.

Études vietnamiennes, No. 24, Hanoi, 1970.

Ferlus, Michel, "Les langues du groupe autroasiatique-nord", *Asie du Sud-Est et monde insulindien* (ASEMI), 5, 1, 1974, pp. 39–68.

Freud, Sigmund, *Works,* vol. 14, Standard Edition, London, 1957, Hogarth Press.

Forest, Alain, *Cambodge. histoire d'une colonisation sans heurt (1897–1920),* Paris, L'Harmattan, 1981.

Foucher, Alfred, *La Vieille route de l'Inde, de Bactres à Taxila,* Paris, 1942–1948, 2 vol.

Frédéric, Louis, *Dictionnaire de la civilisation indienne,* Paris, 1987, Laffont.

Gallasch, Börries, ed., *Ho-Tschi-Minh Stadt, Die Stunde Null,* Hamburg, 1975, Rowohlt.

Gauteron, M. and Pimont, E., *Les Réfugiés khmers dans la région parisienne,* mémoire d'ethnologie, Paris VII, 1976.

Gerini, Colonel G.E., *Researches on Ptolemy's Geography of Eastern Asia,* London, 1909.

Gluckman, Max, *Custom and Conflict in Africa,* Oxford, 1956.

—— *Order and Rebellion in Tribal Africa,* London, 1963.

Gourou, Pierre, *La Terre et l'Homme en Extrême-Orient,* Paris, 1972 (2nd ed.), Flammarion.

Greif, Jean-Jacques, "S.O.S. Réfugiés", *Marie-Claire,* March 1982.

Guide Pratique du réfugié, Paris, 1985.

Hall, D.G.E., *A History of Southeast Asia,* Fourth Edition, London, 1981, Macmillan.

Hardy, Yves, "La Guyane, terre d'hospitalité?", *Le Monde,* Dec. 29 and 31, 1978.

Heder, Stephen, *Pol Pot and Khieu Samphan,* Centre of Southeast Asian Studies Working Paper 70, Monash University, 1991.

Hémery, D., *Révolutionnaires vietnamiens et pouvoir colonial en Indochine,* Paris, 1975, Maspero.

See also Chesneaux.

Henderson, William D., *Why the Vietcong Fought,* Westport, 1979, Greenwood.

Henri, Yves, *Économie agricole de l'Indochine,* Hanoi, 1932.

Herman, Edward S., see Chomsky.

Hickey, Gerald C., *Village in Vietnam,* New Haven, 1964.

—— *Sons of the Mountains* and *Free in the Forest,* both in *Ethnohistory of the Vietnamese Central Highlands,* New Haven, Yale University Press, 1982, 2 vol.

Hochino, Tatsuo, *Pour une histoire médiévale du Moyen Mékong,* Bangkok, 1986, Duong Kamol.

Hô Chi Minh, *Écrits,* Hanoi, 1971.

Hu Nim, *Les Services publics économiques au Cambodge*, thèse de droit, Phnom Penh, 1965.
See also Chandler, Kiernan and Boua.

Imbert, Jean, *Histoire des institutions khmères*, Phnom Penh, 1961.

Isaacs, Harold, *The Tragedy of the Chinese Revolution*, Stanford, 1951; rev. 1961, Stanford University Press.

Johnson, Chalmers A., *Peasant Nationalism and Communist Power*, Stanford, 1962, Stanford University Press.

Joleaud-Duval, *La Colonisation française en Annam et au Tonkin*, Paris, 1899.

Joyaux, François, *La Chine et le règlement du premier conflit d'Indochine, Genève 1954*, Paris, 1979, Sorbonne.

Kampuchea Today, An eyewitness report from Cambodia, Chicago, Dec. 1978, *Call* Pamphlets.

Keng Vannsak, *Recherche d'un fonds culturel khmer*, Thèse, Paris, Sorbonne, 1971.

Khien Theeravit, *Thailand's Response to the Vietnamese Aggression in Kampuchea*, Tokyo, June 1981, Kampuchea Conference.

Khieu Samphân, *L'Économie du Cambodge et ses problèmes d'industrialisation*, thèse de droit, Paris, 1959. See Laura Summers' translation: *Cambodia's Economy and Industrial Development*, Ithaca, 1979, Cornell University Southeast Asia Program Data Paper No. 111.

Khin Myo Chit, *Anawhrata of Burma*, Rangoon, 1970.

Kiernan, Ben, *How Pol Pot came to Power*, London, 1985, Verso.

—— *Cambodia: The Eastern Zone Massacre*, New York, no date, Columbia University.

—— "An Overview of the Cambodian Genocide", paper prepared for the Yale Cambodia Conference (Feb. 1992).
See also Chandler; Thion.

Kleinpeter, Roger, *Le Problème foncier au Cambodge*, Paris, 1937.

Kouchner, Bernard, *Charité Business*, Paris, 1986, Pré aux Clercs.

Krisher, Bernard, see Norodom Sihanouk.

Kropp, Manfred, "'Grecs' et Européens. Note de lexicographie éthiopienne", *Semitica*, 33, 1983.

Lafont, P. B. and Po Dharma, *Bibliographie Campa et Cam*, Paris, 1989, L'Harmattan.

Lamant, Pierre L., *L'Affaire Yukanthor. Autopsie d'un scandale colonial*, Paris, 1989, Société d'histoire d'outre-mer.

Lamotte, Étienne, *Histoire du bouddhisme indien, des origines à l'ère saka*, Louvain, 1958, Université de Louvain.

Land Mines in Cambodia, The Cowards' War, New York, 1991, Asia Watch & Physicians for Human Rights.

Land Reform in Vietnam, Stanford Research Institute, Stanford, 1968, 6 vol.

Laurent, Maurice, Col., *L'Armée au Cambodge*, Paris, 1968, PUF.

La Vallée-Poussin, Louis de, *L'Inde aux temps des Mauryas et des barbares, grecs scythes,parthes et yue-tchi*, Paris, 1930, de Boccard.

Law, B.-C., *Kshatriya Tribes of Ancient India*, Calcutta, 1923.

Lê Chau, *La Révolution paysanne du Sud Vietnam,* Paris, 1966, Maspero.

Leclère, Adhémar, *Recherches sur le droit public des Cambodgiens,* Paris, 1894.

Lefebvre, René, *L'Économie agricole du royaume du Cambodge*, Phnom Penh, 1969, FAO.

Lê Huu Khoa, *Les Vietnamiens en France, insertion et identité*, Paris, 1985, CIEM, L'Harmattan.

Lejeune, Camille, *Régime de la propriété foncière en pays annamite*, thèse de droit, Paris, 1904.

Lemkin, Raphael, *Axis Rule in Occupied Europe: Laws of Occupation, Analysis of Government, Proposals for Redress*, New York, 1944, Columbia University Press.

Lew, Roland, *1949, Mao prend le pouvoir,* Brussels, 1981, Complexe.

Livre noir, faits et preuves des actes d'agression et d'annexion du Viêt-n am contre le Kampuchea, Phnom Penh, Sept. 1978, 116 pp. (authored by Pol Pot).

McAlister Jr., John, see Mus.

Martel, Gabrielle, *Lovea, village des environs d'Angkor,* Paris, 1975, École Française d'Extrême-Orient.

Marx, Karl, *Œuvres*, II, Paris, 1968, Gallimard, La Pléiade.

Mason, Linda and Brown, Roger, *Rice, Rivalry and Politics. Managing Cambodian Relief*, Notre Dame, 1983, University of Notre Dame.

Maspero, Georges, *Le Royaume de Champa,* reprint, Paris, 1988, École Française d'Extrême-Orient.

Maspero, Henri, *Etudes historiques*, Paris, 1950, Musée Guimet.

Mau Say, "Les Institutions cambodgiennes de crédit", *Annales de la Faculté de Droit de Phnom Penh*, IV, 1962.

Meile, Pierre, "Les Yavanas dans l'Inde tamoule", *Journal asiatique,* 1940-41.

Michael, Franz, *The Tai Ping Rebellion, History and Documents*, Seattle, University of Washington Press, 1966.

Moura, J., *Le Royaume du Cambodge*, Paris, 1883, E. Leroux, 2 vol.

Mus, Paul, *Viêt-Nam: sociologie d'une guerre*, Paris, 1952, Seuil.

—— *L'Angle de l'Asie*, Paris, 1977, Hermann.

Mus, Paul and McAlister Jr., John, *Les Viêtnamiens et leur révolution*, Paris, 1972, Seuil (a version widely different from *The Vietnamese and Their Revolution*, New York, 1970, Harper & Row, by the same authors).

Naville, Pierre, *La Guerre du Vietnam*, Paris, 1949.

Ndongo Bidyogo, Donato, *Historia y tragedia de Guinea Ecuatorial*, Madrid, 1977, Cambio 16.

Népote, Jacques, *Le Palais du roi Norodom I. Histoire (1860-1973) et description, suivie de l'analyse structurale de la symbolique du palais royal de Phnom Penh*, Thèse 3ᵉ Cycle, Nanterre, 1973.

Ngô Kim Chung and Nguyên Dúc Nghinh, *Propriété privée et propriété collective dans l'ancien Viêtnam*, translation and presentation by Georges Boudarel, Lydie Prin, Vû Cân and Ta Trong Hiêp, Paris, 1987, L'Harmattan.

Nguyên Dúc Nghinh, see Ngô Kim Chung.

Nguyên Khac Viên, *Expériences vietnamiennes*, Paris, 1970.

Nguyên Ngoc Giao, "Réfugiés ou immigrants: facteurs politiques et facteurs économiques", *Vietnam*, Paris, No. 4, décembre 1981.

Nguyên Thanh Nha, *Tableau économique du Vietnam aux dix-septième et dix-huitième siècles*, Paris, 1970, Cujas.

Nguyên Thê Anh, "Thiên-y-A-Na, ou la récupération de la déesse cham Pô Nagar par la monarchie confucéenne viêtnamienne" in *Cultes populaires et sociétés asiatiques*, ed. by A. Forest, Y. Ishizawa and L. Vandermeersch, Paris, L'Harmattan, 1991, pp. 73-86.

Nguyên Thi Dinh, *No Other Road to Take,* translated by Mai V. Elliott, Ithaca, 1976, Cornell University South East Asia Program.

Nhu Phong, "Intellectuals, Writers, Artists", *The China Quarterly*, No. 9, January–March, 1962.

Norodom Sihanouk, *Chroniques de guerre... et d'espoir*, Paris, 1979, Hachette/Stock.

—— *Souvenirs doux et amers*, Paris, 1981, Hachette/Stock.

—— *Prisonnier des Khmers rouges*, Paris, 1986, Hachette.

—— *Sihanouk Reminisces. World Leaders I Have Known*, with Bernard Krisher, Bangkok, 1990, Duang Kamol.

[Nuon Chea], "Statement of the CPK to the CWP of Denmark, July 1978", introduced by Laura Summers, *The Journal of Communist Studies*, 3,1, March 1987.

Osborne, Milton E., *Strategic Hamlets in South Vietnam: A Survey and Comparison*, Ithaca, 1965, Cornell University.

—— *The French Presence in Cochinchina and Cambodia; Rule and Response, 1859–1905*, Ithaca, 1969, Cornell University Press.

Osborne, Robin, *Indonesia's Secret War, The Guerrilla Struggle in Irian Jaya*, Sydney, 1985, Allen and Unwin.

Pe Maung Tin, transl., *The Glace Palace Chronicle of the Kings of Burma*, Oxford, 1923, repr. Rangoon, 1960.

People's Revolutionary Tribunal held in Phnom Penh for the Trial of the Genocide Crime of the Pol Pot-Ieng Sary Clique, Phnom Penh, 1988, 311 pp.

Peschoux, Christophe, *Les "nouveaux" Khmers rouges (1979-1990), Reconstruction du mouvement et reconquête des villages*, Paris, 1992, L'Harmattan.

Peyronie, H. and Schneider, B., eds., *55 Témoignages sur le Cambodge en lutte, 1970-72*, no place [Rennes?], no date [Dec. 1972?], 160 pp. Authors include J.L. Bonniol, J. Brunel, F. Corrèze, P.M. Danquigny, F. Davreu, F. Decarpentry, F. Dupuis, P. Guérin, J.-M. Hélary, C. Legac, F. Luton, J. Mémin, H. Peyronie, B. Schneider, S. Thion and D. Yvetot.

Picq, Laurence, *Au-delà du ciel, cinq ans chez les Khmers rouges*, Paris, 1984, Barrault.

Pimont, E., see Gauteron.

Pin Yathai, *L'Utopie meurtrière, un rescapé du génocide cambodgien témoigne*, Paris, 1980, Laffont. (The US version of this book differs greatly.)

Po Dharma, see Lafont.

Pol Pot, see *Livre noir*. Also Chandler, Kiernan and Boua.

Ponchaud, François, "A la recherche d'une patrie (Accueil des réfugiés asiatiques en Asie et en France)", *Echanges France-Asie*, 1977.

—— *Cambodia: Year Zero*, New York, 1978, Holt, Rinehart and Winston.

—— "Viêt-nam — Cambodge, 'une solidarité militante fragile'", *Les Temps Modernes*, No. 402, January 1980.

—— "Les réfugiés d'Indochine dans la tourmente politique de l'Asie", *Mission de l'Eglise*, No. 60, juin 1983.

See also Ajchenbaum; Bonvin.

Pottier, Richard, see Condominas.

Pou, Saveros, *Guirlande de Cpap'*, Paris, 1988, Cedoreck, 2 vol.

Prin, Lydie, see Ngô Kim Chung.

Prud'homme, Rémy, *L'Économie du Cambodge*, Paris, 1969, PUF.

Prügel, Peter, *Südostasien-Flüchtlinge in Frankreich*, Konstanz, Fachgruppe Soziologie, University of Konstanz, August 1986.

Quelquejay, Chantal, see Bennigsen.

Quinn, Kenneth M., "Political Change in Wartime. The Khmer Krahom Revolution in Southern Cambodia, 1970-74", *Naval War College Review*, Spring 1976.

Randle, Robert F., *Geneva 1954, the Settlement of the Indochina War*, Princeton, 1969.

Réalités cambodgiennes, 23 April 1971.

"Refugees: the Pull Factor", *Far Eastern Economic Review*, 17–23 July 1981.

Réfugiés du Sud-Est asiatique. Accueil et formation des réfugiés du Sud-Est asiatique en France, Paris, 1980, Centre national de documentation pédagogique-Migrants.

Retbøll, Tørben, "Kampuchea and the 'Readers' Digest'", *Bulletin of Concerned Asian Scholars*, 11, No. 3, 1979.

Robequain, Charles, *L'Evolution économique de l'Indochine française*. See the English translation: *The Economic Development of French Indochina*, London, OUP, 1941.

Roux, André, "L'acquisition de la propriété par la possession en droit foncier cambodgien", *Annales de la Faculté de Droit de Phnom Penh*, IV, 1962.

Sarin Chhak, *Les Frontières du Cambodge*, Paris, 1966, Dalloz.

Sarkisyanz, Immanuel, *The Buddhist Background of the Burmese Revolution*, The Hague, 1965, Nijhoff.

Savitry Sorasinh, *Les Difficultés de vivre une double culture pour un réfugié laotien*, mémoire BEP, Mont-de-Marsan, 1986.

Schafer, Edward H., *The Vermilion Bird, T'ang Images of the South*, Berkeley, University of California Press, 1967.

Schneider, B., see H. Peyronie.

Seanglim Bit, *The Warrior Heritage. A Psychological Perspective of Cambodian Trauma*, El Cerrito (Cal. 94530), 1991, published by the author (5210 Gordon Ave.).

Secher, Reynald, see Babeuf.

Sellers, Nicholas, *The Princes of Hà-Tiên (1682–1867)*, Brussels, 1983, Thanh Long.

S.E.T.E.F., Ministère du Travail, *Etude concernant l'installation des réfugiés du Sud-Est asiatique hors des grandes agglomérations urbaines*, juillet 1981.

Shawcross, William, *Sideshow, Kissinger, Nixon and the Destruction of Cambodia*, New York, 1979, Simon and Schuster.

—— *The Quality of Mercy: Cambodia, Holocaust and Modern Conscience*, London, 1984, André Deutsch.

Simon-Baruh, Ida, "Minorités en France: populations originaires des pays de l'Asie du Sud-Est", *Pluriel*, 32, 1982.

Sisowath Thomico, "Norodom Sihanouk and the Khmer Factions", *Indochina Report*, No. 9, Singapore, 1987.

Smith, Adam, *The Wealth of Nations*, London, 1970, Penguin.

Snow, Edgar, *The Other Side of the River*, London, 1970.

Summers, Laura, "Co-operatives in Democratic Kampuchea", unpublished paper. See also Khieu Samphân; Nuon Chea.

Tambiah, S. J., *World Conqueror and World Renouncer*, Cambridge, 1976, Camb. U.P.

Thai Van Khiem, "La Plaine aux cerfs et la Princesse de jade", *Bulletin de la Société des Études indochinoises*, 4, 1959.

Thion, Serge, "The Social Classification of Peasants in Vietnam", *Asian Thought and Society*, New York, Dec. 1977.

—— "The Cambodian Solution to the Third Indochina War", *Cornell Review*, No. 6, Summer 1979.

—— "Despote à vendre", *Les Temps Modernes*, 402, Jan. 1980, pp. 1254–68.

—— "Le Cambodge, la presse et ses bêtes noires", *Esprit*, Sept. 1980, pp. 95–111.

Thion, Serge and Kiernan, Ben, *Khmers rouges! Matériaux pour l'histoire du communisme au Cambodge*, Paris, 1981, Albin Michel.

Thomas, Roland, *L'Évolution économique du Cambodge, 1900-1940*, Thèse IIIe cycle, Paris VII, 1979.

Truong Chinh and Vô Nguyên Giap, *The Peasant Question*, translated by Christine P. White, Ithaca, 1974, Cornell University Southeast Asia Program Data Paper No. 94.

Turner, Robert F., *Vietnamese Communism*, Stanford, 1975, Hoover Institute.

Vasu, S. C., *The Ashthâdhyâyi of Pânini*, 12 vol., repr. New Dehli, 1962.

Vickery, Michael, *Cambodia after Angkor, The Chronicular Evidences for the Fourteenth to the Sixteenth Centuries*, Ph.D., Yale, 1977.

—— "Democratic Kampuchea: CIA to the Rescue", *Bulletin of Concerned Asian Scholars*, 14, 4, 1982.

—— *Cambodia, 1975–1982*, Boston, 1984, South End Press.

—— Review of Condominas' *From Law to Mon*, *Thai-Yunnan Project Newsletter*, 13, June 1991.

Vô Nguyên Giap, see Truong Chinh.

Vo Thi Tri Thuy, *L'Insertion en France des réfugiés du Sud-Est asiatique*, Aix, mémoire IUT, 1983.

Vu Can, "Les luttes populaires contre le régime US-Diem de 1954 à 1960", *Etudes vietnamiennes*, Hanoi, No. 18–19, 1968.
See Ngô Kim Chung; Corrèze.

Weber, Max, *The Religion of China*, New York, 1968.

White, Christine, see Truong Chinh.

Wijeyewardene, Gehan, see Condominas.

Wittfogel, Karl A., *Das erwachende China*, Vienna, 1926.

—— *Wirtschaft und Gesellschaft Chinas*, Leipzig, 1931.

—— *Oriental Despotism*, New Haven, 1957, Yale University Press.

Workshop on Reconstruction and Development, (coll.), Penang, 1991.

Woodside, Alexander Barton, *Vietnam and the Chinese Model, A Comparative Study of Vietnamese and Chinese Government in the First Half of the Nineteenth Century*, 2nd ed., Cambridge, Mass., 1988, Harvard University Press.

Y Phandara, *Retour à Phnom Penh*, Paris, 1982, Métaillé.

List of Abbreviations

ASALA Armenian Movement of Liberation
ASEAN Association of Southeast Asian Nations
CNE Comité National d'Entraide
CPH Centre Provisoire d'Hébergement
CPK Communist Party of Kampuchea
CWS Church World Service (USA)
DK State of DemocraticKampuchea (1975–9)
FTA France Terre d'Asile
FUNK French acronym of NUFK
GVN Government of (South) Vietnam, in Saigon
ICP Indochinese Communist Party
KPNLF Khmer Peoples National Liberation Front
NGO Non Governmental Organization
NHK Japanese television network
NLF National Liberation Front of South Vietnam
NUFK National United Front of Kampuchea
OFPRA Office Français de Protection des Réfugiés et Apatrides
PCF Parti communiste français
PRK People's Republic of Kampuchea (Phnom Penh)
PRP People's Revolutionary Party
RPR Rassemblement Pour la République
SIPAR a French educational NGO in the border camps
SNC Supreme National Council
UN United Nations
UNAMIC United Nations Advance Mission in Cambodia
UNTAC United Nations Transitional Authority in Cambodia
UNHCR United Nations High Commission for Refugees
VC/NVA Viet Cong/ North Vietnamese Army

Index

Index